HOUSING
MARKETS
AND THE
ECONOMY

HOUSING MARKETS AND THE ECONOMY

Risk, Regulation, and Policy

ESSAYS IN HONOR OF KARL E. CASE

Edited by
EDWARD L. GLAESER
AND
JOHN M. QUIGLEY

L LINCOLN INSTITUTE
OF LAND POLICY
CAMBRIDGE, MASSACHUSETTS

Library of Congress Cataloging-in-Publication Data

Housing markets and the economy : risk, regulation, and policy : essays in honor of
   Karl E. Case / edited by Edward L. Glaeser and John M. Quigley.
      p.   cm.
   Papers from a conference sponsored by the Lincoln Institute of Land Policy,
   held in Dec. 2007.
   Includes index.
   ISBN 978-1-55844-184-2
   1. Housing—United States—Congresses.   2. Housing policy—United States—
Congresses.   3. Housing—Prices—United States—Congresses.   4. Housing—
Law and legislation—United States—Congresses.   I. Case, Karl E.
II. Glaeser, Edward L. (Edward Ludwig), 1967–   III. Quigley, John M., 1942–
HD7293.H678   2009
333.33'80973—dc22   2008043990

Designed by Westchester Book Composition

Composed in Electra LH Regular by Westchester Book Composition in Danbury,
Connecticut. Printed and bound by Puritan Press in Hollis, New Hampshire.
♻ The paper is Rolland Enviro 100, an acid-free, 100 percent recycled sheet.

MANUFACTURED IN THE UNITED STATES OF AMERICA

Contents

Figures

Tables

Foreword

The Lincoln Institute of Land Policy sponsored and supported the conference "Housing and the Built Environment: Access, Finance, Policy," held in December 2007, and the subsequent publication of this volume, for several reasons. First, the scope of the chapters in this volume is fittingly wide, ranging from useful empirical studies to policy-relevant theoretical conjectures while still addressing mainly housing market issues. Second, the timing of the conference and this volume is opportune, taking place during the ongoing deflation of the U.S. housing bubble and associated financial crisis linked to the remarkable contagion effects of subprime mortgages and their securitized investment vehicles. Third, Chip Case, the honoree of this conference, has many long-standing ties to the Lincoln Institute. Many years ago the Institute wisely supported Chip's dissertation on the property tax in Boston, and more recently the Institute benefited from Chip's service as a distinguished member of the Institute's Board of Directors.

As noted by the editors in their introductory chapter, while Chip's interests are wide ranging, much of his work has been strongly linked to the housing market and associated issues such as price measurement, market efficiency, housing market behavior and its macroeconomic linkages, capitalization of local public services in housing prices, and property taxation. It is difficult to overstate Chip's contributions to the analysis of housing markets, particularly his formulation (along with Robert Shiller) of the repeat sales price index for housing. Indeed, the development of this price index and its growing coverage across locations and over time underpins most serious quantitative work on U.S. housing markets today, including the work reported in this volume. More accurate information about housing prices has improved our ability to measure housing market volatility and the effects of policy interventions in the housing market.

Perhaps the next challenge for housing market analysts is to assess the causes of the recent housing bubble. While much attention has been given to its financial sector causes, such as low interest rates and extension of credit to poorly qualified customers, land and housing policy at the local level—particularly restrictions on housing supply—seems also to have played a role. Housing market restrictions may have contributed to the widespread misconception that housing prices "could not go down." Ironically, those metropolitan housing markets that had the strongest restrictions on land and housing supply seem to be faring better during the post-bubble correction than metropolitan markets with few restrictions and rapid increases in supply. Analyses such as those in this volume provide the foundation needed to increase our understanding of how land and housing policy—both national and local—affects housing markets.

Gregory K. Ingram
President and CEO
Lincoln Institute of Land Policy

Part
I

INTRODUCTION

1

Karl E. Case, Housing, and the Economy

EDWARD L. GLAESER
JOHN M. QUIGLEY

This volume collects 10 original essays honoring the career and the contributions of the influential economist Karl Case, whose work links real estate markets and movements in the broader economy. His work has considered the boom-and-bust cycles in real capital investment and their relationship to regional performance and the macro economy. But it has also considered the consequences of these cycles and the risks they impose on the actors in the housing market. In part, this work led him to consider institutional reform and the implications of regulating housing markets for households and housing suppliers. The topics treated in this book reflect many of the concerns raised in Case's academic writings.

Better known throughout the profession as "Chip" Case, Karl Case matriculated at Miami University (Ohio) and later at Harvard University. In between, he served as an officer in the U.S. Army Medical Corps in Viet Nam. He completed his doctoral dissertation in economics in 1977 under the supervision of Richard Musgrave and John Kain and subsequently joined the faculty of Wellesley College, where he has served for three decades. He is currently the Katherine Coman and A. Barton Hepburn Professor of Economics at Wellesley.

Case's doctoral dissertation formed the basis for his 1978 book, *Property Taxation: The Need for Reform*. This book analyzed the variations in effective property tax rates within and between jurisdictions in Massachusetts, offering a blueprint for reform of the institutions that determine local tax appraisal, property tax assessment, and tax policy. This early research identified the qualities he would be known for throughout his professional career: deep knowledge of real-world institutions, keen attention to empirical detail, and a clear focus on behavior and policy.

Case has written four other books, including the highly acclaimed undergraduate text *Principles of Economics* (first published in 1989), undertaken in collaboration with Ray Fair.

Case's analysis of "The Market for Single-Family Homes in Boston, 1979–1985" (1986), and his subsequent paper with Robert Shiller, "Prices of Single Family Homes Since 1970" (1987), introduced improved methods of measuring asset prices. These methods, so-called weighted repeat sales price indices, are now the standard techniques used by government and private industry to track housing prices in the United States and in other countries as well. One of the great virtues of these indices, when compared to their hedonic counterparts, is that they depend far less on researchers' discretionary choices. These techniques have diffused rapidly. For example, they have been used to describe the course of housing prices in Amsterdam for the past 350 years (Eichholtz, 1997), to value private-equity start-up firms (Hwang, Quigley, and Woodward, 2005), and to record the price movements of paintings by the Dutch masters (Goetzmann, 1993), among many other applications.

These methodological contributions led directly to work on price dispersion and the equilibrium tendencies in spatially disbursed housing markets. The development of these price measures permitted direct investigations of market efficiency using micro data on prices. A major investigation of "The Efficiency of the Market for Single-Family Homes," also undertaken with Robert Shiller (1989), demonstrated how slowly equilibrium in the housing market was achieved. This treatment of market efficiency was an important development, and it remains the single most influential paper Case has produced.

In a related set of papers, Case analyzed the incidence of excess returns to housing investment (Case and Shiller, 1990), the distributional effects of housing booms and busts (Case and Cook, 1989), and the role of taxes in dampening speculative behavior in the housing market (Case, 1992). The magnitude and importance of house price fluctuations in affecting consumer welfare led to his important paper explicating the relevance of "Index-Based Futures and Options Markets in Real Estate" for housing and the real estate market (Case, Shiller, and Weiss, 1993). This paper is not among Case's most widely cited academic works, but it did lead to the practical development of institutions to mediate risk in the housing market. Consumers and investors now trade options on Case-Shiller Home Price Indices for a dozen cities on the Chicago Mercantile Exchange.

In tandem with his studies of housing dynamics, Case has conducted a series of empirical analyses linking local public finance to housing outcomes, especially school expenditures and school quality. His most widely cited paper in local public finance, "Property Tax Limits, Local Fiscal Behavior, and Property Values" (2001), undertaken with Katherine Bradbury and Christopher Mayer, concerns tax reform in Massachusetts.

It is a curse to live in interesting times. Case's career and prior work have made him the natural expositor and interpreter of the turmoil in the housing market after 2006. A once-overlooked Brookings paper he wrote, "Real Estate and the Macroeconomy" (2000), compared the volatility of house prices to the volatility in common stocks. In this paper, Case also exhibited the wide variety of short-run house price dynamics across different markets. This paper also emphasized the transmission of economic shocks through the construction sector—a mechanism that was subsequently observed more directly when housing starts declined from 2.3 million in 2006 to 500,000 in 2008. The Brookings essay also drew attention to the wealth effect of housing, that is, the propensity of homeowners to increase consumption in response to capital gains in the housing market. This work was subsequently extended by Case and his collaborators in "Comparing Wealth Effects," an empirical analysis using a panel of U.S. states and developed countries (Case, Quigley, and Shiller, 2005).

Case's analysis of housing market dynamics includes a more recent Brookings paper, "Is There a Bubble in the Housing Market?" (2003). Some of the conclusions of this paper seem almost prophetic a half-decade later. Importantly, however, this research was informed by analysis of a detailed survey of new home purchasers in four U.S. metropolitan areas. As this book goes to press, Case is distributing the fifth wave of this valuable survey to new home purchasers in Los Angeles, Boston, San Francisco, and Milwaukee.

It could not be more appropriate for a volume in honor of Karl Case to begin with a chapter by his longtime collaborator and business partner, Robert Shiller. Their long-term collaboration includes a mission to deepen the financial market so that individuals can hedge their investments in residential real estate. As Shiller points out in chapter 2, real estate is a $20 trillion market, and large groups of the population have the bulk of their wealth tied to a single volatile asset: their home. Yet, these households have little means of hedging the risk that arises from leveraged ownership of a particular house. Case and Shiller saw the development of derivatives, tied to the market prices of housing, as creating large social value by allowing homeowners to share some of their house value risk with investors and other market participants.

If there were to be a market for real estate index derivatives, then there needed to be clearly defined indices of real estate prices. As Shiller explains in his chapter, Case and Shiller's development of repeat sales indices represented an attempt to create a reliable and transparent alternative to hedonic price indices that could provide the basis for a financial instrument. The National Association of Realtors' (NAR's) monthly data on new home sales is the primary public data series that delivers price information at high frequencies (i.e., more often than once per year), but the NAR does nothing to correct for housing quality—and quality varies significantly over time and across markets.

So-called hedonic price methods provide one means of correcting for quality, but they give a great deal of discretion to the econometrician and are, inevitably, subject to a great deal of debate and ambiguity. Debate and confusion would be anathema to an index underlying a publicly traded security. Repeat sales indices have the great virtue of being enormously straightforward and eliminating econometric discretion. Case and Shiller's development of repeat sales indices made possible the development of a derivatives market tied to regularly measured, quality-adjusted real estate prices.

But even with these indices, the development of real estate derivatives has been a slow process. Shiller describes its tortuous pace, slowed down by a scandal in London, and he offers several explanations for why these markets have not matured more rapidly. One explanation, associated with Todd Sinai and Nick Souleles, is that home ownership is itself a hedge against changes in future housing costs. Although Shiller accepts this point, he also argues that surely there must still be millions of people, especially those who anticipate selling within five or 10 years, who would benefit from hedging their house price risk.

A second theory is that people are simply risk loving, which makes them uninterested in foregoing potential gains to hedge themselves against downside risk. Shiller also doubts the power of this explanation and instead argues that the root problem is that real estate index derivatives markets just have not yet become sufficiently liquid. Essentially, he is arguing that there is a coordination failure—people would like to trade if others are trading, but if volume is too small then no one enters the market. If this view is correct, then it is hard not to think that in the long run this coordination problem will be solved, and Case and Shiller's idea will eventually develop into a thriving market that provides hedging opportunities for millions of homeowners.

Timothy Riddiough's discussion of Shiller's essay distinguishes between the distinct, but related, notions of market efficiency and the insurance benefits of hedging. He demonstrates that the development of price indices by Case and Shiller has done much to improve the efficiency of the housing market. These efficiency gains, he argues, are independent of the insurance benefits to hedging that arise from the diversification of risk.

In Robert Van Order's commentary, he describes a variety of alternatives to the price indices developed by Case and Shiller, concluding that the methodology employed in producing the latter index is simply superior to the alternatives. He, too, professes bewilderment at the slow development of the futures market. He fervently hopes that this new market will take off, "although, given that my house will always go up in value, I am sure that I shall never want to use it."

In chapter 3, the second essay in this volume, Andrew Caplin, William Goetzmann, Eric Hangen, Barry Nalebuff, Elisabeth Prentice, John Rodkin, Tom Skinner, and Matthew Spiegel discuss a demonstration in one city (Syracuse, New York) in which home equity insurance was offered to homeowners. The authors' interest in helping homeowners reflects financial economists' concern with the losses arising from "missing markets." However, starting in the 1970s, community builders in Illinois thought that home equity insurance offered a means of protecting communities against the flight of homeowners eager to "cash out" before prices dropped. These plans, one of which was implemented in Oak Park, offered homeowners extremely generous insurance at low cost that was meant to be funded out of general property tax revenues. Over time, the success of the program implemented in Oak Park meant that this program was phased out, but it served as a model for the authors' pilot program implemented in Syracuse.

In Syracuse, the interest in home equity insurance also came from community builders, rather than financiers, and funds were available to subsidize the program. One of the goals of home equity insurance was to create more incentives for local renters to become homeowners. The essay describes the different elements involved in designing a home equity program for Syracuse. Unlike the Oak Park plan, the Syracuse plan tied home equity insurance to a repeat sales index rather than the price of an individual home. The use of an index, like that designed by Case and Shiller, reduces the scope for malfeasance or moral hazard by sellers. The legal challenges that had to be overcome to offer the product were considerable, and the authors describe these in great detail. The essay illustrates a particular and concrete setting where hedging home risk might be particularly appealing both to homeowners and policy makers.

In chapter 4, the third essay in this volume, Todd Sinai investigates the hedging demand for real estate index derivatives by using a classical model. A core insight of Sinai's work has been that renting is not necessarily less risky than owning. Everyone comes into the world needing to procure housing, and renters are continuously exposed to the risks of changes in future housing costs. Homeowners also face risks associated with changing housing prices, but those risks are realized only when the owner sells. The risk at sale, in turn, depends on the owner's residential arrangements after the sale and ultimately on the correlation between the price of the owner's current home and the price of the owner's future home. If the two homes, the current and the intended residence, are within the same metropolitan area, then the prices are certainly highly correlated, and there would be little value from hedging metropolitan area housing price risk.

If the owner is planning on moving across metropolitan areas, then the risk depends on the correlation in prices across those housing markets. Sinai empirically examines the correlation across those areas and concludes that it is rather high. For people who are planning on moving, at least to a relatively similar place, this mitigates the desire to hedge. Sinai concludes that the strongest demand for hedging should come from the elderly, who will be selling their residences at death and not moving anywhere else. But even that demand can be mitigated if older owners have children who are themselves renters and need hedging against housing costs.

In chapter 5, the fourth essay in this volume, Edward Glaeser and Joseph Gyourko address the no-arbitrage relationships that underlie all economic attempts to understand housing prices. This essay argues that the pure financial no-arbitrage relationship, which defines the margin between owning and renting, helps little in analyzing house price fluctuations. Although there are certainly people on the margin between owning and renting, the inability of researchers to measure all of the unobservable elements involved in the owning–renting decision makes the empirical use of that margin quite difficult.

Instead, the Glaeser–Gyourko essay argues that the spatial no-arbitrage condition, which requires that people be indifferent between different houses in different locations, offers a more solid grounding for analyzing housing price fluctuations. This viewpoint emphasizes that researchers should ask not whether prices are too high in relation to rents or the level of income in the country as a whole, but instead whether the price differences between two areas are too high in relation to differences in income and amenities available. The essay discusses empirical work, using this framework, that supports Case and Shiller's long-standing empirical finding that there is too much predictability of housing prices, and especially too much short-term momentum in prices, to be compatible with a perfectly rational model.

The fifth and sixth essays analyze the impact of credit innovations in the housing market. In chapter 6, Chris Mayer and Karen Pence turn to the subject of subprime mortgages. Over the past five years, subprime mortgages exploded in importance within the credit market. They seem to have been associated first with the boom in housing prices and then with a subsequent collapse in the price of housing. Mayer and Pence undertake the task of measuring the presence of subprime mortgages and then understanding the geography of those mortgages.

Because there is no formal definition of subprime mortgages, even basic measurement of subprime lending is difficult. Mayer and Pence use three different sources of data: high-cost loans reported under the Home Mortgage Disclosure Act (HMDA), data collected by the Department of Housing and Urban Development (HUD) on subprime lenders, and data from subprime mortgage pools gathered by First American Loan Performance. Although the three sources do not always agree—for example, the HMDA data report that there were almost a million more subprime mortgages in 2005 than are reported by either HUD or First American—the pattern of magnitudes of the variables that explain concentrations of subprime lending over space are similar.

The Mayer and Pence study documents at least five important facts about subprime lending. First, subprime loans were remarkably concentrated in particular metropolitan areas. Second, subprime lending was particularly prevalent in areas with booming housing markets, as measured by rising prices or the extent to which permits were issued for new construction. Third, subprime lending was more common in places with more poor and unemployed people. Fourth, subprime lending was more common in areas with higher home ownership rates. Fifth, there is a strong link between the subprime lending in a geographic area and the share of minorities residing in that area. These are important facts that can help us think about what happened in the explosion of higher-interest lending.

The commentary by C. F. Sirmans and Kerry Vandell on this timely research emphasizes the importance of Mayer and Pence's normalization of subprime loans per housing unit. This normalization clearly leads to an underestimation of the extent of subprime borrowing in largely renter-occupied areas, and it overestimates the extent of subprime lending in high-growth, high-price-appreciation areas. Sirmans and Vandell also point out that a broader definition of subprime mortgages would include many additional loans—option adjustable rate mortgages, interest-only mortgages, and a variety of second liens. Currently available data mask many of these distinctions and inevitably underestimate the incidence of exotic and subprime loans.

Chapter 7, by Stuart Gabriel and Stuart Rosenthal, also analyzes the impact of lending to poorer Americans who were not always served by traditional banks. Their essay analyzes the impact of the Community Reinvestment Act (CRA) and the Government-Sponsored Enterprises Act (GSEA) on home ownership and lending in the areas targeted by these pieces of legislation. Both acts require lenders to target lending toward poorer, traditionally underserved areas, with the aim of increasing lending within those areas. The two acts both have a narrow geographic focus that enables Gabriel and Rosenthal to use a spatial discontinuity research design to compare abutting tracts, some of which are defined as underserved and others of which are not.

Gabriel and Rosenthal find that underserved tracts experience an increase in GSE origination of conforming loans and a decrease at the same time in the origination of nonconforming loans. Gabriel and Rosenthal find exactly the opposite effect when they analyze the CRA. Nonconforming loans increase in the underserved areas and conforming loans decrease. Overall, they find that these interventions have no appreciable influence on the overall home ownership rate, which calls into question the value of these pieces of legislation.

The commentary by Lawrence Jones emphasizes the novelty of the essay by Gabriel and Rosenthal, namely their emphasis on the net change in home ownership in targeted areas, not merely the extent of lending.

The seventh essay continues on the topic of federal housing interventions that may affect distressed neighborhoods. In chapter 8, Ingrid Ellen, Katherine O'Regan, and Ioan Voicu turn the spotlight on the Low-Income Housing Tax Credit (LIHTC). Since 1986, the LIHTC has been the major federal program aimed at building new housing for poorer Americans. The program uses tax expenditures authorized under the tax code to subsidize new building, but that building must provide homes for poorer Americans. In some cases, the new housing must also be located in poorer areas. Two common criticisms of the act are that it concentrates poverty by building houses for poor people in poor areas and that low-income housing reduces the values of neighboring properties.

The evidence presented by Ellen, O'Regan, and Voicu calls these criticisms into serious question. Although LIHTC funding does encourage building in places that are poorer than the average census tract in the United States, the places chosen for investment are less poor than the average tract occupied by poorer Americans. As a result, the LIHTC actually helps to reduce residential segregation by income, at least relative to other federal housing programs such as Section 8 Vouchers. Ellen, O'Regan, and Voicu also find that housing prices tend to increase in areas that are close to LIHTC projects, which clearly rebuts the notion that these projects hurt their neighborhoods. Instead, the LIHTC seems to be contributing to neighborhood revitalization. Although many contentious issues surrounding the LIHTC remain, this essay provides a careful refutation of two important criticisms.

Daniel McMillen's commentary demonstrates that the LIHTC construction program cannot be expected to have significant effects upon the overall spatial concentration of poverty; there is just not enough new construction in large metropolitan areas for there to be large effects. Despite this, the LIHTC program can exert significant effects on smaller geographical areas. And the operation of the program does seem to be reducing segregation in these areas.

The eighth essay turns from national policy interventions in the housing market to more local interventions, specifically local land use controls. In chapter 9, John Quigley, Steven Raphael, and Larry Rosenthal present an overview of the literature on land use controls, and they present an index of land use restrictions in the San Francisco Bay Area based on a detailed survey of local land use officials. Over the past 40 years, land use controls have become more restrictive in many parts of the country. California has been a leader in restricting new development through local growth controls and statewide environmental rules. It is thus a natural place to study the impact of local land use controls.

The Berkeley Land Use Regulation Index combines information on explicit rules, average delays, and the political actors who are involved in the zoning process. Although many outsiders tend to see northern California as an antigrowth monolith, the index shows that there is considerable heterogeneity within the region. The essay also shows a strong connection between land use restrictions and higher prices and rents. Places that build less housing are more expensive. The entitlement process alone raises housing prices by $23,000 in the Bay Area.

In his discussion of this essay, Richard Green points out a potentially important reason why the statistical models explaining the effects of land use regulation on housing prices are more powerful than those explaining the effects of regulation on market rents. The user cost of capital (i.e., the ratio of rent to value) depends on interest rates, property tax rates, maintenance costs, and expectations about growth. These factors probably do not vary much within a metropolitan area, especially in California, where property taxes are mandated by state law. But marginal tax rates vary greatly within a region, especially in the San Francisco Bay Area (as per capita incomes vary from $22,000 a year in Oakland to $112,000 in Atherton). This increases the variability of house prices relative to rents within the region.

In his commentary, Stephen Malpezzi stresses the importance of understanding the determinants of the variation in regulatory stringency documented by Quigley, Raphael, and Rosenthal.

Chapter 10, the ninth essay in this volume, is by Ann Schnare, a respected consultant on housing policy and a longtime associate of Case, and Robert Kulick. Schnare and Kulick analyze competition among real estate agents. Although it is often alleged that the multiple listing service acts to enforce a cartel that keeps real estate commissions fixed, Schnare and Kulick present evidence suggesting that there is often significant flexibility and competition on price. This evidence certainly does not mean that the real estate industry is fully competitive, but it is not consistent with a view of the real estate brokerage industry as a tightly organized cartel.

The final essay in this volume is by Nancy Wallace and Case's graduate school classmate, Donald Walls. In chapter 11, Wallace and Walls exploit an important new data set reporting an annual time series of essentially all employment in all U.S. metropolitan areas by firm size and employment type. They exploit this unique resource to analyze the microeconomic determinants of the so-called rank-size rule, which seems to govern the size distribution of cities in developed countries. The point of departure for the Wallace–Walls analysis is the observation that the dynamics of job creation and destruction are inconsistent with the rank-size relationship, also known as Zipf's law. Wallace and Walls investigate the apparent dependence of establishment size and employment growth, as well as the effects of financial market frictions and industry-specific human capital on the linkage between size and employment growth. They find important effects of industry-specific capital and capital-labor ratios in explaining mean reversion in the growth and size relationships among firms and also in the aggregate economy. The data analyzed in this essay offer many more rich opportunities to explore economic development and metropolitan growth.

The 10 essays in this volume reflect broadly the intellectual pursuits of Karl Case—the operation of the housing market, its links to financial markets and the broader economy, and the role of policy in improving the efficiency and fairness of the market. We are pleased to dedicate their contributions to our friend and colleague, and this dedication is seconded by the discussants and the many participants in the 2007 policy conference in Cambridge on Housing and the Built Environment.

REFERENCES

Bradbury, Katherine, Karl E. Case, and Christopher Mayer. 2001. "Property Tax Limits, Local Fiscal Behavior, and Property Values: Evidence from Massachusetts Under Proposition 2½." *Journal of Public Economics* 80(2) (May): 287–311.

Case, Karl E. 1986. "The Market for Single-Family Homes in Boston, 1979–1985." *New England Economic Review* (May/June): 38–48.

———. 1992. "Taxes and Speculative Behavior in Land and Real Estate Markets." *Review of Urban and Regional Development Studies* 4(2): 226–239.

———. 2000. "Real Estate and the Macroeconomy." *Brookings Papers on Economic Activity* 2: 119–162.

Case, Karl E., and Leah Cook. 1989. "The Distributional Effects of Housing Price Booms: Winners and Losers in Boston, 1980–89." *New England Economic Review* (March/April): 3–12.

Case, Karl E., John M. Quigley, and Robert Shiller. 2005. "Comparing Wealth Effects: The Stock Market Versus the Housing Market." *Advances in Macroeconomics* 5(1) (March).

Case, Karl E., and Robert Shiller. 1987. "Prices of Single Family Homes Since 1970: New Indexes for Four Cities." *New England Economic Review* (September/October): 45–56.

———. 1989. "The Efficiency of the Market for Single-Family Homes." *American Economic Review* 79(1) (March): 125–137.

———. 1990. "Forecasting Prices and Excess Returns in the Housing Market." *Journal of the American Real Estate and Urban Economics Association* 18(4): 253–273.

———. 2003. "Is There a Bubble in the Housing Market?" *Brookings Papers on Economic Activity* 2: 299–362.

Case, Karl E., Robert J. Shiller, and Allan N. Weiss. 1993. "Index-Based Futures and Options Markets in Real Estate." *Journal of Portfolio Management* 19(2) (Winter): 83–92.

Eichholtz, Piet M. A. 1997. "A Long Run House Price Index: The Herengracht Index, 1628–1773." *Real Estate Economics* 25(2): 175–192.

Goetzmann, William N. 1993. "Accounting for Taste: An Analysis of Art Returns over Three Centuries." *American Economic Review* 83(5): 1370–1376.

Hwang, Min, John M. Quigley, and Susan Woodward. 2005. "An Index for Venture Capital, 1987–2003." *Contributions to Economic Analysis and Policy* 4(1): Article 13.

Part

II

HOUSING RISKS AND CHOICES

2

Derivatives Markets for Home Prices

ROBERT J. SHILLER

The near absence of derivatives markets for real estate, particularly for single-family homes, is a striking anomaly that cries out for explanation and for action to change the situation. In the United States alone, the value of real estate held by households is approximately $20 trillion, an amount rivaling the stock market. And yet, the number and variety of derivative instruments available for real estate are miniscule compared to those of stocks. The proper hedging of real estate risks is of utmost importance. The current world financial crisis, which began in early 2007 and which by 2008 produced the failure of the biggest mortgage finance institutions in history, Fannie Mae and Freddie Mac, along with general financial distress unseen since the Great Depression, has at its roots the failure to manage real estate risks properly.[1] And the failure of risk management can be traced squarely to the absence of liquid markets where real estate risks can be hedged.

Risk management theory has never assumed that only stock and bond risks should be managed. All economic risks should be managed. There are many kinds of economic risks, however, that are not managed, and real estate risk is high on the list. The recent subprime mortgage crisis might be described as the result of failure to manage risks properly. Research by Karl Case and John Quigley (2007) shows that decreases in recent and projected home prices

The author thanks David Blitzer, John Hartigan, Terry Loebs, Jonathan Reiss, Steve Rive, Aniket Ullal, and Ronit Walny for helpful comments.

1. See Shiller (2008).

have repercussions on the financial markets that are far more important than the direct wealth effects on the economy. If any factor will push the U.S. economy into recession in 2008, it will be the financial consequences of the housing decline. The repercussions of major changes in real estate prices go far beyond the risk of recession because they impinge on the well-being of hundreds of millions of people who are often locked into highly mortgage-leveraged positions in their individual homes.

BEGINNINGS OF DERIVATIVES MARKETS

Case and I have been working and thinking about real estate risk, and how it might be better managed, for 20 years. We effectively began our public advocacy for real estate futures markets in our 1989 paper on the efficiency of the market for single-family homes. In that paper, we showed that well-constructed repeat sales home price can accurately capture trends in the real estate market (more on this under "Repeat Sales Indices" in this chapter). The paper also found that these repeat sales indices—which, unlike previous indices, are not subject to the "noise" caused by change in mix of sales—are extremely autocorrelated and forecastable, with a forecast R-squared at a one-year horizon of about one-half. We attributed this forecastability to the profound illiquidity of the market. Much subsequent research (for example, Glaeser and Gyourko, 2006, and Gyourko, Mayer, and Sinai, 2006) confirms the inefficiency of the market for homes.

Professional investors find it very costly to trade in this market and to maintain an inventory of homes as investments. Thus, they can neither take advantage of the forecastability of home prices nor pursue actions that would enforce the efficiency of the market. The problem has been the total absence of derivatives markets for real estate prices. Extensive derivatives markets for mortgages exist, but, until very recently, no derivatives markets at all have been tied to real estate prices. If such markets could be created, they might ultimately lead toward more liquidity in the cash markets. With this thinking began Case's and my mission to create just such markets.

We thought that if a liquid futures market (or another kind of derivatives market) could be established for single-family homes, it might provide the financial infrastructure to bring forth a number of new financial instruments. Later, in my book *Macro Markets* (1993a), and in subsequent books *The New Financial Order* (2003) and *The Subprime Solution* (2008), I described some of these—home equity insurance, down-payment insurance on home mortgages, and price warranties on new homes—and how they might allow the rationalization of a number of businesses. Some of these instruments have since been put in place (see, for example, Goetzmann et al., 2007), but their success has been limited by the absence of hedging markets.

Karl Case, Allan Weiss, and I began our campaign to launch futures markets on single-family homes in 1990. We named ourselves the Index Research Group, but by June we were the Case Shiller Weiss Research Group. We presented our idea at the Coffee, Sugar and Cocoa Exchange (which had previously launched the innovative, but ultimately unsuccessful, consumer price index futures market) in August 1990 and at the Chicago Board of Trade in November 1990. In November 1991, along with partner Charles Longfield, we created Case Shiller Weiss, Inc., a firm whose sole purpose was to produce home price indices designed expressly to settle financial contracts. The discussions with the Chicago Board of Trade led to an alliance between it and our firm to study the possibility of launching home price futures.

The Board did a telephone survey of potential traders in 1993. It concluded that people were willing to sell real estate futures but not willing to buy, so they became reluctant to launch the products at that time. We argued with them that it is probably easier to discover short interest than long interest in a prospective new market, for the short interest is shown by those people who own real estate and have a hedging need, whereas long interest is exhibited by those who want merely to add real estate to their investment portfolios and cannot feel any particular interest in investing in the contracts until they know what the price is and how it relates to other investment returns. Despite our arguments, however, the Board ultimately decided not to launch the home price futures.

In 1991 the London Futures and Options Exchange (London Fox) beat us to the market, although not as competitors because they launched in a different country. The Exchange attempted to create futures markets for both single-family homes and commercial real estate. However, over the few months in which these markets were open, there was little trade. The rapid demise of these markets was due not directly to the low volume, but to efforts to pad the volume. When it was discovered that traders were doing wash trades to pad the volume numbers, the markets were shut down in a scandal. People I spoke to in London in 1991 expressed disappointment that this wash-trading scandal had shut down the markets before they had been open long enough to be given a real test. Indeed, the failure of these markets did not prove anything about the ultimate viability of such markets, although it created a bad precedent and slowed down the launch of our own markets by many years.

The beginnings of a worldwide boom in home prices in the late 1990s led to renewed interest in markets for home values. In the United Kingdom, City Index launched a spread betting market in single-family homes in 2001; this was quickly followed by another spread betting market launched by IG Index in 2002. Although both of these markets were shut down by 2004, attempts have since been made to reopen property spread betting markets in the United Kingdom—for example, by Cantor Index, which has launched spread betting on U.K. home prices (www.spreadfair.com).

Goldman Sachs opened a market in 2003 for covered warrants on U.K. home price indices on the London Stock Exchange that were settled in terms of the Halifax home price indices. However, as of 2004, the open interest was very small, roughly the amount that one would expect if only 100 houses were hedged. It has been hard to get hedging markets started for real estate.

In 2004, Hedgestreet.com created markets for single-family homes, among other markets, on a dedicated Web site aimed at consumers. The site allowed trading in "hedgelets," which were, in effect, $10 bets on the direction of home prices, bets that could be used (if very many such bets were made by one homeowner) to hedge movement in home prices. John Nafeh, the founder of Hedgestreet.com, believed that people would use these hedgelets to help insulate them from economic risks. However, the site was not a success, and trading has been shut down and replaced with mock trading only.

In May 2006 the Chicago Mercantile Exchange (now the CME Group, after the 2007 merger with the Chicago Board of Trade), in collaboration with the firm MacroMarkets LLC that Allan Weiss, Sam Masucci, and I founded, launched futures and options markets on the home price indices that Case and I pioneered, now called the Standard and Poor's/Case-Shiller Home Price Indices. These indices are produced by Fiserv, Inc., the company that purchased Case Shiller Weiss, Inc. in 2002 and continues to produce the thousands of Case-Shiller Home Price Indices by county, zip code, and price tier. Futures contracts, with a February quarterly cycle of expiration dates and settled at $250 times the index, were launched for 10 U.S. cities and an aggregate index. This market has been much more successful and credible than its predecessors. The total notional value of futures and options traded from inception through 21 November 2007 is $612 million. Substantial trades continue: for example, in the week of 5–9 November 2007, a notional value of $2,782,600 was traded. However, the futures' open interest in the 10 contracts together, which peaked at $109 million in February 2007, has fallen with each contract expiration and stood at $20 million as of mid-2008. Between contract expirations, the open interest has been growing at a good, steady rate, cumulating to a 39 percent increase in the three months since the 31 August 2007 expiration, thus pointing to some signs of hope for the growth of these contracts. The longer maturities (from one to five years) that were added in September 2007 may enhance the product's utility.

New markets for commercial real estate have also emerged. In London, the Investment Property Databank (IPD) has begun to be used for derivatives products, for which the global notional outstanding value of property derivatives trades has reached £11.5 billion (de Terán 2007). A swaps market for real estate has begun to develop in the United States, where a company called Radar Logic has found some success in creating home price derivatives for single-family homes with its RPX index, which is based on the median of a maximum likelihood estimate of the distribution of all home prices sold in the time period per square foot of floor space (existing, new, and condominium).

On 2 November 2007, the CME Group announced that it was expanding its suite of real estate indices to include the S&P/GRA Commercial Real Estate Indices, which are a joint venture of Standard & Poor's and Global Real Analytics/Charles Schwab Investment Management, the indices spearheaded by Robert Edelstein. The S&P/GRA index is not a repeat sales index because the authors conclude that there are too few sales of commercial real estate for such a method.[2] Their method uses weighted average transaction prices per square foot, and indices are traded for five major U.S. regions (Northeast, Mid-Atlantic South, Midwest, Desert Mountain, and Pacific West) and four property sectors (apartment, office, retail, and warehouse). Listings for futures contracts for all nine of these contracts and for horizons out as far as five years were posted on 29 October 2007, but trade of these indices so far has gone nowhere.

REPEAT SALES INDICES

The most important innovation making real estate derivatives markets possible has been advances in index technology, notably the advance of electronic technology for recording home sales prices and the invention and development of repeat sales home price indices. The repeat sales indices are the natural extension of existing stock price indices, like the S&P 500. The changes through time in the S&P 500 Index are based on changes in the price of individual stocks. If individual stock prices do not change, then the index does not change.

The S&P 500 Index level does not go up if there is a higher volume of sales in higher-priced stocks; the index is expressly designed not to be affected by sales of the individual stocks, only by the changes in their prices. However, for

---

2. However, as announced in October 2007, David Geltner and Henry Pollakowski of MIT and the company REAL have partnered with Moody's to produce commercial real estate indices. See Geltner and Pollakowski (2007).

real estate, the nontrading problem (the problem that a property or share is not traded at all for some time) is much more severe and requires explicit attention.

Karl Case had an important insight in his 1986 paper: the repeat sales method allows us to construct home price indices that control for quality change in an objective and systematic way. He independently rediscovered the repeat sales (or repeated measures) price index method, which was previously described by Wyngarden (1927), Wenzlick (1952), and Bailey, Muth, and Nourse (1963). The repeat sales method was not received with any enthusiasm when proposed by these authors. As far as we know, no ongoing effort to produce a repeat sales home price initiative was ever launched before we did that. But Case convinced me that the repeat sales method was essential, and thus the natural method for index number construction, as I will expand on here (see Case and Shiller, 1988, 1990, 1993; Palmquist, 1980).

The repeat sales method was criticized by Mark and Goldberg (1984) as throwing away too much data because only homes that provide sales prices at two different dates can be used. With hedonic methods, in contrast, every single sales observation can be used as an input to the index. It may sound from this that hedonic methods have an advantage, but, except for cases in which data are very sparse or there is reason to think that repeat sales are highly unrepresentative, that is not so. Hedonic and repeat sales methods can also be combined (see Shiller, 1993b).

I remember Case convincing me that for the purpose of creating indices for settlement of financial contracts, the repeat sales method is the only way to go. He maintained that he could make a price index do anything one might want by choosing hedonic variables to that end. The problem is that there are too many possible hedonic variables that might be included, and if there are n possible hedonic variables, then there are n-factorial possible lists of independent variables in a hedonic regression, often a very large number. One could strategically vary the list of included variables until one found the desired results. Looking at different hedonic indices for the same city, I saw substantial differences, which must have been due to choices the constructors made. Thus, the indices have the appearance of hypotheses rather than objective facts. One is reminded of Ed Leamer's paper "Let's Take the Con Out of Econometrics" (1983), in which he remarked on the multitude of tricks that econometricians use to get the results they want, and what they sometimes seem to want is just to come up with a different result.

Hedonic variables can come into significance in a regression for spurious reasons. For example, it has been reported that in hedonic regressions explaining home prices, a dummy for air conditioning sometimes has the wrong sign, allegedly in at least one instance, because houses on the shore, where there are cool breezes, are less likely to have air conditioning and more likely to be more valuable because they are on the shore. Thus, if air conditioning becomes more common over the years, a price index based on hedonic regression that includes the air conditioning dummy but excludes a variable representing proximity to shore could show a spurious downtrend in price. If an econometrician wanted to score points by contradicting earlier indices, a search over the set of all possible hedonic regressors for the right combination of regressors might well achieve this. This can leave the public confidence in the indices in disarray by creating an impression that no one knows what home prices are doing.

As I argued in *Macro Markets*, one may think of the repeat sales home price index method as a hedonic regression where there is one dummy hedonic variable for each house and no other hedonic variables. That is, we can think of the repeat sales regression method as taking each sale price as an observation for the dependent variable (so that the number of observations equals the number of all single sales, whether in pairs or not) and using as independent variables a complete set of time dummies (one for each period) and a complete set of house dummies (one for each house, the ith dummy being the numeral 1 only if the sale represents the ith house). Any house that is sold only once is in effect "dummied out" in such a regression and has no effect on the results. In that sense, we are not throwing away data by using repeat sales methods, but rather using all the data with a very complete set of hedonic variables that is defined in a systematic way that eliminates all possible discretion in choosing hedonic variables.

Square footage of property is just an example of one hedonic variable, and taking as an index some indicator of price per square foot is, in effect, running a hedonic regression and constraining the coefficient of this variable to be one and the constant term to be zero, so that no regression need be calculated at all. There are so many other hedonic variables, such as square footage of lot and quality of neighborhood, that the price per square foot alone is only one of very many quality measures. The constant term in a hedonic regression of price on the number of square feet of floor space will certainly be a nonzero constant term, which differs across neighborhoods and property types.

It is very important to get the index number construction method right when one starts trading real estate derivatives. One anomalous reading from an index that has inadequate controls for quality mix could cost traders millions of dollars and create bad feeling for the entire concept of real estate derivatives.

As an exercise, to add some perspective on the potential importance of repeat sales, from January 2003 to December 2007 I computed a monthly volume-weighted median price of the 500 stocks that constitute the S&P 500

Index. I used 12-month average volume of sales for each stock as the weight of its price in calculating the median. This is doing something analogous to what the National Association of Realtors (NAR) does when it computes the median price of existing homes. In contrast, the S&P 500 Index takes careful account of the changing number of shares outstanding for each stock, and when stocks are added or removed from the index, the divisor is adjusted appropriately so that there is no sudden spurious jump in the index. But for this exercise I dispensed with a divisor altogether and let the sales volume for each stock determine the weight it got in the index. The NAR, of course, has no divisor because it takes no account of changes in the mix of homes and makes no other adjustments for possible jumps in the index caused by sudden changes in the mix of sales. My resultant stock price index looks quite different from the S&P 500. The correlation coefficient between the monthly changes in the volume-weighted median and the change in the S&P 500 was only 0.38. Moreover, the standard deviation of the monthly percentage change in the volume-weighted median was more than twice as high as that of the S&P 500.

This exercise with the 500 stocks in the S&P 500 Index has, to my knowledge, not been tried before. Apparently no one would choose a volume-weighted stock price index if they had a choice, so no one does it, and all stock price indices are repeat sales indices. (Volume-weighted indices have been used for special purposes — for example, in constructing measures of the mispricing of options. Volume weighting has been used so that mispricing of insignificantly traded options does not overly affect the measure of mispricing. The volume-weighted stock price has also been used in studies of transaction costs.)

Repeat sales methods thus do not use new-home prices. This is a potentially important advantage when compared with other indices that incorporate both new and existing home prices. A problem with including new-home prices could at times be severe: the median price of a new home on the market changes over time, as market conditions and the supply of new homes change. If high-quality homes with plenty of land in wealthy neighborhoods in good school districts are selling well at some times, then new-home prices will at those times be higher than usual, even if there is no change at all in the price of individual existing homes.

Between May 2006 and December 2007, the monthly ratio of new sales to existing sales (the former from the U.S. Census Bureau, the latter from the NAR) ranged between 10.4 percent and 18.2 percent, a significant variation. But the fraction constituting new sales is relatively low, and the difference in price (the median new-home sales price being only 10.5 percent higher, on average) is such that the weighting anomalies have not been large. The presence of new sales along with existing sales could, however, become an important problem for median price indices of home prices in the future if either the fraction of sales or the relative price of new homes varies greatly.

The problem with raw new-home sales prices is that they are a virtually meaningless series, for they represent a constantly changing thing. New homes are built in times and places where the market is strong, and hence are highly unrepresentative of home prices, even of newer-home prices. Certainly, new homes will not be built at all in areas where home prices have declined far enough that price is below construction cost. Looking at median new-home prices as an indicator of the market is like looking at the median price of a piece of fruit sold as an indicator of the fruit market, without regard for the fact that the varieties of fruit sold change over time.

There are other important changes in the mix of homes sold. According to the Massachusetts Association of Realtors, the fraction of Boston-area home sales that were condominiums rose from 26.3 percent in 1998 to 49.5 percent in 2005, a near doubling of the fraction of condos. Condominiums are very different from single-family homes, and if price is corrected for the number of square feet of floor space, may have a very different relation to square feet than do single-family homes, which have land as well.

We of course do not have data on all dimensions of change in mix. But the data we do have suggests that change in mix can be very important and should be dealt with carefully. The best method available to take account of change in mix is the use of repeat sales indices. We have also been producing repeat sales method separately for price tier (low, medium, or high-priced homes) and property type (single-family or condominium); anyone who wants a specific mix of these types should use a weighted average of such repeat sales indices.

OTHER INDICES

Because of these problems, the Census Bureau has produced since 1964 a "Constant Quality (LaSpeyres) Price Index of New One-Family Houses Under Construction." The correlation between the monthly change in their median new-home price and the monthly change in their Constant Quality Index from May 2006 to December 2007 has been only 0.11. This figure is surprisingly low and indicates the sharp changes in mix that occur month to month. It is remarkable that the news media seem to accept the latest median new-home price number while largely ignoring the Constant Quality Index, when the former is so heavily driven by what must be simply noise.

In the current (2005) incarnation of the Constant Quality Index, the Census Bureau uses, in addition to the average number of square feet of floor area in the house, the log of square feet and 49 other variables that indicate quality and geographical location. The Bureau uses census region, construction method, exterior wall material, heating system and air conditioning form, parking facilities, finished basement, number of bathrooms, number of fireplaces, and so on. It is unlikely, however, even with all these variables, that they can really get a representative price of a constant-quality new house, because change is the essence of new houses, as they are built in the precise microgeographical area and with precise features that represent current buyer interests.

A repeat sales index such as the Case-Shiller index solves all these problems by following individual homes through time. One could also add additional hedonic variables to a repeat sales regression, as long as these variables change over time for individual houses (otherwise there would be multicollinearity). In *Macro Markets* I called such a regression a hedonic repeated-measures regression. However, any such method is inherently tied to taking account of important hedonic variables that change through time for an individual house, and it does not appear that there are obvious candidates for such variables at present.

There are other ways in which repeat sales indices could be improved. Childs, Ott, and Riddiough (2002) have shown a method that deals with noise in asset prices by creating a time-filtered value that takes account of autocorrelation. Genesove and Mayer (1997) have shown a regression method that corrects equilibrium home prices for bias from homeowners holding out for a better price. Case and Quigley (1991) have shown a different way of combining hedonic and repeat sales methodology. The index methodology is something that may be changed somewhat in the future to reflect better methodology, although we need to be conservative in our adjustment of methods—and wary of any methods that might involve judgment or the possibility of manipulation—if we are to maintain the trust of the market.

Of course, we have to throw away data if we want to measure some theoretical quantity accurately. That is what futures markets, in fact, systematically do when they narrowly define the kind of commodity that may be delivered in fulfillment of a futures contract. In wheat futures, for example, one may be required to deliver hard winter wheat of a certain kind and quality, without being able to substitute soft summer wheat. The futures exchanges make these rules because they know that otherwise the price of the wheat delivered would be erratic, for at some times one kind of wheat would be delivered and at other times another grade would be.

A Regret-Theory Approach to Understanding Obstacles to Hedging Real Estate Prices

In the United Kingdom, the spread betting markets were shut down just at the time that home prices had begun to fall in 2004 after a huge boom. In December 2004 I asked John Austin, who was manager of the property spread betting at IG Index, why the firm had shut down the market. He said, "We're only getting one-way sentiment." The volume of trade was rapidly falling off, he continued, and it was as if everyone had the same opinion about the U.K. housing market—that it would decline and hence there was no basis for trade. This view would turn out to be rather ironic, for in fact the U.K. property market had a remarkable turn of fortune and prices began to increase rapidly again starting in 2005.

But it seems that Austin was trying to say to me that people who might have traded were of two views: there were those who hoped to take short positions in a non-backwardated market, and those who hoped to take long positions in a backwardated market. But there were few crossings of orders, and therefore very little trade.

I also asked him why he thought there was relatively little volume in these bets even before the drop in home prices, for, when they launched these contracts, the market in the United Kingdom was rising. Would one not think that, in a time of such attention to housing market conditions, a substantial number of people would want to hedge their homes? Austin replied that IG Index had never promoted spread betting as a hedging device and that virtually all of their customers were in it for sport or amusement, not hedging.

Note that the theory he presented for the relatively low volume of the IG Index property spread betting market is analogous to that which is often used to describe the tendency of volume of sales on the housing market itself to decline in times of falling prices. The oft-cited theory is that homeowners are reluctant to realize a loss on their house and so hold out, trying to wait until the market provides them with the profit they want. They simply regret having bought at a high price and wish to avoid the pain of regret by avoiding selling. Regret theory (Loomis and Sugden, 1982) can model this behavior, and the prospect theory of Kahneman and Tversky (1979) yields similar implications.

Genesove and Mayer (1997) showed, with data on Boston condominium sales, that indeed those homeowners who bought when home prices were higher than currently held out longer than did homeowners who bought when prices were lower. It appears that there is a pain of regret at selling at a loss, and so people take steps to avoid this pain, even if it means not selling the property for a long time. Psychologists have documented that pain of regret is actively avoided, even if the means of doing so involve deliberate self-deception.

Case and I have been surveying recent home buyers and sellers, asking those who had trouble selling their house why they did not lower their price, as follows:

> 23n. If your property did not sell, presumably it might have if you had lowered the asking price more. If you considered doing so but decided not to, can you say why?
>   1. My house is worth more than people seem to be willing to pay right now.
>   2. I can't afford to sell at a lower price.
>   3. By holding out, I will be able to get more later.
>   4. I didn't want to pay off my low-rate mortgage.
>   5. Other: _____

In our 2007 survey, only 27 of 300 respondents reported having had trouble selling their prior house and chose to answer this question. But, for what it is worth, 9 of them picked the first response, 9 picked the second response, 3 picked the third response, 0 picked the fourth response, and 6 picked the fifth response. Eighteen of them picked the first two responses, answers which would appear to be consistent with regret theory, and only 3 picked the third response, which would be a purely rational economic motivation.

Psychologists say that the pain of regret is something people like to avoid. If they have made a mistake that has lost them money, they do not want to think about it.

It is now clear that in a down market, such as London in 2004, which turned out in fact to be a harbinger of a serious down market in future years, owners of real estate are going to lose substantially because of the inertial nature of housing markets. One has already lost the expected amount, in effect, if one is not going to sell the property, and the loss is painful to watch. Therefore, the natural hedgers would like to tune out and just forget about it.

Suppose the London housing market is expected to lose 10 percent over the next year. That is already a given. A hedger, however, is supposed to want to hedge against the risk that it will go down 20 percent. So, the hedger sells a futures contract. If the price of the house goes down 20 percent, the hedger is rewarded by the futures contract, so that total loss on the house is only 10 percent. But, on the other side, if home prices don't go down at all, then the hedger still loses 10 percent.

Maybe that is what John Austin was discovering. If he lowers the price so far that it would cause hedgers to lose if prices drop only 5 percent, they just do not want to think about that.

Kahneman and Tversky, the authors of prospect theory, say that people are risk lovers for losses, that they are willing to take big risks to try to get off scot-free, with no loss. If one takes a short futures contract on real estate in a down market, the possibility of getting off scot-free is eliminated. Perhaps that is why people do not want to do it. They do not want to face up to the fact that they have lost money.

The reason property is so different from other markets is that it must sometimes endure deep discounts because there are expectations of big price change. Other markets for liquid assets are also nearly random walks. Oil is an example of an existing futures market that may more closely resemble the futures market for housing. The NYMEX (New York Mercantile Exchange) futures market for light, sweet crude oil has been in backwardation about half the time.

A LACK-OF-HEDGING-DEMAND THEORY FOR THE SLOWNESS OF REAL ESTATE DERIVATIVES TO DEVELOP

Another theory has been proposed to explain the relative lack of success of hedging markets for real estate: owner-occupants, if not other investors, are self-hedged and hence do not need to hedge their risks. In its simplest form, the argument is that people generally expect to live in a house forever, and so if they will never sell their property, the price it attains in the market is irrelevant to them. If that is the case, then hedging their home price risks might actually create problems rather than solve them, for should home prices rise, then a homeowner who had shorted the market would have to come up with money to pay on the risk management contract.

Sinai and Souleles (2004) and Sinai (2007) argued that for owner-occupants, purchasing a home may be a way of hedging volatility of rent risk. They showed evidence that in cities with more volatile rent, home ownership rates are slightly higher. It is indeed plausible that one motive for owning a home could be to hedge rent risk.

Even if there is a self-hedging aspect to holding real estate, it is certainly not the case that every owner-occupant is at optimal exposure to real estate risk. There are many special situations. Some people are nearing retirement and planning to leave the housing market, and may be worried about the amount of money that will be available to them in retirement. Some are counting on reverse mortgages to sustain them in retirement and are worried about the amount that they can get. Some people are living in geographic areas with volatile housing markets and contemplating moving to another area. Some are contemplating moving to a volatile area. Some are renting and hoping to buy soon. Some own and plan to trade up soon. Some own a second or third home that they are fixing up, and they wish to use their skills in fixing up the home rather than in predicting the real estate market. Some work in the construction industry and have exposure to the housing market beyond what they get through their home. Some are concerned that a possible fall in the real estate market will wipe out their home equity and make it impossible for them to sell and move, as well as to borrow against their home.

And, of course, owner-occupants are hardly the only players in the single-family home market. There are professionals in real estate: builders, electricians, plumbers, and others whose fortunes depend on real estate. There are the portfolio managers, including managers of hedge funds, who have in effect leveraged positions in housing because of their strategy in the market for residential mortgage-backed securities (RMBSs) or collateralized debt obligations (CDOs). And there are the mortgage insurers and the remains (after the government conservatorship of Fannie Mae and Freddie Mac) of the government-sponsored enterprises (GSEs) who guarantee mortgages and who are vulnerable to changes in home prices. Defaults on mortgages may be thought of as exercises on options, and these options become "in the money" when home prices fall. Home prices thus explain a substantial portion of mortgage defaults (Case and Shiller, 1996; Deng, Quigley, and Van Order, 2000).

THE PROSPECTS FOR REAL ESTATE DERIVATIVES

I do not believe that either regret theory or the lack-of-hedging-demand theory is the primary reason for the slowness in growth of the derivatives markets for real estate.

The regret theory just does not seem powerful enough to be a long-term obstacle to the hedging of housing market risk. During a housing downturn, the decline in volume of sales in the cash market for homes is typically no more than 40 percent. If we applied that ratio to the volume of trade in single-family home derivatives in the present market, it would suggest that there still should be a huge market.

Moreover, the lack-of-hedging-demand theory also does not seem powerful enough. Given all the special reasons discussed in the preceding section that different people have for concerns that they are over- or underexposed to real estate risk, it is inconceivable that there would be no interest in hedging real estate risk. This is especially so at present, when talk about the real estate market is everywhere and a subprime mortgage crisis related fundamentally to that market is described as the biggest risk facing the national economy. I think the difficulty is, rather, more that there are problems inherent in getting any new market started, problems that are heightened when the new market is very unusual.

The principal problem, as I see it, in the CME futures market is that it just does not have enough liquidity. I spoke to institutional investors who considered placing substantial orders on our CME futures contracts, but these people reported to me that they saw relatively large bid-asked spreads and only small positions offered. One of them told me that, on looking at the book, he decided to wait a year and look again. The greatest problem here is the dearth of market makers committed to the CME futures, and capital market hiccups this year have not been exactly conducive to institutions assuming and trading new exposures.

Starting a new market is like opening a nightclub. Lots of people will want to come if lots of people are there. But, if few people are there, few people will want to come. Somehow, nightclubs do get started. So too, do real estate futures markets, but it takes time. The liquidity of the futures and options markets may be enhanced as other derivatives—such as index-linked notes, forwards, and swaps—take hold.

Given the current lack of liquidity in the backwardated futures markets, the regret-theory explanation of low volume of trade that is characteristic of declining housing markets may be amplified at the present time. With little liquidity, the prices in these markets are not regarded as authoritative; they do not form a standard of value that is widely cited. Hence, people do not see the loss predicted in these markets as a sunk cost; they do not view these as givens. They may think that they can avoid the pain of regret by choosing to ignore them.

The lack of liquidity in the current markets may also amplify the willingness of people to neglect their hedging demands and to imagine that they are doing enough to hedge their real estate risks. If one can do nothing to hedge one's real estate risks, then one spends very little time developing one's thinking about these risks. After the risks can be hedged, only then will thinking about the need for hedging develop, and only then will expertise on how to hedge these risks be promulgated.

Once liquidity develops further in the real estate hedging markets, one might expect to see less of a problem from regret and more of a willingness on the part of investors to think hard about how they should be hedging their real estate risks. At that point, one may hope to see derivatives markets for real estate come into their full flower.

REFERENCES

Bailey, Martin J., Richard F. Muth, and Hugh O. Nourse. 1963. "A Regression Method for Real Estate Price Index Construction." *Journal of the American Statistical Association* (December): 933–942.

Case, Bradford, and John Quigley. 1991. "The Dynamics of Real Estate Prices." *Review of Economics and Statistics* 73(1) (February): 50–58.

Case, Karl E. 1986. "The Market for Single-Family Homes in Boston, 1979–1985." *New England Economic Review* (May/June): 38–48.

Case, Karl E., and John M. Quigley. 2007. "How Housing Booms Unwind: Income Effects, Wealth Effects, and Feedbacks Through Financial Markets." Unpublished paper, Wellesley College.

Case, Karl E., and Robert J. Shiller. 1988. "Prices of Single Family Homes Since 1970: The Experience of Four Cities." *New England Economic Review*.

———. 1989. "The Efficiency of the Market for Single-Family Homes." *American Economic Review* 79(1) (March): 125–137.

———. 1990. "Forecasting Prices and Excess Returns in the Housing Market." *Journal of the American Real Estate and Urban Economics Association Journal (AREUEA Journal)* 18(3): 253–273.

———. 1993. "A Decade of Boom and Bust in Single-Family Home Prices: Boston and Los Angeles, 1983–1993." *Revue d'Economie Financiere* (December): 389–407. Reprinted in *New England Economic Review* (March/April 1994): 40–51.

———. 1996. "Mortgage Default Risk and Real Estate Prices: The Use of Index-Based Futures and Options in Real Estate." *Journal of Housing Research* 7(2): 243–258.

Childs, Paul D., Steven H. Ott, and Timothy J. Riddiough. 2002. "Optimal Valuation of Noisy Real Assets." *Real Estate Economics* 30(3): 385–414.

Deng, Yongheng, John M. Quigley, and Robert Van Order. 2000. "Mortgage Terminations, Heterogeneity, and the Exercise of Mortgage Options." *Econometrica* 68(2) (March): 275–301.

de Terán, Natasha. 2007. "Property Derivatives Market Ready to Explode." *Dow Jones Financial News Online*, November 23.

Geltner, David, and Henry Pollakowski. 2007. "A Set of Indices for Trading Commercial Real Estate Based on the Real Capital Analytics Transaction Prices Database." Cambridge MA: MIT Center for Real Estate, September 26.

Genesove, David, and Christopher Mayer. 1997. "Equity and Time to Sale in the Real Estate Market." *American Economic Review* 87(3) (June): 255–269.

Glaeser, Edward L., and Joseph Gyourko. 2006. "Housing Dynamics." National Bureau of Economic Research Working Paper No. 12787, December.

Goetzmann, William, Andrew Caplin, Eric Hangen, Elisabeth Prentice, John Rodkin, Matthew Spiegel, and Tom Skinner. 2007. "Home Equity Insurance: A Pilot Project." Paper presented at the Lincoln Institute of Land Policy Conference "Housing and the Built Environment: Access, Finance, Policy," December.

Gyourko, Joseph, Christopher Mayer, and Todd Sinai. 2006. "Superstar Cities." National Bureau of Economic Research Working Paper No. 12355, July.

Kahneman, Daniel, and Amos Tversky. 1979. "Prospect Theory: An Analysis of Decision Under Risk." *Econometrica* 47(2): 263–291.

Leamer, Edward. 1983. "Let's Take the Con Out of Econometrics." *American Economic Review* 73(1) (March): 31–43.

Loomis, Graham, and Robert Sugden. 1982. "Regret Theory: An Alternative Theory of Rational Choice Under Uncertainty." *Economic Journal* 92 (December): 805–824.

Mark, Jonathan H., and Michael A. Goldberg. 1984. "Alternative Housing Price Indices: An Evaluation." *Journal of the American Real Estate and Urban Economics Association (AREUEA Journal)* 12(1) (Spring): 30–49.

Palmquist, Raymond B. 1980. "Alternative Techniques for Developing Real Estate Price Indexes." *Review of Economics and Statistics* 62 (August): 442–480.

Shiller, Robert J. 1993a. *Macro Markets: Creating Institutions for Managing Society's Largest Economic Risks*. Oxford: Oxford University Press.

———. 1993b. "Measuring Asset Value for Cash Settlement in Derivatives Markets: Hedonic Repeated Measures Indices and Perpetual Futures." *Journal of Finance* 68 (July): 911–931.

———. 2003. *The New Financial Order: Risk in the 21st Century*. Princeton, NJ: Princeton University Press.

———. 2008. *The Subprime Solution: How Today's Global Financial Crisis Happened and What to Do About It*. Princeton, NJ: Princeton University Press.

Sinai, Todd. 2007. "The Risk of Home Ownership." Unpublished paper, University of Pennsylvania.

Sinai, Todd, and Nicholas Souleles. 2004. "Owner-Occupied Housing as a Hedge Against Rent Risk." Unpublished paper, University of Pennsylvania.

Wenzlick, Roy. 1952. "As I See the Fluctuations in the Selling Prices of Single-Family Residences." *The Real Estate Analyst* 21 (December 24): 541–548.

Wyngarden, Herman. 1927. "An Index of Local Real Estate Prices." *Michigan Business Studies* (Ann Arbor: University of Michigan) 1(2).

Commentary

Timothy J. Riddiough

No one has done more than Chip Case and Bob Shiller to focus economists and policy makers on the importance of the market for single-family homes. And they do more than just talk about weaknesses in the market—they try to do something about them in order to change things for the better. Their work, which bridges academic scholarship and real-world application, and which is really a fantastically important initiative, has led to the development and refinement of the repeat sales method for price indexing and home valuation as well as the beginnings of hedging markets for the most important investment in the lives of many individuals and families. In the spirit of Keynes, their cumulative work is a monumental effort to make the irrational more rational, to shorten the long run, and to change the facts in order to help the rest of us change our minds.

Robert Shiller's chapter, "Derivatives Markets for Home Prices," has two primary objectives. First, it looks backward to summarize contributions related to analyzing the relative efficiency of the housing market; second, it looks forward to make the case for the continued development of derivatives markets for home prices.

Because of the chapter's dual perspectives, it is important to clearly distinguish between the distinct but related notions of market efficiency and hedging-insurance benefits. Market efficiency of housing is usually judged in the context of classical asset pricing, in which the market is deemed to be efficient when it is sufficiently difficult to predict future home prices on the basis of historical information. As Professor Shiller reminds us, it is well known that the market for single-family homes is far from efficient. This is because of market frictions, including most prominently search and related transaction costs, high storage costs that are defrayed only through personal consumption or renting, and an inability to sell short the underlying asset.

These frictions in the underlying asset market make it difficult to execute riskless arbitrage, which would otherwise produce a more informationally efficient market. All is not lost, however, since well-constructed indices, such as those that utilize Case and Shiller's repeat sales method, can affect market outcomes. That is, the information generated by this type of index is a public good available for consumption by any and all market participants. Self-interested capital allocation decisions can, and presumably will, be affected by information contained in the index, thus affecting transaction prices to improve the efficiency of the market. An additional attraction would be a forward market on house prices, since the forward market offers (presumably unbiased) predictions of future house prices that can then feed back to further improve capital allocation decisions going forward.

Hedging and insurance benefits that accrue to individual homeowners from the development of a housing derivatives market are different from capital allocation outcomes related to market efficiency. Hedging and insurance benefits of derivatives market development come in two somewhat different forms. First, given that markets in aggregate are inevitably incomplete, an accessible derivatives market can help consumers diversify and otherwise hedge against fundamental economic risks they face in consumption and investment decision making. Second, such a market can assist in short-term idiosyncratic risk management. For example, an individual can engage in retirement planning by longing home price futures in a retirement destination and shorting home price futures in the current location. Now, although informational efficiency and hedging are two different things, it is true that the development of a hedging market can improve informational efficiency in the underlying market. Moreover, experience to date suggests it may also be true that the underlying reference market must be sufficiently efficient before a derivatives market on that product can get some traction. Hence, the need to pay close attention to both sides of this same coin, as Professor Shiller does in this chapter and in his related work.

Given the rather obvious risk management benefits, Professor Shiller wonders in his chapter why consumers have yet to embrace a derivatives market on home prices. My view on the disconnect is that, in terms of dealing with the macro risks in an asset pricing context, there is much we do not understand about the dual role of housing as both a consumption good and an investment good. Consumer hedging demand depends prominently and simultaneously on labor income, mobility, capital constraints, adjustment costs, and the general covariance structure of returns to housing and investable securities. The effects of labor income and mobility strike me as particularly important but relatively unexplored factors. For example, mobility is crucial, because it affects the homeowner's investment horizon and therefore the demand to insure against certain adverse outcomes and not others.

Indeed, risk is about adverse consequences, and risk management is about strategies and tactics to mitigate adverse consequences. One basic principle of risk management is to embrace risks over which one has control and to shift or otherwise mitigate risks over which one does not have control. We have a certain amount of control over the value of our human capital, but less control over the value of our housing capital. Yet, based on survey results and a current lack of interest in housing derivatives, many homeowners apparently act as if they believe they have significant control over the value of their house. Puzzling. You can lead a horse to water, but you can't make it drink.

Maybe the lack of derivatives product demand from consumers is related to its complexity. Individual insurance needs differ greatly depending on circumstances. A 25-year-old MBA student in the Midwest who is planning to relocate to the East Coast has different hedging needs from a 35-year-old homeowner with 95 percent leverage on his or her house and no college education, and from a 50-year-old homeowner with no mortgage who wants to retire to Florida at age 65. Product complexity, a lack of scale, and idiosyncratic hedging demands cry out for expert advice. I submit that, even among a group of highly educated housing economists, there are any number of things we do not know about our own housing hedging demands as related to actual product availability and affordability. This reality suggests that a significant intermediation infrastructure will likely be required to meet the needs of the consumer market. Getting the infrastructure right will require addressing costs associated with potential conflicts and agency—not an easy task.

Chip Case and Bob Shiller have dedicated a significant portion of their extraordinary professional lives to making housing markets more efficient and laying a foundation for associated insurance markets. To date, they have certainly made a difference, and will undoubtedly have even greater impact in the future. Their work brings to mind the Lucas critique, which recognizes that most everything is endogenous. As scholars, some wonder whether they are truly endogenous or just engaged in an intellectual parlor game. Not so with Case and Shiller. *Endogenous* seems to be, as they say in the movies, their middle name.

Commentary

ROBERT VAN ORDER

Robert Shiller's chapter has two parts: a brief history of the Case-Shiller collaboration and the Case-Shiller Home Price Index, and a discussion of the problem of getting a futures market in house prices off the ground. The former is clear and interesting, and I have nothing much to add to it. My comments are about the index and the futures market.

I certainly agree with the potential need for a hedging vehicle. The recent economic downturn is certainly an example of a situation in which it would have been useful (albeit perhaps at the expense of more write-downs by banks). Homeowners generally have a very large share of their net worth in an undiversified position in real estate—although as the Sinai and Souleles paper (2004) suggests, the risk may be less severe, but more complicated, than just the risk of prices falling. There are numerous reasons to want to short real estate, especially real estate in a particular place. Less clear are reasons to want a long position or enough confidence in the index for speculators to want to take long positions.

I also agree that the repeat sales technique is the right one, and that eschewing hedonic controls is a good idea. A critical factor in any index used for trading is that it be as transparent as possible, with as little room for fiddling as possible.

I might also add that the repeat sales technique has been useful for some time. While I was at Freddie Mac in the late 1980s, one of my colleagues, Robin Grieves, read the 1989 Case-Shiller article published in the *American Economic Review*, and a light went on: We could do the same thing with our database of millions of home loans. This was not only a neat idea, but the repeat sales index also did a far better job of explaining our defaults over time (by way of explaining borrower equity over time) than did any other available index. This was the genesis of the Freddie Mac index, the joint Fannie Mae–Freddie Mac index, and the Office of Federal Housing Enterprise Oversight (OFHEO) index.

HOW DOES THE INDEX WORK?

The Case-Shiller index is probably the best of the available home price indices for the futures market. It is more comprehensive than the OFHEO index in that it includes houses funded with subprime and jumbo loans as well as houses not funded with loans. Including subprime and jumbo loans probably removes a bias present in the OFHEO index, particularly in downturns, because subprime and jumbo loans probably are more volatile and fall faster than others. A concern has been that the indices will not catch a downturn fast enough because at first only the "lucky" houses will trade. The sharp decline in the Case-Shiller index lately suggests that this may not be a worry after all.

A problem, instead, might be that it falls too much in a downturn. This cycle will be crucial in terms of future operation of the futures market. If it appears that the index went down too much, for instance, because it contained too many fire-sale and trashed, defaulted properties, then it will be hard to work with in the future.

Who Wants It?

I, too, do not really understand why the futures market has not gotten off the ground. Perhaps it was (unfounded) optimism about ever-rising prices, and perhaps that will change soon.

Some answers are probably in the Sinai and Souleles paper and Shiller's discussion of it. The paper suggests that housing is actually a hedge against rent increases, and one should think of home ownership in terms of a string of purchases. If current house price moves in sync with next house price, there is no risk. (This is not true if price falls and equity needed for down payment on the next house vanishes.)

Perhaps the most likely way for the market to work is with cross-hedges — that is, homeowners taking short positions in the city where they live while simultaneously taking long positions in the cities they think they will move to. This has the potential to work in a way that does not require many long positions in real estate as a whole. Perhaps there should be specific contracts that are short in one place and long overall, or long in specific places — although, with thin volume, that may be hard to do.

I agree with the nightclub opening analogy, but the question is: Why is volume falling?

So, it is a mystery why the futures market has not done well. Maybe the current downturn will help. In any event, I hope the futures market does take off; although, given that my house will always go up in value, I am sure I shall never want to use it.

3

Home Equity Insurance: A Pilot Project

ANDREW CAPLIN
WILLIAM GOETZMANN
ERIC HANGEN
BARRY NALEBUFF

ELISABETH PRENTICE
JOHN RODKIN
TOM SKINNER
MATTHEW SPIEGEL

There are, by now, a large number of theoretical plans that promise both to improve the operation of housing finance markets and to increase the general public welfare. Yet, cases in which these ideas have borne practical fruit are few and far between. This chapter describes just such a case. It outlines the process by which the broad idea of home equity insurance—an idea with deep historical roots—has evolved into a product that is currently available for purchase in the city of Syracuse, New York. This chapter shows just how intricate the process of reform is, and suggests that a profound convergence of interest is needed to make even the most theoretically attractive products feasible.

The initial impetus for our project was the poor performance of the economy of Syracuse in the 1990s. The local political and business communities were willing to consider innovative proposals to halt the pattern of urban decline, and our home insurance project is the result. This project required a rich collaboration among not only the coauthors of this chapter, but many others besides.

Ours is not the first home price insurance plan. An important precursor was offered by the City of Oak Park, Illinois in the early 1970s. Yet, for reasons outlined in the section on home equity insurance, this plan and its more

We thank Barry Adler, Douglas Rae, Zhong Yi Tong, and Joe Tracy for their valuable comments. Caplin thanks the Fannie Mae Foundation for grant support. All authors thank the participants in the 2007 Lincoln Institute conference in honor of Chip Case.

recent variants could not be used as a template for our project. One major drawback of these plans is that they severely restrict the right of sale in order to ensure that adequate effort is put into the sale of the home and that the home is adequately maintained. To avoid these restrictions, we early on embraced a suggestion due to Shiller and Weiss (1999): that product payouts should be based on changes in a home price index, rather than on changes in the price of individual homes.

The key question of how we chose among available indices is outlined in the two sections on index performance. The first of these sections outlines the simple criteria that we used in assessing index performance, while the second explains how an analysis of these criteria led us to select a zip code repeat sales index for the project in Syracuse. As discussed therein, the key limitation in the pilot project is the need to use an "off-the-shelf" product rather than to design our own index from scratch. In the long run, market expansion hinges on improving the design of these indices.

In the section on estimating payouts, we create simulations for our proposed insurance product. In the course of these simulations, we present additional elements of product design, specifying in particular the precise contingencies in which payments will be made, as well as any restrictions on the use of the product, such as a minimal period of occupancy. With these details understood, we move to a discussion of additional considerations affecting the setting of price and ensuring the capital adequacy of the program.

The process of product design is intricately interwoven with the need to fit with the various rules and regulations governing financial transactions in general and housing finance and insurance in particular. The nature of these regulatory constraints on product design is detailed in the section on the topic.

"Looking Forward" addresses the more general importance of our pilot project. If the program in Syracuse succeeds, it will bring financial and economic stability to city residents, as well as to the broader community. It may also spur increased interest in the city among financial institutions that may otherwise have been reluctant to participate in neighborhood revitalization. Such a success might inspire replication in other declining cities, and might also have a profound impact on public policy. All of those who believe that home ownership is a valid route to wealth accumulation will be better able to make this argument if the extreme risks on the downside can be mitigated.

In the end, we believe that our research may have significance that extends beyond the particulars of home price insurance. There are many reform proposals in the housing finance arena, yet few of them get translated into practice. Maybe what is needed to produce further reforms is a dramatic example of an idea being taken all the way from the drawing board to the marketplace. If so, ours may not be the final story of success in translating theoretical ideas for housing finance reform into practice. According to the most optimistic vision, we may be standing on the threshold of a revolution in the U.S. system of housing finance.

THE ECONOMICS OF HOME EQUITY INSURANCE

Home equity is the single largest component of wealth for the majority of American households. Yet, there is virtually no way for the average family to insure itself against drops in home value and the ensuing destructive financial loss. Much of U.S. housing policy has focused on helping Americans own a home, but relatively little has focused on helping protect them against the risk that home ownership entails. The need for mitigating this collective risk would seem to be an obvious one, and yet somehow the perils of home ownership have only recently been explored in the literature of economics.

Goetzmann (1993) quantifies the volatility of the single-family home in the investment portfolio and finds that home investment can expose the household to high risk—where risk is measured by asset volatility. Ambrose and Goetzmann (1998) suggest a substantial subsidy is required to make home ownership attractive to low-income households. Caplin (1999) and Goetzmann and Spiegel (2002) document the significant fraction of long-term drops in the real value of homes in many U.S. housing markets historically. Indeed, these documented historical risks of home ownership have led economists to try to explain the high-home-ownership puzzle and offer solutions to the risk that home ownership represents.

There are a number of possible explanations for the puzzle of high home ownership in the United States. A complete survey is well beyond the scope of this chapter. However, demographic trends, private value for ownership, and a government policy of encouraging ownership (as part of the American Dream) all potentially play a role. Given the social and governmental forces pressing Americans toward home ownership—including tax policy—it may be worth asking whether behavioral finance helps explain the puzzle. Do homeowners truly understand the potential for price declines? Might some cognitive dissonance after buying prevent them from considering the risks of loss? Perhaps, instead, economists themselves do not quite understand the risk—or lack thereof—to home ownership.

A recent, novel perspective on the home ownership puzzle takes this latter tack. Sinai and Souleles (2005) observe that housing is a hedge against local rent risk. For households confronting a volatile rental market, without the inability to contract for the long term, owning a home is a means to hedge rent risk. Sinai and Souleles's model suggests that households trade off asset risk for net income risk. It is an appealing solution to the home ownership puzzle to the extent that the realization of asset values can be deferred, whereas rent increases cannot. However, the dominance of a "rent-hedging" motive versus building long-term equity through portfolio choice depends on the specification of household preferences and is an empirical issue the authors have continued to explore. The current housing crisis, with its rash of foreclosures, indicates that these two risks cannot truly be decoupled. Home ownership is a hedge against rent risk only when there is no bankruptcy. Nevertheless, rent hedging might be an important explanation for the propensity to buy rather than rent.

Given that housing represents a significant risk to the long-term household investment portfolio—regardless of the benefit it provides in hedging the fluctuation in local rents—one puzzle implicit in our research agenda is why home equity insurance does not already exist. Quite simply, a market for sharing risk appears to be missing. The lack of an institution for risk sharing is often more of a puzzle for economists thinking in terms of equilibrium rather than taking an institutional perspective. However, the question is a legitimate one: perhaps there is no demand for hedging home price risk because the risk is not there, or the rent-hedging motive trumps the equity-hedging motive. The experiment in home equity insurance described in this chapter can be thought of as an empirical attempt to probe this question. We put the demand for home equity insurance to the test by supplying a market for risk sharing where previously one did not exist.

As such, our study builds on the work of other economists who have proposed new markets and mechanisms for addressing housing risk and sought to put them to the test. Shiller and Weiss (1999) proposed home equity insurance. Caplin, Chan, Freeman, and Tracy (1997) proposed housing partnerships. Englund, Hwang, and Quigley (2002) quantified the potential benefit of hedging, particularly for low-income households, in the context of exploring the possibility of a hedging market in Sweden. What is distinct about both this group of researchers and a growing circle of others working on the problem is their willingness to push beyond the realm of academic discourse to try and change the market. Indeed, the hope that such hedging could be brought to the market originally motivated Chip Case and Bob Shiller to develop a futures product for housing markets in the United States.

BACKGROUND TO THE PROJECT

Once a thriving industrial city that peaked at 250,000 inhabitants in 1950, Syracuse suffered significant population losses starting in the 1950s with the decline in its manufacturing base. The economy of Syracuse and other cities in the upstate New York region continued to decline during the 1990s, while the rest of the country was on the upswing. According to U.S. Census Bureau figures, the city of Syracuse lost 10 percent of its population from 1990 to 2000, declining from 164,000 to 147,000 residents.

Concomitant to the loss in population and in manufacturing activity, the Syracuse housing market also declined precipitously. From the fourth quarter of 1988 to the fourth quarter of 1997, home prices in Onondaga County (specifically in Syracuse and several of its suburbs) dropped by 16.5 percent in nominal terms. Half of all homeowners in the county who sold their homes in 1997 did so at a loss. As homeowners left the city, many city neighborhoods were left with an overwhelming preponderance of investor-owned properties: by 2000, the home ownership rate in Syracuse stood at just 40 percent, whereas the number of vacant properties had risen to more than 1,000.

Given the long history of decline and even greater fears for the future, Congressman James Walsh issued an urgent challenge to revitalize the distressed neighborhoods in Syracuse. One outcome of this was that the Syracuse Neighborhood Initiative (SNI) was set up in 1999. SNI is a collaborative effort between the City of Syracuse, local and national nonprofit community development organizations, and private-sector leaders to revitalize neighborhoods in Syracuse and to reclaim and reduce the city's substantial stock of vacant buildings.

At the behest of Congressman Walsh, Neighborhood Reinvestment Corporation (NR) was called in to provide assistance to SNI. NR is a public, nonprofit organization that was chartered by Congress to help revitalize the nation's distressed, older communities. For nearly 25 years, it has provided funding, training, technical assistance, and program monitoring to a network of more than 225 local nonprofits working in more than 2,000 communities across the country. The nonprofits engage in a variety of activities, including home ownership education and lending, affordable housing development and management, economic development, neighborhood revitalization, and community building.

In November 1998, NR conducted a symposium in Syracuse called "What Works" to provide examples to Syracuse stakeholders of programmatic strategies and best practices for addressing such a soft market and to foster dialogue.

This symposium introduced the community to the SNI and began to lay the groundwork for solutions. One key question asked was why there was not more interest among renters in buying their homes, given that homes were so affordable (in 2001 the median sale price for a home in Syracuse was only $60,000). One of the sessions in the symposium focused on the home equity insurance programs that had started in Oak Park and that had been replicated in several Chicago neighborhoods, as well as a number of other areas (see the section on home equity insurance for a complete discussion of these cases). The programs in Illinois were seen as providing particularly instructive examples, because the neighborhoods in which the home equity insurance has been offered have generally enjoyed strong housing markets and have stabilized as racially diverse, mixed-income areas.

After the symposium, the City of Syracuse and SNI asked NR to do a follow-up study to explore the potential of an equity insurance program in Syracuse. NR's resulting report further buttressed the case for such a program. The authors of the report found that a major factor in the decline of Syracuse was population loss to the surrounding suburban areas. Moreover, through interviews and surveys, evidence was gathered that fear of continuing price declines in city neighborhoods was, in and of itself, contributing to the disinvestment.

In most markets, a fall in price leads to an increase in demand. But in the real estate market, a decline in price may further depress demand as home buyers become concerned that home ownership will prove to be a bad investment. Real estate agents in Syracuse reported that home buyers were shying away from city neighborhoods because they perceived buying there as a bad investment, and existing owners in the city were looking for a chance to get out before they lost everything. Even today, feedback from focus groups suggests that many potential home buyers consider it a near certainty that prices in Syracuse will continue to decline.

Given the high level of fear in the atmosphere, NR believed not only that an equity protection program might encourage new investment in Syracuse neighborhoods, but also that it would help protect the many families who were already homeowners in Syracuse. These owners included many low- and moderate-income households who had purchased homes through government-subsidized programs, only to see their equity put at serious risk. Overall, NR concluded that by making it safe for potential and current homeowners to invest in a home, an equity assurance program would directly address one of the main barriers—risk to the home buyer's equity—to reinvesting in older urban neighborhoods like those in Syracuse.

With the conceptual case clear, SNI asked NR to take the lead in developing an insurance product for use in Syracuse. Following up on this, the two NR staff members who are coauthors of the report—Beth Prentice, the director of the NR's New York and Puerto Rico district office, and Eric Hangen, a member of the district staff—took on the task of designing a program appropriate for Syracuse. Beth and Eric contacted researchers at the Yale School of Management and met with an interdisciplinary team from Yale and New York University (NYU) that was interested quite broadly in housing, finance, and urban issues. Ultimately, the project was structured as a joint venture between the Yale School of Management and NR. It involved the active efforts of researchers from Yale, NYU, and Real Liquidity, Inc.

. In addition to those listed as authors of the report, the research team at various times included Professor Douglas Rae of the Yale School of Management and Professor Barry Adler of NYU. The Department of Housing and Urban Development (HUD) provided home mortgage data, and Freddie Mac provided additional data, along with research, legal, and marketing assistance.

The academics in the team were largely motivated by a desire to participate in the development of an innovative product to mitigate a problem of great theoretical and practical importance: real estate risk. Theoretically, the benefits to risk sharing in the residential real estate market appear overwhelming. Empirically, Goetzmann (1993), Flavin and Yamashita (2002), and Englund, Hwang, and Quigley (2002) have confirmed the magnitude of these benefits, not only in the United States but also overseas. In addition, the notion that such products might encourage ownership is supported by results of Rosen, Rosen, and Holtz-Eakin (1984) concerning the impact of home price risk in reducing the incentive to own. Moreover, academics have proposed several different market structures in addition to simple insurance to enable this risk sharing to take place. In addition to proposing the broad development of insurance markets, Case, Shiller, and Weiss (1993) analyzed the potential value of a market in futures contracts tied to regional home price indices, allowing households and institutions to hedge by taking short positions in these derivatives contracts. Caplin et al. (1997) suggested setting up "housing partnerships" that would allow far broader ownership and risk sharing in the housing sector. The project therefore held a natural fascination for those of us interested in how to translate these theoretical ideas into practice.

HOME EQUITY INSURANCE: A HISTORICAL PERSPECTIVE

The roots of home equity insurance go back to at least 1925 when section 453hh was added to the Civil Code in California. This code regulated land value insurance. After minor amendments in 1933, land value insurance was codified into the California insurance code in 1935. Four years later, it reached a sudden, and apparently ignominious, end. All sections of the land value insurance code were repealed, and transacting in land value insurance was made a felony. In a unanimous vote on 20 June 1939, land value insurers changed from constituting a regulated industry to constituting criminal enterprises. The records do not explain this radical change of status.

The first actual home equity insurance program in the United States was started by the Department of Defense in 1966, in the Demonstration Cities and Metropolitan Development Act of 1966.[1] This ongoing program protects military personnel and civilian contractors from loss in home value caused by the closing of a nearby military installation.

Marcus and Taussig (1970) and Yarmolinsky (1971) were the first to propose general home equity insurance programs. In both proposals, the payout to the purchaser was based on the difference between the insured value and the actual sale price of the home. Marcus and Taussig envisioned financing this insurance from the public purse, whereas Yarmolinsky suggested that policies should be written by the commercial insurance industry and then reinsured by the federal, state, or local government. Yarmolinsky suggested a pilot program, with administrative costs covered by a local government or foundation that would also guarantee the policy risk, if the insurer fails. Oak Park, Illinois, an incorporated village on Chicago's northwest edge, launched just such a program in 1978.

In 1973, a women's group named First Tuesday formed in Oak Park to discuss efforts to racially integrate. They realized that the panic of declining home value that led to "white flight" was a major hurdle to orderly racial integration of Oak Park. To defuse the panic, First Tuesday had, by 1977, convinced the village to implement a home equity assurance program, in concept nearly identical to the program described by Yarmolinsky in 1971. In 1978 Oak Park launched the program, backed by a property tax; 99 households enrolled in the first four months. The Oak Park experiment with home equity insurance became the model on which other home equity insurance programs were based for the next 20 years.

After much ethnically charged debate, in 1988 the state legislature passed the Illinois Home Equity Assurance Act, which allowed local precincts in Chicago[2] to pass binding referenda creating local tax districts to support home

---

1. Public Law 89-754, section 1013 (80 Stat. 1255, 1290).

2. The Illinois Home Equity Assurance Act limits its purview to cities of one million or more people (section 65 ILCS 95/2 [2003]), so Chicago is the only city in Illinois to which it applies. Smaller cities in Illinois can, like Oak Park, charter home equity insurance programs on their own, but the state statute enabled neighborhoods within Chicago to charter programs under the state code and bypass Chicago politics.

equity insurance programs. Since then, plans have been offered in various other districts of the city.

The first question for the team was whether or not we could adapt these existing programs to the Syracuse context. Superficially this seemed to be a promising possibility. However, the more we explored the details of these plans, the more obvious it became that the answer was no. Hersh (2001) provides the most up-to-date description of these programs, although there remains no comprehensive presentation anywhere in the literature.

The apparent attractiveness of these plans is easy to understand. In the original Oak Park plan, for a one-time fee of $175, the participants were offered the opportunity to claim back 80 percent of any losses after they had owned their homes for a minimum of five years. This price to the individual participant was set well below estimates of program cost, so that the costs of executing the program had to be raised through a general tax levied on all homeowners in the neighborhood.

In many respects, the Oak Park program appears to have been a great success. Prices in the neighborhood generally have risen, and apparently there has never been a single insurance claim against the program. In fact, the program appears to have been a victim of its own success. The neighborhood is now so successful that the program is no longer offered, in part with the rationale that the mere presence of the plan may suggest a fear that is no longer relevant. According to Mahue (1991), "The Oak Park program's . . . participants now have dwindled to 99, most of whom are original members. . . . Furthermore, administrators no longer promote the program, citing that the speculation and uncertainty caused by such promotions could trigger a 'where there's smoke, there's fire' response among home owners."

The other plans set up under the broader Illinois law offer even more coverage than did the original one. For a one-time fee of no more than $200, the programs cover 100 percent of the losses on sale of one's residence after the five-year waiting period. Following the lead of Illinois, there are other programs current or pending in Baltimore, Pittsburgh, and in two communities in Missouri—Ferguson and Florissant. All of these plans offer participants coverage of their entire loss after a five-year holding period. However, the programs outside Illinois remain very small: there is little supporting legislation, and in some cases the funding base remains unclear. In essence, the only case that is developed well enough to offer design lessons is the Illinois case, and it is this case that we investigated in more detail.

One of the most remarkable features of the Illinois programs is the limited number of households who purchase the insurance, despite the fact that the price involves a heavy component of subsidization. Hersh reports that there were 1,500 households who initially used equity assurance in Oak Park, a number that had fallen by a factor of 10 by the year 2000. Even according to these numbers, which may in fact be overstated, only 15 percent of owner-occupants chose to avail themselves of this subsidized insurance.[3] In the other municipalities in which it has been offered, the take-up rates have generally been below 10 percent.

Why would there be such limited demand for such an apparently important and attractive product? The reason is obvious as soon as one looks at just two of many product details.

Limited Coverage

The first product feature that might restrict homeowner interest is that the insurance applies only to strictly local fluctuations. According to the Illinois Home Equity Assurance Act, the insurance is "intended to provide relief only from specifically local adverse housing market conditions within the territory of the program as they may differ from municipal-wide, regional, or national housing conditions" (65 ILCS 95/3).

Given the intent to cover only local fluctuations, the program can be temporarily suspended if there is a "5 percent annual decline in the median value of existing houses in any 12 month period for the nation, Midwest region, State of Illinois, or municipality in which the program is located according to statistics published by NAR" (65 ILCS 95/13).

Thus, the program specifically excludes the type of wholesale price fall that occurred in the city of Syracuse.

Restrictions on Sale

A second major problem with these plans is that they impose onerous payout conditions. Insurance is based on the *actual* transactions price. This means that a whole section of the Illinois law (section 8) has been written to prevent excessive or fraudulent claims. Each individual program has nine commissioners appointed by the mayor of the municipality in question. Home sales that trigger a claim need to be vetted by this committee. The first step in this process is for the homeowner to submit a "notice of intent to sell," which may then trigger an appraisal for a possible write-down of the guaranteed value (if

---

3. Unfortunately, there is no definitive report on these programs, so that even the number of enrollees is a subject of dispute. According to Mahue (1991), there were never more than 150 members in the Oak Park program.

the property is deemed to have deteriorated since purchase). After filing this notice, the owner must list the home for sale according to program guidelines "at a price that can be reasonably expected to attract buyers."

If the property is not sold at guaranteed value in 90 days, the homeowner must file a "notice of intent to claim." The commission then requires the owner to submit to a new 60-day listing, with municipality-wide advertising at the price *the commission* sets. If during these 60 days an offer is made that is below the guarantee, the commissioners have three working days to approve or reject the offer. If they fail to act, this is tantamount to rejection. In cases of disagreement, the result is arbitration as set out in section 10 of Illinois law.

Given the limitations on access and the restrictions in the right of sale, it is no wonder that take-up rates have remained small. In fact, the complexity of the claims process may in part explain the apparent success of the program, at least as measured by the miniscule number of claims against the insurance funds.

Even though the Illinois programs may be of doubtful value to individual homeowners, this does not mean that they are of no value to the community. Indeed, it can be argued that the chief value of the Oak Park plan was precisely that its mere existence added to confidence. The initial introduction of equity assurance was in large part designed to reassure existing homeowners that the Oak Park neighborhood would not be allowed to decline.[4] The theory is that preventing neighborhood decline is much like preventing a bank run. Without this type of protection in place, people might sell in advance of any negative reality, and their fear of decline may become a self-fulfilling prophecy.

If the program works as a confidence-building device, then one might expect it to be very popular at the community level, even if there is limited demand from individual homeowners. Unfortunately, this does not seem to be the case for the programs in Illinois. Any municipality may vote to institute just such a program, yet very few have done so.

One possible reason for communities to be skeptical of the value of these programs is an entirely rational fear of high administrative and insurance costs. As stressed by Mahue (1991), the programs are expensive to administer, and there is no capital stock to support any policy payouts. Thus, if values in the neighborhood were in fact to decline significantly and trigger a high volume of claims, the money would have to come from a special tax assessment levied on all property owners, regardless of whether they had chosen to

---

4. Along with providing protection against a sudden decline in neighborhood property values, the program restricted the public display of for-sale signs, with the goal of not alarming existing homeowners.

participate in the program. This would be particularly inappropriate in Syracuse, where property tax rates are already high relative to much of the United States.

Contemplating the fallout from a serious decline in real estate prices raises one potentially alarming possibility concerning these programs. It seems possible that a severe downturn would make the programs insolvent. In turn, fear of insolvency might trigger a rush to sell at the early stage of the downturn, in order to make a claim prior to insolvency. The neighborhood would decline in part because of a "run" on the insurance fund, with the initial claims stoking fear of further decline and therefore triggering new claims in a self-fulfilling downward spiral.

The problems alluded to above made clear to the team that we would have to start our task of product design without relying excessively on the example of Illinois. The transactional complexity of the plan also suggested to us that it would be better to use a plan based on a home price index rather than one based on individual home prices. Shiller and Weiss (1998) provide additional quantitative arguments in favor of index-based techniques on the grounds of moral hazard in maintenance.

EVALUATING INDEX PERFORMANCE: A SIMPLE APPROACH

In this section, we set out the main criteria that we use to assess the performance of any given index in terms of its ability to provide homeowners with protection declines in the value of their homes. Before outlining these criteria, we introduce one key feature of product design that plays a crucial role in these evaluations.

There are a great many different ways in which one can offer insurance against home price declines. The key issue that distinguishes these various different forms of insurance is the condition under which the funds are actually paid out. In principle, one could offer a fully flexible product that allowed the insurance to be claimed at any point, treating it as a pure financial option. On the other end, one might offer a policy allowing claims only in very few contingencies. One specific product variant discussed by Case and Shiller requires that in order to claim, the household in question not only has to sell its current home, but also has to purchase a new home at least 50 miles away from the home being sold.

After much internal discussion, the research team decided that the best option would be to mimic one aspect of the Oak Park program, and allow exercise at point of sale, without reference to future purchase behavior. Simulations suggested that by allowing exercise at will, the price that would have to be charged for the insurance would become prohibitive. For this same reason, we also rejected such intermediate options as allowing exercise upon termination of a specific mortgage. Fortunately, evidence from focus groups suggests that most people believe that the most important point at which to receive an insurance payment is the point of sale, so that this restriction apparently would do little to lower consumer interest. With respect to restrictions on movement, we believed that such restrictions would not lower program costs sufficiently to justify its somewhat onerous terms.

Another option discussed by Case and Shiller is a product in which the index-based insurance is paid out only to those who lost money at point of sale. We worried that this would set up bad incentives with respect to maintenance and improvements. We wanted to provide positive incentives for homeowners to maintain and improve their homes. In addition, we thought that potential customers would find the product particularly attractive if they could make a profit on the sale of the home should they have taken particularly good care of it, even if their neighborhood declined.

Given the assumption of exercise at point of sale, the fundamental input to any measure of index performance is actual or simulated data on repeat sales data for the homes in a given area over some fixed period indexed by t, with $0 \leq t \leq T$. The universe of repeat sales in the given area for the given period is indexed by $i \in I$. The precise source of this data varies from case to case, depending on whether we are looking at a particular historical event or simulating future events.

Repeat sale transactions can be partitioned into those involving sale at a (strict) loss and those involving sale at the purchase price or above, I_L and I_G respectively. The date of purchase in repeat sale i is $t_0(i)$ and the date of sale is $t_1(i)$, with corresponding prices $p_0(i)$ and $p_1(i)$. The level of the particular price index under study throughout the period is $P(t)$. Note that although the universe under study comprises repeat sales, the underlying index may be constructed on the basis of any amount of additional information, including hedonic measures of housing characteristics, transaction prices in surrounding areas, and broader economic indicators.

The question of interest hinges on how well insurance that is based on the value of the index covers individual losses given all of the above fundamental data. Here we make one key simplifying assumption: we assume that index insurance is purchased by all homeowners in the area in an amount that precisely corresponds to the initial value of their home. If their home value was to be perfectly aligned with the index, this would imply that they were 100 percent insured.

In practice, we allow households to buy index insurance different in value than the value of the home itself. A household that is particularly concerned with not suffering losses may decide to purchase insurance corresponding to an amount in excess of the face value of the home. The additional insurance increases the proportion of losses that is going to be covered. This implies that a whole set of different performance criteria, based on the extent of coverage chosen, is associated with any given insurance product. We believe that our calculations, based on universal purchase of insurance equal to the face value of the home captures the essence of what is available with a given index, but it must be borne in mind that there may in fact be richer options available.

Given these assumptions, we can compute the actual insurance payout for each repeat sale in the sample. Specifically, the *index-based insurance payout* on transaction i is

$$\pi(i) = \max\left\{\left[\frac{P(t_0(i)) - P(t_1(i))}{P(t_0(i))}\right] p_0(i), 0\right\}.$$

Having computed these payouts for each transaction i, the first question concerns how well actual losses are covered (*coverage*).

- Definition 1: The (*average loss*) *coverage* of the index is defined as

$$C = \frac{\displaystyle\sum_{i \in I_L} \pi(i)}{\displaystyle\sum_{i \in I_L} [p_0(i) - p_1(i)]}.$$

This definition involves averaging up individual loss coverage according to the dollar amounts of the loss. Doing so measures what fraction of a loss is covered on average. Note that in calculating this measure, we do *not* average a payment of 200 percent to one homeowner and 0 percent to another and call this 100 percent coverage. Instead, we take the more conservative approach and count only payments that cover the actual loss.

A second important determinant of index performance concerns whether the index inadvertently pays out significant funds to those who have in fact not suffered losses (*efficiency*).

- Definition 2: The *efficiency* of the index is defined as

$$E = \frac{\sum\limits_{i \in I_L} \pi(i)}{\sum\limits_{i \in I} \pi(i)}.$$

Efficiency measures the fraction of total payouts that went to people who lost money on their sales. The efficiency number may understate "true" efficiency if there are homeowners who profit on their sale only because of specific investments that they made in improvements.[5]

Our measures of coverage and efficiency are computed on a per dollar basis. They measure, respectively, how much of each dollar of losses is covered, and how much of each dollar of payouts goes to those who incurred losses. In addition to these per dollar measures, we need measures of total program costs, both actual and ideal. To measure the actual payout costs of a given index, we compute the *payout ratio* as the ratio of nondiscounted payouts to the initially insured value of housing. This is the cost of paying claims, without taking account of administrative costs and capital requirements.

- Definition 3: The *payout ratio* is defined as

$$P = \frac{\sum\limits_{i \in I} \pi(i)}{\sum\limits_{i \in I} p_0(i)}.$$

This measure of actual program costs needs to be contrasted with the costs of a program that perfectly targets actual losses. We label this the *loss ratio*.

- Definition 4: The *loss ratio* is defined as

$$L = \frac{\sum\limits_{i \in I_L} [p_0(i) - p_1(i)]}{\sum\limits_{i \in I} p_0(i)}.$$

---

5. We are only measuring nominal losses. Thus many of the people who made money in nominal terms will have lost money in real terms. We do not include these individuals in our calculation, further lowering reported efficiency.

The coverage, efficiency, loss ratio, and payout ratio are related by the identity

$$P = \frac{L.C}{E}.$$

In the next section, using both actual and simulated data, we will explore the manner in which various indices perform according to the above criteria in Syracuse and other parts of the country. Of course, the indices that one gets using fixed geographic categories, such as the zip code, will never be quite as precise as one might get by using an expert system in which true neighborhood boundaries are tracked over time. It will therefore always be of interest to consider also how any given index does against such an expert system.

Neighborhood-Level Heterogeneity

The starting point for the analysis of neighborhood-level heterogeneity is some *ex ante* division of the geographic area in question into smaller neighborhoods. In many cases, neighborhood boundaries may be well known to all who inhabit a given area, and yet be entirely different from the basis on which the indices are constructed. For example, in Syracuse, city records show a division into 20 distinct residential neighborhoods with significant levels of owner occupancy. The boundaries between neighborhoods bear no relation to standard zip codes. One should expect to find similar subdivisions in any reasonably large geographic area. This raises the obvious question of whether a given index performs well or badly in terms of its treatment of the various different underlying neighborhoods.

What are the appropriate measures of how well a given index is performing at the neighborhood level? Clearly, one wants to achieve similar levels of coverage in all neighborhoods. An index that has 80 percent coverage in one submarket and 20 percent coverage in a second of equal size is clearly inadequate in the second submarket even if the average coverage of 50 percent is deemed acceptable. One also wishes to achieve similar levels of efficiency in all neighborhoods. An index that covers 50 percent of losses in two different regions may nevertheless systematically misdirect far more funds in one of the neighborhoods than in the other. Hence, one technique for gauging neighborhood-level heterogeneity is to recalculate measures of coverage, efficiency, and payout ratios at this level.

Important as it is to repeat these measures at possibly ever more refined levels, we believe that it may also be important to measure heterogeneity of index performance separately from the notion of how well and efficiently losses are covered. In conceptual terms, an index has heterogeneous performance at the neighborhood level if, and only if, it contains within its borders two or more geographically and demographically distinct subregions, identifiable ex ante, that have experienced fundamentally divergent price dynamics. In the next section we present a preliminary analysis of neighborhood heterogeneity in the Syracuse context.

Refining the Criteria

It is clear that the simple criteria outlined above are far from the last word on how to measure index performance. For example, our effectiveness measure is weighted by the size of the loss. There are other useful definitions available in which the losses are measured in real terms, averaged across transactions rather than on a dollar-for-dollar basis, or measured in some other more utility-relevant fashion. Such alternatives are potential areas for long-term research.

Even as we refine our theoretical criteria for ideal index performance, we must bear in mind that actual transaction histories contain a great deal of noise. Some sales are not truly at arm's length, so that the corresponding transaction prices are essentially meaningless. In other cases, homes are left to deteriorate, and it is this that accounts for declines in price. In yet others, radical improvements account for price increases. Hence, we would neither expect nor desire to achieve 100 percent effectiveness in practice. In particular, we have no desire to protect individuals from their own failure to either maintain their home or to put in the effort required to sell it at a fair market price. We want to protect people from market conditions, not from moral hazard.

INDEX PERFORMANCE IN THREE HISTORICAL EPISODES

In this section, we address the fundamental question of index choice for our Syracuse equity insurance program. Time and resource constraints, as well as the need for a consistent available data source, imposed one profound limitation on our adoption of an index for the project. All of these computations are carried out using various geographically defined repeat sales indices that are not of our construction. The broadest is the Office of Federal Housing Enterprise Oversight's (OFHEO's) Metropolitan Statistical Area–level (MSA-level) index. Somewhat narrower is the Mortgage Risk Assessment Corporation's (MRAC's) index at the county level. The narrowest involves the use of MRAC zip-code-level indices.

There are many reasons why we will ultimately have to take a more hands-on role in generating the methods used to construct the indices. One crucial issue is that all available indices use repeat sales methodology. With this methodology, indices have significant measurement error in the short run. In fact, the level of the index for a particular month is revised over time as new trades are realized. In the computations below, we use, throughout, the value of the index as computed at the end of the sample period, which may differ significantly from its value as computed on a real-time basis.

Measurement error is of great importance to those who are offering index-based insurance, as it adds extra volatility into an index. Because protection essentially is a put option, it becomes more expensive where there is more noise. Our geographically specific repeat sales indices are particularly good candidates for this form of error, as they may be based on a small number of highly idiosyncratic transactions and they ignore vast amounts of available information. Information relevant to the value of the index in a specific time and place can be found in transactions that occur in surrounding geographic areas, in ensuing time periods, and in entirely different markets. There may be additional information contained in the volume of transactions. How best to construct an index for insurance purposes is an issue that is in need of greatly increased analysis.

With respect to the specific indices that are being compared, one would expect the use of finer geographic resolution to improve index performance, at least until the point where the improved specificity is swamped by measurement error, given the small number of trades that actually take place. Note that the presence of significant measurement error at the zip code level is suggested by the facts presented in table 3.1. It is well known that there is positive serial correlation in real estate returns. This is reflected in the increase in annualized volatility at longer horizons in an index of U.S. real estate values.

TABLE 3.1 Standard Deviation of Returns at Different Time Horizons

	Annualized standard deviation (percent)			
	One quarter	One year	Two years	Five years
Stocks	14.6	14.7	13.4	14.4
U.S. real estate	2.2	3.0	3.8	3.8
MSA real estate	3.4	5.0	6.4	6.7
Zip code	10.2	8.7	8.5	8.4
Zip code large MSAs	10.8	10.0	10.4	10.9

NOTE: MSA=metropolitan statistical area.
SOURCES: Ibbotson Associates/Morningstar, OFHEO, and MRAC.

This same increasing pattern of volatility is present at the MSA level. However, it is reversed at the zip code level, suggesting that mean reversion in rates of return implied by measurement error at this level is overwhelming the serial correlation. Table 3.1 shows that this effect is no longer so significant when we look at the largest zip codes by population.

There is one last choice to be made. Because there were practical limits to our ability to obtain data on repeat sales, we had to be selective about choosing the historical episodes of particular importance to the evaluation of index performance. Clearly, Syracuse in the 1990s is the central case to be understood. Beyond that, our selection process was strongly influenced by our view that the fundamental goal is to provide protection to, and build confidence in, those in markets that may decline in the future. We would like homeowners to be confident that their investment will remain more or less intact in the face of such a decline. Hence, our primary empirical concern is with the coverage of losses in the face of a systematic regional downturn. Syracuse in the 1990s is not the only case of such a downturn, so it is of interest to perform calculations of coverage, efficiency, and payout ratios for other areas that have had similar patterns of decline. To this end, we use data from MRAC on repeat sales in two other geographic locations that experienced sizable home price declines, namely New Haven County since the mid-1980s and Los Angeles County in the early 1990s.

Syracuse

Table 3.2 illustrates the coverage, efficiency, and payout ratio for actual repeat sales in Onondaga County from 1991 to 2001. We have data on 3,323 repeat sales transactions. This represents all recorded transactions in the county, excluding those that have the very highest and lowest 3 percent of returns on an annualized basis; these we treat as outliers.[6] On average, the homes in the sample were purchased for an initial price of $83,902. When we compute the total of all losses on homes that fell in price, it averages $6,288 per transaction (including those in which there were gains). It is the ratio of these losses to the initial price of the homes that accounts for the recorded loss ratio of 7.49 percent in table 3.2.

The results in table 3.2 present our three different underlying indices: OFHEO's MSA-level index, the MRAC index for Onondaga County, and the MRAC zip code indices. There are 15 different zip codes in Onondaga

---

6. Our general findings are robust to various different rules for defining outliers.

TABLE 3.2 Index Performance in Syracuse

Syracuse (N=3,253)	Coverage (percent)	Efficiency (percent)	Payout ratio (percent)	Loss ratio (percent)
OFHEO	12.1	55.0	1.64	7.49
MRAC county	31.3	53.6	4.38	7.49
MRAC zip	42.3	50.1	6.33	7.49

NOTES: OFHEO=Office of Federal Housing Enterprise Oversight; MRAC=Mortgage Risk Assessment Corporation.
SOURCES: OFHEO and MRAC.

FIGURE 3.1 Index Plot for Selected Zip Codes: Onondaga County and the Syracuse MSA

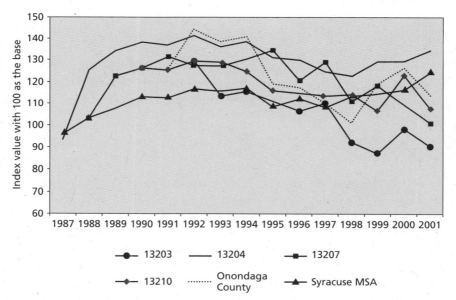

SOURCES: Office of Federal Housing Enterprise Oversight and Mortgage Risk Assessment Corporation.

County, of which eight are entirely contained in the city of Syracuse itself and two more overlap the city. Figure 3.1 shows the different patterns that these various indices have taken during the 1990s.

As one might hope, the coverage level of the indices increases significantly as the geographic definition of the index area is narrowed. The MSA index covers only 12 percent of losses, whereas the county-level index covers more than 30 percent, and the zip code index more than 40 percent, of all losses. There is relatively little difference in efficiency among the indices. In all cases, in fact, roughly 50 percent of the money paid out appears to compensate sellers for actual losses. Given that efficiency remains similar regardless of the index used, there is a close link between coverage and payouts. The low coverage of the MSA index is reflected in a low payout ratio of well under 2 percent, whereas the high coverage of the zip code index is reflected in a payout ratio in excess of 6 percent.

Given that the zip code indices provide so much better coverage than the broader indices, it is natural to wonder whether even further refinements should be considered. What happens when we look at the neighborhood-level heterogeneity of our zip code indices? Are there ex ante identifiable geographic and demographic divisions within Syracuse in which the index performs particularly poorly or particularly well? To assess this, we use the division of Syracuse into 20 residential neighborhoods as used by the city planning office. The neighborhoods are delineated as areas set off with strong boundaries, and are recognized by residents as well as by the planning office.

In looking for neighborhood-level heterogeneity, we use data on all 3,323 transactions. For each such transaction, we compute the "drift"—i.e., the difference between the realized return on the repeat sale and the return on the index over the same period. We then sort repeat sales by neighborhood, so that we get a complete empirical distribution of our measure of drift for each of the 20 neighborhoods in Syracuse. We then look for patterns in the drift within a given neighborhood. A preliminary examination of this data produces no evidence that this drift had any systematic relationship to the underlying neighborhood structure. In almost all of the neighborhoods, the median level of drift is very close to zero. In the case of Syracuse, at least, drift from the zip code index appears to be related only to what happened at an extremely local level, below even the neighborhood level.

New Haven and Los Angeles

Our data for New Haven cover the New Haven MSA, comprising New Haven and Middlesex counties. The data contain all repeat sales from 1985 to 2001. Again, the 3 percent highest and lowest returns are excluded. This leaves us with more than 30,000 repeat sales and an average purchase price of close to $150,000. As indicated in table 3.3, the average loss experienced in this sample amounted to almost 10 percent of the purchase price.

Table 3.3 shows that both the effectiveness of coverage and the efficiency at all three geographic index levels is substantially higher than for Syracuse.

In New Haven, the OFHEO index provides coverage of more than 30 percent while achieving more than 70 percent efficiency. Both the MRAC county and zip-code-level indices achieve more than 55 percent coverage levels and efficiency levels higher than 60 percent. In contrast to Syracuse, the New Haven zip code levels achieve only a modest increase over the county indices in effectiveness of coverage, suggesting that fluctuations in home prices during this time took place more at a county-wide level rather than at a zip code level.

Although there is far less improvement in coverage at the zip code level in New Haven than in Syracuse, the zip code indices still appear to have had a somewhat better performance history than the county indices. They achieve a modest increase in coverage and a 10 percent higher level of efficiency. Combining the small increase in coverage with the increase in efficiency, the zip code indices result in greater loss coverage at lower cost than the county index.

Our data for Los Angeles in table 3.4 cover all repeat sales for the years 1988 to 2001, excluding the usual "outliers." The sample includes more than 300,000 repeat sales with an average purchase price of more than $210,000. The average loss in this sample was a little over $20,000, or 9.5 percent of the average pur-

TABLE 3.3   Index Performance in New Haven

New Haven	Coverage (percent)	Efficiency (percent)	Cost (percent)	All losses (percent)
OFHEO	31.7	72.4	4.19	9.58
MRAC county	55.9	61.0	8.77	9.58
MRAC zip	58.7	66.1	8.50	9.58

NOTES: OFHEO=Office of Federal Housing Enterprise Oversight; MRAC=Mortgage Risk Assessment Corporation.
SOURCES: OFHEO and MRAC.

TABLE 3.4   Index Performance in Los Angeles

Los Angeles	Coverage (percent)	Efficiency (percent)	Cost (percent)	All losses (percent)
OFHEO	32.8	69.5	4.52	9.56
MRAC county	47.0	63.6	7.06	9.56
MRAC zip	49.8	67.8	7.03	9.56

NOTES: OFHEO=Office of Federal Housing Enterprise Oversight; MRAC=Mortgage Risk Assessment Corporation.
SOURCES: OFHEO and MRAC.

chase price. The effectiveness of coverage and the efficiency at all three geographic index levels are again higher than for Syracuse. At both the county and the zip code level, coverage is close to 50 percent, and efficiency is almost 68 percent at the zip code level. As with New Haven, the zip code index achieves slightly higher efficiency than the county index, and at slightly lower cost.

ESTIMATING INSURANCE PAYOUTS

Given the above results, it was natural for us to propose that the zip code index be used in developing the insurance product in Syracuse. In the next two sections, we provide various methods of understanding the past and possible future costs of providing this form of insurance. In this section, we focus in particular on the payouts that are likely to be involved when insurance is offered using this index.

Our concern with payouts requires us to substantially broaden our analysis beyond the cases of Syracuse, New Haven, and Los Angeles. It becomes important to consider a larger universe of geographic areas, not merely to focus on those that ex post turned out to have a slump. From MRAC, we have data on actual zip code price indices from more than 9,000 zip codes in the country. These zip codes represent 69 percent of the population of the United States and 83 percent of the value of the nation's housing stock based on 1990 census data. All of these zip codes are used in the analysis that follows.

In addition to broadening our geographic coverage, we must move away from data on actual repeat sales by neighborhood and come up with a broader and more general characterization of homeowner mobility, as it is this that determines the volume of claims against the program to provide insurance based on the zip code index. In all of the simulations that follow, we estimate mobility in the simplest possible fashion, using a constant moving rate of some 10 percent per year. Clearly, refinements to this procedure can be considered in future research, as can the question of how the availability of the insurance product itself might affect mobility.

With this mobility assumption in place, it quickly became apparent that a high proportion of losses is incurred in the very earliest years of the program's operation because these are the years in which the probability of a decline in the index is the highest. The combination of the cost implications and the policy goal of ensuring neighborhood stability led us to follow the lead of the existing programs and to impose a minimum period of occupancy. We imposed a minimum occupancy period of three years, while also allowing for health-based exceptions to this minimum occupancy period. In all of the simulations that follow, we estimate the costs of insurance that is available upon sale of the home after this minimum occupancy period expires.[7]

Although mobility has important impacts on the costs of insurance, the dominant determinant of payouts is the dynamic pattern of zip code indices. As outlined below, we use two very different approaches to assessing home price dynamics.

- *Historical*: Our first procedure uses historical price indices for all of our zip codes, together with the assumed mobility rates, to estimate the claims that would have arisen to an insurer writing business in any given year since 1980.
- *Simulation Based*: Our second procedure involves estimating simple models of the dynamics of home prices at the zip code level. We then run Monte Carlo simulations to generate time paths for the evolution of the home price index.

Historical Indices

We consider insurance written in each year from 1986 to 1997 in each zip code for which data are available.[8] Given the constant hazard rate (moving rate) of 10 percent per year after the end of the three-year occupancy period, we can then compute losses by year in any given year in any given zip code. We can then aggregate these to get an estimate of the present value of losses to date on each such insurance contract. In doing this, we use a nominal interest rate of 6 percent per year. Figure 3.2 shows the average of these present value computations across all zip codes for each book year.

Clearly, there is substantial fluctuation in the present value of payouts, depending on the year in which the insurance is issued. Insurance from the mid-1980s would have resulted in very low payouts, yet insurance issued in the late 1980s and early 1990s would have experienced claims approaching 200 basis points (bps). Because of the overall healthy economy in the 1990s and the concomitant rise in home prices, minimal loss experience is recorded for recent book years. When we average across all markets and all years of issuance since the beginning of 1986, the present value of insurance payouts

---

7. In addition to the minimum period, our insurance product expires 30 years after its issuance. This has minimal impact on payouts because the numbers remaining at this late date are so low, as is the probability of prices remaining below their initial value.

8. The MRAC data begin in the early 1980s. However, we use 1986 as our starting point because the early years suffer from relatively sparse coverage and more volatile index estimates. In addition, estimates from a period of higher inflation, such as the early 1980s, are not a useful guide to the future costs of such insurance.

FIGURE 3.2 Insurance Claims to Date by Year of Issuance

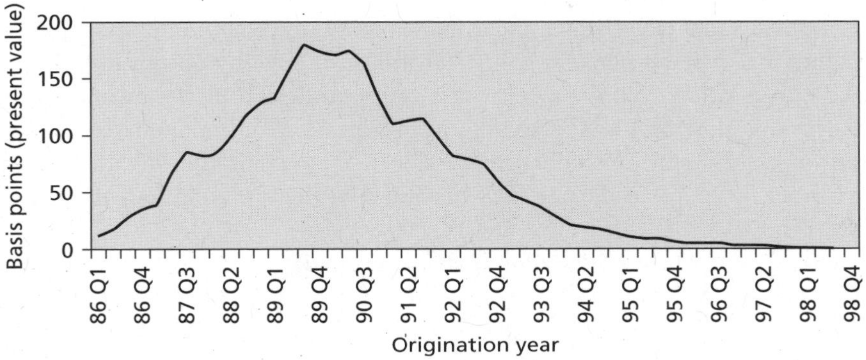

SOURCE: Authors' calculations using data from the Mortgage Risk Assessment Corporation.

to date is a mere 60 bps. Note that this average reflects the imputed claims to date and is therefore likely to significantly underestimate ultimate payoffs for insurance issued in recent years. One simple method to correct for this issue is to use the average claim by time period since origination of the policy and then sum these to generate the average historical loss. After making this adjustment, the average imputed national historical loss is 79 bps in present value terms.

Simulating Future Movements in the Syracuse Index

Valuable as the above findings are, the period under study (1986 to 2000) may not be ideal as a guide to future expectations. The recent decline in inflation is one specific factor that might drive up losses in the future as compared to the historical imputed loss experience, as our product provides nominal price protection for homeowners. Another unique feature of the survey period is that it covers the entire boom period of the 1990s. Hence, pricing design must consider systematic changes in loss performance in the future.

Our initial expectation was that we could directly estimate a time series model of monthly real returns at the zip code level. Measurement error rendered the results unsatisfactory (the mean reversion induced by measurement error obscured the well-known positive serial correlation in returns). Given this, we used two different approaches to estimate the dynamics of home prices.

Our first approach was to assume that annual real returns on housing at the zip code level are described by a simple lognormal distribution with increments that are serially uncorrelated. For the Syracuse market, we make the assumption that there is no expected appreciation of real home prices. This means that we estimate the average rate of nominal home price appreciation at 2 percent per year going forward, in line with consensus expectations of inflation. With respect to the standard deviation, we estimate this over a long horizon for all zip codes in the sample. We find a quarterly standard deviation of 4.2 percent (comprising 3.0 percent at the MSA level and a further 3.0 percent deviation of the index at the zip code level from the MSA index).[9]

There is an obvious limitation of the lognormal approach described above. There is a great deal of evidence of positive momentum in housing returns. To allow for this, our second approach involves estimating an AR(8) model of the dynamics of prices at the MSA level. We then layer on top of this an additional zip-code-level risk (itself assumed to be serially uncorrelated) over and above the MSA price index.

Having estimated by both techniques the price dynamics at the zip code level, we generated 1,000 future price paths for each of the eight zip codes contained entirely within the city of Syracuse, as well as the associated losses for each zip code on each time path. Figure 3.3 illustrates the evolution of losses averaged across zip codes for each of the two approaches.

Using the 6 percent annual rate of interest, we estimate that the present value of losses is 121 bps when we use the lognormal approach and 74 bps using the more intricate AR(8) approach. The reason that the AR(8) approach provides a lower estimate of the cost of insurance written today is that the recent increase in Syracuse home prices provides a positive momentum to the estimated price series. In our pricing and program design approach, we adopted the more conservative of these two approaches. We believe this is appropriate because there are a number of offsetting costs that we have not explicitly modeled.[10]

---

9. While we are aware that there is considerable evidence for momentum in the evolution of home prices, we believe that the presence of the three-year lockout period for claims makes the assumption of an efficient housing market without correlated returns being a reasonable simplifying assumption. Although we neglect the presence of momentum to determine near-term price movements, we do include the impact that momentum has on our volatility estimates. Thus, the estimated zip code volatility is based on volatility at a two-year horizon translated back to a quarterly measure.

10. For instance, we assume no change in homeowner moving behavior beyond the assumed hazard rate of 10 percent in response to the presence of equity assurance. In addition, we assume that the deviations from the MSA index of the zip code indices within the city where the product is offered are independently distributed.

FIGURE 3.3 Projected Claims Following Origination: Two Different Indices

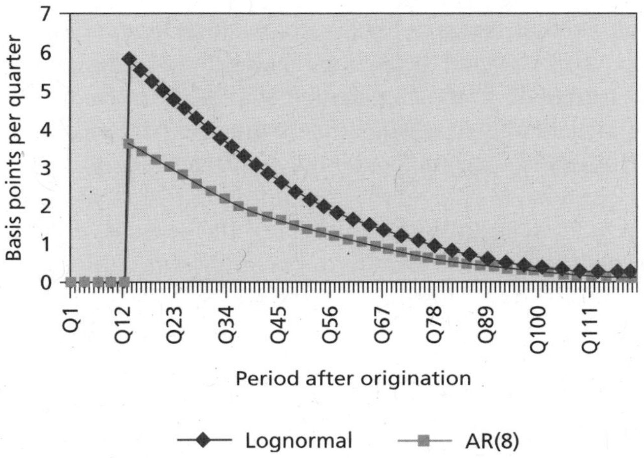

Conceptual Limitations of the Analysis

There are, of course, any number of technical alternatives to be considered that may change the above conclusions concerning insurance payouts. Yet, provided that we base our analysis on historical data, it is unlikely that the above conclusions concerning future program costs will be radically altered. The deeper issue is that the insurance we are offering has properties that cannot be entirely predicted in advance. We simply do not know enough about the underlying determinants of home prices to obtain a reliable description of future dynamics. This becomes especially important given that the availability of insurance may itself have profound effects on the pattern of returns on real estate. Given the current limitations in our ability to accurately model these feedback effects, we are left with little alternative but to rely on simulations based on the historical pattern of returns.

One of the key issues that we leave out of the formal analysis is the possibility alluded to in our prior discussion of existing insurance plans in the section "The Economics of Home Equity Insurance." There we outlined a case in which pessimistic beliefs about the future solvency of the insurance fund might lead to a wave of selling, which would validate the initial fears and set up a self-perpetuating cycle of decline. Unfortunately, history does not provide any reliable way for us to assess the likelihood of such an outcome.

Even contemplating the possibility of a run of some kind suggests a number of points of caution. First, we need to limit the amount of protection that is offered for a given level of initial capital in order to reduce the rational basis for the initial fears. One method for setting this limit is analyzed in the next section. Second, we need to consider whether in an expanded program, the insurance contract, and the capital needs should be designed explicitly to lessen the chances of a run. The chance of a local run causing a significant loss of capital would become insignificant in a truly national program. However, that still leaves open the possibility of a statewide, or even nationwide, collapse of confidence leading to a self-fulfilling fear of an impending collapse of the underlying insurance program. In the section "Looking Backward" later in this chapter, we return to the implications this may have for the long-run expansion of the insurance market.

MORE ON COSTS AND PRICES

There is more to setting the price of insurance than determining the average cost of payouts. One important design issue with our Home Equity Protection (HEP) product was the choice of how the product would be purchased (more on this in the section "Product Design and the Regulatory Environment" under "Is It Insurance?"). Shiller and Weiss (1999) focused attention on insurance products in which the protection is purchased on a short-term basis, similar to fire or theft insurance. Instead, our implementation has a one-time fee covering the full thirty-year life of the insurance product. We believed that using an annual fee would risk destroying the fundamental pooling required for insurance to be efficient. Those who lived in markets that were increasing in value would swiftly cancel their insurance, leaving in the pool only those with high risk. Hence, for the insurance to remain viable, fees for those who selected to stay in the program would have to be commensurately higher. Of course, there are more intricate dynamic paths of prices that may be worth considering in the future. In addition, there is clearly room for the product to sell at different prices in different markets, depending on future market prospects. However, in the present program these considerations would merely add additional confusion to a product that is already somewhat more novel than is comfortable for many consumers.[11]

---

11. The same remark applies to the idea of index insurance payouts to the rate of price appreciation. Case and Shiller proposed that any insurance program should include such indexing right from the outset. Hard as it is for consumers to understand insurance based on one index, we believed that it would be exponentially more difficult for them to understand if two different indices were involved. Not only would the product be more complex if it compensated for real losses, but it would also be far more expensive to supply.

Given that we had decided to charge for the product on a once-off basis (albeit with financing available), the next question was "how much"? In determining how this price was set, it is important to bear in mind one source of funding entirely specific to this project, as well as a constraint defined by the social goal of providing insurance at a relatively low cost to a not especially affluent target group. Of course, in the long run we would like to calculate the appropriate price to charge in a purely privately funded program. The computations that follow tell an important part of that story, but many new questions would need to be addressed before such a launch could be successfully carried out.

The specific funding for the program we launched consists of a $5 million HUD grant to SNI, obtained by Congressman Walsh. The intent was that this entire block of funds be used as capital for the program. With opportunity comes responsibility. The role of the program is to make the insurance available at a relatively low cost to all current and potential home buyers in the Syracuse area, regardless of income. Hence, the price is constrained to not exceed a level that might cause demand in the low- and moderate- income families within the target group to be unacceptably low. Using evidence from local focus groups, it became clear that interest among our target group might drop off considerably if the price exceeded 2 percent of the initial value of the home. In fact, a price of 1.5 percent of the face value of insurance purchased was thought by most respondents to provide decent value for money. Hence, this is the price we work with in the remainder of the calculations that follow.

The key question that we had to address once the size of the initial capital for the program was set at $5 million and the price of the insurance was set at 1.5 percent of the protected value was precisely how much insurance we could afford to write without excessive risk to the capital adequacy of the program. This depends critically on the volatility of payouts, as well as on the analysis of unfortunate tail events. We now describe our methodology for analyzing these tail events, and the implications for the amount of insurance that can be written with the given level of capital.

Certain data are fixed at the outset. We fix the initial $5 million in capital, and also fix the price of insurance as 1.5 percent of the face value of the insurance purchased. In addition, we assume a 6 percent return on invested assets. We also take account of direct program expenses, estimated at 30 bps per annum.

With these data fixed, we simulate a wide variety of different possible paths for the future evolution of returns on the zip code index. For each such path, we calculate payoffs in each year assuming that a certain fixed amount of insurance is issued at a constant annual rate for the first five years, with no additional insurance being written thereafter. Subtracting these payoffs and program costs from the initial capital, up-front premiums, and accrued investment returns gives us a dynamic path for the evolution of the total funds that remain for meeting future insurance obligations.

As the amount of annual insurance issued increases, the path of remaining funds shifts because of both increased costs and revenues and a rise in potential future payouts. In the typical case, there will be some finite maximum to the amount of insurance that can be offered in each of the five years before the fund itself ends up running out of money. Paths are indexed by $p \in P$, and we let $M(p)$ denote the corresponding maximum amount of annual insurance contracts that can be issued. By definition, provided no more than $M(p)$ of insurance is issued in the first five years, the program will never run out of capital on path p.

With price paths ordered in this manner, we select the paths that are in the most demanding 1 percent in terms of how little insurance they allow to be offered in order to ensure that the program remains solvent throughout the period: we look at the first percentile of the distribution of $M(p)$. Provided the amount of insurance issued is no higher than this value, our simulations indicate that the program will remain solvent for the entire 30-year period covered by the insurance in 99 percent of cases. Following this method, we determine that we are able to write $24 million per year of insurance for five years, or a total of $120 million in insurance with the $5 million of initial capital, while still maintaining a 99 percent probability of remaining solvent over the subsequent 25 years.

Figure 3.4 illustrates the evolution of capital over time for the median case and for specific 1 percent, 5 percent, and 10 percent worst-case loss scenarios. By design, the 1 percent worst-case scenario exhausts the program's capital down to zero at the end of 30 years. However, in the 5 percent and 10 percent worst-case scenarios, not only does the program not run out of capital, but capital substantially exceeds the initial $5 million at the end of 30 years. Capital does decline in both the 5 percent and 10 percent cases during the peak loss periods, as losses and expenses exceed new premiums plus the program's investment income. However, capital bottoms out before the end of year 15 even without any new business written. In addition, note that in these two cases capital is never below the initial level of $5 million.

To put these loss scenarios in perspective, figure 3.5 shows the evolution of average prices in each of the 1 percent, 5 percent, 10 percent, and median loss scenarios. As can be seen from the figure, the 1 percent loss scenario represents a pretty dire housing market, much worse than Syracuse has experienced in recent years. In the 1 percent worst-case scenario, prices decline

FIGURE 3.4 Capital in Various Scenarios

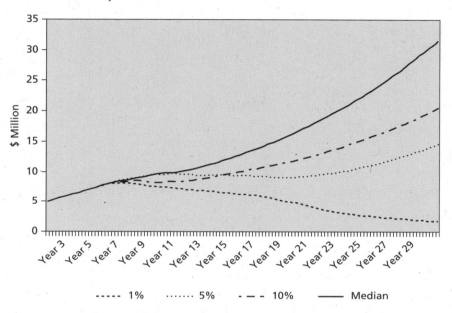

SOURCE: Authors' calculations using data from the Mortgage Risk Assessment Corporation.

FIGURE 3.5 Price Paths Associated with Different Paths of Capital

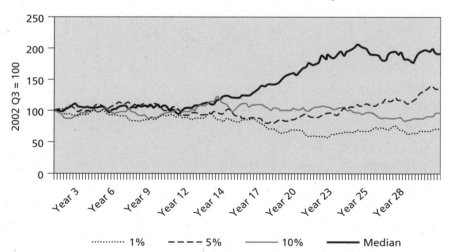

SOURCE: Authors' calculations using data from the Mortgage Risk Assessment Corporation.

by close to 40 percent in the first 20 years. Even at the end of the 30-year period, prices are 30 percent below their initial starting point. The 5 percent and 10 percent worst-case scenarios also show prolonged periods of significant price weakness, with peak-to-trough declines of 30 percent. Of note is that in this example the 5 percent loss scenario shows a stronger long-term housing market than the 10 percent loss scenario, with prices in the former ending 35 percent above their starting level as opposed to 2 percent below their starting level in the latter. This illustrates the importance of the pattern of home price movements in determining the projected losses from the program.

PRODUCT DESIGN AND THE REGULATORY ENVIRONMENT

At the same time as we were developing the product and pricing parameters described in the previous section, we were also exploring the regulatory challenges that would be involved in any product offering. Of course, offering a new financial product is not easy, as there are many regulatory requirements that must be met before a new product of this nature can be launched. These requirements are particularly stringent in New York State. Although it is doubtless that those who set up these regulatory requirements were well-intentioned, the resulting rules often miss their intended mark and instead end up causing confusion and delay. We hope that a successful launch of this equity protection product may provide some guidance to the regulators in New York State in their ongoing efforts to modernize and update the regulatory environment. In the present environment, it appears that these regulations may be inadvertently preventing the development of financial products that could be of tremendous social value if properly regulated.

Is It Insurance?

Our first conjecture was that the financial regulations to which we would be subjected would be the insurance regulations. Yet, as we met with New York State regulators, who were very helpful, we found that the matter was more intricate than it appeared. Initial discussions with the regulators concerning the insurance status of our product were inconclusive. Although there were legal authorities who did not consider our product to be insurance, there were others who believed that the rules were not so clear-cut.

Given the confusing nature of the underlying laws, the worst of all possibilities would have been to be left in a gray area, uncertain as to the ultimate classification of equity insurance. Because the New York State Insurance Commissioner, Greg Serio, and his senior staff could see the social value of the product that was being proposed, they removed us from this gray area. They kindly took the time to review the case very carefully and provided a specific letter of opinion. This letter stated that the product that we ultimately designed does not fall under the realm of insurance regulatory law, at least in the State of New York.

What prevents our product from being classified as insurance? According to the State of New York, under the definition of an insurance contract (Art. 11, Sect. 1101), the insurer is obliged to pay money on the "happening of a fortuitous event in which the insured has . . . a material interest which will be adversely affected by happening of such event."

The key words in the definition are "fortuitous event" and "material interest." Insurance regulators worry about the moral hazard potential of insurance contracts. Thus, it is essential that the insured not have any ability to influence the outcome of what is being insured. A fire or a theft may be regarded as a fortuitous event, but sale of a home at a loss is not deemed fortuitous. After all, the sale of the home—and therefore the exercise of this equity protection policy—is under the direct control of the homeowner. The fact that the homeowner can decide *when* to collect, even if he or she is required to take some costly action such as sell the home, means that the event is not fortuitous.

The second reason why the offered protection is not insurance is that the homeowner does not have any material interest in the local real estate index. Although the value of the index may be highly correlated with the value of a person's home, it is entirely possible for one's home to go up in value while the index falls. The lack of a 1–1 material interest means that HEP functions essentially as a derivative or a hedge, and, hence, is not insurance.[12]

It appears that the intent of the regulations is to distinguish between insurance (good) and gambling (bad). To avoid any possibility that the insurance laws could be interpreted as legitimizing private lotteries, the law prohibits insurance products that provide derivative-like protection on financial products. Unfortunately, this applies equally to desirable insurance products such as weather insurance and home price insurance as it does to gambling.

---

12. From an economist's perspective, this definition is not easy to justify. The local index, rather than the individual home index, is used precisely to avoid the moral hazard problems that so worry regulators. The current regulation would almost be like saying that bidders on eBay do not have a material interest in their bids, as they will pay the second-highest bid and not their own! One of the great lessons of modern economics is to find ways to preserve incentives while offering protection. We would encourage insurance laws to embrace this approach rather than to reject it.

The letter of opinion stating that our product was not insurance gave us the green light to move forward and explore entirely different channels for delivering it. However, the difference in status has some unfortunate implications. It denies consumers the additional sense of safety they might derive from knowing that there was an agency involved in guaranteeing the capital adequacy of providers. Some such agency, private or public, will be necessary if the market is to expand beyond the trial stage. The lack of certification of this type is reflected in the naming of the product. Rather than being called "insurance" or "assurance," our product is called "Home Equity Protection." This provides consumers with a good description of the product without misleading them into thinking they are purchasing a regulated insurance product.

Is It a Mortgage?

Having discovered relatively early on that our product was not likely to be deemed insurance, we were somewhat concerned that we might find ourselves subject to even more stringent regulation, or even thought to be offering an altogether inadmissible product. To avoid such a status, we explored the idea of writing the equity protection directly into a mortgage. To this end, we designed an equity protection mortgage that operates just like a price-level adjusted mortgage (PLAM), but with adjustments to the outstanding mortgage balance based on the level of the local home price index rather than the general price level.[13]

As we designed it, adjustment in the mortgage balance would go only one way—down. The outstanding balance would fall in line with a change in the real estate index. The mortgage note itself would detail the calculation of the precise change in the balance when this index fell between the initial date that the mortgage was initiated and the trigger date, as determined by the home itself being sold. On the supply side, we envisaged these mortgages as being packaged into pools that would be very attractive on the secondary market. The ultimate supplier of the underlying equity protection would make payments first to the mortgage holder. The individual selling the home would receive only payments over and above those required to pay off the underly-

---

13. A PLAM is a mortgage in which the principal adjusts in relation to some index, such as inflation. In certain high-inflation countries, mortgages are written in real terms and so the payments due and the outstanding balance both adjust with inflation. This allows the borrower to pay the real rate of interest rather than the nominal rate. Mortgages become less onerous, as fewer of the payments are front loaded. The regulatory concern appears to have arisen because these mortgages may have negative amortization in the early years. Although it is surely important for borrowers to be aware that this might occur, it is economically absurd to pass an outright ban on negative amortization. By construction, PLAMs have positive amortization in real terms, even if they do not in nominal terms.

ing mortgage. The equity protection would therefore offer additional security to the underlying holders of the mortgage-backed securities, with the premium possibly being passed back to borrowers in the form of a reduced rate of interest.

A second attractive feature of our HEP mortgage proposal is that it makes clear a connection between equity assurance, private mortgage insurance (PMI), and Federal Housing Administration (FHA) insurance. FHA and PMI programs make payments to lenders in case the homeowner defaults. Frequently, this default is accompanied, or triggered, by a reduction in the value of the home. By helping to protect the net equity in the property, an equity protection mortgage would, in certain circumstances, substitute a small cost of prevention (equity protection) for the large cost of the cure (PMI or FHA insurance).

Although an equity protection mortgage or a HEP product are similar to FHA/ PMI insurance in that they offer protection to lenders, an important distinction is that FHA/PMI programs insure only the lender, not the borrower, in cases of default. With PMI and FHA insurance, the benefit to the borrower is indirect. The value of FHA and PMI products to the borrower is that they enable the borrower to gain access to well-priced home mortgage loans with less than 20 percent down payment. Demand for these products is driven entirely by the mandates of the lenders. In contrast to these FHA and PMI programs, a HEP mortgage would directly protect homeowners from loss. Because our product is designed so that the equity protection payouts go first to any lender, rather than directly to the homeowner, these mortgages would offer lenders an equity protection benefit that might reduce the need for and cost of FHA insurance and PMI. Of course, such a change would have to survive scrutiny by HUD, Fannie Mae, and Freddie Mac, as well as their Congressional overseers. This was an angle that we were keen to pursue.

Unfortunately, our investigation of this issue was stopped in its tracks. Attractive as our HEP mortgage might be, it ran afoul of New York State banking regulations. New York State makes all forms of PLAM illegal.[14] Because our HEP mortgage would have been ruled to be a variant of the PLAM, it was deemed illegal by extension. This seems to be a prime example of regulation having just the opposite of its intended effect.

---

14. The case against our "PLAM" in the context of home equity insurance is even weaker than the general case against a PLAM indexed to the rate of inflation. Our proposed product could reduce the outstanding balance due to a decline in property values. Although an adjustment to the principal is possible, the adjustment would only be favorable to the homeowner. It is hard to see how banning such a product protects homeowners.

Fortunately, the banking superintendent, Elizabeth McCaul, and her senior staff understood the value of the equity protection idea and were extremely helpful to us in reviewing the regulations and making a quick determination on how to proceed with our equity protection ideas in a manner that would survive regulatory scrutiny.

No, It Is Something Else!

In the end, HEP is written as a stand-alone product that is neither insurance nor a mortgage. Legal analysis has also concluded that HEP is not a security for securities regulation purposes, as it is not intended or marketed to consumers as a way of generating a gain or profit but rather as a way of protecting against a loss.

Our stand-alone product retains one design feature that was initially proposed in the days when we believed that we would be offering the protection in combination with a mortgage. The product is structured so that a mortgage lender, if one exists, will have priority in getting the protection payment. This is similar to the case of fire insurance on a home on which the mortgage lender is the first payee. The homeowner gets the full value of the payment in the form of a reduced mortgage obligation, and may get even further benefit in reduced interest rates that reflect the enhanced quality of credit (or reduced risk) extended to these households.

By putting the lender first in line, we intend to make clear to suppliers of capital the benefits of lending to homeowners who have purchased equity protection. In fact, we believe that it will be important to research the overlapping risk between HEP and FHA/PMI. Of course, both FHA insurance and PMI protect against some risks that HEP does not. In particular, they protect lenders from the expense involved with removing the owner from the home, the missed interest payments, and possible distressed re-sale prices, given the likely lack of homeowner maintenance during the default and foreclosure period. Ultimately it may be of value to both price equity protection and FHA/PMI products to protect both borrowers and lenders against idiosyncratic events, such as job loss and divorce, that lead to default as well as against market forces that lead to falling home prices. We would expect cost savings to result for the purchaser of any such pooled product.

With the details of product definition pinned down, there remained a number of vital steps that had to be taken before the product could in fact be launched. One important issue was to identify an institutional home for the project. NR was able to identify an ideal candidate. Home Headquarters Inc. (HHQ), a local NeighborWorks affiliate of NR in Syracuse, offered a ready vehicle to deliver the product. Their Web site, www.equityhq.org, provides a good description of the product offering and a set of frequently asked questions.

On 30 July 2002, a press event to launch the program was held by Congressman Walsh and Mayor Matthew Driscoll. On this date, Deborah Woods, a dental hygienist, became the first person to purchase protection against a general market loss in her home equity. The press event was held at her home to dramatize the fact that the product was immediately available.

LOOKING FORWARD

A major priority in future research is to assess the success or failure of the project. Precisely how best to measure these aspects of the program is a great challenge in and of itself. Some of the benefits go to individual purchasers, and to this extent success may be reflected in the level of private demand for the product and satisfaction with its ex post performance. Yet there are also community-wide benefits, which may be somewhat more difficult to assess. In fact, there are those who believe that the program can succeed even if very few households choose to buy the equity protection. The case of Oak Park suggests that, by building confidence, HEP may produce profound social benefits even if there is little private demand. Understanding the potential confidence-building effects of equity protection is an important question left for future research.

As highlighted in the previous section on index performance in three historical episodes, a key limitation of the current product is the reliance on an index that may not be optimal on a real-time basis. There is a profound need for additional research on index design, and several authors of this chapter intend to contribute to this design effort. In fact, the pressure to improve index design may be crucial to expansion of richer markets in real estate–related assets.

Although recognizing that success itself may be difficult to measure, it is nevertheless of interest to speculate on the future ramifications of the project, should it be judged to succeed. We believe that the potential benefits to those in the city of Syracuse are self-evident. The fact that ownership in the city of Syracuse has been correctly perceived as a poor investment in recent years has surely held back the rate of home ownership. To the extent that the availability of equity protection reduces the attendant risk and thereby boosts ownership rates, the benefits would extend to the larger community. If the HEP product is able to make home ownership more attractive in Syracuse, it should be expected to bring the broader benefits of community involvement that are so strongly associated with ownership. At the same time, the combination of the increase in ownership rates and the decrease in default rates due to the presence of the protection may stabilize the financial community's investment in the area, and thereby increase the extent of this community's involvement with the central city area. Of course, a reduction in defaults is itself important in preventing buildings from becoming abandoned and being a blight on the rest of the community. Finally, the increase in stability in central-city Syracuse would be very good news for the broader metropolitan area: it would enhance the long-term viability of the entire area, prevent further erosion in the tax base, and potentially stabilize the flow of tax revenues.

Any success in Syracuse would surely provoke interest in other communities needing similar help. Identifying these communities is a high priority in any future efforts aimed at project expansion. There are several key issues involved in this identification effort. First, one needs to assess different cities for a combination of declining property values, abandonment, low home ownership rates in distressed neighborhoods, high rates of default or foreclosure, and potential homeowners' reluctance to move into these neighborhoods. Second, it is important to find other parts of the country that would provide diversification benefits for financial participants interested in supplying the product. Third, institutional infrastructure is required. There must be a set of local and national organizations that are willing to promote and develop the product as needed for the particular community. Finally, one needs to investigate the legal and regulatory barriers that may operate in states other than New York, to ensure that the appropriate products are developed.

Although the introduction of HEP was targeted to the moderate-priced homes in Syracuse, we expect there will be similar demand across the price spectrum. One of the team members, Barry Nalebuff, has written, with Ian Ayres, about the HEP product in a column in Forbes Magazine (Ayres and Nalebuff, 2002). In addition to describing the basic product and its price, this article concludes by asking readers to indicate their level of interest in the product. The results to date suggest that, among more affluent households, there may be great interest in the type of home price protection that we introduced in Syracuse. This interest appears to be particularly pronounced among those who do not as yet own homes. Indeed, we have e-mails suggesting that there are some households for whom the lack of availability of any form of protection represents the major barrier standing in the way of home ownership. If the responses to the poll are in any way indicative of attitudes in the broader population, there may well be room for a national HEP market that operates on a for-profit basis. Of course, many new issues will arise in assessing the potential operation of such a market, and we hope that these also may be addressed in the near future.

As further evidence for the potential level of interest in equity protection at a national level, we conducted a nonrepresentative national Internet survey of recent home buyers concerning their general concerns when buying their home. More than 70 percent of respondents reported that whether homes in the neighborhood hold their value is very important to their decision on where to buy a home. There was no other single factor that was deemed this important by such a large proportion of buyers. In addition to this general statement of priorities, a significant minority of 13 percent of respondents indicated that HEP would encourage them to purchase in a neighborhood they liked, but where property values were seen as "shaky."

The advent of home price protection would have profound ramifications for other parts of the housing finance system. In the current market, those who do not have sufficient cash to place a large down payment on their homes must purchase PMI. PMI is clearly of great benefit in terms of stabilizing the financial system, and yet does little to help the borrower who ends up in default and with tremendously compromised credit. An important subject of research as the HEP market develops is the extent to which the product lowers default rates and thereby reduces the need for PMI. Prevention is surely better than cure, and if protection is able to prevent homeowners from going into such deep negative equity positions, it may enable lenders to reduce their purchases of PMI without in any way compromising the safety of the financial system.

The plan's success may have a broader impact on public policy. For some time now, the consensus has been that promoting home ownership provides one of the most important vehicles for encouraging wealth building among less-well-off households. Yet, with ownership come profound financial risks. It can be argued that no one benefits if a household is provided with a subsidy for purchasing a home, but then finds that their home has fallen in value because of declines in the local or national economy.

Although this argument paints a rosy picture of the ramifications of success, it would be remiss to ignore negative possibilities. Some people may be uneasy at the market impact of HEP in the case even of a relatively mild fall in prices. The likelihood, in such a case, would be that there would be more households selling their homes than in the existing market. Historically, in the midst of a downturn, people have been trapped in their homes because of negative equity. With equity protection in place, they would no longer be trapped, and thus the local housing market may experience a bout of sales in the midst of a downturn. On balance, we view this as an improvement over the status quo: allowing mobility is good public policy, especially in the event of job losses. However, those who remain in the neighborhood may not agree with our positive assessment.

Altogether more serious than the orderly rundown just alluded to is the possibility of a panic, referred to already in the section on the historical perspective to home equity insurance. In this scenario, fear of a future suspension of the program triggers a run, leading ultimately to the collapse of the program. It would be absolutely tragic if the future of HEP products foundered because of undercapitalization of the initial program. It is for this reason that we will remain very conservative in setting limits on product availability until there is a longer historical record with which to work, and until we have deepened our understanding of possible feedback effects.

Fear of a run is a major consideration motivating program expansion beyond the Syracuse area. Such an expansion will allow for better pooling of risks. With superior pooling, there would be no reason for a decline in one small geographic area to threaten the capitalization of the protection, as such declines would be of negligible significance in a national context.

Although geographic diversification can remove the fear of a local price decline causing a run, there remains that question of what would happen in the face of a major decline in the value of housing, either at the national level or in a large state such as California. There is simply no way for an insurance product to provide protection against such a large-scale event, as it is essentially a nondiversifiable risk. In such situations, funds to pay the insurance cannot be made available, except by governmental bailout. The situation here is no different than for insurance against other major events, such as earthquakes or acts of terrorism. Whether explicit or implicit, any offer of insurance against such contingencies can be made void by an event of unprecedented magnitude.

One possible way to address the problems that would arise with a large-scale market meltdown is to consider radical changes in product design. The goal of these changes would be to maintain the essential risk-sharing benefits of equity protection, without requiring any party to make a promise to deliver payments that they may in fact be unable to keep. Our HEP mortgage is one simple product that has this feature. With this form of mortgage, the losses in home value result in lower payments to those holding the mortgages. In principle, these mortgages could be priced up front to include a discount for possibly catastrophic later falls in the value of housing at the national level. These mortgages should be bundled into securities and sold onto the secondary market. In this manner, the ultimate holders of the mortgage-backed securities would wind up providing insurance to homeowners, but at no stage would anyone be providing a second party with a promise that could not be kept.

With suitable imagination, it may be possible to construct far richer state-contingent housing finance products that would serve all of the functions of home price insurance, without some of the drawbacks—such as the need for high reserves—and the possibility of runs. As we consider the possibility of yet more ambitious efforts at market reform, we are drawn back to the question of whether or not the U.S. housing finance market is ready for more profound innovations. For such innovations to occur, changes need to be made in the underlying rules of the innovation game. In particular, the regulatory environment is in need of an overhaul. Although the New York State regulators provided us with great assistance in threading the regulatory needle, the rules that they are enforcing appear somewhat dated. We hope that our project spurs a revision of the regulations with a view to encouraging innovation, while nevertheless maintaining necessary oversight. Provided that all parties are willing to learn the hard lessons from our experience, there may well be room for major innovations in housing finance in the United States.

LOOKING BACKWARD

Given the initial investment in the project, it has so far been a modest success. As of May 2006, 120 homeowners had purchased HEP. This amount is far short of an estimated capacity of $120 million over five years. The 120 policies written suggest that customers understood the product and were willing to pay something substantial for it. On the other hand, the slow growth in public interest, even at an effectively subsidized rate, suggests that it has remained a marginal program for most Syracuse homeowners.

From the perspective of its funders, the effectiveness of the program is not necessarily measured by its pervasiveness but by positive neighborhood externalities, local home price stabilization, and increased home ownership. At this point, no program evaluation addressing these issues has taken place. A look at the OFHEO indices for Syracuse and another upstate city, Albany (figure 3.6), suggests two things. First, that Syracuse housing prices have fared relatively well since program inception. Second, that the 2007 downturn in housing prices has not yet severely tested the financial strength of the program.

Since the initial development of HEP, the authors of this chapter have occasionally been contacted by financial institutions seeking to launch similar products. Although these efforts may well bear fruit—particularly given the renewed awareness across the United States that housing prices can actually go down—we are not yet aware of a private-sector launch of a significant HEP program. This is surprising, given our "proof of concept" and the availability of

FIGURE 3.6 OFHEO Indices: Syracuse and Albany, 1996–2007

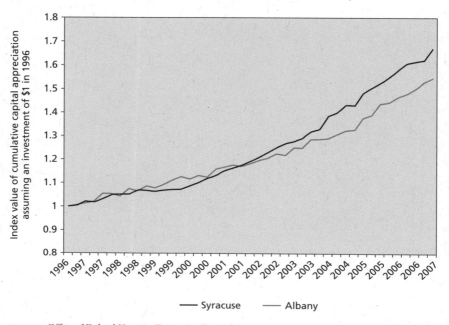

Syracuse — Albany —

SOURCE: Office of Federal Housing Enterprise Oversight.

housing futures that could be used to hedge shocks to home prices in major metropolitan areas. Considering recent turmoil, perhaps these plans have simply been put on hold by financial institutions.

The development of HEP has been particularly interesting from the point of view of housing econometrics. The trade-off between geographical focus and repeat-sales index accuracy has long been an issue of academic interest. In this case, we had to confront the very real problems presented by local indices—not just accuracy, but issues of when an index updates, what to do about revisions, how to deal with institutional change, and a host of other practical issues that put flesh on the bones of purely econometric challenges.

CONFERENCE DISCUSSION

The lively conference discussion of the HEP project at the 2007 Lincoln Institute conference focused largely on the initiative as experimental economics. A group of housing researchers were given an opportunity to understand how economic agents addressed housing risks. The conference participants were keen to examine the data collected in more detail to test such theories as whether homes were purchased to insure against rent increases and how sensitive homeowners were about the fee structures, as well as other product features. We hope to be able to investigate such fruitful suggestions in the future. Certainly we anticipate renewed government and private sector enthusiasm for understanding homeowners' choices regarding risk.

REFERENCES

Ambrose, Brent W., and William N. Goetzmann. 1998. "Risks and Incentives in Underserved Mortgage Markets." *Journal of Housing Economics* 7(3): 274–285.

Ayres, Ian, and Barry Nalebuff. 2002. "Price Protect Your Home." "Why Not?" column, *Forbes* magazine, August 28. http://www.forbes.com/2002/08/28/0829whynot.html.

Caplin, Andrew. 1999. "Housing Asset Portfolios and the Reform of the Housing Finance Market." *TIAA-CREF Research Dialogues* 59 (February).

Caplin, Andrew, Sewin Chan, Charles Freeman, and Joseph Tracy. 1997. *Housing Partnerships*. Cambridge, MA: MIT Press.

Case, Karl E., Robert J. Shiller, and Allan N. Weiss. 1993. "Index-Based Futures and Options Markets in Real Estate." *Journal of Portfolio Management* 19(2) (Winter): 83–92.

Englund, Peter, Min Hwang, and John Quigley. 2002. "Hedging Housing Risk." *Journal of Real Estate Finance and Economics* 24(1–2): 167–200.

Flavin, Marjorie, and Takashi Yamashita. 2002. "Owner Occupied Housing and the Composition of the Household Portfolio over the Life Cycle." *American Economic Review* 92(1): 345–362.

Goetzmann, William. 1993. "The Single Family Home in the Investment Portfolio." *Journal of Real Estate Finance and Economics* 6: 201–222.

Goetzmann, William N., and Matthew Spiegel. 2002. "The Policy Implications of Portfolio Choice in Underserved Mortgage Markets." In Nicholas P. Retsinas and Eric S. Belsky, eds., *Low-Income Homeownership: Examining the Unexamined Goal*, 257–274. Cambridge, MA: Harvard Joint Center for Housing and Urban Studies Conference; Washington, DC: Brookings Institution Press.

Hersh, Liz. 2001. "Summary Report on Home Equity Assurance." Issued to the Urban Affairs Task Force of 10,000 Friends of Pennsylvania. http://www.10000friends.org/Web_Pages/Resources/HomeEquityAssuranceReport10-01.doc.

Mahue, Michelle. 1991. "Housing Equity Assurance Programs." *ORER Letter, Office of Real Estate Research, University of Illinois at Urbana–Champaign* (Summer Edition): 12–13.

Marcus, Matityahu, and Michael K. Taussig. 1970. "A Proposal for Government Insurance of Home Values Against Locational Risk." *Land Economics* 46 (November): 404–413.

Rosen, Harvey, Kenneth Rosen, and Douglas Holtz-Eakin. 1984. "Housing Tenure, Uncertainty, and Taxation." *Review of Economics and Statistics* 66: 405–416.

Shiller, Robert, and Allan Weiss. 1998. "Moral Hazard in Home Equity Conversion." Cowles Foundation Discussion Paper 1177. New Haven, CT: Cowles Foundation.

———. 1999. "Home Equity Insurance." *Journal of Real Estate Finance and Economics* 19(1): 21–47.

Sinai, Todd, and Nicholas Souleles. 2005. "Owner-Occupied Housing as a Hedge Against Rent Risk." *The Quarterly Journal of Economics* 120(2): 763–789.

Yarmolinsky, Adam. 1971. "Reassuring the Small Homeowner." *The Public Interest* 22: 106.

4

Spatial Variation in the Risk of Home Owning

TODD SINAI

To casual observers, home owning often appears risky. They note that the typical preretirement household (in the 2004 Survey of Consumer Finances) has about 45 percent of its net worth tied up in housing wealth—and those house values can be volatile. In fact, between the end of 2005 and the end of 2007, real house prices fell by more than 15 percent, according to the 10-city composite S&P/Case-Shiller Home Price Index. Even expert analysts of housing markets typically concern themselves with the risk of house price declines. Indeed, chapters 2 and 3 in this volume address ways to mitigate the asset price risk of housing through the use of house price derivatives or home equity insurance.

Recent research has emphasized that this focus on asset price volatility yields an incomplete picture of the risk of home owning. Sinai and Souleles (2005) highlight two additional components of that risk. First, renting, which is the alternative to owning, is itself risky. Although homeowners take on asset price risk, they avoid uncertainty about the total rent they would have to pay as renters. Second, households face uncertainty about the cost of future housing if they ever move. When an owner sells his or her home and purchases another, the risk the owner faces is due to uncertainty about the difference in the prices of the two homes. If the two homes were in independent markets, there

I am grateful to Yongheng Deng, David Geltner, Ed Glaeser, and conference participants for helpful comments. The Research Sponsors Program of the Zell-Lurie Real Estate Center at Wharton generously supported this research.

would be risk both from selling in the current market and purchasing in the next. If the housing markets moved together, any change in the price of a home in a household's current city could net out the price changes of the home purchase in a subsequent city, reducing the sale or repurchase risk. That is, owning one home can hedge against uncertainty in the price of a household's next home if the prices of the two homes covary positively (Cocco, 2000; Han, forthcoming; Ortalo-Magné and Rady, 2002; Sinai and Souleles, 2005).

In this chapter I consider all three of these determinants of housing risk (rent volatility, price volatility, and the average covariance of house price growth with other housing markets), document where and for whom home owning might be risky, and discuss the conditions under which hedging housing price risk through the use of housing derivatives would or would not be valuable for a homeowner. One source of variation in the riskiness of home owning is location: the volatility of the housing market varies widely across metropolitan statistical areas (MSAs). This volatility is reflected both in rents and house prices because they are endogenously related, as stressed by Meese and Wallace (1994) and Sinai and Souleles (2005). I first provide evidence suggesting why some housing markets are more volatile than others, showing that the difference in volatility results from more variable underlying demand combined with an inelastic housing supply. I then estimate the rent and house price volatilities across MSAs, using the standard deviation of an MSA's log annual rents or log prices after removing its time trend. That standard deviation for log rent ranges from 0.011 in a low-volatility market, such as Pittsburgh, to 0.136 in a high-volatility market, such as San Jose. The estimated standard deviation for log prices follows a similar pattern, ranging from 0.012 (Indianapolis) to 0.146 (San Jose). Indeed, I find that rent volatility and house price volatility are highly correlated across MSAs, as would be expected if house prices are determined endogenously by rents. All of these facts are unchanged if one computes the standard deviation using the annual growth rate of rents or prices or the growth rate over longer horizons, such as five years. Although the estimated standard deviations decline as the horizon lengthens, the relative magnitudes across MSAs remain the same.

Another factor in housing risk that varies across MSAs is the covariance between an MSA's house price changes and those in the rest of the country. I estimate that almost every MSA in the data has house price growth that, from 1990 through 2002, on average covaried positively with the house price growth in the other MSAs. This implies the asset price risk of owning is mitigated by the natural hedge between the sale price of the current house and the purchase price of a future house. This point has long been recognized for within-market moves where the covariance is assumed to be high (e.g., Cocco, 2000), but the positive cross-MSA covariances indicate that there is a hedging value even when a household may move out of its MSA. Although this empirical point was made by Sinai and Souleles (2005), in this chapter I estimate how the covariances differ across MSAs. The average correlation in real house price growth with other MSAs ranges from 0.034 (Seattle) to 0.636 (Richmond), with covariances between 0.015 (Seattle) and 0.046 (Boston). In addition, I find that MSAs with higher price volatilities tend to have higher covariances of house price growth with other MSAs. Thus, the MSAs with the highest house price volatilities have the most valuable natural hedge against house price risk in future MSAs. That pattern indicates that the hedging property of home owning reduces the net house price volatility, especially for the most volatile markets. Because of this, buying a home in a more volatile market might reduce lifetime housing risk on the net price if that home is a better hedge against house price uncertainty in some future market.

Because the net risk of home owning involves trading off the three different sources of risk, none of these risks should be considered in isolation. Indeed, since rent volatility and house price volatility are positively correlated within MSAs, the relative risk of owning is usually mitigated because taking on greater sale price risk typically entails avoiding commensurately larger rent risk. And, because higher volatility markets covary more with future markets, the asset price risk is attenuated. The element that links these risks is a household's probability of moving. A household that plans never to move should place greater weight on avoiding rent risk, whereas mobile households should care more about sale price volatility and the natural hedge that owning a house provides for future houses. Thus, I combine the risk parameters to illustrate how the difference between the volatility of renting and the volatility of owning varies across MSAs for households with different expected mobilities. I conclude that when expected lengths of stay are short and the correlation of house prices with the next residence is low, the risk of renting could dominate that of owning.

The evidence in this chapter has important implications for the role of housing derivatives for homeowners and may help explain some of the low utilization of house price hedges documented in chapters 2 and 3. Because every household has to live somewhere, the natural hedge provided by the house undoes risk—the risk of the cost of obtaining housing—that households are "born" with. For a household that might move, whether to another MSA or within the same housing market, owning a home typically provides at least a partial hedge against the cost of a future home. In fact, households that use housing derivatives or home equity insurance to lock in their current house price may actually unhedge themselves, because they would reduce to zero the covariances of their current house price with their subsequent house price. Such households would face less risk than renters because they would lock in rental costs in their current markets, but more risk than owners because, like renters, they would be unhedged against the costs of future houses. And among households that plan never to move, they may face low house price volatilities in the first place, they may have heirs who value the hedge against their own housing costs embodied in their parents' home, or they may place little weight on the sale price of their home because the sale is so far in the future. Instead, the best use of housing derivatives by existing homeowners may be to enhance the hedging benefit of owning a house rather than to substitute for it. This could be done by supplementing the natural hedge owning a house provides by raising the house price covariance for mobile households in low-covariance markets or by locking in house prices for immobile households without children.

This point, which applies most when the quantity of housing consumption is held constant, is not intended to minimize the other potentially valuable uses of housing derivatives (Case, Shiller, and Weiss, 1993; de Jong, Driessen, and Van Hemert, 2007; Geltner, Miller, and Snavely, 1995; Voicu, 2007). For example, households that are short future housing, such as those composed of renters or the underhoused, could use derivatives to hedge their future increases in housing consumption. Households that have sold one home but not yet purchased their next one could use derivatives to lock in the relative house prices. Households that plan never to move and whose heirs live in uncorrelated markets, or seniors who need to lock in wealth for retirement consumption or who intend to downsize, could form a market for home equity insurance. Investors, such as developers or institutions exposed to housing market risk, might wish to hedge their exposure, and speculators seeking diversification may wish to increase theirs.

The rest of this chapter proceeds as follows: In the next section, I outline a simple conceptual framework for thinking about housing risk. The section "Why Does Rent Variance Differ Across Metropolitan Areas?" delves into why housing markets differ in their volatilities. Next, "How the Risks of Owning and Renting Vary Across Metropolitan Areas" estimates rent and house price volatility by MSA, then turns to the covariances in house price growth across MSAs. In "The Net Volatility of Renting," I incorporate household mobility to estimate the net risk of owning versus renting, and in "Where and When Is There Risk of Owning?" I discuss the findings. "The Implications for House Price Derivatives" describes what the results from this chapter imply for the housing derivatives. A brief conclusion follows.

Conceptual Framework

To provide some intuition behind how various sources of volatility contribute to housing risk, I adapt the conceptual framework from Sinai and Souleles (2005). That framework starts with the notion that every household needs a place to live. The decision the household faces is how to obtain its desired level of housing services at the lowest risk-adjusted cost: i.e., either rent, or own. The total cost of renting a home is the present value of the annual rents paid. The total cost of owning is the present value of the purchase price minus the present value of the sale price when the owner moves out.

In a riskless, frictionless equilibrium, the market would set house prices so that the present values of owning and renting were equal (Meese and Wallace, 1994). But housing costs are far from certain. Annual rent is determined by the intersection of household demand for housing services and the supply of housing. It fluctuates because of shocks to local housing demand that, in concert with the elasticity of housing supply, determine the rent level that clears the housing market.

Because of this rent volatility, renting yields an uncertain total cost of obtaining housing services. Renting is akin to purchasing housing services on the spot market. Because renters do not know what future rents will be, the present value of their rental payments is uncertain. But the total cost of home owning is uncertain as well. Although a homeowner essentially prepays the present value of expected future rents and thus avoids the uncertainty over the spot housing market, the future sales value of the home is unknown.

In the Sinai and Souleles framework, households live in two houses, the first in city A and the second in city B (cities A and B could be the same). A household stays in each house for N years and after $2N$ years it dies. Both future rents and house prices are uncertain, although they are correlated with each other and across MSAs, as I will discuss later. To choose between renting and owning, households compare their lifetime risk-adjusted cost of renting to the risk-adjusted cost of buying.

From a homeowner's perspective, the lifetime ex post cost of owning is

$$C_O \equiv P_0^A + \delta^N(\tilde{P}_N^B - \tilde{P}_N^A) - \delta^{2N}\tilde{P}_{2N}^B.$$

The P_0^A term is the initial purchase price in city A, which is known with certainty. The middle term, $\delta^N(\tilde{P}_N^B - \tilde{P}_N^A)$, is the difference between the sale price of the house in A at time N and the purchase price of the house in B at time N. The tilde denotes that both prices are uncertain. Because the move from A to B occurs N years in the future, the sale and subsequent purchase prices are discounted at rate δ^N. The last term, $\delta^{2N}\tilde{P}^B_{2N}$, is the uncertain residual value of the house at the time of death. It, too, is discounted, as death occurs $2N$ years in the future.

For a renter, the lifetime cost of obtaining housing services is the present value of all future rents,

$$C_R \equiv r_0^A + \sum_{n=1}^{N-1} \delta^n \tilde{r}_n^A + \sum_{n=N}^{2N-1} \delta^n \tilde{r}_n^B.$$

The first year's rent, r_0^A, is known with certainty. The remaining rents in city A are uncertain, and so the ex post present value is $\sum_{n=1}^{N-1} \delta^n \tilde{r}_n^A$. The move to city B occurs after year N, and thus those rents are discounted yet further, yielding an ex post present value of $\sum_{n=N}^{2N-1} \delta^n \tilde{r}_n^B$.

From this initial setup, we can derive two key measures of housing risk. The risk of renting comes from not having locked in the future price of housing services, so the present value of the future rent stream is unknown. It turns out that the cost of the risk of renting is proportional to the present value of the sum of the variance of rent innovations,

$$\pi_R \approx \frac{\alpha}{2}\left(s_A^2 \sum_{n=1}^{N-1} \delta^{2n} + s_B^2 \sum_{n=N}^{2N-1} \delta^{2n} \right), \tag{4.1}$$

where s_A^2 is the variance of the rent risk in market A, s_B^2 is the variance of the rent risk in market B, and α is a proportional scaling factor.

For owners, risk comes from uncertainty over the sale price of the first house and the purchase price and sale price of the second house,

$$\pi_O \equiv \frac{\alpha}{2}\left[\delta^{2N} \frac{(1-\rho)^2}{1+\rho^2}(\sigma_A^2 + \sigma_B^2) + \delta^{4N}(\sigma_B^2) \right], \tag{4.2}$$

where ρ is the correlation in house price shocks between cities A and B and σ_A^2 and σ_B^2 are, respectively, the variance in house prices in those two cities. The first house is sold N years in the future for some uncertain amount. However, at the same time, the household has to purchase a house in B. Because of that, the net risk is due to the difference between the sale price in A and the purchase price in B. However, since the sale and repurchase occur N periods in the future, and the terminal sale another N periods after that, the risk is discounted.

If city A and city B have highly correlated house prices, so that ρ is close to 1, the first sale and subsequent purchase is nearly a wash because $\dfrac{(1-\rho)^2}{1+\rho^2} = 0$ when $\rho = 1$. If the two markets are relatively uncorrelated, the sale and subsequent house repurchase are riskier. In that case, the magnitude of the risk depends on the variances of house prices in city A and city B. In the extreme case of completely uncorrelated housing markets, $\rho = 0$, we see that $\dfrac{(1-\rho)^2}{1+\rho^2} = 1$: the owning risk depends solely on the sum of the variances. When $\rho = -1$, so the house prices in the two markets are perfectly negatively correlated, the sale and repurchase volatility is twice as large as the sum of the variances.

As we turn to the data, it will be convenient to rewrite equation 4.2 as

$$\pi_O \equiv \frac{\alpha}{2}\left[\delta^{2N}(\sigma_A^2 + \sigma_B^2 - 2g(\operatorname{cov}(A, B))) + \delta^{4N}(\sigma_B^2)\right] \qquad (4.3)$$

In equation 4.3, g( ) is increasing.

For ease of exposition, these equations assume that rents and prices follow separate white-noise processes. This convenience requires two simplifications. First, the risks of renting and owning should be correlated because house prices are endogenously determined by rents in a given market when households equate the expected utilities of renting and owning. Sinai and Souleles (2005) show that, assuming inelastic supply, house prices should capitalize the expected present value of future rents plus a premium for the hedging value of home ownership. Because of this endogenous relationship, house price volatility should be a function of rent volatility and the two should be correlated. In any case, the endogeneity of rents and house prices does not affect the intuition that households trade off the two sources of risk when making their tenure choice. Rather, it affects the likelihood that the risk of renting outweighs the house price risk or vice versa. In the end, these are empirical questions that will be examined later in this chapter.

Second, shocks to rents (or prices) are likely to be persistent. Persistent rent shocks lead to a larger effective risk of renting, because an early rise or fall in rent is more likely to be sustained throughout a household's entire stay. However, because the persistence is capitalized into house prices, the volatility of those prices would increase as well. On the other hand, the resulting greater persistence in house prices implies a higher correlation between the purchase and sale prices of the home in city B, reducing the net volatility of owning that second home. The qualitative discussion of the sources of risk does not depend on the degree of persistence. However, the empirical analogs to the rent and price variance and the covariance terms in the previous equations may. We will turn to that question in the section on the risks of owning and renting.

It also bears mentioning that this framework assumes away a number of interesting complications, such as whether income and rents covary (Davidoff, 2006) or whether there are time-varying discount rates. However, the hedging intuition exposited here operates in addition to these other issues.

In the remainder of this chapter, I will show how the underlying parameters—rent variance, price variance, and house price correlations and covariances—differ across MSAs. In addition, I will compare the risk of renting in equation 4.1 to the risk of owning in equations 4.2 and 4.3 as a way of illustrating how the interaction of the parameters varies across MSAs.

WHY DOES RENT VARIANCE DIFFER ACROSS METROPOLITAN AREAS?

In the conceptual framework outlined earlier, housing markets have varying degrees of volatility that are expressed in rents and endogenously through prices. The cross-MSA variation in rent volatility should be due to differences in demand volatility and housing supply elasticities. We expect MSAs that have volatile housing demand, presumably caused by shocks to local economic growth, will also have more rent variance. MSAs with more inelastic housing supply should also exhibit higher rent variance as the housing or apartment stock is less able to adjust to demand fluctuations.

This view is supported by table 4.1, where we regress the standard deviation of detrended rents (i.e., rents after normalizing out the trend) in an MSA on a proxy for the volatility of demand for space and on proxies for the elasticity of housing supply. The rent variable we use comes from surveys of Class A apartment buildings conducted quarterly by REIS, Inc. and reported as an annual average by housing market. For each market, we detrend the 1989–1998 rent series by MSA and compute the standard deviation of the residual. The demand proxy is the detrended standard deviation in aggregate employment for the MSA that corresponds to each REIS housing market. We proxy for the inelasticity of supply of living space with two variables from Mayer and Somerville (2000): whether the MSA charges impact fees to developers and the number of months it takes to ob-

TABLE 4.1 Factors that Affect Rent Variance

	(1)	(2)	(3)	(4)
Standard deviation of	0.52		0.42	0.08
MSA employment	(0.17)		(0.18)	(0.29)
Impact fees		0.0084	0.0061	−0.0061
		(0.0026)	(0.0027)	(0.0068)
Months for permit		0.00069	0.00040	
		(0.00036)	(0.00037)	
Standard deviation of				0.63
employment × use				(0.35)
impact fees				
Constant	0.010	0.011	0.011	0.014
	(0.003)	(0.003)	(0.003)	(0.005)
Adjusted R-squared value	0.19	0.29	0.38	0.41
Observations	43	38	37	38

NOTES: Dependent variable is the detrended standard deviation of real rents, as defined in the text. Standard errors are in parentheses. Sample year is 1998. MSA = metropolitan statistical area.

tain a building permit. The former raises construction costs so that developers would wait for a larger increase in rents before adding more housing stock. The latter reduces the speed with which developers can respond to demand shocks and adds uncertainty to the development process, which is another cost of construction.

Variation in demand for space has a strong effect on rent variance. In the first column, we include only the standard deviation of MSA employment on the right-hand side. This leaves us with a sample of 43 MSAs in 1998, which is the entire REIS sample during this period. The coefficient on employment volatility is positive and significant, with a coefficient of 0.52 (0.17), and the regression has an R-squared value of 0.19. Thus, an MSA with a one standard deviation higher employment volatility (0.008 on a mean of 0.019) has a one-half standard deviation higher rent volatility.

Our proxies for whether supply is inelastic in the MSA also appear to affect rent volatility. In the second column, we use the indicator variable for whether the MSA charges impact fees and the time-to-obtain-permit variable as covariates. Our sample size falls to 38, as the supply elasticity variables are not available for all MSAs in the REIS sample. The impact fee dummy has a strong and statistically significant effect on rent variance, with an estimated coefficient of 0.0084 (0.0026). Presumably, our impact fee variable proxies for other deterrents to development in the market, as well. The estimated coefficient on the length of time to obtain a development permit variable has the expected positive sign, 0.00069 (0.00036), and is significant at the 93 percent confidence level.

In the third column, we show that both the demand- and supply-side factors have an effect on rent variance in the MSA by including all three covariates. The point estimate on the standard deviation of employment changes only slightly, falling to 0.42 (0.18). The impact fee dummy remains statistically significant: its estimated coefficient of 0.0061 (0.0027) implies that the standard deviation of rent is approximately 30 percent higher than the mean of 0.020 in markets in which impact fees are charged. The coefficient on the development permit variable falls in magnitude to 0.00040, reducing its t-statistic to just over one, so it is not statistically distinguishable from zero. The R-squared value increases to 0.38, suggesting that we are able to account for a substantial portion of the variation across MSAs in rent variance with this small set of explanatory variables.

Although the regression in the third column suggests that both demand variance and supply inelasticity contribute to rent variance in a given market, we anticipate that both factors must work in concert to create high rent variance. In other words, demand fluctuations may be innocuous if housing supply can easily adjust, and inelasticity of supply would be moot if demand were not volatile. We provide a crude test of that hypothesis in the fourth column by interacting the impact fee dummy variable with the employment variance variable. Indeed, only the interaction term is statistically significant in that regression, showing that the standard deviation of employment affects rent variance only in markets with impact fees. The point estimate of 0.63 (0.35) is significant at the 90 percent confidence level. Of course, these regressions are intended only to be suggestive, given the small number of MSAs, limited proxies for the elasticity of supply, and our inability to control for unobserved heterogeneity across MSAs.

How the Risks of Owning and Renting Vary Across Metropolitan Areas

Because of the factors described in the previous section, the volatility of rents and house prices varies considerably across MSAs. The covariances and correlations with other MSAs vary as well, likely because of the extent that an MSA is exposed to national demand shocks.

In this section, we estimate each MSA's real rent and real house price volatilities, and the average correlation and covariance of their house price growth with that of the other MSAs. As in table 4.1, the annual rent data come from REIS. Our annual house price data come from an index of repeat sales of houses with conforming mortgages available from the Office of Federal Housing Enterprise Oversight (OFHEO). Combining the two yields 42 MSAs for which we have consistent data in both data sets. We convert from nominal to real values using the Consumer Price Index (CPI) less shelter. The two housing series are believed to understate true housing market volatility because the liquidity of the housing market declines with rents and prices in a downturn (Stein, 1995). That reduced liquidity is costly, but is not capitalized into market prices because only a selected sample of properties trade. Fisher, Geltner, and Pollakowski (2006) construct a constant-liquidity apartment rent index and show that, at the national level, the volatility of the latent rent is greater than the volatility of the observed rent. However, the data sets we use cover a long period (1980 to the present) and a large number of MSAs (44 in the REIS data and 136 in the OFHEO data), so they are the best options for our application. Because in the end we are concerned with the relative risk of owning and renting, as long as the percent bias in the estimated volatility is approximately the same across MSAs and for both the rent and house price series, it should net out.

That rent risk varies considerably across MSAs is documented in table 4.2, which reports several different estimates of rent volatility by metropolitan area. A low standard deviation of rent in an MSA implies that fundamentals are not that volatile. In that case, there is less inherent uncertainty about total rental costs. Because rent risk should reflect unanticipated changes in rents, each column reflects a slightly different assumption about the underlying rent process.

The first column lists the standard deviation of log real rent after the MSA-specific trend has been removed. Implicit in this specification is a model of rents where they have a constant expected growth rate within an MSA with independent and identically distributed (i.i.d.) deviations around the trend. By using logs, the standard deviation is calculated as a percent of the rent and so the measured risk is not affected by the level or average growth rate of rents. In this column, the underlying rent variance is calculated over the 1990–2002 period. Some MSAs, such as Palm Beach (0.017), Detroit (0.019), and Pittsburgh (0.011), have very low standard deviations of rent. Others, such as San Jose (0.136), San Francisco (0.121), Oakland (0.102), and New York (0.082), exhibit high rent volatility.

In the second column, we estimate the standard deviation of annual real rent growth. Implicit in this measure is the assumption that households expect rents to be the same as last year, so rents follow a random walk. In general, the estimated volatility is lower than in the previous column, especially in the most cyclical markets, such as Boston, New York, and Los Angeles, because sustained deviations from the trend lead to a higher estimated standard deviation

TABLE 4.2 Real Rent Volatility by MSA

MSA	1990–2002 standard deviation of detrended log real rent	1990–2002 standard deviation of growth rate of annual rent	1990–2002 standard deviation of growth rate of five-year sum of rent	1981–1993 standard deviation of detrended log real rent
Atlanta	0.035	0.019	0.012	0.052
Austin	0.042	0.040	0.015	0.127
Baltimore	0.038	0.013	0.009	0.048
Boston	0.085	0.048	0.020	0.099
Charlotte	0.046	0.011	0.017	0.044
Chicago	0.022	0.019	0.006	0.059
Cincinnati	0.019	0.012	0.005	0.048
Cleveland	0.017	0.011	0.006	0.044
Columbus	0.020	0.014	0.008	0.030
Dallas	0.034	0.020	0.017	0.038
Denver	0.024	0.028	0.015	0.066
Detroit	0.019	0.016	0.005	0.033
District of Columbia	0.069	0.030	0.013	0.041
Fort Lauderdale	0.014	0.010	0.003	0.016
Fort Worth	0.030	0.018	0.014	0.037
Houston	0.028	0.014	0.009	0.083
Indianapolis	0.014	0.010	0.007	0.023
Jacksonville	0.026	0.015	0.007	0.015
Kansas City	0.026	0.015	0.009	0.086
Los Angeles	0.080	0.026	0.014	0.075
Memphis	0.032	0.011	0.011	0.034
Miami	0.026	0.017	0.006	0.026
Milwaukee	0.016	0.015	0.004	0.023
Minneapolis	0.039	0.021	0.012	0.055
Nashville	0.044	0.011	0.013	0.077
New York	0.082	0.041	0.025	0.038
Oakland–East Bay	0.102	0.109	0.031	0.060
Orlando	0.034	0.007	0.005	0.035
Palm Beach	0.017	0.015	0.002	0.026
Philadelphia	0.029	0.014	0.004	0.039
Phoenix	0.039	0.009	0.013	0.054
Pittsburgh	0.011	0.016	0.002	0.020
Portland	0.015	0.017	0.010	0.041
Richmond	0.034	0.013	0.007	0.045
Sacramento	0.077	0.040	0.012	0.075
St. Louis	0.027	0.016	0.002	0.034
San Antonio	0.029	0.012	0.003	0.076

(*continued*)

TABLE 4.2 *(continued)*

MSA	1990–2002 standard deviation of detrended log real rent	1990–2002 standard deviation of growth rate of annual rent	1990–2002 standard deviation of growth rate of five-year sum of rent	1981–1993 standard deviation of detrended log real rent
San Diego	0.077	0.027	0.009	0.066
San Francisco	0.121	0.103	0.048	0.055
San Jose	0.136	0.170	0.056	0.058
Seattle	0.047	0.027	0.020	0.055
Tampa–St. Petersburg	0.029	0.009	0.007	0.028
Correlation with column 2:	0.846		0.909	
Correlation of columns 1 and 3:		0.863		

in the first column but can yield a relatively lower estimated standard deviation in the second column. In Los Angeles, for example, the estimated standard deviation of real rents fell from 0.080 in the first column to 0.026 in the second. By contrast, San Jose's estimated standard deviation of real rents rose from 0.136 in the first column to 0.170 in the second.

In the third column, we take a different approach to estimating the rent volatility. Rather than estimating the volatility of the underlying rent shocks (which we would then aggregate up to total rent volatility over the entire residence spell, using equation 4.1), we estimate the volatility of the present value of the rents over a five-year horizon. Using a discount rate of 1/0.96, we compute the present value of the rental cost over the prior five years for each year in each MSA. We then compute the standard deviation of the annual growth in that rent total. This approach estimates the volatility of apparent rent, rather than the underlying rent shocks. To the extent that rents mean-revert at a high frequency, the volatility of the total rent should be lower than the sum of the rent volatilities.

This approach typically yields a lower estimated rent volatility than in either of the prior two columns. The declines in the San Francisco Bay Area MSAs are especially notable, with the estimated standard deviations falling by as much as one-third. For example, in San Jose, the estimated standard deviation of rent falls from 0.170 to 0.056 between the second and third columns. In most other MSAs, the decline is much more muted.

Despite the declines in the estimated rent volatility in the second and third columns, the relative volatility across MSAs stays fairly constant across the two columns. The correlation between the first two measures of rent volatility is

0.85, between the second and third measures is 0.91, and between the first and third measures is 0.86.

The pattern of rent risks across MSAs can also differ over time, as can be seen in the last column of table 4.2, which reports the standard deviation of the detrended log real rents estimated over the 1981–1993 period. During that era, Texas cities such as Austin, Houston, and San Antonio had much higher rent volatilities. The Bay Area cities had considerably lower rent volatility.

In table 4.3, we repeat this exercise for real house prices, with the first column reporting the standard deviation of detrended (by MSA) log real house prices over the 1990–2002 period. The California cities again have the highest estimated volatilities. For example, the estimated house price volatility in San Jose is 0.146 and in Los Angeles it is 0.132. By contrast, Cincinnati has an estimated 0.015 standard deviation; in Indianapolis it is 0.012. Midrange cities include those in Florida (Miami, for example, comes in at 0.50), the Northwest (Seattle has a 0.057 estimated volatility), and the Mid-Atlantic (Baltimore's is 0.051).

The second column of table 4.3 reports the estimated standard deviation of annual house price growth. For many cities, this estimate is similar to the first column. For others, where house prices tend to have sustained deviations from trend rather than higher-frequency fluctuations, the estimated volatility falls considerably. Such cities include those in California, Boston, and New York. Even so, the correlation between the estimated standard deviations in the first two columns is 0.97.

The third column uses a longer difference — five years — when calculating the average annual growth to try to mimic the longer holding period of a homeowner. According to the "Conceptual Framework" section, within-holding period fluctuations in house prices should not matter. Thus, for someone with a longer holding period, high-frequency house price changes that net out with each other may be less important than sustained deviations. The estimated annual standard deviations using five-year average growth rates are typically lower than those using one-year growth rates. However, the relative degree of volatility across MSAs remains stable. The estimates in the third column are highly correlated with those in the second column — 0.91 — and even the first and third columns have a 0.88 correlation.

As with rents, we see that the period over which the standard deviation is estimated can matter quite a bit. The last column of table 4.3 follows the same estimation procedure as the first column, but uses the 1981–1993 period. The estimated standard deviation of house prices rises from 0.037 to 0.141 in Austin, Texas, from 0.039 to 0.067 in Dallas, and from 0.061 to

TABLE 4.3   Real House Price Volatility by MSA

MSA	1990–2002 standard deviation of detrended log real HPI	1990–2002 standard deviation of annual growth of HPI	1990–2002 standard deviation of five-year growth rate of HPI	1981–1993 standard deviation of detrended log real HPI
Atlanta	0.040	0.035	0.026	0.042
Austin	0.037	0.038	0.047	0.141
Baltimore	0.051	0.038	0.022	0.079
Boston	0.112	0.079	0.057	0.204
Charlotte	0.028	0.023	0.016	0.044
Chicago	0.028	0.023	0.015	0.066
Cincinnati	0.015	0.015	0.010	0.031
Cleveland	0.013	0.013	0.003	0.045
Columbus	0.014	0.014	0.008	0.033
Dallas	0.039	0.032	0.033	0.067
Denver	0.043	0.037	0.039	0.064
Detroit	0.050	0.028	0.021	0.121
District of Columbia	0.083	0.055	0.033	0.093
Fort Lauderdale	0.071	0.054	0.027	0.026
Fort Worth	0.031	0.026	0.028	0.051
Houston	0.046	0.032	0.024	0.087
Indianapolis	0.012	0.015	0.007	0.052
Jacksonville	0.049	0.037	0.029	0.044
Kansas City	0.032	0.031	0.026	0.023
Los Angeles	0.132	0.078	0.059	0.157
Memphis	0.021	0.028	0.018	0.037
Miami	0.050	0.047	0.019	0.041
Milwaukee	0.015	0.014	0.006	0.041
Minneapolis	0.055	0.041	0.030	0.017
Nashville	0.040	0.031	0.025	0.055
New York	0.090	0.066	0.043	0.182
Oakland–East Bay	0.143	0.081	0.056	0.122
Orlando	0.052	0.038	0.022	0.026
Palm Beach	0.071	0.052	0.028	0.030
Philadelphia	0.061	0.045	0.030	0.110
Phoenix	0.031	0.038	0.033	0.041
Pittsburgh	0.022	0.024	0.007	0.021
Portland	0.049	0.029	0.016	0.085
Richmond	0.029	0.025	0.015	0.039
Sacramento	0.131	0.079	0.050	0.129
St. Louis	0.030	0.029	0.021	0.047
San Antonio	0.020	0.032	0.030	0.081

(*continued*)

TABLE 4.3 *(continued)*

MSA	1990–2002 standard deviation of detrended log real HPI	1990–2002 standard deviation of annual growth of HPI	1990–2002 standard deviation of five-year growth rate of HPI	1981–1993 standard deviation of detrended log real HPI
San Diego	0.137	0.079	0.054	0.110
San Francisco	0.142	0.085	0.060	0.154
San Jose	0.146	0.098	0.060	0.149
Seattle	0.057	0.044	0.027	0.108
Tampa–St. Petersburg	0.057	0.043	0.028	0.031
Correlation with column 2:	0.974		0.914	
Correlation of columns 1 and 3:		0.879		

NOTE: HPI = House Price Index.

0.110 in Philadelphia, for example. However, in many cities the estimated standard deviation remains unchanged over the time periods.

Because house prices should be determined endogenously from rents, in MSAs with low rent risk there should also be low house price volatility. In a simple model of rents, even if there is persistence in the rent process, the standard deviation of rents and prices should be the same when measured in percentages. Even so, there are a number of practical reasons why rent and price volatility might differ within an MSA. For example, changes in the discount rate might affect the pricing multiple applied to rents differentially across markets, as argued in Himmelberg, Mayer, and Sinai (2005), Mayer and Sinai (forthcoming), and, in the commercial real estate context, by Geltner and Mei (1995). Or, the differences could be the result of speculative bubbles, as in Case and Shiller (2003); inefficiencies, as in Case and Shiller (1989); capital markets, as in Pavlov and Wachter (2007); or an unspecified overpricing, as in Campbell et al. (2007).

More prosaically, differences between rent and house price volatility could be due to the underlying samples in the rent and house price series. REIS surveys "class A" apartments in each market, which are the nicest available, to obtain rents. The OFHEO uses transaction and appraisal-based valuations from repeat observations of properties with conforming mortgages. As Smith and Smith (2006) point out, these two samples potentially are not comparable, because houses and apartments are very different. This issue might lead us to find differences between the observed rent volatility and the observed house price volatility, whereas there should be no difference in the underlying true risks. Even with that handicap, we observe highly correlated rent and price volatilities.

To the Smith and Smith (2006) argument, Glaeser and Gyourko (see chapter 5 in this volume) add that differences in tax treatment of homeowners and landlords, among other factors, lead to an inability to arbitrage rents and house prices. If this were the case, the true rent volatility could deviate from the true house price volatility. In the analysis that follows, I will use the actual rent and house price volatilities, thus allowing the two risk concepts to differ.

House price volatility indeed is highly correlated with rent volatility. The correlation between rent volatility and price volatility, as reported in the first columns of tables 4.2 and 4.3, is 0.87. The second columns, which use the higher-frequency variation of annual growth rates, have a 0.72 correlation. This close relationship can be seen in figure 4.1, where the data from the first columns of tables 4.2 and 4.3 are plotted against each other. MSAs with a higher standard deviation of detrended log real rent also have a higher standard deviation of detrended log real house prices over the 1990–2002 period. The slope of the regression line that is plotted through the data is 1.2 (with a standard error of 0.11) and the adjusted R-squared value is 0.74.

FIGURE 4.1   Relationship of House Price Volatility to Rent Volatility, 1990–2002

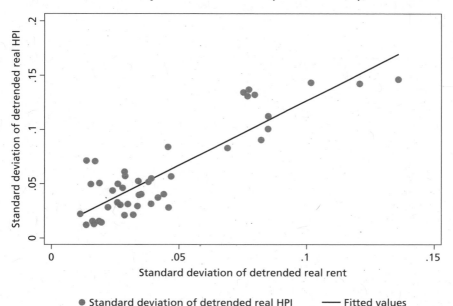

NOTE: HPI = House Price Index.

Even so, there are some notable MSAs in which price risk diverges from rent risk. In Miami, the standard deviation of detrended log rent is 0.026 but the standard deviation of detrended log price is almost twice as high, at 0.050. In San Diego, the standard deviation of rents is 0.077, whereas for prices it is 0.137. And in Fort Lauderdale, the standard deviation is just 0.014 for rents but 0.071 for prices.

It is important to note that we are considering only how the estimated rent volatilities and price volatilities are correlated across metropolitan areas and not whether year-to-year rent and price changes covary within an MSA. The "Conceptual Framework" section shows that households trade off rent and price volatility when making their tenure decisions, and the high-frequency comovement of rent and price changes does not enter their decisions. That parameter may be more relevant in other contexts, such as in Davidoff (2006).

From equation 4.3, we know that selling a house in city A is risky only to the extent that house prices there do not covary much with house prices in city B. If they covaried perfectly, there would be no house price risk upon leaving city A because all the sale proceeds would be used to purchase the home in B. If the covariance were zero, a household would be exposed to the uncertainty of the sale price in A plus the purchase price in B.

Indeed, it is possible that if both the price variance in city A and the covariance between cities A and B increased together, on net the risk of buying a home in A could be *reduced*. That occurs because the sale price volatility in A affects net risk only to the extent that it is independent of the house-purchasing risk in B.

It turns out that the correlation in house prices with the market varies widely across MSAs, so to assess the true risk of renting versus owning, one needs to consider the particular MSA he or she is living in. Table 4.4 reports several estimates of the average of the correlations of each MSA's house prices with the other MSAs in the sample over the 1990–2002 period. In the first column, the correlation is computed using the annual real house price growth from the OFHEO index. Some MSAs—such as Richmond with 0.636, Chicago with 0.595, and Miami with 0.550—have relatively high correlations. Others are much lower: Austin has a 0.243 correlation, Seattle's is 0.034, and Portland's is negative.

In the second column, we estimate the correlations using average house price growth rates over a five-year period. The longer period is intended to better correspond to the holding period for some owners. That is, owners may not care about the year-to-year correlation in house prices as long as prices are correlated at the time of sale or repurchase. The pattern of correlations across MSAs is similar whether we use one-year or five-year growth rates, with a correlation of 0.89.

As equation 4.3 showed, the covariance in house prices should be more relevant than the correlations to the hedging value of owning a house. A pair of cities can be highly correlated, but one could have more volatility than the other, making them poor hedges for each other. The covariance better measures whether the benefit of house price movements in one city undoes the cost of house price movements in another.

In table 4.5, we provide estimates of the average of the square roots of each MSA's covariances with all the other MSAs. We use the same underlying concepts to measure house price growth as in table 4.4. In the first column of table 4.5, cities like San Diego, Boston, and New York have high average covariances, and thus houses there have more value as a hedge against the price of houses if the household were to move. The hedging value is low in Cleveland, Seattle, and Portland. In fact, Portland's average covariance over the 1990–2002 period was negative, hence the square root is not listed. Using five-year growth rates, we obtain lower estimates of the square root of the covariances, but the correlation between columns 1 and 2 is 0.94.

This wide range of average covariances means that a city like Austin can have a larger effective price risk even if its actual rent and price volatilities are not high because the sale price is unhedged. By contrast, in Washington, DC, where the average correlation is 0.591 and the average covariance is 0.039, the high price volatility hedges the home owner in part against house price movements in other cities.

THE NET VOLATILITY OF RENTING

It is becoming apparent that the parameters that enter equation 4.3 are not independent of each other across MSAs. For example, metropolitan areas with high rent volatility also have high house price volatility. These correlations mean that the volatility of owning, net the volatility of renting, needs to take into account how the parameters interrelate.

One important correlation from the perspective of the hedging value of owning is that the very MSAs that have higher house price volatility (and thus present a greater risk of owning) also tend to have higher pairwise covariances with other markets, providing a hedge against subsequent house purchases that mitigates the initial house price risk. Figure 4.2 plots MSAs in risk-covariance space. On the y-axis is the standard deviation of detrended

TABLE 4.4   Average House Price Correlations Among MSAs, 1990–2002

| | Mean correlation | |
MSA	In real annual HPI growth	In real five-year HPI growth
Atlanta	0.598	0.536
Austin	0.243	0.225
Baltimore	0.563	0.336
Boston	0.597	0.562
Charlotte	0.469	0.464
Chicago	0.595	0.379
Cincinnati	0.578	0.530
Cleveland	0.479	0.416
Columbus	0.549	0.483
Dallas	0.596	0.447
Denver	0.339	0.352
Detroit	0.366	0.474
District of Columbia	0.591	0.396
Fort Lauderdale	0.599	0.554
Fort Worth	0.620	0.446
Houston	0.508	0.459
Indianapolis	0.554	0.498
Jacksonville	0.601	0.535
Kansas City	0.555	0.488
Los Angeles	0.564	0.316
Memphis	0.490	0.461
Miami	0.550	0.505
Milwaukee	0.483	0.445
Minneapolis	0.594	0.539
Nashville	0.369	0.321
New York	0.611	0.550
Oakland–East Bay	0.476	0.427
Orlando	0.612	0.548
Palm Beach	0.621	0.555
Philadelphia	0.607	0.343
Phoenix	0.535	0.441
Pittsburgh	0.383	0.268
Portland	−0.398	−0.452
Richmond	0.636	0.517
Sacramento	0.287	0.262
St. Louis	0.609	0.540
San Antonio	0.489	0.265
San Diego	0.555	0.418
San Francisco	0.440	0.436
San Jose	0.385	0.445
Seattle	0.034	0.148
Tampa–St. Petersburg	0.628	0.551
Correlation with column 2:	0.893	

NOTE: HPI = House Price Index.

TABLE 4.5 Average House Price Covariances Among MSAs, 1990–2002

MSA	Mean square root of the covariance	
	In real annual HPI growth	**In real five-year HPI growth**
Atlanta	0.029	0.020
Austin	0.020	0.014
Baltimore	0.031	0.017
Boston	0.046	0.031
Charlotte	0.020	0.014
Chicago	0.025	0.014
Cincinnati	0.019	0.012
Cleveland	0.015	0.006
Columbus	0.017	0.010
Dallas	0.029	0.020
Denver	0.023	0.018
Detroit	0.021	0.017
District of Columbia	0.039	0.022
Fort Lauderdale	0.038	0.021
Fort Worth	0.026	0.018
Houston	0.027	0.018
Indianapolis	0.017	0.010
Jacksonville	0.032	0.021
Kansas City	0.026	0.018
Los Angeles	0.045	0.027
Memphis	0.022	0.014
Miami	0.033	0.016
Milwaukee	0.017	0.008
Minneapolis	0.033	0.022
Nashville	0.019	0.013
New York	0.042	0.027
Oakland–East Bay	0.044	0.029
Orlando	0.032	0.019
Palm Beach	0.038	0.022
Philadelphia	0.035	0.019
Phoenix	0.028	0.019
Pittsburgh	0.020	0.008
Portland	.	.
Richmond	0.026	0.016
Sacramento	0.037	0.023
St. Louis	0.028	0.018
San Antonio	0.025	0.013
San Diego	0.046	0.028
San Francisco	0.043	0.030
San Jose	0.043	0.030
Seattle	0.015	0.014
Tampa–St. Petersburg	0.035	0.021
Correlation with column 2:	0.935	

NOTE: HPI = House Price Index.

FIGURE 4.2 Standard Deviation of Real Annual House Price Growth Versus Average Covariance of Real Annual House Price Growth with Other MSAs

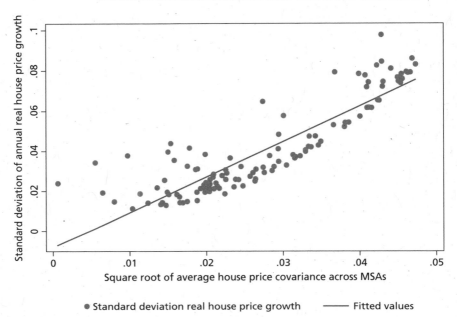

● Standard deviation real house price growth　　——— Fitted values

NOTE: MSAs= metropolitan statistical areas.

log house prices, computed over the 1990–2002 period. On the x-axis is the average of the square root of the MSA's pairwise covariances in its log real house price growth with each of the other MSAs' log real house price growth, computed for 126 metropolitan areas from the OFHEO data. The relationship is strongly positive, with a tight clustering of MSAs (the dots) around the fitted regression line. The estimated slope on the line is 1.77 (standard error of 0.081) and the adjusted R-squared value is 0.78. We obtain quantitatively similar results using covariances computed using five-year growth rates.

In some sense, the result in figure 4.2 is not surprising, as only MSAs with high variances can have high covariances. But it emphasizes a crucial point: house price volatility inherently hedges homeowners against the same price volatility in other markets. Without it, homeowners are exposed to the vagaries of house prices wherever they move.

To evaluate the relative volatilities of renting and owning, we need to combine the various risk and correlation parameters at the MSA level, as there is so much cross-MSA heterogeneity and the parameters interact nonlinearly. In table 4.6, we take the difference between equations 4.1 and 4.2 to compute the net volatility of renting. A more positive coefficient means that renting has more volatility than owning. Larger numbers (in absolute value) mean that there is more overall volatility. The intent is not to measure the actual cost of the risk of owning versus renting, but to provide an index that incorporates several MSA-specific parameters into one. The only parameters that do not vary across MSAs are δ and α. We assume $\delta = 0.96$ and $\alpha = 2$, and use the parameters estimated using the one-year growth rates in rents and house prices.

Results from Sinai and Souleles (2005) suggest that, on average, the risk-based demand for home owning increases with expected length of stay in the house and with greater intensity when housing market risk is larger. That is because a short-duration homeowner avoids few rent risks but has asset price risk arriving early (and thus being large in present value), whereas a long-duration homeowner avoids many rent risks—frontloaded in time and thus more significant in present value—and takes one price risk far in the future. The greater the market volatility, the more emphatic is that trade-off. That is, when the rent and price volatilities are small, there is little risk from either owning or renting and the net risk does not vary much with expected length of stay. Conversely, in MSAs with high rent risk, prices will be volatile as well, and there will be considerable risk from owning for a short duration or renting for a longer duration.

In keeping with the notion that expected length of stay affects the relative risks of renting and owning, we evaluate each MSA in terms of five different expected durations. As can be seen in table 4.6, the volatility of renting increases in relation to the volatility of owning as expected duration increases. Beyond that, there is considerable heterogeneity across MSAs in the magnitude of the risks and the slope with duration. Sacramento and Seattle, for example, are the most volatile MSAs in which to own for a short duration, with a net volatility of -0.004. Although Seattle has only moderate rent and house price volatility, its price growth has a low covariance with other MSAs, so a short-duration owner risks changes in house prices both in Seattle and in the city he or she moves to without being able to offset them against each other. Sacramento has a very high house price volatility (0.079 standard deviation), which the natural hedge of its moderate covariance (the square root of its covariance is 0.037) cannot undo. As expected durations rise, the expected price volatility declines and the expected rent volatility increases, so the relative volatility of owning falls. Given the greater volatility of Sacramento's housing market, the net volatility changes more rapidly with duration there.

TABLE 4.6 Net Rent Volatility by MSA and Expected Length of Stay

MSA	Expected length of stay (years)				
	2	5	10	15	20
Atlanta	−0.001	0.002	0.003	0.004	0.005
Austin	−0.001	0.005	0.010	0.014	0.016
Baltimore	−0.001	0.001	0.002	0.002	0.003
Boston	0.001	0.008	0.015	0.020	0.022
Charlotte	−0.001	0.001	0.002	0.002	0.002
Chicago	−0.001	0.002	0.004	0.004	0.005
Cincinnati	−0.001	0.001	0.002	0.003	0.003
Cleveland	−0.001	0.001	0.002	0.002	0.002
Columbus	−0.001	0.001	0.002	0.003	0.003
Dallas	−0.001	0.002	0.004	0.005	0.005
Denver	−0.001	0.002	0.006	0.007	0.008
Detroit	−0.002	0.001	0.002	0.003	0.003
District of Columbia	−0.001	0.003	0.006	0.008	0.009
Fort Lauderdale	−0.002	0.000	0.002	0.002	0.002
Fort Worth	−0.001	0.002	0.003	0.004	0.004
Houston	−0.001	0.001	0.002	0.003	0.003
Indianapolis	−0.001	0.001	0.002	0.002	0.002
Jacksonville	−0.001	0.001	0.003	0.003	0.003
Kansas City	−0.001	0.001	0.003	0.003	0.003
Los Angeles	−0.002	0.002	0.005	0.006	0.007
Memphis	−0.001	0.001	0.002	0.002	0.002
Miami	−0.002	0.001	0.003	0.004	0.004
Milwaukee	−0.001	0.001	0.003	0.003	0.003
Minneapolis	−0.001	0.002	0.004	0.005	0.005
Nashville	−0.002	0.000	0.002	0.002	0.002
New York	0.000	0.006	0.011	0.015	0.017
Oakland–East Bay	0.008	0.038	0.072	0.095	0.110
Orlando	−0.002	0.000	0.001	0.002	0.002
Palm Beach	−0.001	0.001	0.002	0.003	0.003
Philadelphia	−0.001	0.001	0.002	0.003	0.003
Phoenix	−0.002	0.000	0.001	0.002	0.002
Pittsburgh	−0.001	0.001	0.003	0.003	0.003
Portland	−0.006	−0.003	0.000	0.002	0.002
Richmond	−0.001	0.001	0.002	0.003	0.003
Sacramento	−0.004	0.002	0.009	0.012	0.015
San Antonio	−0.001	0.001	0.002	0.002	0.002
San Diego	−0.002	0.002	0.005	0.007	0.008
San Francisco	0.007	0.034	0.065	0.086	0.099
San Jose	0.023	0.093	0.177	0.232	0.269
Seattle	−0.004	0.000	0.004	0.006	0.007
St. Louis	−0.001	0.001	0.003	0.003	0.004
Tampa–St. Petersburg	−0.001	0.001	0.002	0.002	0.002

Another example is San Jose, which has extremely high rent and price volatility. In San Jose, the net volatility of renting increases very rapidly with expected duration in the house, from 0.02 at two years' duration to 0.27 at 20 years' expected duration. By contrast, low-volatility places like Memphis experience little change in the net volatility of renting as expected duration increases. In Memphis, the net volatility ranges from -0.001 to 0.002.

Where and When Is There Risk of Owning?

This low relative volatility of home owning arises in part because owning a house hedges the consumption need for a place to live. In equilibrium, when the present value of housing costs rise, so must house prices, exactly undoing the increases. Empirically, it appears that this linkage between rents and prices more or less holds at the MSA level. Because of this linkage between the price of housing and the consumption value, there is no net gain in household net worth, if consumption holds constant, when house prices rise. Although the housing wealth increases, so does the future rent liability, on net, leaving no change in net worth. To see why that is, consider a household whose house has appreciated in value. Could it increase its lifetime consumption while holding housing service consumption constant? If it sold its house, it would have to repurchase one that provided the same level of housing services in the same market—and that house would have gone up in price just as much as the existing house, leaving the household no better off. If it sold and did not repurchase, the household would have to rent, which, risk adjusted, would be just as costly in present value as owning. And, if it borrowed against its now-higher housing equity to finance consumption, the borrowing would have to be paid back, merely resulting in changing the timing of consumption. This may be the reason many researchers find a low marginal propensity to consume (MPC) out of housing wealth (Skinner, 1989, 1996).[1]

One category of households that potentially could gain from this increase in house prices are homeowners who anticipate moving. However, if their house prices covary with other markets', their house price capital gain is offset by an increase in the purchase price of their next house.

Indeed, the households that could gain the most from an increase in house prices are the elderly—for whom the present value of the residual

---

1. One notable exception is Case, Quigley, and Shiller (2003), who find a high MPC out of housing wealth.

value of their house when they expect to die is greater than zero—if they have a limited bequest motive (Li and Yao, 2007). Such households can transfer wealth from their heirs to themselves by spending housing capital gains. For example, if they sold their homes and rented instead, the present value of future rents would be less than their sale price because they had relatively few years left to live. Or, they could borrow against their homes, leaving their heirs to settle the debt position. Campbell and Cocco (2007) find that, consistent with this possibility, the largest marginal propensity to consume out of housing wealth is among older homeowners, whereas there is a zero MPC for younger homeowners. However, for elderly households with children, the bequest motive can yield a positive hedging value of home owning if the children live in a housing market that covaries positively with the parents'.

Still, the largest risk from home owning comes toward the end of life, when more of the value of the house could be extracted from the estate and used for current consumption. Sinai and Souleles (2008) estimate how much housing equity could be used for nonhousing consumption, depending on a household's age. They find that the median 62- to 69-year-old could extract almost 50 percent of housing equity as long as he or she did not want to leave a bequest, although 40 percent of households could not extract any equity at all. By contrast, by age 90 to 94, almost all home-owning households could extract housing equity, with a median value of 76 percent. Considering that national house prices rose 50 percent between 2000 and 2007, the amount of equity available for consumption by older households increased significantly. Should house prices decline, there would be commensurately less residual value of the house to consume. This uncertainty of house prices even makes the timing of the decision to extract equity risky (Sun, Triest, and Webb, 2006).

THE IMPLICATIONS FOR HOUSE PRICE DERIVATIVES

Using house price derivatives to lock in house prices looks appealing at first glance because it could eliminate one of the risks in equation 4.2, the volatility of the sale price. By buying a house and using such derivatives to effectively lock in its value, one could avoid both rent risk and sale price risk.

However, as can be seen in equations 4.2 and 4.3, eliminating asset price fluctuations in city A does not necessarily reduce the risk of owning, and possibly could increase it. That is, house price risk in both the current and the future markets affect the risk of owning, attenuated by their covariance. Hedging the volatility of house prices in the current market eliminates a portion of the aggregate uncertainty, but also reduces the covariance, which makes the effective volatility higher.

Consider, for example, a homeowner who intends to move to a new home in the same market. If her housing value is unhedged, then the volatility in the sale price exactly offsets the volatility in the purchase price, at least to the degree that the volatility is due to marketwide demand shocks rather than idiosyncratic factors, resulting in a volatility-free wash sale. But if she locks in the value of her current home to avoid sale price uncertainty, she is exposed to all the changes in the market cost of housing services. A similar thing happens if the homeowner intends to move to another market. Owning a house, in most cases, would at least partially hedge the uncertainty about house prices in the future city. But locking in the current house price would undo the natural hedge of home owning. The only way to truly avoid house price risk is to lock in the asset value until one dies (assuming any children do not value a hedge against housing costs in their bequest). That would require hedging house prices in both the current and future locations, as in Voicu (2007).

This counterproductive aspect of the derivatives-based hedge may help explain why there are so few long-term leases in the United States (Genesove, 1999). A long-term lease averts rent risk and leaves the asset price risk with the landlord. But a mobile household should want to retain the asset price uncertainty to hedge future housing costs.

The greatest value of a housing derivatives–based hedge, then, may be in complementing the natural hedging aspect of house price volatility rather than trying to undo it. One such way may be to use such derivatives to lock in the *relative* price of two locations, either in the short run to eliminate risk in between selling in one market and buying in the next (or vice versa), or in the long run if the household knows its sequence of housing locations and is not completely hedged by owning a home. This application would enhance the hedging aspect of home ownership by eliminating risk from the timing of the buy/sell transaction. Another use may be for households who are too short or too long future housing consumption, such as renters or the underhoused, who would like to trade up to larger homes, or for the overhoused who would like to downsize to smaller homes in the future. Of course, housing derivatives can still provide a hedging benefit for investors and lenders, as they are not naturally hedged through the consumption value of ownership.

CONCLUSION

Fluctuations in housing markets manifest themselves in uncertain rents and house prices. This chapter considered how that volatility varies across metropolitan areas. Using several measures, we found considerable heterogeneity across MSAs in rent and house price volatility. The two volatilities are highly correlated, as would be predicted by a model where house prices were determined endogenously by rents. That correlation in volatilities implies that for a household with a long enough expected length of stay in a house, owning will involve less volatility than renting because homeowners can avoid the uncertainty of future rents, and the risk of the future sale price is smaller in present value.

In addition, in many MSAs, the house price volatility provides a natural hedge for the price of housing in other MSAs. In fact, the greater the house price volatility in the housing market, the better it hedges prices in other MSAs. This hedging benefit of home owning helps mitigate the house price risk in the current market.

The implication of these results is that the role of housing derivatives in locking in asset values for homeowners is limited. That is because, for most households, home owning provides a natural hedge due to the implicit short position in housing that all households are born with. Putting a collar on house price volatility would actually unhedge a homeowner.

This analysis has ignored two important features of housing market risk. The first is that households control whether to adjust their housing consumption. In that case, if a homeowner uses derivatives to hedge housing price volatility and market housing costs fall, she can choose to move to a larger house, whereas if housing costs rise she can remain instead in her current house at her current level of consumption. The second is leverage. In the presence of housing debt and liquidity constraints, the risks of house price volatility may be exacerbated (Chan, 2001; Genesove and Mayer, 1997, 2001; Hurst and Stafford, 2004; Lustig and Van Nieuwerburgh, 2005; Stein, 1995). Even so, the risk-hedging benefits of home ownership that we have outlined in this chapter should remain even with these other risks of home owning.

REFERENCES

Campbell, John, and Joao Cocco. 2007. "How Do House Prices Affect Consumption? Evidence from Micro Data." *Journal of Monetary Economics* 54(3) (April): 591–621.

Campbell, Sean, Morris Davis, Joshua Gallin, and Robert F. Martin. 2007. "What Moves Housing Markets: A Variance Decomposition of the Rent-Price Ratio." Mimeo, University of Wisconsin, July.

Case, Karl, John Quigley, and Robert Shiller. 2003. "Comparing Wealth Effects: The Stock Market Versus the Housing Market." Mimeo, University of California, Berkeley, May.

Case, Karl, and Robert Shiller. 1989. "The Efficiency of the Market for Single-Family Homes." *American Economic Review* 79(1) (March): 125–137.

———. 2003. "Is There a Bubble in the Housing Market?" *Brookings Papers on Economic Activity* 2: 299–362.

Case, Karl E., Robert J. Shiller, and Allan N. Weiss. 1993. "Index-Based Futures and Options Markets in Real Estate." *Journal of Portfolio Management* 19(2) (Winter): 83–92.

Chan, Sewin. 2001. "Spatial Lock-In: Do Falling House Prices Constrain Residential Mobility?" *Journal of Urban Economics* 49(3) (May): 567–586.

Cocco, Joao. 2000. "Hedging House Price Risk with Incomplete Markets." Mimeo, London Business School, September.

Davidoff, Thomas. 2006. "Labor Income, Housing Prices and Homeownership." *Journal of Urban Economics* 59(2) (March): 209–235.

de Jong, Frank, Joost Driessen, and Otto Van Hemert. 2007. "Hedging House Price Risk: Portfolio Choice with Housing Futures." Mimeo, New York University, August 8.

Fisher, Jeff, David Geltner, and Henry Pollakowski. 2006. "A Quarterly Transactions-Based Index (TBI) of Institutional Real Estate Investment Performance and Movements in Supply and Demand." Mimeo, MIT Center for Real Estate, May.

Geltner, David, and Jianping Mei. 1995. "The Present Value Model with Time-Varying Discount Rates: Implications for Commercial Property Valuation and Investment Decisions." *Journal of Real Estate Finance and Economics* 11(2): 119–136.

Geltner, David, Norman Miller, and Jean Snavely. 1995. "We Need a Fourth Asset Class: HEITs." *Real Estate Finance* 12(2) (Summer): 71–81.

Genesove, David. 1999. "The Nominal Rigidity of Apartment Rents." National Bureau of Economic Research Working Paper No. 7137, May.

Genesove, David, and Christopher Mayer. 1997. "Equity and Time to Sale in the Real Estate Market." *The American Economic Review* 87(3): 255–269.

———. 2001. "Loss Aversion and Seller Behavior: Evidence from the Housing Market." *Quarterly Journal of Economics* 116(4): 1233–1260.

Han, Lu. Forthcoming. "The Effects of House Price Uncertainty on Housing Demand: Empirical Evidence from the U.S. Housing Markets." *Journal of Urban Economics.*

Himmelberg, Charles, Christopher Mayer, and Todd Sinai. 2005. "Assessing High House Prices: Bubbles, Fundamentals, and Misperceptions." *Journal of Economic Perspectives* 19(4) (Fall): 67–92.

Hurst, Erik, and Frank Stafford. 2004. "Home Is Where the Equity Is: Mortgage Refinancing and Household Consumption." *Journal of Money, Credit and Banking* 36(6): 985–1014.

Li, Wenli, and Rui Yao. 2007. "The Life-Cycle Effects of House Price Changes." *Journal of Money, Credit and Banking* 39(6) (September): 1375–1409.

Lustig, Hanno, and Stijn Van Nieuwerburgh. 2005. "Housing Collateral, Consumption Insurance, and Risk Premia: An Empirical Perspective." *Journal of Finance* 60(3) (June): 1167–1219.

Mayer, Christopher, and Todd Sinai. Forthcoming. "Housing and Behavioral Finance." In *Implications of Behavioral Economics on Economic Policy*. Boston: Federal Reserve Bank of Boston.

Mayer, Christopher, and Tsur Somerville. 2000. "Land Use Regulation and New Construction." *Regional Science and Urban Economics* 30(6): 639–662.

Meese, Richard, and Nancy Wallace. 1994. "Testing the Present Value Relation for Housing Prices: Should I Leave My House in San Francisco?" *Journal of Urban Economics* 35(3): 245–266.

Ortalo-Magné, François, and Sven Rady. 2002. "Tenure Choice and the Riskiness of Non-Housing Consumption." *Journal of Housing Economics* 11 (September): 266–279.

Pavlov, Andrey, and Susan Wachter. 2007. "Aggressive Lending and Real Estate Markets." Mimeo, Wharton School, University of Pennsylvania.

Sinai, Todd, and Nicholas Souleles. 2005. "Owner Occupied Housing as a Hedge Against Rent Risk." *Quarterly Journal of Economics* 120(2) (May): 763–789.

———. 2008. "Net Worth and Housing Equity in Retirement." In John Ameriks and Olivia S. Mitchell, eds., *Recalibrating Retirement Spending and Saving*, 46–77. Oxford: Oxford University Press.

Skinner, Jonathan. 1989. "Housing Wealth and Aggregate Saving." *Regional Science and Urban Economics* 19(2) (May): 305–324.

———. 1996. "Is Housing Wealth a Sideshow?" In David Wise, ed., *Advances in the Economics of Aging*, 241–268. Chicago: University of Chicago Press.

Smith, Gary, and Margaret Hwang Smith. 2006. "Bubble, Bubble, Where's the Housing Bubble?" *Brookings Papers on Economic Activity* 1: 1–63.

Stein, Jeremy. 1995. "Prices and Trading Volume in the Housing Market: A Model with Downpayment Effects." *Quarterly Journal of Economics* 110 (May): 379–406.

Sun, Wei, Robert Triest, and Anthony Webb. 2006. "Optimal Retirement Asset Decumulation Strategies: The Impact of Housing Wealth." Mimeo, Boston College Center for Retirement Research.

Voicu, Cristian. 2007. "Optimal Portfolios with Housing Derivatives." Mimeo, Harvard Business School, May 1.

5

Arbitrage in Housing Markets

EDWARD L. GLAESER
JOSEPH GYOURKO

Like the economic study of financial and labor markets, the economic analysis of the housing sector relies on "no-arbitrage" relationships. Case and Shiller (1987, 1989, 1990) were pioneers in the study of housing price dynamics, and they emphasized a financial no-arbitrage condition in which investors earn equal risk-adjusted returns by investing in housing or other assets. Poterba (1984) and Henderson and Ioannides (1983) focus on the no-arbitrage condition between renting and owning a home. Alonso (1964) and Rosen (1979) examine the implications for housing prices implied by a spatial no-arbitrage condition where individuals receive similar net benefits from owning in different places.

The spatial equilibrium condition is at the heart of modern urban economics and has enjoyed much success in predicting the distribution of prices and density levels within and across metropolitan areas (Muth, 1969; Roback, 1982). Yet, this no-arbitrage condition yields disturbingly imprecise predictions about price levels, at least by the standards of financial economics. Spatial equilibrium models clearly imply that housing should cost more in more pleasant climes, but they cannot tell us whether people are overpaying for California sunshine. Moreover, the heart of the model lies in spatial compar-

Our analysis is grounded on many of Karl (Chip) Case's insights over the years. Helpful comments were provided by James Brown and Cornelia Kullman. We also appreciate the excellent research assistance of Andrew Moore on this project.

ison, so it could never help us understand whether national housing prices are too high or too low.

In evaluating housing price levels, many economists have been drawn to a more financial approach that relies on there being no predictable excess return on being an owner rather than a renter. This approach seems to offer much greater precision than the spatial equilibrium approach because it appears to yield clear predictions about the relationship between the annual user cost of home owning and the annual cost of renting. If we know the owner's income tax bracket and ability to itemize deductions, the fraction of leverage on the home, the mortgage interest rate, the maintenance and depreciation expenses, the risk premium associated with housing, and expected housing price growth, then we can compare price and rents to determine whether house prices are "too high." Recent research in this vein includes Smith and Smith (2006), McCarthy and Peach (2004), and Himmelberg, Mayer, and Sinai (2005).

Case and Shiller (1989) were pioneers in documenting the predictability of housing markets. In their discussion of that predictability, they also rely on a financial no-arbitrage condition. Some of their calculations suggest the presence of excess returns for investors that run counter to the efficient markets hypothesis. Thus, a financial approach has been used widely in the analysis of housing markets.

In this chapter, we reexamine the strengths and weaknesses of both the spatial and financial equilibrium approaches to the analysis of housing markets. The next section, "The Spatial Equilibrium Model," argues that the traditional urban framework cannot provide much insight into issues such as the appropriateness of price levels. "The Arbitrage of Buying and Renting" then turns to the financial approach. We first argue that it makes sense to conflate the rent-own no-arbitrage relationship with the purely financial no-arbitrage analysis of Case and Shiller (1989). In both cases, the key prediction of the absence of arbitrage is that there will not be excess predictable returns for owning.

Our primary conclusion, however, is that the empirical (not conceptual) robustness of the financial approach is weaker than many may realize. For example, the home-price-to-rent ratio predicted by the buy-rent no-arbitrage condition is quite sensitive to variation in different factors that are difficult to measure accurately, such as the level of maintenance costs, the degree of risk aversion, future price growth, and expected tenure. "The Arbitrage of Buying and Renting" section highlights that what we consider to be reasonable variation in the parameter values of these variables easily can generate well over 30 percent differences in the predicted ratio between home prices and rents.

The importance of unobserved factors is highlighted by simultaneously examining two financial no-arbitrage conditions: a prospective investor in a home must be indifferent between the choice of becoming a landlord or investing in some other asset; and a prospective renter must be indifferent between renting and owning. As landlords have no advantage comparable to the tax shield provided by home ownership, landlords should not be willing to pay as much as an owner-occupant for the same unit of housing, at least if the landlord has the same maintenance cost and cost of capital as an owner-occupant. Our calculations suggest that owner-occupants who itemize on their income taxes should be willing to pay about 40 percent more than landlords for the same property if they both face the same costs. This gap may reflect higher maintenance costs for landlords or higher capital costs for some renters, but whatever the true explanation, any reconciliation requires that unmeasured attributes account for a 40 percent difference in predicted home-price-to-rent ratios.

Contrasting the user cost of owning with the cost of renting also implicitly assumes the direct comparability of owned units to rental units and of owners to renters. However, the section "Differences in the Owner-Occupied and Rental Stocks" later in this chapter documents that rental units tend to be very different from owner-occupied units and that renters are different from owners in economically meaningful ways. For example, the vast majority of owned units are single-family detached dwellings, whereas rental units are highly likely to be part of a denser multifamily building. The average owner-occupied housing unit is about double the size of the typical rental unit, according to the *American Housing Survey* (AHS) of the U.S. Census Bureau. In addition, rental and owner-occupied units also often are sited in different parts of the metropolitan area. Rental units tend to be closer to the urban core and are more likely to be in less attractive neighborhoods (as evaluated by residents surveyed in the AHS). These spatial differences may affect both the predicted level of prices and the expected level of future price appreciation.

Some researchers, such as Smith and Smith (2006), have made truly heroic efforts to ensure that their rental and owner-occupied properties are comparable, but this effort is not feasible for large-scale statistical work that involves all the key markets in the country. Furthermore, given the large observable differences between rented and owned units, we suspect that unobservable differences are also considerable. Moreover, even these units are not truly comparable, because the demand for owned units comes from a different section of the population than the demand for rental units. For example, owner-occupiers are substantially more likely to be richer, married, and have minor children in the home. Data from the most recent AHS also show that the median income of owner households is twice that of renter households. Other sources indicate that income volatility is much greater for owners in general and for recent home buyers in particular. All this suggests that there are related, but not precisely comparable, demand schedules for owning and renting, further implying that rents and prices need not be all that highly correlated over time.

The section "Risk Aversion and the One-Period No-Arbitrage Condition" turns to the problems that make it difficult to use the short-term, no-arbitrage relationship implied by the ability to delay purchase or sale. Although there may not be many people on the margin between being a lifelong renter and a lifelong owner, it certainly could be possible to arbitrage in the housing market by postponing a home purchase simply by remaining a renter or delaying a transition to rental status by not selling immediately.

However, the ability to arbitrage by delaying the transition from rental to owning status in a declining market is limited by risk aversion and the high volatility of housing prices. Although it well may be reasonable to assume a household is risk neutral with respect to any single stock, the same is not true for housing, because it is the dominant asset for most households. If a buyer knows that she will have to buy, delaying the purchase creates a large amount of volatility in wealth because house prices vary so much even over annual periods. Our calibrations show that reasonable amounts of risk aversion will lead one not to delay a purchase, especially in the more expensive and volatile coastal markets.

However, risk aversion does not counterbalance the gains from delaying a sale when transitioning to rental status, largely because existing owners are likely to have much greater wealth. Although homeowners looking to sell and then rent are a group that could arbitrage on the rent-own margin, less than four percent of owners actually ever transition to renting (Sinai, 1997). The small and select group of people who do so severely limits the influence of this arbitrage channel to equalize the returns to owning and renting. Thus, it is quite possible that substantial random shocks to housing prices will not be arbitraged away by changing the timing of a purchase or sale.

All this leads us to conclude that the relevant indifference relationships between owning and renting are not as tight as a purely financial perspective might indicate. We do not doubt that there is a clear theoretical indifference relationship between the two types of housing, but key variables are sufficiently difficult to measure that this approach is very unlikely to be able to convincingly conclude that the price of housing is too high or too low when compared to the cost of renting. Of course, this does not mean that the financial approach provides no valuable insights and should be abandoned.

The equilibrium price of a durable asset like housing will always depend, at least partially, on financial variables such as interest rates.

Rather, our skepticism about the empirical precision of the own-versus-rent no- arbitrage condition and the no-excess-returns no-arbitrage condition leads us toward an approach that combines the spatial no-arbitrage condition with aspects of the asset market perspective. This still does not yield precise implications about price levels, but it does generate implications about the moments of housing price changes and new construction.

In the section "Using Price and Rent Data Together to Understand Housing Markets," we describe the results of Glaeser and Gyourko (2006), using the spatial no-arbitrage condition in combination with a no-excess-profits condition for builders to understand housing dynamics. Those results strongly support the finding of Case and Shiller (1989) that there is too much high-frequency positive serial correlation in price changes. And, just as Shiller (1981) finds too much variation in stock prices relative to dividends, we find that there is too much volatility in price changes relative to changes in fundamentals in the expensive coastal markets. Finally, we describe how to make more use of rental data in these exercises.

The Spatial Equilibrium Model

The spatial equilibrium model requires homeowners (or renters) to be indifferent across different locations. If housing consumption is fixed, then we can write the utility function as $U(Y_i - R_i, A_i)$, where Y_i represents income, R_i is the cost of housing, and A_i represents a vector of j location-specific amenities. The term $Y_i - R_i$ represents cash after housing costs, and we are assuming that nonhousing prices are constant across space. The spatial equilibrium assumption implies that $U(Y_i - R_i, A_i)$ is constant across space, or

$$dR_i = dY_i + \frac{1}{U_1} \sum_{j=1}^{J} \frac{\partial U}{\partial A_j} dA_{i,j} \tag{5.1}$$

where $A_{i,j}$ denotes the different elements in the vector of amenities. Differences in housing prices across space are associated either with different income levels or different amenity levels. The spatial equilibrium assumption allows us to treat one area within the United States as a reservation locale, and we denote its income as $\underline{Y}$, its housing prices as $\underline{R}$, and its amenity levels as $\underline{A}_j$ for each amenity j. We then use a first-order Taylor approximation to find that

$$R_i \approx \underline{R} + (Y_i - \underline{Y}) + \frac{1}{U_1} \sum_{j=1}^{J} \frac{\partial U}{\partial A_j}(A_{i,j} - \underline{A}_j).$$ (5.2)

In each location, the housing cost is approximately equal to the housing cost in the reservation locale plus the difference in income between location i and the reservation locale plus the sum of all of the amenity differences times the marginal utility of each amenity divided by the marginal utility from income.

Although this equation implies a tight, even one-for-one, relationship between the changes in the flow of housing costs and housing prices, it does not directly tell us about the level of prices at any given time. It might be possible to use this to look at rent differences over space, but for reasons that we will discuss later, we think that renters and rental units are sufficiently unrepresentative of a metropolitan area that we are skeptical about using rents in this fashion. If we want to use this equation to deal with prices, we need to make further assumptions that relate housing prices with per period housing costs.

Following Poterba (1984) and others, the per period cost of housing can be written as $(1-\tau)(r+p)H(t) - [H(t+1) - H(t)]$, where $H(t)$ denotes housing prices at time t, τ denotes the income tax rate, r denotes the interest rate, and p denotes the local property tax rate. If we make the heroic assumption that we are in a steady state where housing prices are expected to be constant over time, then the per period housing costs are just $(1-\tau)(r+p)H(t)$, or $\mu H(t)$, where μ denotes a fixed ratio between housing prices and housing costs, or $(1-\tau)(r+p)$. If housing prices were known to appreciate at a fixed rate α, then the value of μ is $(1-\tau)(r+p) - \alpha$.

If we know the value of μ, then the model makes a hard quantitative prediction about the relationship between changes in income and home prices. Specifically, every dollar increase in income should be associated with a $\frac{1}{\mu}$ increase in housing costs. The relationship between housing costs and incomes across metropolitan areas in 2000 is shown in figure 5.1. Although the slope is undeniably positive, the coefficient is 5.6 (standard error of 0.99), meaning that a \$1 increase in income is associated with a \$5.60 increase in housing prices.[1] This would be compatible with the model if μ were equal to 0.18. However, this number is higher than standard user cost estimates, which range from 7.5 percent to 12 percent. Such user costs would suggest

---

1. The underlying data are from our 2006 working paper, which uses information on 116 metropolitan areas for which we have consistent price and income data over more than two decades. The home price data are for the median-quality home from the 1980 census, with the home value in 2000 reflecting the appreciation in the OFHEO repeat sales index for each metropolitan area. Median family income is from the 2000 decennial census. All values are in \$2,000.

FIGURE 5.1 House Prices and Incomes Across Metropolitan Areas, 2000

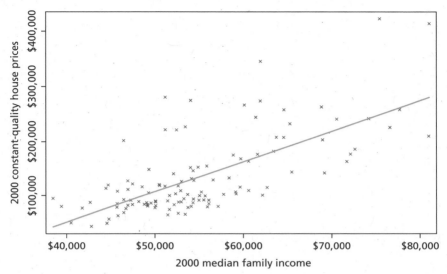

SOURCE: U.S. Census Bureau (2000).

that the coefficient on income should lie between 8 and 12, yet we generally find that it is far lower.[2]

We can still save the spatial equilibrium model by appealing to omitted variables. For example, higher-income places might also have lower amenity values, especially if the higher income levels are compensating for lower amenities, as in Rosen (1979). Alternatively, higher prices might not accurately reflect different housing costs because we are ignoring any heterogeneity in expected housing cost appreciation. Thus, the spatial equilibrium model is salvageable, but any claims about its tight precision are not. The one numerically precise implication that comes out of the model does not seem to fit the data, and if the model is correct, then unobserved variables must be quite important.

In addition, predictions about prices and amenities are never particularly tight. Certainly, the model predicts that prices should rise with positive amenities, as indeed they do. Figure 5.2 shows the positive connection between housing prices and median January temperature across the same sample of metropolitan areas in 1990. However, there is no external estimate of the value of

---

2. Different cross sections and data generate different results, of course. If we use 1990 data, the coefficient estimate increases to 6.2, but that still implies higher user costs than most researchers believe are sensible.

FIGURE 5.2 House Prices and Winter Warmth Across Metropolitan Areas, 1990

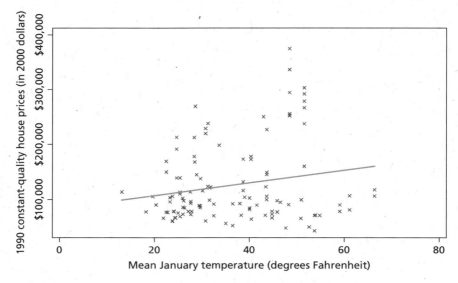

SOURCES: United States National Climatic Center (1971–2000); U.S. Census Bureau (2000).

$\dfrac{1}{U_1}\dfrac{\partial U}{\partial A_j}$ that would enable us to know whether the observed relation of a home price that is higher by $1,158 (standard error of $549) for each extra degree of winter warmth is too high or too low. Indeed, housing price regressions of this kind are generally used to provide such estimates because nothing else is available.

By first differencing the linear approximation to the spatial no-arbitrage relationship, we also gain predictions about the dynamics of housing prices:

$$R_{i,t+1} - R_{i,t} \approx \Delta_t + Y_{i,t+1} - Y_{i,t} + \frac{1}{U_1}\sum_{j=1}^{J}\frac{\partial U}{\partial A_j}(A_{i,j,t+1} - A_{i,j,t}) \quad (5.3)$$

where

$$\Delta_t = \underline{R}_{t+1} - \underline{R}_t - (\underline{Y}_{t+1} - \underline{Y}_{j,t}) - \frac{1}{U_1}\sum_{j=1}^{J}\frac{\partial U}{\partial A_j}(\underline{A}_{j,t+1} - \underline{A}_{j,t}).$$

This equation implies that changes in housing costs should be tightly connected to changes in income and changes in amenities. However, it does not directly tell us about the level of prices. Moreover, assuming that we are in a steady state in which housing prices are fixed is logically inconsistent with a regression that is examining heterogeneity in housing price changes. If we want to use this equation to deal with prices, we need to make further assumptions that relate housing prices with per period housing costs. In particular, we need to make assumptions about the extent to which housing price changes are expected or unexpected.

At one extreme, we can assume that any shocks to income or amenities are completely unexpected. In that case, the model predicts that a \$1 increase in income will continue to be associated with a $\frac{1}{\mu}$ dollar increase in housing prices. This assumption is surely counterfactual, as local income changes are quite predictable (Glaeser and Gyourko, 2006).

The other extreme is to assume that local income changes are entirely known in advance. To create simple closed-form solutions, we can go so far as to assume that amenities and housing costs in the reservation locale are constant over time and that the gap in income between location i and the reservation locale is growing by $g_{i,Y}$ dollars per period. In this case,

$$ H_{i,t} \approx \frac{1}{\mu} \left(\underline{H} + (Y_{i,t} - \underline{Y}_t) + \frac{1}{U_1} \sum_{j=1}^{J} \frac{\partial U}{\partial A_j} (A_{i,j} - \underline{A}_j) \right) + \frac{g_{i,Y}}{\mu^2} \qquad (5.4) $$

and

$$ H_{i,t+1} - H_{i,t} \approx \frac{(Y_{i,t+1} - Y_{i,t}) - (\underline{Y}_{t+1} - \underline{Y}_{j,t})}{\mu}. $$

Expected income changes will have exactly the same impact on housing price changes as unexpected income changes, as long as those income changes are part of a long-run trend in income appreciation.

An intermediate option that yields a slightly different result is to assume that there is a one-time increase in income between time t and $t + 1$ that is anticipated, but that there will not be any more shocks to income after that point. In that case, the impact of housing changes is much smaller:

$$ H_{i,t+1} - H_{i,t} \approx \frac{(Y_{i,t+1} - Y_{i,t}) - (\underline{Y}_{t+1} - \underline{Y}_{j,t})}{1 + \mu}. $$

Price changes will exist, and they will be predictable, but they will be much smaller than in the case where price changes are unexpected or where they reflect a long-run trend. Because we know little about the information that people have about income shocks, the model does not deliver a tight relationship between housing price changes and income changes. Instead, the implied coefficient could range from $\frac{1}{\mu}$, which could be more than 10, to $\frac{1}{1+\mu}$, which is less than 1.

Figure 5.3 plots the actual relationship between home price changes and income changes across metropolitan areas between 1980 and 2000 for the same 116 metropolitan area sample used above. Home prices again use the 1980 census median value as the base value, with the relevant Office of Federal Housing Enterprise Oversight (OFHEO) metropolitan area price index used to scale prices over time. The change in income is the 20-year difference in median family income between the 1980 and 2000 censuses. As expected, the figure shows a robust positive relationship, with a coefficient of 5.1 (standard error of 0.42) from a simple regression of 20-year price changes on 20-year income changes. Happily, this number lies between 1 and 10, so it does not reject the spatial equilibrium model. However, the bounds implied by the model are so loose that it would have been shocking for the model to be rejected.

In sum, we have shown that the spatial no-arbitrage condition fails to yield tight predictions about the relationship between housing prices and income,

FIGURE 5.3   Twenty-Year Changes in House Prices and Incomes, 1980–2000

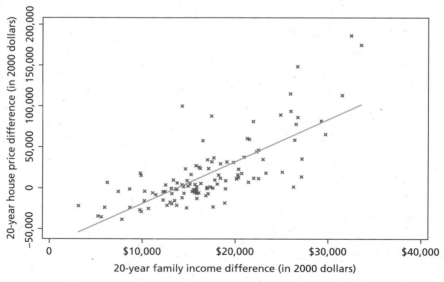

SOURCE: U.S. Census Bureau (1980–2000).

which we treat as the "fundamental" in that model. This weakness surely plays a role in explaining why real estate economists have been attracted to other no-arbitrage relations, which we consider next.

THE ARBITRAGE OF BUYING AND RENTING

Case and Shiller's (1989) pioneering work on housing price dynamics discusses the no-arbitrage conditions for both buyers and for investors. The no-arbitrage condition for buyers is usually a no-arbitrage condition between buying and renting; this may involve either a lifetime indifference or an indifference between buying (or selling) and renting for a short time. Case and Shiller (1989) themselves emphasize the decision of a buyer to purchase today or to wait for a year. They also discuss the possible decision of a buyer who is looking at whether to increase housing consumption. In this case, estimating the costs of delay must include an estimate of the inconvenience associated with consuming too little housing. As that inconvenience level surely is impossible to measure directly, this approach cannot offer much precision, and we are not surprised that subsequent work has focused primarily on the owner-renter no-arbitrage condition. We will focus on that condition first, and then turn to the investor's no-arbitrage condition.

The simplest version of the financial approach to housing involves a one-period indifference condition in which consumers receive the same return from owning or renting the identical housing unit. We will later emphasize that risk aversion is likely to be far more important in the context of housing markets than it is in financial assets, but we begin with a representative risk-neutral individual who is considering buying a home at time t and leaving the city with probability one at time $t + 1$. The buyer must pay property taxes of p times the housing price H. The interest rate at which this person can both borrow and lend is given by r. Both property taxes and interest payments are deductible for owner-occupants. If we further assume that this person earns $Y(t)$ dollars and faces a marginal tax rate of τ, then the owner's user cost of housing will equal $(1 - \tau)(r + p)H(t) - [H(t + 1) - H(t)]$. If the same individual rents, housing costs equal $R(t)$.

Poterba (1984) and others have emphasized additional costs of housing, too. For example, the average owner spends nearly \$2,100 per year on maintenance, although there is substantial measurement error in this variable (Gyourko and Tracy, 2006). In addition, this observable component of maintenance misses the time and effort that owner-occupants put into caring for their homes. The economic depreciation of a home is also difficult to measure.

Of course, ownership may also bring with it hidden benefits such as the ability to customize the housing unit to one's own needs. We let $\delta H(t)$ denote the net unobserved costs of being an owner-occupant, or one's own landlord, as it were.

With these costs, indifference between owning and renting for a risk-neutral resident implies that $R(t) = [(1 - \tau)(r + p) + \delta]H(t) - E[H(t + 1) - H(t)]$, where the final term represents the expected capital gain on the housing unit. Iterating this difference equation and imposing a transversality condition on housing prices yields the familiar formula that prices are the appropriately discounted sum of rents:

$$H(t) = \sum_{j=0}^{\infty} \frac{R(t + j)}{(1 + (1 - \tau)(r + p) + \delta)^{j+1}}.$$

As this equation shows, it is impossible to determine the appropriate price of housing as a function of rents without knowing the long-term path of rents. Because expected future rents are certainly unobservable, this in turn creates ambiguity in the formula. One approach is to assume that rents will rise at a constant rate a, so that $R(t + j) = (1 + a)^j R(t)$. If so, then equation 5.5 holds

$$H(t) = \frac{R(t)}{(1 - \tau)(r + p) + \delta - a}. \tag{5.5}$$

Equation 5.5 is also implied by a one-period no-arbitrage relationship if housing prices are expected to increase at a rate of "a" over the next period (i.e., $E[H(t + 1)] = (1 + a) H(t)$). Thus, this formula does not require individuals to be indifferent between owning and renting over their lifetimes or rents to continue to rise at a fixed rate forever.

This ratio can then be used to predict housing values if rents, true maintenance and depreciation, interest rates, property tax rates, marginal income tax rates, and expected capital gains are known, and if unobserved influences on user costs are small in magnitude.[3] Drawing on Himmelberg, Mayer, and Sinai (2005) for some baseline numbers, if $\tau = 0.25$, $r = 0.055$, $p = 0.015$, $\delta = 0.025$, and $\alpha = 0.038$, the nominal price-to-rent ratio is 25.[4]

---

3. It is noteworthy that Poterba (1984), who generally is credited with introducing this model into mainstream economics, neither considered the own-rent margin nor equated the utility flow from owning with the observed rental price of a home. He used the user cost formula to determine the cost to owners; the results then shift the demand for the quantity of housing.

4. This is only slightly higher than the ratio predicted by the more complex formula used by those authors.

Even abstracting from risk aversion, to which we will return later in the chapter, there is a reasonable amount of uncertainty about what true maintenance, expected appreciation, and even the relevant interest and tax rates are. For example, if expected appreciation actually is one percentage point higher, the multiple increases by about one-third to 34, and larger changes can be generated by incorporating relatively minor adjustments to the other parameters. Although a one-percentage-point increase in permanent rent appreciation may be a big number, a one-percentage-point increase in expected price appreciation over a one-year period represents a much more modest change. Thus, any reasonable sensitivity analysis is going to result in a fairly wide bound for what prices "should be" in a given market.[5] This wide bound means that it will be very difficult to convincingly evaluate whether prices seem rational purely on the basis of the financial no-arbitrage condition.

DIFFERENCES IN THE OWNER-OCCUPIED AND RENTAL STOCKS

One underappreciated problem with using the rent-own no-arbitrage condition to make inferences about housing prices is that rental units are generally quite different from owner-occupied housing and that renters and owners are very different people. These stylized facts, which are documented in the para-

---

5. We have greater faith in the value of the comparative statics suggested by equation 5.5 than in its ability to justify the level of prices. However, there is considerable debate in the literature over one important result involving the impact of interest rates on home prices. Equation 5.5 suggests a powerful relationship between interest rates and home prices, and McCarthy and Peach (2004) and Himmelberg, Mayer, and Sinai (2005) have relied on it to justify previously high home prices at least partially as a function of historically low interest rates. In contrast, Shiller (2005, 2006) argues that there is no economically or statistically significant relationship between home prices and interest rates over any reasonably long period. When we regressed the real value of the median quality home from 1980 (using the OFHEO index as previously described) on the real seven-year interest rate using data from the last 30 years, the results indicated that a one-percentage-point increase in interest rates is associated with only a 2 to 3 percent rise in home prices. The R-squared value is 0.12, which is well below the nearly two-thirds of variation in home prices that can be accounted for by metropolitan area fixed effects. However, this is a very complex issue that cannot be definitively answered within the confines of such a simple static model. For example, one can imagine a dynamic setting in which interest rates mean-revert and in which homeowners either can refinance loans or expect to sell and buy another home within a few years. In that context, temporary rises in rates need not lead to substantially higher debt service costs (in present value terms) that are capitalized into lower house values if refinancing costs are low and borrowers believe rates will drop in the relatively near future. Of course, borrowers will not want to refinance mortgages obtained during periods of abnormally low rates. Still, the extent to which temporary drops in interest rates are capitalized into high prices will be mitigated by the expected length of tenure on the margin. In general, mean reversion in interest rates implies that we should see far less connection between current rates and home prices than is predicted by the constant interest rate version of the model (Glaeser and Gyourko, 2006). In addition, we would expect interest rates to have relatively little impact on house prices in elastically supplied markets where prices tend to be pinned down by construction costs, which themselves are determined primarily by labor and materials costs, not capital costs (Glaeser and Gyourko, 2006; Himmelberg, Mayer, and Sinai, 2005).

TABLE 5.1 Comparing the Owner-Occupied and Rental Housing Stocks

	Owner-occupied housing	Renter-occupied housing
Single-family detached unit type (percent)	64.3	17.7
Located in central cities (percent)	30.5	45.7
Rating their neighborhoods as excellent[a] (percent)	45.6	34.2
Median household income in 2005	$53,953	$24,651
Married households with minor children (percent)	27.6	15.4

NOTES: Data are from the 2005 *American Housing Survey* unless otherwise noted.

[a] We label a neighborhood as excellent if the survey respondents gave it a rating of 9 or 10 on a 1–10 scale.

graphs immediately following, are important because mismeasurement of unit quality makes it hard to compare rents and home prices, and the fact that the demand for these types of these units comes from different types of people likely matters for expectations about future housing prices.

We begin by documenting a number of physical characteristics of owner-occupied and rental units in table 5.1. We rely primarily on the 2005 AHS. Perhaps the most striking fact about renting and owning is the very strong correlation between unit type and physical structure. The 2005 AHS shows that 64.3 percent of owner-occupied housing units were of the single-family, detached-unit type, whereas only 17.7 percent of rental units were of that type. The vast majority of rental units are in multiple-unit buildings, not single-unit, detached dwellings.

Naturally, these types of units are of very different sizes. Figure 5.4, which is taken from Glaeser and Gyourko (2008), plots the median square footage of owned versus rented units using data from the last 20 years of the AHS. The median owner-occupied unit in the United States is nearly double the size of the median rented housing unit. Per person consumption of space also varies widely by tenure status. Housing consumption per capita among owner-occupied households is now more than 700 square feet, whereas that for renters is about 450 square feet (Glaeser and Gyourko, 2008).

Not only are the owner-occupied and rental stock physically quite different from one another, but the two types of housing also tend to be located in different parts of the metropolitan area, as well as in different-quality neighborhoods. The suburban dominance of owner occupancy is highlighted in the second row of table 5.1. Fewer than one-third of all owned units were in the central cities of metropolitan areas, according to the 2005 AHS. Ownership has become more widespread in America's central cities, but nearly half of all rental units still are located in cities (row 2, column 2 of table 5.1).

FIGURE 5.4 Housing Unit Size: Owner-Occupied Versus Rental Units

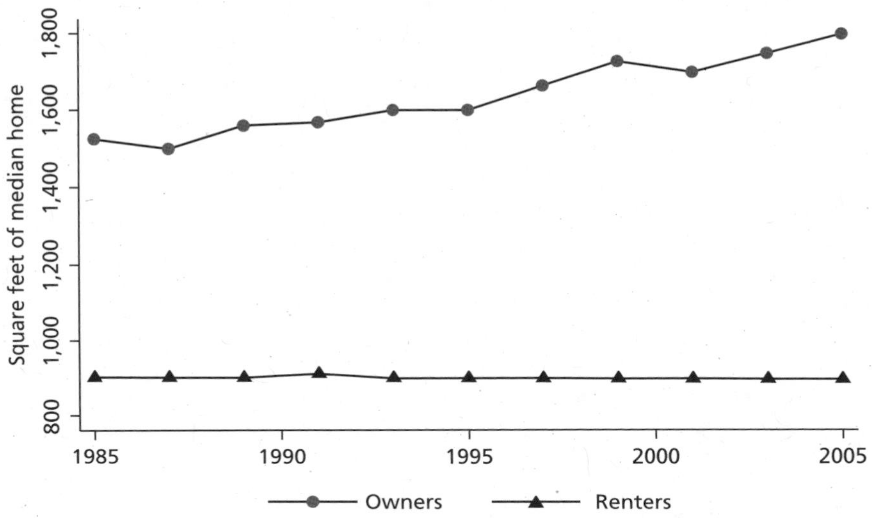

SOURCES: Glaeser and Gyourko (2008), figure 2.1. Data from U.S. Census Bureau (1985–2005).

Owner-occupied units tend to be in better neighborhoods, too. The AHS asks its survey responders to rate their neighborhoods on a scale from 1 to 10. Just looking at those who gave their neighborhoods very high scores of 9 or 10 shows that almost one-half of owners believe they live in the highest-quality areas, whereas only one-third of renters feel the same way (row 3, table 5.1).

Just as owned units are different from rented units, owner-occupants are quite different from renters. Perhaps most important, owners are substantially richer. The median nominal income of owner-occupied households was $53,953, whereas it was $24,651 for renter households, according to the 2005 AHS (row 4, table 5.1). Household types also tend to differ systematically by tenure status, as indicated by the fact that the probability an owner-occupied household is a married couple with minor children present is nearly double that of a renter household (bottom row of table 5.1).

There are at least two reasons why the characteristics of owners should influence the price-to-rent ratio. First, because owner-occupied housing tends to be surrounded by other owner-occupied housing and because the characteristics of neighbors is likely to be an important influence on price, occupant characteristics themselves should be thought of as an often unobserved factor influencing both home prices and rents. Second, since the price of owner-occupied housing depends on what you can sell that housing for next period, the characteristics of owner-occupants will affect current price because they will affect the state of demand in future periods.

For example, the higher volatility of incomes among owner-occupants will surely have an impact on expectations about future demand for owner-occupied housing. Comparing the incomes, over time, of recent buyers in the Home Mortgage Disclosure Act (HMDA) data with that for the mean in an area as reported by the Bureau of Labor Statistics (BLS) finds the volatility of recent buyer income roughly double that of the average income in the same market (Glaeser and Gyourko, 2006). A similar pattern can be seen specifically for the New York City market in the New York City Housing and Vacancy Survey (NYCHVS) data. A simple regression of the income of recent buyers (defined as those who bought within the past two years) on Bureau of Economic Analysis (BEA)–reported per capita real income for that market finds that recent buyer income goes up by $1.29 for every $1.00 increase in BEA-measured income. Moreover, the same source reveals that renter household incomes are less volatile than average. They increase by only $0.47 for every $1.00 rise in per capita income in the city.[6]

Taken literally, all this indicates that the variance of income shocks for renters is only a small fraction of that for owners or for the general population. If so, rent series should be more stable than house prices. On the aggregate level, Leamer (2002) has emphasized that home prices have grown much more quickly than rents. In the 44 markets for which we have both consistent rent data from a prominent industry consultant and constant-quality repeat sales indices, table 5.2 documents that the annual appreciation rate for housing since 1980 is 1.9 percent, whereas that for rents is only 0.5 percent.[7] Table 5.2 also reports results for a handful of representative major markets in which price growth typically is at least double that of rent growth. Similar patterns with relatively low rent volatility also exist if one breaks the data into different time periods.

---

6. Because the NYCHVS provides much smaller samples, the regression results are based on averages of individual respondents over two-year windows. Effectively, there are only nine observations after averaging, and although the regression coefficients are statistically significant, one clearly does not want to make too much of this. The underlying regression results are available upon request.

7. The rental series is from REIS, Inc. The company does not report a constant-quality series, but their data are consistently measured in the sense that they reflect the answers to a question about asking rents on higher-quality apartment complexes in major U.S. markets. Rent data are very rare, and little analysis of the robustness of such series exists. We found that the REIS asking rent series is strongly positively correlated with the rent subindex of the local Consumer Price Index (CPI) that the Commerce Department computes for approximately 25 areas nationwide. REIS also reports an "effective rent" series that allegedly reflects discounts or premiums being charged to tenants. That series is not positively, and sometimes is negatively, correlated with the local CPI rent subindex numbers. Hence, we do not use it in any of the analysis reported here.

TABLE 5.2 Comparing House Price and Rental Growth in 44 Markets with Continuous Rent Data from REIS, Inc., 1980–2006

	Average annual rent growth (percent)	Average annual price growth (percent)
44 markets	0.51	1.88
San Francisco	1.96	3.93
Boston	2.06	4.37
Los Angeles	1.29	3.62
Atlanta	0.22	1.06
Chicago	0.83	2.20
Phoenix	−0.20	2.19

NOTES: Rent data are from REIS, Inc. Home price appreciation rates are computed from the Office of Federal Housing Enterprise Oversight price index. All data are in real terms.

One explanation for the mismatch in the growth of housing prices and rents is that housing prices represent the cost of accessing higher-quality housing units, while rental prices represent the cost of accessing lower-quality units. Rising incomes and rising income inequality could easily mean that demand has increased more for higher-quality units. Gyourko, Mayer, and Sinai (2006) argue that housing prices have risen more steadily for metropolitan areas with higher amenity levels.

Of course, an empirical mismatch between home price growth and rent growth still could be explained by a purely financial model if other factors such as interest rates or expected house price appreciation themselves are changing. We have already noted the debate about the role of interest rates, so that remains an unsettled issue. There also is not much convincing evidence that the differences between home prices and rents are positively correlated with price appreciation. A proper user cost model implies that the user costs of housing minus rents should equal expected home price appreciation.

In table 5.3, we report the results from regressing actual home price appreciation on the gap between user costs and rents, using the user cost data from Himmelberg, Mayer, and Sinai (2005).[8] Over one-, three-, and five-year horizons, there is a negative, not a positive, relationship between actual home price appreciation and the change in home prices forecast by a user

8. We thank Todd Sinai for providing the underlying data. Because we need user costs before expected housing appreciation, we added back their appreciation component, which is based on the long-run average annual real appreciation rate between 1940 and 2000 in Gyourko, Mayer, and Sinai (2006). We then create a shorter-run expected price change variable by multiplying the user costs before the appreciation figure by the real value of a 1980-quality home and then subtracting real asking rents. The house price variable is computed by scaling the mean house value in each market as reported in the 1980 census by the OFHEO repeat sales index appreciation for each year. The rent data are from REIS, Inc, and are discussed above.

TABLE 5.3 Is Actual Real House Price Appreciation Consistent with Forecasts from a User Cost Model?

1-year horizon $(P_{i,t+1} - P_t)$: $\beta = -0.81$; $n = 1119$, $R^2 = 0.40$, cluster by MSA
(0.22)

3-year horizon $(P_{i,t+3} - P_t)$: $\beta = -9.60$; $n = 358$, $R^2 = 0.57$, cluster by MSA
(0.83)

5-year horizon $(P_{i,t+5} - P_t)$: $\beta = -14.03$; $n = 224$, $R^2 = 0.64$, cluster by MSA
(1.14)

NOTES: $P_{i,t+n} - P_{i,t} = \alpha + \beta^*(F_{i,t+1} - F_{i,t}) + \delta^*Year_t + \eta^*MSA_i + \varepsilon_{i,t}$ where $P_{i,t+n} - P_t =$ change in real house prices in market I, and $F_{i,t+1} - F_{i,t} =$ one-period change in real house prices forecast by user cost model. See Himmelberg, Mayer, and Sinai (2005) for the details behind the user cost calculation. MSA = metropolitan statistical area.

SOURCE: Data on user costs were provided by Todd Sinai and are identical to data used in Himmelberg, Mayer, and Sinai (2005).

cost model. Although Shiller-type animal spirits certainly could be behind this, our point simply is that there is no strong evidence that variation in the relationship between prices and rents is systematically related to accurate assessments of house price appreciation.

This leads us to conclude that the home price and rent series can be understood as the costs of two different types of housing. The differences seem so large that it probably is best to think of them as reflecting different demands for two related, but not directly comparable, markets. Of course, there still will be some sort of indifference relationship between owned and rental housing, but quantifying this relationship in the way suggested by the standard user cost approach will overstate the empirical precision of the approach. Essentially, the indifference relationship appears to be sufficiently weak that there is abundant opportunity for the measured financial costs of owning to diverge significantly from those of renting.

THE IMPORTANCE OF OMITTED COSTS

Smith and Smith (2006) represent the best effort that has been made to deal with the often stark differences in rental versus owner-occupied units. However, their approach still faces the problem that owners and renters are likely to be quite different people. Moreover, this work also needs to deal with the challenge that unobserved factors in equation 5.5, such as maintenance costs, may be very important and could lead to quite different predictions about the appropriate relationship between housing prices and rents.

Both theory and data suggest that unobserved influences on user costs are likely to be large in magnitude. A rental property must involve two different agents—the renter and the landlord—and both of them have relevant no-arbitrage conditions. The renter must be indifferent between renting and owning. The landlord must be indifferent between owning a housing unit and renting it out and investing one's capital in something else. This no-arbitrage condition implies a second way of evaluating the appropriate price of housing, but the price implied by the investor's no-arbitrage condition will be very different from the price implied by the renter's no-arbitrage condition, unless omitted variables are quite important.

To illustrate this, we assume that the investor also has the ability to borrow at interest rate r. The relevant no-arbitrage condition is that the net present value of revenues from the property is zero. Gross revenues equal the rent received each period, or $R(t)$. Property taxes on the unit are the same as for an owner-occupant. However, we allow for net maintenance costs to differ, so that they equal $\delta_I H(t)$ for the investor. Profits are taxed, but the tax rate is irrelevant if there are zero profits. Hence, the zero profit condition is given by equation 5.6,

$$R(t) + E[H(t + 1) - H(t)] - (r + p + \delta_I)H(t) = 0. \tag{5.6}$$

The same zero profit condition holds if the investor either can lend money at rate r or buy a house, with all revenues being taxed at a rate τ_I. The relevant indifference condition is given by $(1 - \tau_I)rH(t) = (1 - \tau_I)[R(t) - (p + \delta_I)H(t) - E\{H(t + 1) - H(t)\}]$, which again yields equation 5.6. Thus, the tax rate on the investor does not affect the relationship between prices and rents in this simple model.

Iterating equation 5.6 and imposing a transversality condition implies that

$$H(t) = \sum_{j=0}^{\infty} \frac{R(t + j)}{(1 + r + p + \delta_I)^{j+1}}.$$

This leads to the following analogue to equation 5.5:

$$H(t) = \frac{R(t)}{r + p + \delta_I - a}. \tag{5.5'}$$

There are two ways to use equations 5.5 and 5.5'. First, we can assume that $\delta = \delta_I$ and ask how much bigger the price-to-(net) rent ratio should be for owner-occupants than for landlords. For owner-occupants, the no-arbitrage condition predicts a price-to-net rent ratio of $\dfrac{1}{(1-\tau)(r+p)+\delta-a}$. For the investor-landlord, the price-to-net rent relationship predicted by the no-arbitrage condition is $\dfrac{1}{r+p+\delta-a}$. The two relationships are the same only when the owner-occupier does not deduct interest and taxes.

However, the housing literature that uses the rent-own no-arbitrage decision to deduce housing prices generally assumes that owners are deducting interest.[9] Recall that using Himmelberg, Mayer, and Sinai's (2005) assumptions for our parameter values finds that the price-to-rent ratio given by $\dfrac{1}{(1-\tau)(r+p)+\delta-a}$ is about 25 ($\sim 1/.0395$). However, the investor-landlord's no-arbitrage condition implies a price-rent ratio of $\dfrac{1}{r+p+\delta-a}$, which equals 17.5. This means that owner-occupants should be willing to pay about 45 percent more for the same home than should a landlord (25/17.5 ~ 1.45).

One way of interpreting this is that if we think that the price-to-rent ratio eliminates arbitrage between renting and owning, then housing is nearly 50 percent too expensive to eliminate the arbitrage between being a landlord and other forms of investment. This gap increases in environments with higher appreciation or inflation because the tax subsidy to owner-occupants rises with inflation (Poterba, 1984). If expected inflation increases so that the nominal interest rate rises to 8 percent and the rate of appreciation equals .063 instead of .038, then the ratio $\dfrac{1}{(1-\tau)(r+p)+\delta-a}$ rises to over 30, while the ratio $\dfrac{1}{r+p+\delta-a}$ remains at 17.5. Indeed, it is relatively easy to envision environments in which the price-to-rent ratio implied by the owner-occupant's no-arbitrage condition literally would be double that implied by the investor's no-arbitrage condition.

---

9. Data on itemization by tenure status is not directly reported by the Internal Revenue Service, but it is only natural to presume that homeowners are more likely to itemize. Nationally, only 35.7 percent of all tax returns filed in 2005 were itemized. Given the nearly 69 percent home ownership rate estimated for that year, at least half of owners did not itemize, even if we assume that all itemizers own their home. However, itemization rates are higher in areas with higher house prices, which is consistent with more owners in those markets being able to deduct local property taxes and mortgage interest payments. For example, 39.9 percent of California returns, 38.8 percent of New York returns, and 45.2 percent of New Jersey returns were itemized in 2005.

There are many possible ways that we can reconcile these seemingly in-compatible predictions about price-to-rent ratios. We wrote the model so that different maintenance and depreciation rates could do the job. The two no-arbitrage conditions will imply the same price-to-rent ratio when $\tau(r + p) = \delta - \delta_p$, or when the difference in the maintenance rates just equals the difference in the tax advantage provided to owner-occupants. If $\tau = 0.25$, and $r + p = 0.07$, this would mean that the maintenance costs are 0.0175 higher for the owner-occupant than for the landlord. Only if it costs more for the owner to keep up his home can we explain why landlords would ever buy and rent at the same prices that make owner-occupants indifferent between owning and renting.

A second way to reconcile the two no-arbitrage conditions is by assuming that the landlord's cost of capital is lower than the owner-occupant's. Perhaps the marginal buyer has more difficulty making a down payment or negotiat-ing the loan process. If maintenance costs were the same, then landlords would need to face interest rate costs that were 175 basis points lower than those for prospective tenants in our simple example.

Alternatively, risk tolerance might differ between owners and landlords. Perhaps the marginal buyer has a relatively short time horizon in the city and does not want to face the risk of housing price shocks (Sinai and Souleles, 2005), whereas landlords are diversified and remain immune to those shocks. There are many unobserved factors that could explain the seeming incom-patibility of the two no-arbitrage conditions.

Our point is that unobservable elements must be quite important in hous-ing markets because they need to explain a difference of more than 40 percent in the price-to-rent ratios predicted by the landlord's and the owner-occupant's no-arbitrage conditions. The magnitude of these unobserved factors makes us wary of believing these conditions can be used to answer definitively whether prices are too high or too low.

RISK AVERSION AND THE ONE-PERIOD NO-ARBITRAGE CONDITION

We now turn to the impact of risk aversion on the one-period no-arbitrage condition between owning and renting. Although owners and renters gener-ally are quite different people, individuals are often both renters and owners over the course of their lives. When they transition from renting to owning, or the reverse, individuals have the opportunity to delay purchase, or sale, to exploit predictability in housing prices. Case and Shiller (1989) specifically focus on the ability to exploit excess returns by delaying consumption for one period.

In this section, we argue that the ability to exploit any predictable excess returns is compromised by the interaction between risk aversion and the volatility of housing prices. Whereas individuals may be effectively risk neutral with respect to one individual stock that represents a small share of their overall portfolio, housing usually is the dominant asset for most homeowners. Normal year-to-year variation in housing prices can create significant swings in an individual's total wealth. The magnitude of these swings creates an incentive for anyone who knows that she is going to buy next year to buy today instead, as well as for anyone who knows that he is going to sell next year to sell today. Thus, there appear to be even more limits to arbitrage in the housing market than there are in the financial markets (Shleifer and Vishny, 1997).

Consider the case of a household that knows with certainty that it eventually will own a home in a given market, and assume that it can either buy at time t or wait until time $t + 1$. To simplify the notation, we abstract from local property taxes and assume away any unobserved costs associated with maintenance or other aspects of owning. The only two flow costs remaining are debt service, where the interest rate still is denoted as r, and known maintenance and depreciation, which is denoted as M.

We assume that this household is maximizing its expected wealth, denoted as $E(V(Wealth_{t+1}))$, where $Wealth_{t+1}$ refers to wealth net of housing costs as of time $t + 1$. By assumption, the household must have bought a home by that date. If the household buys at time t, its wealth at time $t+1$ is predictable. The household's total welfare will equal $V((1 + (1 - \tau)r)$ $(Y - H(t)) - M(t))$. If it rents at time t and then buys, its wealth at time $t + 1$ will be stochastic and will equal $E(V((1 + (1 - \tau)r)Y - R(t) - H(t + 1)))$.

To calibrate the model, we will use a second-order Taylor series expansion for the function $V(.)$ and assume that $H(t + 1) = H(t) + \overline{H(t + 1) - H(t)} + \varepsilon(t)$, where $\varepsilon(t)$ is mean zero and $\overline{H(t + 1) - H(t)}$ is the predictable component of the change in housing prices. With these assumptions, delay makes sense only if

$$(1 - \tau)rH(t) + M(t) - R(t) - \overline{H(t+1) - H(t)}$$
$$> \frac{\sigma Var(\varepsilon)}{(2 - z\sigma)((1 + (1 - \tau)r)(Y - H(t)) - M(t))} \tag{5.7}$$

where σ denotes the coefficient of relative risk aversion, i.e.,

$$\sigma = -\frac{((1+(1-\tau)r)(Y-H(t))-M(t))V''((1+(1-\tau)r)(Y-H(t))-M(t))}{V'((1+(1-\tau)r)(Y-H(t))-M(t))},$$

and z represents the ratio of expected one-period gains from delaying to total wealth if the individual does not delay, i.e.,

$$z = \frac{(1-\tau)rH(t)-\overline{H(t+1)}-H(t)-R(t)+M(t)}{((1+(1-\tau)r)(Y-H(t))-M(t))}.$$

Equation 5.7 provides a useful bound for the plausible amount of expected losses that would justify waiting one year given reasonable values of risk aversion. The standard deviation of annual housing price changes in our sample of 116 metropolitan areas is just over \$9,100. If the coefficient of relative risk aversion is 2, and if we assume nonhome wealth of \$50,000 for a person buying at time t, then the expected gains from waiting would need to be at least \$1,750.[10] Thus, risk aversion causes the plausible gulf between the user costs of owning and rental housing costs to increase by nearly \$150 per month, even for a renter household with \$50,000 in nonhousing wealth.

To help gauge whether the potential benefit of exploiting short-run predictability can counter this risk aversion affect, we begin by regressing the one-year, forward-looking change in home prices on observables, such as the current home price, and on macroeconomic variables, such as the long-term real rate and real gross domestic product. We also include metropolitan area dummies, so that knowledge of average, one-year price changes also is presumed. All the observables are statistically significant predictors of the coming year's price change. Table 5.4 reports the distribution of predicted one-year changes.[11] Fewer than one-third of the expected one-year changes in house prices are negative (31 percent, to be precise), and only 18 percent of the cases involve expected losses of more than −\$1,750, which is required to generate positive returns to a renter household delaying purchase for one year, given our assumptions.

This calculation, however, assumes that the variation in housing prices is constant across markets, which obviously is not the case. Hence, in the second column of the table, we report the distribution of the total gains resulting from

---

10. To simplify the calculation, this result also assumes that $(1-\tau)rH(t)+M(t)-R(t)=0$, not only that nonhousing wealth or $((1+(1-\tau)r)(Y-H(t))-M(t))=\$50,000$.

11. The precise equation estimated is $P_{i,t+1}-P_{i,t}=\alpha+\beta^*P_{i,t}+\dot\gamma^*10yrRealRate_t+\delta^*RealGDP_t+\eta^*MSA_i+\varepsilon_{i,t}$. All results are available upon request.

TABLE 5.4 Estimating the Benefits of Short-Term Predictability

Percentile	Distribution of one-year price changes[a] $(P_{i,t+1} - P_{i,t})$	Distribution of net gains from delaying purchase[b] $- \overline{H(t+1) - H(t)} - \dfrac{2Var(\varepsilon)}{100,000 + 2H(t+1) - H(t)}$	Distribution of net gains from delaying sale[c] $\overline{H(t+1) - H(t)} - \dfrac{2Var(\varepsilon)}{500,000 - 2H(t+1) - H(t)}$
10th	−$2,698	−$15,352	−$2,864
25th	−$612	−$8,089	−$775
50th	$2,361	−$3,199	$2,144
75th	$6,163	$112	$5,609
90th	$10,802	$2,179	$9,739

NOTES: [a] The underlying specification estimated regresses the one-year, forward-looking change in home prices on a series of observables as follows:

$$P_{i,t+1} - P_{i,t} = \alpha + \beta^* P_{i,t} + \gamma^{*7}/yrRealRate_t + \delta^*RealGDP_t + \eta^*MSA_t + \varepsilon_{i,t}, \text{ where } P_{i,t} \text{ reflects house price in metropolitan area } i \text{ in year } t, 10yrRealRate \text{ is the real interest rate}$$

on seven-year Treasuries (calculated as in Himmelberg, Mayer, and Sinai, 2005), RealGDP is real gross domestic product from the Economic Report of the President, MSA$_t$ is a vector of metropolitan area dummies, and ε is the standard error term.

[b] Net gain from delaying purchase for one year for a renter household with $50,000 in nonhousing wealth and a relative risk aversion coefficient equal to 2. See the discussion in the text for more detail.

[c] Net gain from delaying sale for one year for an owner household with $250,000 in wealth and a relative risk aversion coefficient equal to 2. See the discussion in the text for more detail.

delay for our hypothetical household, using information on price volatility at the metropolitan area level. Predicted price changes still are estimated via the specification with metropolitan area fixed effects, lagged house price, and the other economic variables. However, the variance of ε is computed separately for each metropolitan area by making use of the relevant residuals from the equation used to predict housing price changes. Once again assuming that $(1 - \tau)rH(t) + M(t) - R(t)$ equals zero, $((1+(1 - \tau)r(Y - H(t)) - M(t))$ equals $\$50,000$, and σ equals two, the formula for expected gains minus risk aversion–

related losses then equals $-\overline{H(t + 1) - H(t)} - \dfrac{2Var(\varepsilon)}{100,000 + 2\overline{H(t + 1) - H(t)}}$.

The second column in table 5.4 reports on the distribution of net benefits from our hypothetical renter household that is delaying the purchase of a home for a year. The net benefits are positive in only 26 percent of the cases, and a look at the results by metropolitan areas indicates that it is in the high-price-volatility coastal markets where risk aversion almost always more than counterbalances the gross benefits of waiting to purchase in a declining market. As indicated by the results in column one, house prices are expected to rise in most markets in most years. However, even in the highest-appreciation markets in the northeast region and coastal California, our naïve forecasting equation does generate expected declines in the early 1980s and the early 1990s, when general economic conditions were quite poor. Nevertheless, in no case does our simple calculation show a positive return to delaying purchase in any of the five major coastal California markets in our sample (Los Angeles, San Diego, San Francisco, San Jose, and Santa Barbara). For the Boston and New York City areas, the return to delay is positive only once—in 1980, when forecasted price declines were large enough to outweigh the costs associated with risk aversion.

The reason is the very high volatilities of price changes in these markets. The values of $Var(\varepsilon)$ among these seven large coastal markets range from a low of $\$175$ million in Boston to a high of $\$572$ million in San Francisco. In contrast, the impact of risk aversion is much less in many interior markets. For example, Atlanta's $Var(\varepsilon)$ value is only $\$12.9$ million. Its home prices were expected to fall in only eight of the 26 years for which we can forecast, but in each of those years the return to our hypothetical renter household delaying purchase for a year is positive.

In sum, this arbitrage opportunity has value only if price declines can be expected, and that is not the normal condition in our housing markets. However, even if we reasonably can expect price declines over the coming year in markets such as New York, Boston, and the Bay Area, the volatility of their home price changes is more than enough so that risk aversion eliminates any gain from delaying the purchase of a home. Hence, it seems unlikely that renters considering changing tenure status in these markets will find this potential arbitrage opportunity to be of value.

Of course, there also is the possibility to arbitrage renting and owning among those individuals who are moving from owner-occupied to rental housing. In this case, people could delay a year in order to take advantage of a rising market. To consider this issue more formally, we continue to assume that households maximize $E(V(Wealth_{t+1}))$. If a household sells immediately, its expected wealth is deterministic, and expected welfare will equal $V((1 + (1 - \tau)r)(Y + H(t)) - R(t))$. If the household waits a year, then its time $t + 1$ wealth is stochastic, and expected welfare will equal $E(V((1 + (1 - \tau)r)Y + H(t + 1) - M(t))))$. Again using a second-order Taylor series expansion, we see that it is sensible to wait if and only if

$$\frac{R(t) - (1 - \tau)rH(t) - M(t) + \overline{H(t+1)} - H(t)}{(2 - z_2\sigma)((1 + (1 - \tau)r)(Y + H(t)) - M(t))} > \frac{\sigma Var(\varepsilon)}{} \tag{5.8}$$

where σ continues to denote the coefficient of relative risk aversion, and z_2 represents the ratio of expected one-period gains from delaying to total wealth if the individual does not delay, i.e.,

$$z_2 = \frac{R(t) - (1 - \tau)rH(t) - M(t) + \overline{H(t + 1)} - H(t)}{((1 + (1 - \tau)r)(Y + H(t)) - M(t))}.$$

The impact of risk aversion should be smaller here because wealth should be much larger. To show this more clearly, we now calculate the distribution of gains from waiting a year to sell a home, again computing $Var(\varepsilon)$ at the metropolitan area level. As before, we assume that $(1 - \tau)rH(t) + M(t) - R(t)$ equals zero, and σ equals two, but now we presume that $((1 + (1 - \tau)r)(Y + H(t)) - M(t))$ equals \$250,000. With these assumptions, the expected risk-adjusted gain from waiting a year can be written as

$$\overline{H(t + 1)} - H(t) - \frac{2Var(\varepsilon)}{500,000 - 2\overline{H(t + 1)} - H(t)}.$$

The third column of table 5.4 reports our estimates of the distribution of expected gains from an existing owner delaying sale. Although it often does not make sense to delay a purchase decision to take advantage of falling prices, especially in the more volatile markets, there generally are substantial gains from delaying a sales decision to take advantage of rising prices. More than 70 percent of our observations exhibit positive returns to this potential arbitrage opportunity. Not only are prices expected to appreciate in most cases, but the much larger assumed wealth substantially mitigates the impact of risk aversion so that it rarely counterbalances the benefits of delay even in the most volatile markets. In principle, the population of homeowners looking to sell and rent represents one group that really could arbitrage along the own-rent margin whenever prices are expected to increase.

However, there is a reason to expect that the likely impact of this arbitrage on housing prices is quite small—namely, very few people actually transition from owning to renting. Sinai (1997) documents that transitions from owner-occupant to renter status are quite rare. Working with a 1970–1992 panel of observations from the Panel Study of Income Dynamics, he shows that less than four percent of owners ever engage in such a tenure transition, and of those that do, about one-third transition back to ownership within two years.[12] Hence, we are skeptical that this group can be a real force for creating an equilibrium in which renting and owning returns are equalized.

USING PRICE AND RENT DATA TOGETHER TO UNDERSTAND HOUSING MARKETS

Although we have provided various reasons why it is problematic to use the buy-rent no-arbitrage condition to produce precise predictions about housing prices, we still believe that there is much to be learned from the use of rents and prices together to understand housing dynamics. In this section, we discuss three ways in which these data can be employed to add insight into housing prices.

The first use of rents lies in prediction without theory. Rents may add predictive power to housing price change regressions even if we are not sure why they have this predictive power. Table 5.5 details the results from nine regressions where changes in housing prices have been regressed on initial characteristics. The basic specification is

---

12. Capital gains taxation rules explain the short tenure spells in this case. A household must trade up in value within two years to be able to roll over any gains from the original sale. Our point is not about the arcana of the tax code, but to illustrate that a large fraction of the transitions from owner-occupancy status to rental status are very short-term and probably not related to the arbitrage we are discussing. In addition, Sinai (1997) reports that falls in income have an especially large impact on the probability of this type of tenure transition (see his table 4); this suggests that households making this move are suffering some type of negative income shock rather than trying to arbitrage along the rent-own margin.

TABLE 5.5 Price Changes Within Market Over Time

$$(5.9)\ Log\left(\frac{Price_{t+i}}{Price_t}\right) = \beta_1\ Log(Price_t) + MSA\ Dummies + Year\ Dummies.$$

1-year horizon, $j = 1$
$\beta_1 = -0.034\ (0.013)$, $R^2 = 0.42$, $n = 1144$

3-year horizon, $j = 3$
$\beta_1 = -0.391\ (0.047)$, $R^2 = 0.53$, $n = 1056$

5-year horizon, $j = 5$
$\beta_1 = -0.864\ (0.079)$, $R^2 = 0.71$, $n = 968$

$$(5.9')\ Log\left(\frac{Price_{t+i}}{Price_t}\right) = \beta_2\ Log\left(\frac{Price_t}{Rent_t}\right) + MSA\ Dummies + Year\ Dummies.$$

1-year horizon, $j = 1$
$\beta_2 = -0.110\ (0.015)$, $R^2 = 0.46$, $n = 1144$

3-year horizon, $j = 3$
$\beta_2 = -0.570\ (0.052)$, $R^2 = 0.53$, $n = 1056$

5-year horizon, $j = 5$
$\beta_2 = -0.984\ (0.073)$, $R^2 = 0.70$, $n = 968$

$$(5.9'')\ Log\left(\frac{Price_{t+i}}{Price_t}\right) = \beta_3\ Log(Price_t) + \beta_4\ Log(Rent_t) + MSA\ Dummies + Year\ Dummies.$$

1-year horizon, $j = 1$
$\beta_3 = -0.101\ (0.015)$, $\beta_4 = 0.199(0.039)$
$R^2 = 0.48$, $n = 1144$

3-year horizon, $j = 3$
$\beta_3 = -0.570\ (0.052)$, $\beta_4 = 0.533(0.085)$
$R^2 = 0.59$, $n = 1056$

5-year horizon, $j = 5$
$\beta_3 = -0.984\ (0.073)$, $\beta_4 = 0.578(0.096)$
$R^2 = 0.70$, $n = 968$

NOTES: Standard errors in parentheses. Specifications estimated on 44 metropolitan areas with both Office of Federal Housing Enterprise Oversight home price and REIS, Inc. apartment rent data for 1980–2006. Dependent variable: $Log(P_{i,t+j}/P_{i,t})$; i = metropolitan area i; t = year; j = 1, 3, 5

$$Log\left(\frac{Price_{t+j}}{Price_t}\right) = \beta_1 \, Log(Price_t) + MSA \; Dummies$$

$$+ \; Year \; Dummies. \tag{5.9}$$

We repeat this specification for j equal to one, three, and five years, using the same home price variable described above. As Case and Shiller (1989) first showed us, there is much that is predictable about home price changes simply from knowing previous price levels.

We then repeat this basic specification using the price-to-rent ratio instead of prices themselves, as in equation 5.9':

$$Log\left(\frac{Price_{t+j}}{Price_t}\right) = \beta_2 \, Log\left(\frac{Price_t}{Rent_t}\right) + MSA \; Dummies$$

$$+ \; Year \; Dummies. \tag{5.9'}$$

Note that using the price-to-rent ratio is associated with uniformly higher t-statistics, as well as a higher R-squared value for the one- and three-year price change horizons. Over five-year periods, one cannot reject the null that the elasticity of price changes with respect to the price-to-rent ratio is -1.

The final specification reported in table 5.5 enters prices and rents separately, i.e.,

$$Log\left(\frac{Price_{t+j}}{Price_t}\right) = \beta_3 \, Log(Price_t) + \beta_4 \, Log(Rent_t)$$

$$+ \; MSA \; Dummies + Year \; Dummies. \tag{5.9''}$$

Note that both prices and rents are highly significant at standard confidence levels for high- and low-frequency price changes. Higher levels of rents tend to predict higher price growth, holding prices constant. And, the R-squared values are uniformly higher than in the base case that includes only prices (row 1).

These regressions show that incorporating both prices and rents does improve our ability to explain housing price changes over time. However, as our discussion should have made clear, there are real problems in deciphering the meaning of these results. A particularly naïve view might be that the negative correlation between the price-to-rent ratios and future price growth seems to reject the view given in equation 5.5 that $\frac{H(t)}{R(t)}$ equals one divided by $(1 - \tau)$ $(r + p) + \delta - a$. If that were the case, then higher housing price-to-rent ratios should predict future appreciation, not future depreciation. Clearly, they do not, and especially not over longer time intervals.

One interpretation of these results is that the market is fundamentally irrational and that prices do not inherently contain reasonable expectations of future housing price growth, but instead reflect some kind of irrational exuberance (Shiller, 2005). An alternative interpretation is that rents are telling us about a market that is related, but different from, that of owner-occupied housing. Rents, by and large, reflect the cost of housing in lower-quality homes in the inner city. House values, by and large, reflect the cost of housing in the suburbs. These lower-quality inner city homes are not a perfect substitute for the suburban homes, but they are at least something of a substitute. If higher rents are associated with higher housing price appreciation, this might reflect the fact that rents are giving us new information about the state of the region's economy that is not fully embedded in home prices. Higher rents might well mean that demand is robust not only for high-end housing, but for low-end housing as well, and this could easily mean that the future of a region is brighter. According to this view, the role of rents in the housing price regression does not reflect irrationality, but rather the natural role of providing more information about the future of the region's economic strength.

Although rents can naively be inserted into a regression aimed at maximizing predictive power, it is harder to actually connect housing prices and rents with a structural model to test the model's implications. Glaeser and Gyourko (2006) write down a straightforward model of housing dynamics and then test its implications by using housing prices and permits, but we do not look significantly at rents, for the reasons discussed in the paragraphs that follow. In the model, high-frequency changes in demand for housing are driven by changing economic conditions within a region. We use the model to generate predictions about the moments of price and quantity fluctuations.

Whereas Glaeser and Gyourko (2006) rely on the spatial no-arbitrage condition introduced by Rosen (1979) and Roback (1982), our framework, like any sensible model of changes in housing prices, is not finance free. Interest rates certainly affect housing prices in a purely urban model, and their influence can differ across markets. As Himmelberg, Mayer, and Sinai (2005) emphasize, lower interest rates should increase prices more in places with higher expected rental appreciation. Our model produces a similar comparative static, showing that the impact of expected local income growth on prices will be higher if interest rates are low. Moreover, the impact of changing interest rates on price volatility also will be greater in areas with high income and amenity levels.

Our 2006 paper also highlights that unobservable differences in the information structure can have enormous impact on the predicted high-frequency correlations between prices and new construction. If people recognize economic changes only when they occur (i.e., they are true shocks), then the predicted correlation between contemporaneous price changes and new construction will be almost perfect. However, if people can anticipate these changes a period before they occur, then the predicted correlation between price change and new construction will be almost zero. As outside researchers have little ability to assess the actual information that people have, we believe that these results mean that it makes little sense to look at high-frequency correlations between prices and construction.

We believe it is problematic to focus on high-frequency correlations between rents and housing prices for the same reason. To reiterate, if people learn about economic changes only when they occur, then the correlation between price changes and rent changes will be extremely high; if they learn about them a period or more ahead of time, then this correlation will be significantly lower. In general, this makes us wary about how to properly interpret the correlations between price innovations and rents.

However, the model does deliver important predictions that are more robust toward changes in the information structure. For example, the actual variances of price changes and new construction are implied by the variation in underlying economic shocks, and these relationships are not particularly sensitive to the timing of new information. Our empirical work suggests that the variability of prices for the median market in the United States seems close to the variability predicted by the model. However, the variability of prices for the most expensive models is far too high to be explained by the underlying economic variation. This excess variation is the housing price analogue to Shiller's (1981) finding of excess variation in the stock market.

The model also predicts the autocorrelations of both price and quantity changes. Notably, despite the fact that the model has no irrationality, there is every reason to expect that price changes will be predictable. In the long run, prices are predicted to mean-revert, both because economic shocks appear to mean-revert and because new construction becomes available. In fact, the model predicts a level of mean reversion over five years that is almost identical to the level of mean reversion that we see in the data.

The model is less successful in predicting the high-frequency positive serial correlation that is also a feature of the data. The high-frequency positive serial correlation in the OFHEO data is probably biased upward, because it contains appraisal data and because of inaccuracy in the timing of sales. However, using much better sales data purged of these problems, Case and Shiller (1989) also documented substantial price persistence at high frequencies. This serial correlation is not predicted by our spatial equilibrium model, and we agree with the original Case and Shiller conclusion that this momentum in high-frequency price changes provides a challenge to conventional models of housing price dynamics.

Glaeser and Gyourko (2006) do little with rents, for two reasons. There is good reason to believe that observed rent levels understate the true volatility of rents because of long-term relationships between some landlords and tenants. This understatement becomes even more severe in areas with rent control. Moreover, if the observed data on median or average incomes are informative about the marginal home buyer, they cannot be so about the marginal renter. As noted above, data from the NYCHVS indicate that the variability of renter income is less than one-quarter of the variability of owner income. This lower variability should predict low variation in rents.

How, then, could rents be brought into a model of housing dynamics that started with a spatial no-arbitrage assumption? The first requirement is to have good high-frequency income data for a set of metropolitan areas that reflect the income of potential renters. For some larger metropolitan areas, this potentially could be done with the American Community Survey, but it would be difficult to get a significant sample of metropolitan areas. The second requirement would be to obtain high-frequency data on new rental contracts, preferably involving new tenants. Such data presumably would be free of any implicit (or explicit) longer-term commitments between tenants and landlords.

These tasks are not easy, but they offer some promise of enabling us to use rental data to test the predictions of the spatial no-arbitrage model. Although we recognize the difficulties of these tasks, other approaches that rely more or less exclusively on a no-arbitrage condition between owning and renting seem even less promising.

SUMMARY AND CONCLUSION

Economics forms predictions about housing prices using no-arbitrage conditions, and different researchers have emphasized different ways in which housing prices can be arbitraged. The traditional urban approach has been to emphasize the absence of arbitrage across space, but this approach never delivers too much precision. A more financial approach has emphasized the ability of investors to arbitrage prices and the ability of owners to arbitrage between owning and renting.

The major point of this chapter is that the seeming empirical precision of these more financial approaches is illusory. Although the conceptual ability to arbitrage between owning and renting is clear, the ability to use this insight empirically is limited. Owned units and rented units are extremely different. Unobserved components of housing costs, like maintenance, are quite large. Owners and renters are quite different people, and risk aversion creates a substantial cost, especially to delaying a purchase. For these reasons, we are skeptical that existing rental data can tell us much about the appropriate price of a home.

Instead, we believe that integrating the financial no-arbitrage condition into a spatial equilibrium model offers a more promising approach for understanding the nature of housing markets. Our past work in this area suggests that some seeming anomalies of housing markets, like the high mean reversion of prices over five-year intervals, is quite compatible with a rational spatial equilibrium model. Other seeming anomalies, like high-frequency positive serial correlation of price changes and high volatility in coastal markets, seem to be much harder to reconcile with such a market, just as Case and Shiller (1989) have suggested. It would be possible to bring rents into such a model if we had better data on the income series of potential renters, and if we had better data on new rental contracts. We hope future work will follow this path.

REFERENCES

Alonso, William. 1964. *Location and Land Use*. Cambridge, MA: Harvard University Press.

Case, Karl, and Robert Shiller. 1987. "Prices of Single Family Homes Since 1970: New Indexes for Four Cities." *New England Economic Review* (September/October): 45–56.

———. 1989. "The Efficiency of the Market for Single-Family Homes." *American Economic Review* 79(1) (March): 125–137.

———. 1990. "Forecasting Prices and Excess Returns in the Housing Market." *Journal of the American Real Estate and Urban Economics Association Journal (AREUEA Journal)* 18(3): 253–273.

Glaeser, Edward, and Joseph Gyourko. 2006. "Housing Dynamics." National Bureau of Economic Research Working Paper No. 12787, December.

———. 2008. *Rethinking Federal Housing Policy: How to Make Housing Plentiful and Affordable*. Washington, DC: The AEI Press.

Gyourko, Joseph, Chris Mayer, and Todd Sinai. 2006. "Superstar Cities." National Bureau of Economic Research Working Paper No. 12355, June.

Gyourko, Joseph, and Joseph Tracy. 2006. "Using Home Maintenance and Repairs to Smooth Variable Earnings." *Review of Economics and Statistics* 88(4) (November): 736–747.

Henderson, Vernon, and Yannis Ioannides. 1983. "A Model of Housing Tenure Choice." *American Economic Review* 73(1): 93–113.

Himmelberg, Charles, Chris Mayer, and Todd Sinai. 2005. "Assessing High House Prices: Bubbles, Fundamentals and Misperceptions." *Journal of Economic Perspectives* 19(4) (Fall): 67–92.

Leamer, Edward. 2002. "Bubble Trouble: Your Home Has a P/E Ratio, Too." Mimeo, UCLA Anderson School of Management, June.

McCarthy, Jonathan, and Richard Peach. 2004. "Are Home Prices the Next Bubble?" *Economic Policy Review* 10(3) (December): 1–17.

Muth, Richard. 1969. *Cities and Housing: The Spatial Pattern of Urban Residential Land Use*. Chicago: University of Chicago Press.

Poterba, James. 1984. "Tax Subsidies to Owner-Occupied Housing: An Asset Market Approach." *Quarterly Journal of Economics* 99(4) (November): 729–745.

Roback, Jennifer. 1982. "Wages, Rents, and the Quality of Life." *Journal of Political Economy* 90(4) (December): 1257–1278.

Rosen, Sherwin. 1979. "Wage-Based Indexes of Urban Quality of Life." In Peter Mieszkowski and Mahlon Straszheim, eds., *Current Issues in Urban Economics*, 74–104. Baltimore: Johns Hopkins University Press

Shiller, Robert. 1981. "Do Stock Prices Move Too Much to Be Justified by Subsequent Changes in Dividends?" *American Economic Review* 71(3): 421–436.

——. 2005. *Irrational Exuberance*. Princeton, NJ: Princeton University Press.

——. 2006. "Long-Term Perspectives on the Current Housing Boom." *Economists' Voice* 3(4) (March): 1–11.

Shleifer, Andrei, and Robert Vishny. 1997. "The Limits of Arbitrage." *Journal of Finance* 52(1) (March): 35–55.

Sinai, Todd. 1997. "Taxation, User Cost and Household Mobility Decisions." Mimeo, Wharton School, University of Pennsylvania, December.

Sinai, Todd, and Nicholas Souleles. 2005. "Owner-Occupied Housing as a Hedge Against Rent Risk." *Quarterly Journal of Economics* 120(2) (May): 763–789.

Smith, Margaret Hwang, and Gary Smith. 2006. "Bubble, Bubble, Where's the Housing Bubble?" Mimeo, Pomona College, March.

United States National Climatic Data Center. 1971–2000. *US Climate Normals*. Washington, DC: United States National Climatic Data Center.

U.S. Census Bureau. 1985–2005. *American Housing Survey*. Washington, DC: U.S. Census Bureau.

——. 2000. *Decennial Census, Long Form Housing Characteristics*. Washington, DC: U.S. Census Bureau.

Part
III

HOUSING REGULATION AND POLICY

6

Subprime Mortgages: What, Where, and to Whom?

CHRIS MAYER
KAREN PENCE

T
he housing market has turned sharply throughout the country since 2006. Home prices have swung from steady rates of appreciation to outright declines, while sales and construction of new homes have dropped steeply. Much of this turmoil appears related to the boom and bust in mortgage markets over the last five years.

It was not supposed to work out this way. Securitization and other innovations in mortgage markets led to new loan products with the potential to make home ownership easier and more accessible to buyers who could not access credit previously through conventional means. These so-called subprime and near-prime mortgage products allowed buyers with lower credit scores, smaller down payments, little documentation of income, or all of these to purchase homes. These new products not only allowed new buyers to access credit, but also made it easier for homeowners to refinance loans and withdraw cash from homes that had appreciated in value.

Despite the economic implications of the credit boom and bust, there have been only a handful of studies on who received subprime loans during

The authors wish to thank Alex Chinco, Erik Hembre, Rembrand Koning, Christy Pinkston, and Julia Zhou for extremely dedicated research assistance. We thank Bob Avery, Ken Brevoort, Brian Bucks, Glenn Canner, Karen Dynan, Andreas Lehnert, Kristopher Rengert, Shane Sherlund, Dan Sokolov, and participants at the Homer Hoyt Institute, the American Real Estate and Urban Economics Association Mid-Year Meeting, and the Lincoln Land Institute Conference in honor of Karl (Chip) Case for many helpful comments and thoughts. Chris Mayer especially wishes to thank Chip Case for his friendship and mentorship throughout his career. The chapter represents the opinions of the authors and does not represent the views of the Federal Reserve Board or its staff.

this most recent housing cycle, where these loans were made, and what the loans were used for. In part, the lack of studies is due to data limitations. Timely industry sources of data on subprime loans, such as LoanPerformance (LP), is not freely available to researchers. In addition, there is no consensus among either lenders or researchers about what types of mortgages should be considered subprime.

In this chapter, we begin to fill this void, focusing our empirical analysis in two areas. First, we describe the strengths and weaknesses of three different sets of data on subprime mortgages. These data sets embody different definitions of subprime mortgages. We show that estimates of the number of subprime originations are somewhat sensitive to which types of mortgages are categorized as subprime. Second, we describe what parts of the country and what sorts of neighborhoods had more subprime originations in 2005, and how these patterns differed for purchase and refinance mortgages.

We believe that we are the first researchers to examine this second question—the geographic dispersion of subprime lending—with the LP data, although previous studies have examined this question with other data sets (Avery, Canner, and Cook, 2005; Brooks and Ford, 2007; Calem, Gillen, and Wachter, 2004; Center for Responsible Lending, 2006; Consumer Federation of America, 2006; Scheessele, 2002; U.S. Department of Housing and Urban Development [HUD], 2000). However, analyses of other mortgage topics have also used the LP data (Brooks and Simon, 2007; Demyanyk and Van Hemert, 2008; Gerardi, Shapiro, and Willen, 2007; Keys et al., 2008; Pennington-Cross and Ho, 2006).

Turning to our first focus, we examine three sources of data on subprime mortgages: LP, for mortgages in securitized pools marketed as subprime by the securitizer; the Home Mortgage Disclosure Act (HMDA) for higher-priced mortgages with high interest rates; and HMDA HUD for mortgages originated by lenders specializing in subprime mortgages. The three measures paint quite different pictures of the number of subprime originations. In 2005, the most recent year all three measures are available, the average number of originations per 100 housing units in zip codes in metropolitan statistical areas (MSAs) ranges from 3.6 (LP) to 5.4 (HMDA higher-priced).

The measures also portray the growth in subprime originations differently. The LP measure implies that subprime originations grew seven-fold from 1998 to 2005, whereas the HMDA HUD measure implies that originations tripled during this period. The difference between the two measures appears to stem from growth in subprime securitization during these years. If we restrict the HUD measure to originations that were securitized, the two series track each other closely in most years. These findings suggest that which measure captures the subprime market best may vary as the market structure evolves.

Turning to our second focus, we explore what areas of the country and what types of neighborhoods experienced the most subprime originations. Here, the three measures tell a consistent story. As has been reported in the press, metropolitan areas in Nevada, Arizona, California, and Florida had large concentrations of subprime originations: 10, eight, seven, and six subprime originations, respectively, in 2005 per 100 housing units. These rates, which are based on the LP data, are two to three times the national average in metropolitan areas of 3.6 subprime loans per 100 housing units. Yet, large numbers of subprime mortgages were also originated in other places, including the Washington, DC area, Atlanta, Chicago, Providence, Rhode Island, and parts of Texas.

When we map these origination patterns, three intriguing possibilities emerge. First, subprime originations appear to have only a partial correlation with home price appreciation. Some locations in the Northeast, like New York and Boston, had relatively high home price appreciation, but relatively few subprime mortgages. Second, subprime mortgages were concentrated not only in the inner cities, where lower-income households are more prevalent, but also on the outskirts of metropolitan areas where new construction was more prominent. Third, economically depressed areas in the Midwest do not appear to have high rates of subprime originations, despite their weak housing markets.

When we delve more deeply into this third finding, we find that economically depressed areas in the Midwest had low rates of originations relative to total housing units, but high rates relative to total originations. All previous studies have used total originations as the benchmark. We use total housing units because we think that the option to take out a subprime loan may affect a household's choice to take out a loan at all, as well as its decision on what type of loan to take out. We interpret the difference between the "housing units" and "originations" results as indicating that both prime and subprime originations are elevated in areas with hot housing markets. In contrast, less lending activity occurs in depressed housing markets, and what occurs is more likely to be subprime.

Next, by running cross-sectional regressions on zip code–level data, we explore what types of neighborhoods had the most subprime originations in 2005 and come up with several key results. First, subprime mortgages are concentrated in locations with high proportions of black and Hispanic residents, even controlling for the income and credit scores of these zip codes. Areas with black and Hispanic shares 50 percent higher than the mean are associated with

8 percent and 7 percent, respectively, larger proportions of subprime loans. However, zip codes containing large numbers of minorities appear to have a much higher concentration of these originations. The ninetieth percentile zip code ranked by the share of black residents appears to have 42 percent more subprime loans than the corresponding median zip code, and the ninetieth percentile zip code ranked by the share of Hispanic residents appears to have 33 percent more subprime originations than the median. These results remain relatively consistent whether we compare zip codes across cities or within a given city.

Second, subprime loans appear to provide credit in locations where credit might be more difficult to obtain. Subprime loans are heavily concentrated in zip codes with more mid-level credit scores. They are also more prevalent in counties with higher unemployment rates. The latter result suggests that subprime loans have the potential to be an additional source of credit when economic conditions deteriorate.

Finally, the regressions confirm the correlation suggested by the maps between subprime lending and areas with more new construction and with high home price appreciation in the previous year. These results suggest that subprime lending played a role in the recent housing cycle, although we cannot determine the extent to which subprime mortgages were a cause or a consequence of housing activity.

When we split the sample between refinancing and purchase originations, the results are consistent with our earlier findings. For example, subprime purchase and refinance loans are more prevalent in zip codes with a high share of minorities. The only substantive difference between the samples is that purchase originations are more pronounced than refinancing originations in areas with substantial amounts of new construction.

DATA SUMMARY

LoanPerformance

First American LoanPerformance, a subsidiary of First American CoreLogic, Inc., provides information on securitized mortgages in subprime pools.[1] The data do not include mortgages held in portfolio; securitized mortgages in prime, jumbo, or alt-A pools; or loans guaranteed by government agencies

---

1. FirstAmerican also has a product based on data obtained from loan servicers. We do not use these data, as FirstAmerican does not provide the underlying micro data. We also do not use FirstAmerican's data on loans in securitized jumbo and Alt-A pools because we focus on subprime loans.

such as the Federal Housing Administration and the Veterans' Administration or by government-sponsored enterprises such as Fannie Mae, Freddie Mac, or Ginnie Mae. The data also exclude loans securitized by lenders that do not report to LoanPerformance. Comparing the LP subprime totals to the subprime mortgage-backed securities totals published by Inside Mortgage Finance (Inside Mortgage Finance, 2006) suggests that LP captured around 90 percent of the subprime securitized market from 1999 to 2002 and nearly all of the market from 2003 to 2005.[2]

The guidelines for what type of mortgage can be sold into a subprime pool vary across securitizers. In general, borrowers in subprime pools tend to have low credit scores and high loan-to-value ratios, but a smaller number of borrowers have higher credit scores. On occasion, securitizers include a handful of near-prime or prime loans in these pools.

The data contain extensive information on the characteristics of the loan, such as the mortgage type, the interest rate, the loan purpose (purchase or refinance), and whether the loan has a prepayment penalty. Data on fees are not included. LP has less detailed information about the borrower, reporting the FICO credit score, the borrower's reported debt-to-income ratio, and the extent to which that income is documented. There is relatively little information about the property beyond the sale or appraised price, the type of property, and its state and zip code.

For a few observations, the reported state in which the property is located does not match the zip code. In these cases, we retain the observations for statistics based on the nation as a whole, but drop the observations when we create zip code–level observations. This restriction drops less than 0.4 percent of observations.

HMDA Higher-Priced

Under HMDA, most originators must report basic attributes of the mortgage applications that they receive in MSAs to the Federal Financial Institutions Examination Council. These data are considered the most comprehensive source of mortgage data, and cover an estimated 80 percent of all home loans nationwide (Avery, Brevoort, and Canner, 2007a) and a higher share of loans originated in MSAs. Depository institutions that are in the home lending business, have a home or branch office in an MSA, and have assets over a certain threshold ($35 million in 2006) are required to report these data to the

---

2. Two exceptions are 1998, when LP captured 46 percent of the market, and 2001, when its share was 78 percent.

regulator. Mortgage and consumer finance companies that extend 100 or more home purchase or refinancing loans a year are also required to report for any MSA in which they receive five or more applications. In total, nearly 8,900 lenders reported in 2006.

The share of mortgages covered under HMDA has fluctuated over time with changes in the definitions of MSAs and in the depository asset threshold. The most substantive recent change occurred when new MSA boundaries were drawn in 2004 to reflect the 2000 U.S. Census. These new boundaries added 242 counties to the HMDA coverage area, and the number of reporting lenders correspondingly increased by 9 percent. Although the LP data are reported at the zip code level, HMDA data are reported by U.S. Census Bureau tracts. We describe in the appendix to this chapter how we map Census Bureau tracts to zip codes.

Since 1990, HMDA has contained borrower characteristics such as income, race, and gender, as well as loan characteristics such as the balance, purpose (purchase, home improvement, refinancing), and type (conventional or government-backed) plus the census tract in which the property is located. As suggested in Avery, Brevoort, and Canner (2007b), we classify home improvement loans as refinancings. In 2004, information was added on the spread to the rate on the comparable-maturity Treasury for first-lien mortgages with an annual percentage rate (APR) three percentage points over the Treasury benchmark and for junior liens with an APR five percentage points over the benchmark. Mortgages with a reported spread are commonly called "higher-priced" loans.

Although "higher-priced" is generally considered to be a proxy for "subprime," this definition may capture different shares of fixed- and adjustable rate mortgages (ARMs) because of the "comparable maturity" definition. "Comparable maturity" corresponds to the maturity in the loan contract, not the expected maturity. Thus, an ARM with a contract maturity of 30 years is compared to the rate on a long-term Treasury security, even though the ARM's interest rate may be based on a shorter-term security. As short-term rates are generally below long-term rates, subprime ARMs are likely to be underreported in the data relative to subprime fixed-rate mortgages.

The extent of this bias shifts over time as the slope of the yield curve changes. When the yield curve is flatter and short-term rates are closer to long-term rates, subprime ARMs will be more represented in the data. Avery, Brevoort, and Canner (2007b) suggest that at least 13 percent of the increase in the number of higher-priced loans in the HMDA data between 2004 and 2005 is attributable to a flattening of the yield curve.

An additional possible source of bias is the fact that the spread of mortgage rates relative to Treasuries changes over time. As this spread fluctuates, the three-percentage-point threshold will capture a varying share of the near-prime — and perhaps even some of the prime — market in addition to the sub-prime market.

Finally, the APR definition is susceptible to whether the loan cost comes primarily from interest rates or fees. The calculation assumes that fees are paid over the full maturity of the loan, although most loans — especially subprime loans — are repaid after a shorter period. As a result, some loans that are expensive for the borrower may not be captured under the HMDA higher-priced definition.

"Higher-priced" appears to be a problematic measure in 2004 for reasons beyond the shift in the yield curve slope. Some lenders may have had difficulty complying with reporting the new information in the first year that reporting was required (Bostic et al., 2008). In addition, higher-priced originations are artificially low in 2004 because price information was not required for loans whose application process began in 2003 but concluded in 2004.

HMDA HUD Lender

Before the APR data were added to the HMDA data, researchers typically labeled a loan in the HMDA data as subprime if it was originated by a lender on the Subprime and Manufactured Home Lender list maintained by HUD.[3] The list identifies lenders that specialize in subprime or manufactured home lending. It is designed to be used as a companion to the HMDA data and is available by year from 1993 to 2005. HUD dropped lenders specializing in manufactured housing in 2004 when HMDA added a variable that identified loans backed by manufactured homes. HUD continued the subprime lender list, however, because of concerns that HMDA's higher-priced variable might prove an insufficient proxy for subprime loans.

HUD bases its initial search for subprime lenders by reviewing each lender's HMDA filings. Lenders that have higher denial rates, higher shares of mortgage refinancings, few loan sales to the government-sponsored enterprises, or more higher-priced loans are considered more likely to be subprime lenders. HUD then contacts possible subprime lenders to determine definitively their area of specialization. The list is updated and revised annually on the basis of feedback from lenders, policy analysts, and housing advocacy groups. In 2005, the list contained 210 lenders.

Because not all lenders specialize solely in prime or subprime loans, defining loans as subprime based on the HUD list will inherently misclassify prime

---

3. These data are available at http://www.huduser.org/datasets/manu.html.

loans originated by subprime lenders as subprime and, likewise, subprime loans originated by prime lenders as prime. A few lenders on the list are also primarily near-prime rather than subprime specialists. Gerardi, Shapiro, and Willen (2007) suggest that lenders on the HUD subprime list originate only a few prime loans, so this source of bias should be minor.[4] In addition, we prune many of these nonsubprime loans from the HUD lender measure by dropping loans that were later sold to Fannie Mae, Freddie Mac, the Federal Housing Administration, or Farmer Mac; any mortgages sold to these institutions are likely not subprime. However, we are not able to add subprime loans originated by prime lenders to the HUD measure, which Gerardi, Shapiro, and Willen suggest are a larger source of bias. As a result, we expect the HUD measure to understate the number of subprime originations.

For all three measures, we limit our sample to first-lien, closed-end mortgages collateralized by one-to-four-family properties and originated in zip codes that are in MSAs in the 48 contiguous states and Washington, DC. We exclude loans collateralized by manufactured housing, unless otherwise noted, as some of these loans are underwritten in a manner more similar to automobile loans than mortgages. As the HMDA data do not identify lien status until 2004, we drop from the HMDA data, in all years, mortgages with balances below $25,000 in 2006 dollars, as we suspect that these loans are junior liens.[5]

Other Data Sources

We extract from the 2000 Census the share of residents in each census tract who are black or Hispanic, the number of properties that are owner-occupied, the median income of each tract, and the number of housing units. We define black individuals as those who report being black and not Hispanic. Hispanic individuals are any persons who report being Hispanic. We map these counts to the zip code level as described in the appendix to this chapter. Based on these counts, we calculate a zip code's home ownership rate as the share of owner-occupied properties relative to all housing units. We categorize a zip code's median income relative to other zip codes within its MSA: we sort zip codes within each MSA on the basis of their median income, and then split the zip codes into quintiles. We create dummy variables that indicate the quintile in which each zip code's median income falls.

---

4. See appendix C of Gerardi, Shapiro, and Willen (2007).
5. We do not impose a similar restriction on the LP data, as lien status is reported in all years. About one-half of 1 percent (0.05 percent) of mortgages in our LP sample have balances below $25,000.

We also obtain data on the share of tract residents with high, medium, and low credit scores according to a file provided by Equifax Inc. An individual's credit is assessed with the VantageScore created jointly by the three national credit reporting agencies (Equifax, Experian, and TransUnion). VantageScores range from 501 to 990, with higher scores signifying better credit. The VantageScore was developed so that individuals with identical data across agencies would receive the same credit score. (Because of differences in how the agencies define certain variables, the better-known FICO score developed by Fair Isaac Corporation may take on different values across credit bureaus.) The VantageScore modelers also paid particular attention to generating a reliable credit score for "thin-file" individuals (those with few credit transactions on record).

We consider an individual as having high credit if the VantageScore exceeds 700; medium credit if the score falls between 640 and 700; or low credit if the score lies below 640. Broadly speaking, the high category includes the prime credit market and the upper end of the near-prime market; the middle category includes the lower end of the near-prime market and the upper end of the subprime market; and the low category includes the lower end of the subprime market and those generally ineligible for any mortgage credit. As with the census data, we map these counts to the zip code. When we calculate the shares of individuals in each category, we include all individuals in the zip code except the approximately 10 percent without VantageScores.

We obtain annual county-level data on unemployment rates from the Bureau of Labor Statistics' Local Area Unemployment program; MSA-level data on home price changes from the Office of Federal Housing Enterprise Oversight (OFHEO) all-transactions housing price index; and county-level data on permits for the construction of residential one-to-four-family housing units from the U.S. Census Bureau.

LOAN PERFORMANCE, HIGHER-PRICED HMDA MORTGAGES, AND MORTGAGES BY HUD SUBPRIME LENDERS

Time Trends, 1998–2006

We begin by showing the rise in subprime lending from 1998 to 2006 as depicted by the LP and HUD subprime lender measures (figure 6.1a). Both measures show a substantial increase in subprime originations over this period and a marked acceleration from 2003 to 2005. However, the measures differ in the

FIGURE 6.1A   Subprime Originations by Year

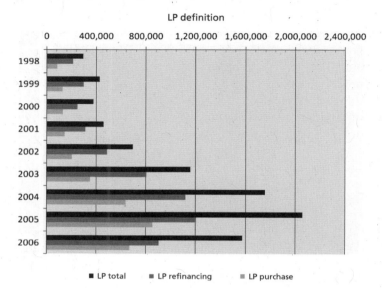

LP definition

Legend: ■ LP total   ■ LP refinancing   ■ LP purchase

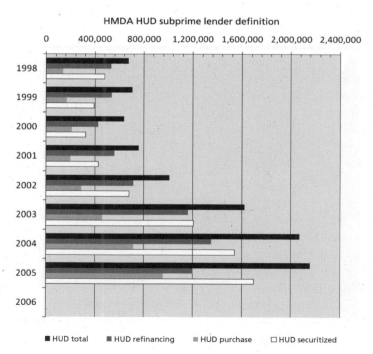

HMDA HUD subprime lender definition

Legend: ■ HUD total   ■ HUD refinancing   ■ HUD purchase   □ HUD securitized

SOURCES: Authors' calculations using data from LoanPerformance and HMDA.

number of originations they record in the late 1990s and early 2000s and thus in how much they suggest that subprime lending increased over the period.

The LP data show around 300,000 subprime originations in MSAs in 1998, with a gradual increase to around 700,000 originations in 2002, a sharp increase to around 2 million in 2005, and then a drop to 1.5 million in 2006. In contrast, the HUD lender measure shows 750,000 subprime mortgage originations in 1998—two and a half times the LP level for that year—and subsequently a moderate rise to 1 million in 2002 and a steep rise to 2.2 million in 2005 (data for 2006 are not available).[6] Although total originations in 2005 are about the same under both measures, the difference in the 1998 levels implies that subprime lending increased nearly seven-fold under the LP measure, but only tripled under the HUD measure. Measuring LP and HUD originations in relation to all mortgage originations in HMDA (figure 6.1b) underscores that the HUD measure captures more subprime originations than the LP measure in the early years of the data.

The difference between the LP and HMDA time trends seems to reflect primarily an increase in the share of subprime mortgages that are securitized, although the share of securitizers that report to LP may change over time as well. To show this, we add the share of HUD subprime mortgages that are securitized to the lower panel of figure 6.1a. We define a subprime mortgage as securitized if the originator does not hold it in portfolio. Thus, we assume that mortgages that an originator sells to another institution are eventually securitized. In the prime market, where more lenders buy and hold whole loans, we would be less comfortable with this assumption. This assumption biases upward our estimate of the number of securitized loans, but it is partially offset by the fact that we miss subprime mortgages that were originated at the end of one year and sold in the next.

The HUD-securitized measure tracks the total LP measure fairly closely for all years except 1998 (when the HUD-securitized measure is larger than the LP measure) and 2004 and 2005 (when the HUD-securitized measure is smaller). The difference between the HUD total and the HUD-securitized bars indicates that about three-fourths of mortgages originated by these lenders were securitized in recent years. The discrepancy in 1998 is consistent with our earlier finding that the LP data appear to be less representative in that year; the fact that the LP measure begins to exceed the HUD-securitized

---

6. The data in this figure, unlike that in all other figures and tables in this chapter, include manufactured housing units for the HUD subprime lender measure. We include these units to make the series consistent over time, as HMDA did not include a way to identify these units until 2004.

FIGURE 6.1B   Subprime Originations as a Share of HMDA Originations

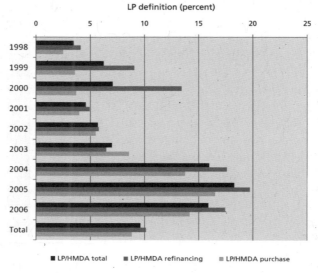

LP definition (percent)

■ LP/HMDA total   ■ LP/HMDA refinancing   ■ LP/HMDA purchase

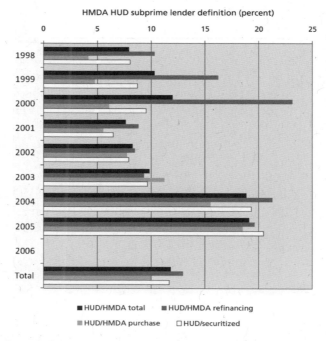

HMDA HUD subprime lender definition (percent)

■ HUD/HMDA total   ■ HUD/HMDA refinancing
■ HUD/HMDA purchase   □ HUD/securitized

SOURCES: Authors' calculations using data from LoanPerformance and HMDA.

measure in 2004 suggests that prime lenders around that time became more active in the subprime market.

Figure 6.1a also suggests that the match between the HUD total and the LP measures in 2005 may be coincidence rather than an indication that the measures are capturing the same pool of mortgages. These measures may match because the number of subprime originations held in portfolio by HUD lenders in 2005 was about the same as the number of subprime mortgages securitized by prime lenders. This conclusion assumes that we are measuring the HUD securitization share accurately.

Time Trends, 2004–2006

For the 2004–2006 period, we also have data from the HMDA higher-priced measure (table 6.1). The higher-priced measure confirms the LP finding that the peak of subprime lending occurred in 2005. For that peak year, the higher-priced measure shows nearly 3 million mortgages, 800,000 to 900,000 more than shown by the LP or HUD lender measures.

The time series pattern for these three years differs across subprime measures. The higher-priced measure nearly doubles between 2004 and 2005, reflecting in part the flattening of the yield curve. The LP measure also shows large gains over these two years. The HUD measure, however, is flat, perhaps because prime lenders—who are not reflected in the HUD data—became more active in the subprime market in the last couple of years. Between 2005 and 2006, the higher-priced measure indicates a slight dip in the number of subprime originations, whereas the LP data report a drop of about 20 percent. The discrepancies across these three measures suggest the difficulties in relying on any single measure to gauge the prevalence of subprime lending.

Trends in Purchase and Refinance Mortgages

All three measures suggest that subprime mortgages are used a bit more for refinancing than for home purchase, as refinancings represent a majority of subprime originations in all years. For example, in 2005 the LP data show 1.2 million refinance mortgages (figure 6.1a and table 6.1), or 58 percent of all LP subprime; the HUD data also show 1.2 million refinance mortgages, or 56 percent of all HUD lender subprime; and the HMDA higher-priced data show 51 percent.

The data also indicate that over the past decade subprime refinance mortgages were a greater share of total refinancings, as reported in HMDA, than subprime purchases were of total purchases (figure 6.1b). As we show later in

TABLE 6.1 Subprime Originations in the LP and HMDA Data, 2004–2006

Year	HMDA total	LP total	HMDA higher-priced total	HMDA HUD subprime total
2004	10,959,872	1,725,466	1,575,342	2,070,631
2005	11,245,059	2,022,038	2,987,451	2,154,212
2006	9,887,994	1,547,155	2,855,954	—
Total	32,092,925	5,294,659	7,418,747	4,224,843

Year	HMDA refinance	LP refinance	HMDA higher-priced refinance	HMDA HUD subprime refinance
2004	6,347,590	1,100,609	949,030	1,353,115
2005	6,089,788	1,182,615	1,521,854	1,197,396
2006	5,176,485	888,783	1,486,475	—
Total	17,613,863	3,172,007	3,957,359	2,550,511

Year	HMDA purchase	LP purchase	HMDA higher-priced purchase	HMDA HUD subprime purchase
2004	4,612,282	624,857	626,312	717,516
2005	5,155,271	839,423	1,465,597	956,816
2006	4,711,509	658,372	1,369,479	—
Total	14,479,062	2,122,652	3,461,388	1,674,332

NOTES: Observations are loan originations. The sample is restricted to first-lien mortgages on properties located in a metropolitan statistical area that are not backed by manufactured housing or by buildings with more than four units. LP are loans that were packaged into subprime mortgage pools. HMDA higher-priced are mortgages with an APR of 3 or more percentage points above Treasury securities. HMDA HUD subprime are loans in the HMDA data originated by lenders on the HUD subprime lender list. HMDA HUD data are not available for 2006. LP = LoanPerformance; HMDA = Home Mortgage Disclosure Act; HUD = Department of Housing and Urban Development.

the chapter, almost all subprime refinances are cash-out refinances, although, in some cases, subprime borrowers may be extracting cash solely to pay their mortgage closing costs. In periods when interest rates are low—such as 2003, when interest rates hit a 30-year low—prime borrowers refinance *en masse* to lower their payments, and subprime borrowers represent a relatively small share of total refinances. In times when interest rates are relatively higher, such as 2000 and 2004 to 2006, fewer prime borrowers refinance, and subprime borrowers play a larger role. From 2004 to 2006, subprime refinance originations, as measured by both the LP and HUD measures, represented 15 percent to more than 20 percent of total refinance originations in HMDA.

Originations per Zip Code

Next, we consider the number of subprime loans originated in 2005 as a percentage of the housing units in that zip code according to the 2000 Census (table 6.2). Depending on the measure, subprime loans were originated on between 3.6 percent and 5.4 percent of housing units in the typical zip code. The geographic dispersion is also quite pronounced. At the ninetieth percentile, anywhere from 7.9 to 10.9 subprime loans were originated in the typical year for every 100 housing units. At the tenth percentile, fewer than 2 subprime loans were originated for every 100 housing units.

TABLE 6.2 Subprime Originations by Zip Code, 2004–2006

		Subprime/100 units			
Variable	Year	Mean	10th percentile	Median	90th percentile
LP	2004	3.1	0.8	2.2	6.6
	2005	3.6	0.9	2.5	7.8
	2006	2.8	0.7	1.9	5.9
	Total	3.2	0.8	2.2	6.8
HMDA	2004	2.8	1.0	2.3	5.4
higher-priced	2005	5.4	1.7	3.9	10.9
	2006	5.2	1.7	3.7	10.3
	Total	4.5	1.3	3.2	9.0
HMDA HUD	2004	3.7	1.2	2.7	7.5
subprime	2005	3.9	1.1	2.6	8.3
	2006	—	—	—	—
	Total	3.8	1.1	2.7	7.8

		Subprime purchases/100 units			
Variable	Year	Mean	10th percentile	Median	90th percentile
LP	2004	1.1	0.2	0.7	2.5
	2005	1.5	0.3	1.0	3.4
	2006	1.2	0.2	0.8	2.6
	Total	1.3	0.2	0.8	2.8
HMDA	2004	1.3	0.4	0.9	2.6
higher-priced	2005	2.9	0.7	1.9	6.2
	2006	2.7	0.7	1.8	5.7
	Total	2.3	0.5	1.5	4.8
HMDA HUD	2004	1.3	0.2	0.8	3.0
subprime	2005	1.7	0.3	1.0	4.1
	2006	—	—	—	—
	Total	1.5	0.3	0.9	3.6

(continued)

TABLE 6.2 *(continued)*

Variable	Year	Subprime refinances/100 units			
		Mean	10th percentile	Median	90th percentile
LP	2004	2.0	0.5	1.4	4.1
	2005	2.1	0.6	1.4	4.5
	2006	1.6	0.4	1.1	3.4
	Total	1.9	0.5	1.3	4.0
HMDA	2004	1.6	0.6	1.3	2.9
higher-priced	2005	2.5	0.9	1.9	5.0
	2006	2.5	0.9	1.9	4.8
	Total	2.2	0.7	1.7	4.2
HMDA HUD	2004	2.3	0.8	1.8	4.4
subprime	2005	2.1	0.7	1.5	4.2
	2006	—	—	—	—
	Total	2.2	0.7	1.6	4.3

NOTES: Observations are zip codes. The sample is restricted to first-lien mortgages on properties located in a metropolitan statistical area that are not backed by manufactured housing or by buildings with more than four units. LP are loans that were packaged into subprime mortgage pools. HMDA higher-priced are mortgages with an APR of 3 or more percentage points above Treasury securities. HMDA HUD subprime are loans in the HMDA data originated by lenders on the HUD subprime lender list. HUD data are not available for 2006. LP = LoanPerformance; HMDA = Home Mortgage Disclosure Act; HUD = Department of Housing and Urban Development.

BY THE MAPS: WHERE ARE SUBPRIME LOAN SHARES THE HIGHEST?

Subprime Originations Relative to Housing Units

To explore the geographic dispersion of subprime lending, we examine maps of the largest 100 MSAs in 2005, as ranked by population (figures 6.2–6.4). Subprime loans were originated throughout the country in this year. We divide zip codes into quintiles based on the number of subprime originations in 2005 relative to housing units in the 2000 census. The patterns described below are similar across the three subprime measures.

The most striking pattern is the extent to which subprime lending was more prevalent in some locations than others. The cutoffs for the quintiles in figure 6.2, based on the LP measure, range from 1.1 subprime originations per 100 housing units and below for the lowest quintile (shaded in light gray) to

4.6 and above for the highest quintile (shaded in dark gray).[7] Concentrations in dark gray are especially pronounced in the West, with Los Angeles (especially Riverside County), Las Vegas, Phoenix, Fresno, Denver, and Salt Lake City showing high concentrations of subprime loans. In the south, much of Florida and Atlanta also exhibit high concentrations of subprime lending. Cities in the Midwest and the Northeast experienced less subprime lending, although even markets less traditionally linked with subprime lending, such as Chicago, Providence, Minneapolis, Norfolk, and Washington, DC, have somewhat high portions of dark gray shading. In tables 6.3 and 6.4, we list the subprime concentrations using the LP measure for all 50 states and the top 100 MSAs by population.

The maps and tables suggest a couple of findings regarding the dispersion of subprime lending. We establish these correlations more conclusively in the later regression analyses. First, subprime loans are prevalent in locations with large amounts of new construction; this is consistent with a link between construction and the expansion of credit. Fast-growing metropolitan areas in states such as Nevada, Arizona, California, and Texas appear to have many subprime originations. Even within metropolitan areas, exurbs often have the highest subprime concentrations. This pattern is especially apparent in California, where the outlying Los Angeles suburbs and the so-called "Inland Empire" of Riverside and San Bernardino counties show large dark gray concentrations (figure 6.5). Although not readily apparent from the national map, a similar— although more muted—pattern exists in other areas, such as the ring at the edge of the Boston metropolitan area and outlying parts of New Jersey.

Second, there is an apparent link between home price appreciation in the previous year and subsequent subprime lending, but the correspondence is certainly not one-for-one. Whereas California, Las Vegas, and Miami saw high rates of appreciation and a great concentration of subprime lending, parts of the Northeast had high rates of home price appreciation but moderate numbers of subprime originations. Similarly, Atlanta had a high concentration of subprime lending in 2005 but relatively little home price appreciation, when compared with other locations. Third, some locations, such as Ohio or Michigan, that have received widespread attention because of large numbers of

---

7. The distribution of subprime originations across zip codes in the maps differs from the distributions described in the section "Loan Performance, Higher-Priced HMDA Mortgages, and Mortgages by HUD Subprime Lenders," because the maps are limited to the top 100 MSAs whereas the section describes our entire sample. The maps are available on the Internet in an interactive fashion at http://www4.gsb.columbia.edu/realestate/research/SubprimeMaps.

FIGURE 6.2   Percentage of Housing Units with Subprime Loan Originations in 2005, LP

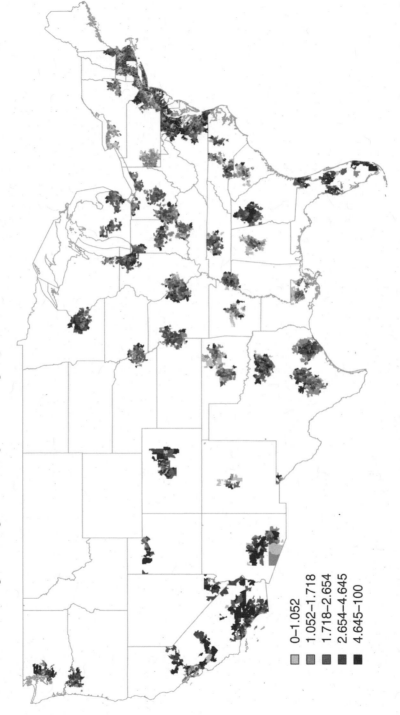

0–1.052

1.052–1.718

1.718–2.654

2.654–4.645

4.645–100

SOURCES: Authors' calculations using data from HMDA, LoanPerformance, and 2000 U.S. Census.

FIGURE 6.3 Percentage of Housing Units with Subprime Loan Originations in 2005, HMDA Higher-Priced

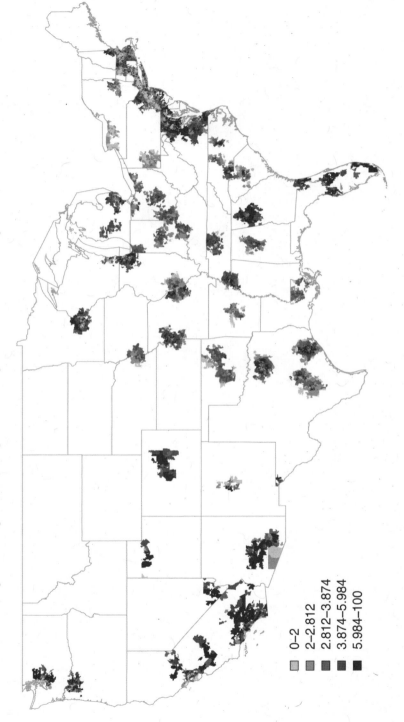

0–2
2–2.812
2.812–3.874
3.874–5.984
5.984–100

SOURCES: Authors' calculations using data from HMDA and 2000 U.S. Census.

FIGURE 6.4   Percentage of Housing Units with Subprime Loan Originations in 2005, HUD Subprime Lender

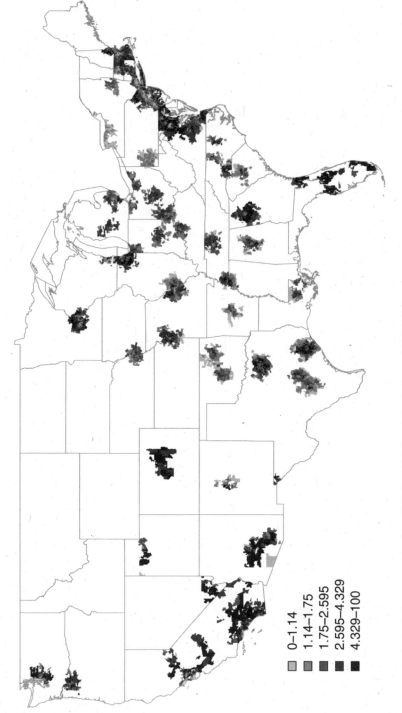

0–1.14
1.14–1.75
1.75–2.595
2.595–4.329
4.329–100

SOURCES: Authors' calculations using data from HMDA, HUD Subprime Lender List, and 2000 U.S. Census.

TABLE 6.3   LP Subprime Originations as a Share of Housing Units by State, 2005

State	Number of subprime loans/ number of units	State	Number of subprime loans/ number of units
Nevada	0.100	Wisconsin	0.030
Arizona	0.077	New Hampshire	0.029
California	0.071	Maine	0.028
Florida	0.062	Ohio	0.026
Rhode Island	0.062	Wyoming	0.026
Maryland	0.061	Indiana	0.025
District of Columbia	0.052	Kansas	0.021
Illinois	0.048	Mississippi	0.021
New Jersey	0.043	New Mexico	0.021
Georgia	0.040	North Carolina	0.021
Utah	0.039	Oklahoma	0.021
Connecticut	0.038	South Carolina	0.020
Colorado	0.037	Iowa	0.019
Virginia	0.036	Kentucky	0.019
Washington	0.035	Nebraska	0.019
Massachusetts	0.034	Pennsylvania	0.019
Michigan	0.034	Alabama	0.018
Minnesota	0.034	Louisiana	0.018
Missouri	0.034	Arkansas	0.017
Idaho	0.033	South Dakota	0.014
Oregon	0.033	Vermont	0.014
Delaware	0.032	Montana	0.012
New York	0.032	North Dakota	0.012
Texas	0.031	West Virginia	0.009
Tennessee	0.030		
Total		0.041	

NOTES: Sample is restricted to first-lien mortgages on properties located in a metropolitan statistical area that are not backed by manufactured housing or by buildings with more than four units. LP subprime loans are loans that were packaged into subprime mortgage pools. LP = LoanPerformance.

foreclosures, do not appear to have particularly large concentrations of subprime loans as compared with other parts of the country.

Subprime Originations Relative to Total Origination

Our finding about the low prevalence of subprime originations in Ohio and Michigan turns out to depend on our choice of housing units rather than on total originations as the denominator. All previous papers in this literature have used total originations. We use housing units as the denominator because the

TABLE 6.4   LP Subprime Originations as a Share of Housing Units by MSA, 2005

	MSA	Number of subprime loans/number of units		MSA	Number of subprime loans/number of units
1	Riverside, CA	0.14	39	Seattle, WA	0.04
2	Bakersfield, CA	0.13	40	Lakeland, FL	0.04
3	Stockton, CA	0.12	41	Boise City, ID	0.04
4	Las Vegas, NV	0.12	42	San Francisco, CA	0.04
5	Modesto, CA	0.11	43	Springfield, MA	0.04
6	Fresno, CA	0.10	44	Minneapolis St Paul, MN–WI	0.04
7	Visalia, CA	0.09			
8	Phoenix, AZ	0.09	45	Bridgeport, CT	0.04
9	Cape Coral, FL	0.09	46	Dallas, TX	0.04
10	Orlando, FL	0.08	47	Kansas City, MO–KS	0.04
11	Miami, FL	0.08	48	Ogden, UT	0.04
12	Sacramento, CA	0.08	49	St Louis, MO-IL	0.03
13	Los Angeles, CA	0.07	50	Hartford, CT	0.03
14	Washington DC, DC–VA–MD–WV	0.06	51	Richmond, VA	0.03
			52	Boston, MA-NH	0.03
15	Chicago, IL–IN–WI	0.06	53	San Jose, CA	0.03
16	Providence, RI–MA	0.05	54	Cleveland, OH	0.03
17	Tampa, FL	0.05	55	Nashville, TN	0.03
18	New Haven, CT	0.05	56	Grand Rapids, MI	0.03
19	Baltimore, MD	0.05	57	Charlotte, NC-SC	0.03
20	Atlanta, GA	0.05	58	Charleston, SC	0.03
21	Jacksonville, FL	0.05	59	Indianapolis, IN	0.03
22	San Diego, CA	0.05	60	Columbus, OH	0.03
23	Milwaukee, WI	0.05	61	Spokane, WA	0.03
24	Palm Bay, FL	0.05	62	Santa Rosa, CA	0.03
25	Virginia Beach, VA–NC	0.04	63	San Antonio, TX	0.03
26	Oxnard, CA	0.04	64	Akron, OH	0.03
27	Detroit, MI	0.04	65	Philadelphia, PA–NJ–DE–MD	0.03
28	Houston, TX	0.04			
29	Tucson, AZ	0.04	66	Allentown, PA–NJ	0.03
30	Worcester, MA	0.04	67	Portland, ME	0.03
31	Memphis, TN–MS–AR	0.04	68	Dayton, OH	0.03
32	New York, NY–NJ–PA	0.04	69	Knoxville, TN	0.03
33	Salt Lake City, UT	0.04	70	Des Moines, IA	0.03
34	Denver, CO	0.04	71	Austin, TX	0.03
35	Poughkeepsie, NY	0.04	72	Chattanooga, TN–GA	0.03
36	Sarasota, FL	0.04	73	Cincinnati, OH–KY–IN	0.03
37	Colorado Springs, CO	0.04	74	Raleigh, NC	0.03
38	Portland, OR–WA	0.04	75	Jackson, MS	0.02

(*continued*)

TABLE 6.4 (continued)

MSA	Number of subprime loans/number of units	MSA	Number of subprime loans/number of units
76 Birmingham, AL	0.02	92 New Orleans, LA	0.02
77 Albuquerque, NM	0.02	93 Scranton, PA	0.02
78 McAllen, TX	0.02	94 Greensboro, NC	0.02
79 El Paso, TX	0.02	95 York, PA	0.02
80 Oklahoma City, OK	0.02	96 Little Rock, AR	0.02
81 Albany, NY	0.02	97 Wichita, KS	0.02
82 Ann Arbor, MI	0.02	98 Harrisburg, PA	0.02
83 Baton Rouge, LA	0.02	99 Durham, NC	0.02
84 Omaha, NE–IA	0.02	100 Madison, WI	0.02
85 Columbia, SC	0.02	101 Greenville, SC	0.02
86 Louisville, KY–IN	0.02	102 Lancaster, PA	0.02
87 Corpus Christi, TX	0.02	103 Augusta, GA–SC	0.01
88 Toledo, OH	0.02	104 Pittsburgh, PA	0.01
89 Lexington-Fayette, KY	0.02	105 Rochester, NY	0.01
90 Youngstown, OH–PA	0.02	106 Syracuse, NY	0.01
91 Tulsa, OK	0.02	107 Buffalo, NY	0.01
Total			0.041

NOTES: The sample is restricted to first-lien mortgages that are not backed by manufactured housing or buildings with more than four units. Subprime loans are loans that were packaged into subprime mortgage pools. We restrict our sample to loans in the top three deciles of MSAs by population. MSA = metropolitan statistical area.

availability of subprime loans may affect the decision to take out a loan as well as the decision of what type of loan to choose. For example, subprime loans may allow some individuals who would have otherwise stayed renters to become homeowners. Subprime loans may also allow some homeowners who would otherwise be liquidity constrained to extract cash from their properties.

When we measure subprime originations in relation to total originations (tables 6.5 and 6.6), states and cities with depressed housing markets move up in the distribution. For example, home prices in Michigan appreciated 3 percent in 2005; Michigan ranked seventeenth among states in subprime originations in terms of housing units, but fifth in terms of originations.[8] In the same year, home prices in California rose 21 percent; California ranked third among

---

8. Home price appreciation estimates are calculated by the authors and based on the change in the OFHEO all-transactions house price index between fourth quarter 2004 and fourth quarter 2005.

FIGURE 6.5   Percentage of Housing Units in Southern California with Subprime
Loan Originations in 2005, LP

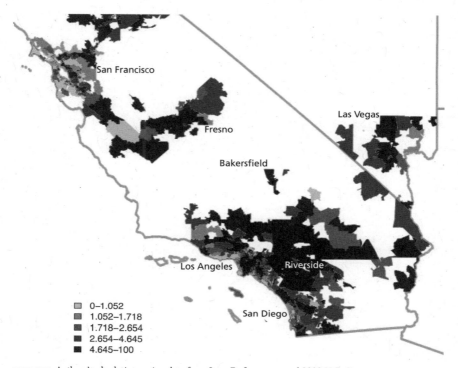

0–1.052
1.052–1.718
1.718–2.654
2.654–4.645
4.645–100

SOURCES: Authors' calculations using data from LoanPerformance and 2000 U.S. Census.

states in subprime originations as related to housing units, but sixteenth as related to originations. Likewise, Memphis, Detroit, and Cleveland have a higher
relative share of subprime originations related to all originations than to housing units. However, some areas rank high under both measures. Nevada has the
highest share of subprime loans relative to both housing units and originations,
and Bakersfield, California ranks second among cities under both measures.

We hypothesize that areas with high home price appreciation and more
new construction may have more mortgage activity of all kinds than do areas
with more depressed housing markets. More new residents may move to rapidly growing areas and purchase homes; more renters may transition to home
ownership, and more investors may purchase properties; more homeowners
may extract their recent home price gains through cash-out refinancings. Because mortgage activity is elevated among both prime and subprime borrow-

TABLE 6.5 LP Subprime Originations as a Share of All Originations by State, 2005

State	Number of subprime loans/ number of loans	State	Number of subprime loans/ number of loans
Nevada	0.25	Pennsylvania	0.16
Florida	0.24	South Carolina	0.16
Michigan	0.24	Utah	0.16
Texas	0.24	Wisconsin	0.16
Tennessee	0.23	Arkansas	0.15
Ohio	0.22	Colorado	0.15
Arizona	0.21	Kansas	0.15
Illinois	0.21	Kentucky	0.15
Indiana	0.21	Nebraska	0.15
Maryland	0.21	Wyoming	0.15
Mississippi	0.21	Idaho	0.14
Missouri	0.21	Iowa	0.14
Rhode Island	0.21	Massachusetts	0.14
California	0.19	North Carolina	0.14
Georgia	0.19	Oregon	0.14
New York	0.19	Virginia	0.14
Oklahoma	0.19	Washington	0.14
Connecticut	0.18	New Mexico	0.13
Louisiana	0.18	New Hampshire	0.12
New Jersey	0.18	South Dakota	0.10
Alabama	0.17	Montana	0.09
District of Columbia	0.17	Vermont	0.08
Delaware	0.16	North Dakota	0.08
Maine	0.16	West Virginia	0.08
Minnesota	0.16		
Total			0.19

NOTES: The sample is restricted to first-lien mortgages on properties located in a metropolitan statistical area that are not backed by manufactured housing or by buildings with more than four units. LP subprime loans are loans that were packaged into subprime mortgage pools. LP = LoanPerformance.

ers, subprime originations may be high in connection with housing units, but not necessarily as a share of mortgage activity.

In contrast, mortgage activity is likely subdued in depressed housing markets: these markets do not attract new homeowners or investors, and existing homeowners have no home price gains to cash out in refinancings. As depressed housing markets often reflect difficult local labor market conditions, more residents of these areas may have trouble qualifying for prime mortgages. As a result, we expect subprime originations to be low with regard to housing units, but

TABLE 6.6   LP Subprime Originations as a Share of All Originations by MSA, 2005

	MSA	Number of subprime loans/number of loans		MSA	Number of subprime loans/number of loans
1	Memphis, TN–MS–AR	0.34	40	Atlanta, GA	0.20
2	Bakersfield, CA	0.34	41	Oklahoma City, OK	0.19
3	Visalia, CA	0.32	42	Providence, RI–MA	0.19
4	Fresno, CA	0.31	43	Tulsa, OK	0.19
5	Detroit, MI	0.29	44	Palm Bay, FL	0.19
6	Miami, FL	0.29	45	Toledo, OH	0.19
7	Houston, TX	0.28	46	Sacramento, CA	0.19
8	Riverside, CA	0.28	47	Columbus, OH	0.19
9	Jackson, MS	0.27	48	Grand Rapids, MI	0.19
10	Las Vegas, NV	0.27	49	New York, NY–NJ–PA	0.19
11	McAllen, TX	0.27	50	Springfield, MA	0.19
12	Cleveland, OH	0.27	51	Knoxville, TN	0.19
13	San Antonio, TX	0.26	52	Virginia Beach, VA–NC	0.19
14	Stockton, CA	0.26	53	Scranton, PA	0.19
15	Orlando, FL	0.25	54	New Orleans, LA	0.18
16	Cape Coral, FL	0.24	55	Sarasota, FL	0.18
17	Jacksonville, FL	0.24	56	Albany, NY	0.18
18	Milwaukee, WI	0.24	57	Philadelphia, PA–NJ–DE–MD	0.18
19	Dayton, OH	0.23	58	Nashville, TN	0.18
20	Tampa, FL	0.23	59	Columbia, SC	0.17
21	Lakeland, FL	0.23	60	Tucson, AZ	0.17
22	Akron, OH	0.23	61	Little Rock, AR	0.17
23	Chicago, IL–IN–WI	0.23	62	Worcester, MA	0.17
24	Dallas, TX	0.23	63	Cincinnati, OH–KY–IN	0.17
25	New Haven, CT	0.22	64	Hartford, CT	0.17
26	Kansas City, MO–KS	0.22	65	Omaha, NE–IA	0.17
27	Phoenix, AZ	0.22	66	Louisville, KY–IN	0.17
28	El Paso, TX	0.22	67	Augusta, GA–SC	0.17
29	Chattanooga, TN–GA	0.22	68	Charlotte, NC–SC	0.17
30	Youngstown, OH–PA	0.22	69	Salt Lake City, UT	0.17
31	Baltimore, MD	0.22	70	Minneapolis St Paul, MN–WI	0.17
32	Corpus Christi, TX	0.22	71	Charleston, SC	0.16
33	Indianapolis, IN	0.21	72	Pittsburgh, PA	0.16
34	Modesto, CA	0.21	73	Richmond, VA	0.16
35	St Louis, MO–IL	0.21	74	Des Moines, IA	0.16
36	Birmingham, AL	0.21	75	Spokane, WA	0.16
37	Baton Rouge, LA	0.21	76	Buffalo, NY	0.15
38	Los Angeles, CA	0.21			
39	Poughkeepsie, NY	0.20			

(continued)

TABLE 6.6 *(continued)*

MSA	Number of subprime loans/number of loans	MSA	Number of subprime loans/number of loans
77 Colorado Springs, CO	0.15	92 Albuquerque, NM	0.14
78 Ogden, UT	0.15	93 Lexington, KY	0.14
79 Austin, TX	0.15	94 Portland, ME	0.14
80 Denver, CO	0.15	95 Seattle, WA	0.13
81 Rochester, NY	0.15	96 Boston, MA–NH	0.13
82 Wichita, KS	0.15	97 Syracuse, NY	0.13
83 Greensboro, NC	0.15	98 Harrisburg, PA	0.12
84 Washington DC, DC–VA–MD–WV	0.15	99 Raleigh, NC	0.12
		100 Ann Arbor, MI	0.11
85 Boise City, ID	0.15	101 San Francisco, CA	0.11
86 Allentown, PA–NJ	0.14	102 York, PA	0.11
87 Bridgeport, CT	0.14	103 San Jose, CA	0.10
88 Oxnard, CA	0.14	104 Santa Rosa, CA	0.10
89 Greenville, SC	0.14	105 Lancaster, PA	0.10
90 Portland, OR–WA	0.14	106 Durham, NC	0.10
91 San Diego, CA	0.14	107 Madison, WI	0.09
Total		0.20	

NOTES: The sample is restricted to first-lien mortgages that are not backed by manufactured housing or by buildings with more than four units. Subprime loans are loans that were packaged into subprime mortgage pools. We restrict our sample to loans within the top three deciles of MSAs by population.
MSA = metropolitan statistical area.

perhaps higher with regard to loan originations. In regression analyses presented later in this chapter, we present evidence consistent with these hypotheses.

However, we cannot rule out the possibility that subprime originations are high relative to housing units in fast-growing cities because of a timing issue: our loan measures are from 2005, whereas our measure of housing units is from 2000. In fast-growing cities, the number of housing units in 2000 may be significantly less than the number of units in 2005, and subprime loan originations will seem more prevalent than they really are.

REGRESSION ANALYSIS: WHERE ARE SUBPRIME LOAN SHARES THE HIGHEST?

Next, we formalize the analysis in the maps, using regressions that examine the factors correlated with the prevalence of subprime loans in MSA zip codes.

Our goal is to describe the types of neighborhoods that saw the highest incidence of subprime lending; we are not asserting a causal relationship between these factors and these originations.

Summary Statistics

As we described the subprime measures earlier, we highlight here the other variables in our analysis (table 6.7). As already noted, we measure zip code income with dummy variables that indicate the quintile within the MSA that each zip code's median income falls into. Although we use these dummy variables in the regressions, we show the distribution of the zip code median income by quintile in table 6.7 to give a sense of the variability in the quintiles across MSAs. Whereas the mean of the bottom income quintile is $15,300, the tenth percentile is $11,300 and the ninetieth percentile is $19,300. The highest income quintile averages $34,000, but ranges from $21,900 to $50,000. The variability of each income quintile rises with the income quintile.

Zip codes exhibit great skewness in the percentage of black and Hispanic residents. Although blacks and Hispanics on average represent 10.7 percent and 10.8 percent, respectively, of the zip code residents, the medians are only 3.6 percent and 4.1 percent. The standard deviations of both variables exceed 16 percent.

The mean and median home ownership rates are 65.2 percent and 67.1 percent in our sample, slightly below the national 2005 home ownership rate of 68.9 percent. Once again, this measure is quite variable, with the tenth and ninetieth percentiles of the distribution of home ownership rates ranging from 45 percent to 83 percent.

The mean unemployment rate is 5.0 percent, quite close to the national average of 5.1 percent, with relatively low variability across counties. However, the amount that home prices appreciated in 2004, the year preceding our data, ranges from 0.5 percent to 17.1 percent, with a median of 5 percent. The variance (7.0 percent) is nearly as high as the mean (7.5 percent). Our measure of new home construction, permits per 100 housing units, also exhibits skewness. The mean number of permits (1.6) is above the median (1.1), with a tenth percentile to ninetieth percentile range of 0.3 to 3.5.

Base Regressions Using LoanPerformance Data

We show first regressions that use LP subprime originations per 100 housing units as the dependent variable (table 6.8). The specification in column one

TABLE 6.7 Sample Characteristics, 2005

Variable	Mean	Standard deviation	10th percentile	Median	90th percentile
LP subprime/100 units	3.6	3.8	0.9	2.5	7.8
LP subprime purchases/ 100 units	1.5	1.8	0.3	1.0	3.4
LP subprime refinances/ 100 units	2.1	2.3	0.6	1.4	4.5
LP subprime refinances for cash-out/100 units	1.9	2.1	0.5	1.2	4.2
LP subprime refinances not for cash-out/100 units	0.2	0.2	0.0	0.2	0.5
HMDA higher-priced subprime/100 units	5.4	5.0	1.7	3.9	10.9
HMDA higher-priced subprime purchases/ 100 units	2.6	3.1	0.6	1.7	5.9
HMDA higher-priced subprime refinances/ 100 units	2.7	2.3	1.0	2.1	5.4
HMDA HUD subprime/ 100 units	3.9	3.9	1.1	2.7	8.4
HMDA HUD subprime purchases/100 units	1.7	2.2	0.3	1.0	4.1
HMDA HUD subprime refinances/100 units	2.2	2.0	0.7	1.6	4.4
Income in zip codes in bottom income quintile	15.3	3.2	11.3	15.3	19.3
Income in zip codes in second income quintile	19.2	3.5	15.2	18.7	23.9
Income in zip codes in third income quintile	21.9	4.2	17.1	21.2	27.7
Income in zip codes in fourth income quintile	25.3	6.0	18.6	24.4	32.9
Income in zip codes in top income quintile	34.0	12.9	21.9	31.1	49.8
Percent with low VantageScore	24.5	12.4	10.4	22.4	41.9
Percent with mid-VantageScore	12.8	3.1	8.6	12.9	16.5
Percent of population black	10.7	17.7	0.4	3.6	30.5
Percent of population Hispanic	10.8	16.3	0.9	4.1	30.1
Percent ownership rate	65.2	14.8	45.3	67.1	82.6

(continued)

TABLE 6.7 *(continued)*

Variable	Mean	Standard deviation	10th percentile	Median	90th percentile
Percent unemployment	5.0	1.3	3.7	4.9	6.4
HPI appreciation in previous year	7.4	7.0	0.5	5.0	17.1
Lagged permits in county/ 100 units	1.6	1.5	0.3	1.1	3.5

NOTES: Observations are zip codes. The sample is restricted to first-lien mortgages on properties located in a metropolitan statistical area that are not backed by manufactured housing or by buildings with more than four units. LP denotes loans that were packaged into subprime mortgage pools. HMDA higher-priced are mortgages with an APR of 3 or more percentage points above Treasury securities. HMDA HUD subprimes are loans in the HMDA data originated by lenders on the HUD subprime lender list. LP = LoanPerformance; HMDA = Home Mortgage Disclosure Act; HUD = Department of Housing and Urban Development; HPI = house price index.

compares total subprime originations in each zip code to originations in other zip codes across the country.

Zip codes in the bottom income quintile and zip codes with higher shares of households in the middle credit category had the highest proportion of subprime loans. A one standard deviation increase in the percentage of households with a VantageScore of 640 to 700 (3.1 percentage points) is associated with a 0.86 increase in the number of subprime originations per 100 housing units, which is a 24 percent increase over the sample average of 3.63. Borrowers with credit scores in this range are the typical market for subprime mortgages. The share of households in the lowest credit category appears to be less related to the number of subprime loans, possibly because the credit of households in this category was below the lending standards of many subprime lenders.

The positive and significant coefficient on the unemployment rate suggests that subprime originations were more prevalent in communities with adverse economic conditions. However, the order of magnitude is moderate: a one standard deviation increase in the unemployment rate (1.3 percentage points) is associated with an 0.22 increase in the number of subprime originations per 100 housing units, or a 6 percent increase relative to the sample mean. Locations with higher home ownership rates also had more subprime loans, with an elasticity close to one-for-one: a 1 percent increase in home ownership rate is associated with an increase of 0.04 additional subprime loans per 100 housing units, about 1 percent of the sample mean.

Even controlling for credit scores and other zip code characteristics, race and ethnicity appear to be strongly related to the proportion of subprime loans in a statistically significant way. A 5.4 percentage point increase in the percent of non-Hispanic blacks—a 50 percent increase relative to the mean—is associated with an 8.3 percent increase in the share of subprime originations in the zip code.[9] A similar 5.4 percentage point increase in the percent of Hispanics— also a 50 percent increase relative to the mean—is associated with a 6.8 percent increase in the proportion of subprime loans. However, skewness in the racial composition of zip codes suggests that subprime originations are much more prevalent in zip codes with large shares of minority residents. Moving from the median to the ninetieth percentile zip code share of black and Hispanic residents (an increase from 3.6 percent to 30.5 percent and from 4.1 percent to 30.1 percent of residents, respectively) suggests an increase in subprime originations of 41.5 percent and 32.9 percent. However, without more information on borrowers' credit constraints and borrowing options, we cannot assess whether these subprime loans displaced lower-cost conventional loans in minority communities or provided additional credit where lending was not previously available.

We believe that we are the first researchers to use LP data to document these differences in the incidence of subprime lending by neighborhood racial composition, although several researchers have found similar results with the HMDA data. Avery, Canner, and Cook (2005), the Center for Responsible Lending (2006), and the Consumer Federation of America (2006) show that minorities are more likely than whites to take out HMDA higher-priced mortgages. The U.S. Department of Housing and Urban Development (2000), Scheessele (2002), and Calem, Gillen, and Wachter (2004) document that subprime loans, as measured by the HUD lender list, are more prevalent in minority neighborhoods. The differences across races generally persist in these studies even after controlling for borrower characteristics, although no study can control fully for all relevant variables. Our results are particularly striking given that they are the first to control, in a consistent manner, for the distribution of credit scores in a given zip code. Avery, Canner, and Cook (2005) find that the racial gap decreases substantially after controlling for the lending institution, but this result raises the further question of why minorities are served disproportionately by higher-priced lenders. The extent to which these differences across races represent steering, discrimination, or unobserved characteristics correlated with race remains an unsettled question.

---

9. We benchmark the impact of race on zip code lending, using a 50 percent increase in the mean instead of a one standard deviation increase, because of the skewness in racial composition. The standard deviation in percent of residents who are black or nonblack Hispanics is about 60 percent larger than the mean.

TABLE 6.8 Incidence of LP Subprime Originations in MSA Zip Codes, 2005

	Subprime loans/100 units		Subprime purchases/100 units		Subprime refinances/100 units	
	(1)	(2)	(3)	(4)	(5)	(6)
Median income is in bottom quintile	1.15**	−0.54**	0.23**	−0.41**	0.91**	−0.13*
	(9.86)	(−4.44)	(3.94)	(−6.60)	(13.72)	(−1.88)
Median income is in second quintile	0.52**	−0.69**	0.030	−0.47**	0.48**	−0.22**
	(6.33)	(−7.59)	(0.71)	(−9.92)	(9.93)	(−4.26)
Median income is in third quintile	0.30**	−0.60**	0.017	−0.35**	0.28**	−0.25**
	(3.89)	(−7.28)	(0.45)	(−8.23)	(6.19)	(−5.31)
Median income is in fourth quintile	0.07	−0.39**	0.013	−0.18**	0.059	−0.21**
	(1.21)	(−5.96)	(0.41)	(−5.32)	(1.62)	(−5.66)
Percent with low VantageScore	−0.002	0.056**	0.010**	0.035**	−0.012**	0.020**
	(−0.28)	(7.37)	(3.19)	(9.34)	(−2.99)	(4.71)
Percent with mid-VantageScore	0.28**	0.41**	0.11**	0.17**	0.17**	0.24**
	(16.01)	(22.80)	(13.18)	(18.32)	(15.81)	(22.97)
Percent of population black	0.056**	0.045**	0.018**	0.011**	0.038**	0.034**
	(17.25)	(13.97)	(12.65)	(7.33)	(17.04)	(16.03)
Percent of population Hispanic	0.046**	0.051**	0.022**	0.018**	0.025**	0.032**
	(13.47)	(13.21)	(13.23)	(10.04)	(12.46)	(14.19)

	(1)	(2)	(3)	(4)	(5)	(6)
Percent ownership rate	0.036**	0.053**	0.013**	0.021**	0.023**	0.032**
	(15.16)	(22.82)	(11.22)	(17.55)	(16.27)	(23.63)
Percent unemployed	0.17**	—	0.06**	—	0.11**	—
	(6.28)	—	(4.61)	—	(6.96)	—
HPI appreciation in previous year	0.21**	—	0.071**	—	0.14**	—
	(28.37)	—	(19.17)	—	(32.81)	—
Lagged permits in United States/100 units	0.51**	—	0.29**	—	0.22**	—
	(18.24)	—	(18.98)	—	(15.39)	—
Constant	−6.94**	−6.94**	−2.79**	−2.93**	−4.18**	−4.03**
	(−21.44)	(−24.16)	(−17.50)	(−19.78)	(−21.96)	(−23.97)
MSA fixed effects	No	Yes	No	Yes	No	Yes
Observations	15,281	15,611	15,281	15,611	15,281	15,611
R-squared value	0.45	0.57	0.33	0.43	0.46	0.60
Mean of dependent variable	3.63		1.51			2.13

NOTES: Dependent variable: LP subprime loans as a percentage of total housing units in 2000. Observations are zip codes. The sample is restricted to first-lien mortgages on properties located in an MSA that are not backed by manufactured housing or by buildings with more than four units. LP subprime denotes loans that were packaged into subprime mortgage pools. For the specifications without MSA fixed effects, we drop 330 zip codes with missing unemployment rate or permit data. LP = LoanPerformance; HPI = house price index; MSA = metropolitan statistical area; * = statistically significant at the .10 level; ** = statistically significant at the .05 level. T-statistics are shown in parentheses.

Finally, the positive and statistically significant coefficients on lagged home price appreciation and new housing permits suggest an interrelationship between subprime lending and the housing boom. A one standard deviation increase in home price appreciation in the previous year is associated with a 39 percent increase in subprime loans, whereas a one standard deviation increase in lagged construction is associated with a 21 percent higher proportion of subprime loans. Other research has documented a relationship between subprime lending and the housing cycle. Mian and Sufi (2008) show that zip codes where previously constrained borrowers subsequently received mortgage credit had higher rates of home price appreciation. Mayer and Sinai (2007) demonstrate that metropolitan areas with higher subprime originations had greater "excess" appreciation in price-to-rent ratios above fundamental values. The extent to which subprime lending either helped cause this housing boom or was a consequence of it remains an open question.

When we compare zip codes within an MSA in our MSA fixed-effects specification (column two), the results are similar to the across-MSA specification. The main exception is the coefficients on the various income quintiles, which suggest that subprime lending was most prevalent in zip codes in the top income quintile, and was lower by about the same amount in zip codes in the bottom four quintiles. As our income quintiles are defined relative to each MSA's distribution, it is a bit surprising that the income coefficients differ so much across the specifications with and without MSA fixed effects. However, the fact that the "percent with low VantageScore" coefficient is so much larger in the specification with MSA fixed effects than in the specification without fixed effects suggests that a correlation between income and credit score may underlie these results.[10] The coefficient on "percent with mid-VantageScore" is about the same in the two specifications—large and statistically significant.

Coefficients on the percent of black and Hispanic residents remain nearly the same as in column one. This result is striking, given that racial and ethnic concentrations vary substantially across MSAs. We drop the controls for home price appreciation, housing permits, and unemployment in this specification, as these effects are primarily identified across MSAs.

The next four columns report the results from separate analyses for purchases and refinancings. In 2005, the year of our analysis, subprime purchases

---

10. Indeed, when we run the fixed-effects specification with only the income variables, the coefficients are almost identical to the equivalent specification without fixed effects. When we then add the credit score variables to the fixed-effects specification, the income coefficients change to values that are similar to the coefficients in the full fixed-effects specification.

represent about 42 percent of originations in the LP data. Because purchases are a smaller share in the LP data, we expect the coefficients in the purchase regressions to be proportionately smaller than the coefficients in the refinancing regression if the correlation between the subprime measure and the covariates was the same for both purchases and refinancings. (Notice that the number of purchase loans plus refinancings sum to total originations, so that the sum of the coefficients in columns three and five adds to the coefficients in column one, and similarly the sum of columns two and four equals column 6.)

Overall, the pattern of subprime lending appears roughly similar for purchase loans as for refinancing. Although the income and credit score variables change a bit across the two mortgage purposes, the general pattern is similar. The race coefficients remain statistically and economically significant in all four specifications, as do those for home ownership rate and unemployment.

The major difference between purchase and refinance mortgages is that lagged construction has a stronger correlation with purchases than with refinancings. The coefficient on lagged construction is larger for purchase loans, even though refinancings represent the bulk of the sample. It is interesting, however, that locations with more new construction still appear to exhibit some additional refinancing activity, possibly because new units provide an additional base for refinancings.

Table 6.9 segments refinancing into "cash-out" and "not for cash-out" categories. Strikingly, cash-out refinancings dominate the sample, with about nine in 10 mortgage borrowers receiving some type of cash back. Even so, the coefficients appear to show similar patterns as in the other regressions.

Regressions with the HMDA Higher-Priced and HUD Subprime Lender Measures

We next use the higher-priced and HUD lender measures of subprime originations relative to housing units as the dependent variables (tables 6.10 and 6.11). Although the choice of subprime measure affects the estimates of the number of originations, as shown in tables 6.1 and 6.2, this choice does not appear to affect the regression results substantively. The factors associated with the incidence of subprime lending are similar across all three measures. However, patterns may diverge more in other years of the data, when the number of subprime originations differs more across measures.

The regressions in table 6.10 use HMDA higher-priced originations in 2005 per 100 housing units in 2000 as the dependent variable. Considerably more HMDA higher-priced loans than LP subprime loans were originated in 2005, so we expect the coefficients in table 6.10 to be, on average, 50 percent

TABLE 6.9 Incidence of LP Subprime Refinancings in MSA Zip Codes, 2005

	Subprime refinances for cash-out/100 units		Subprime refinances not for cash-out/100 units	
	(1)	(2)	(3)	(4)
Median income is	0.85**	−0.088	0.063**	−0.042**
in bottom quintile	(13.70)	(−1.34)	(8.93)	(−6.24)
Median income is	0.44**	−0.20**	0.048**	−0.028**
in second quintile	(9.59)	(−4.02)	(9.14)	(−4.80)
Median income is	0.24**	−0.23**	0.039**	−0.019**
in third quintile	(5.73)	(−5.26)	(8.19)	(−3.75)
Median income is	0.032	−0.20**	0.027**	−0.0082*
in fourth quintile	(0.95)	(−5.86)	(6.91)	(−1.93)
Percent with low	−0.011**	0.017**	−0.0012*	0.0039**
VantageScore	(−3.04)	(4.13)	(−1.80)	(9.20)
Percent with	0.15**	0.21**	0.016**	0.024**
mid-VantageScore	(15.43)	(22.34)	(15.07)	(21.15)
Percent of population	0.035**	0.032**	0.0031**	0.0021**
black	(16.85)	(16.12)	(14.75)	(10.01)
Percent of population	0.023**	0.031**	0.0018**	0.0014**
Hispanic	(12.32)	(14.45)	(10.75)	(6.57)
Percent ownership rate	0.021**	0.028**	0.0033**	0.0035**
	(15.38)	(22.32)	(19.61)	(26.91)
Percent unemployed	0.10**	—	0.0093**	—
	(6.87)	—	(5.60)	—
HPI appreciation in	0.14**	—	−0.00012	—
previous year	(34.69)	—	(−0.47)	—
Lagged permits in	0.19**	—	0.029**	—
United States/no. units	(14.45)	—	(19.59)	—
Constant	−3.87**	−3.61**	−0.31**	−0.42**
	(−21.66)	(−22.99)	(−18.18)	(−23.97)
MSA fixed effects	No	Yes	No	Yes
Observations	15,281	15,611	15,281	15,611
R-squared value	0.48	0.61	0.21	0.34
Mean of dependent variable	1.9		0.22	

NOTES: Dependent variable: LP subprime cash-out or non–cash-out refinances as a percent of units in 2000. Observations are zip codes. The sample is restricted to first-lien mortgages on properties located in an MSA that are not backed by manufactured housing or by buildings with more than four units. LP subprime denotes loans that were packaged into subprime mortgage pools. For the specifications without MSA fixed effects, we drop 330 zip codes with missing unemployment rate or permit data. LP = LoanPerformance; HPI = house price index; MSA = metropolitan statistical area; * = statistically significant at the .10 level; ** = statistically significant at the .05 level. T-statistics are shown in parentheses.

TABLE 6.10 Incidence of HMDA Higher-Priced Subprime Originations in MSA Zip Codes, 2005

	Subprime loans/100 units		Subprime purchases/100 units		Subprime refinances/100 units	
	(1)	(2)	(3)	(4)	(5)	(6)
Median income is in bottom quintile	1.59**	−0.67**	0.57**	−0.59**	1.02**	−0.09
	(9.83)	(−3.92)	(5.34)	(−5.22)	(15.54)	(−1.24)
Median income is in second quintile	0.88**	−0.72**	0.26**	−0.62**	0.62**	−0.11**
	(7.56)	(−5.44)	(3.35)	(−7.04)	(12.50)	(−1.99)
Median income is in third quintile	0.59**	−0.60**	0.18**	−0.47**	0.42**	−0.12**
	(5.14)	(−4.85)	(2.36)	(−5.65)	(8.63)	(−2.46)
Median income is in fourth quintile	0.18**	−0.44**	0.05	−0.30**	0.14**	−0.14**
	(2.09)	(−4.79)	(0.78)	(−4.89)	(3.68)	(−3.83)
Percent with low VantageScore	−0.023**	0.063**	−0.012**	0.035**	−0.012**	0.027**
	(−2.49)	(5.99)	(−2.03)	(5.11)	(−2.83)	(6.29)
Percent with mid-VantageScore	0.49**	0.64**	0.27**	0.37**	0.21**	0.27**
	(20.30)	(25.95)	(17.92)	(22.01)	(19.52)	(25.76)
Percent of population black	0.065**	0.043**	0.030**	0.016**	0.036**	0.028**
	(14.57)	(9.53)	(11.70)	(5.59)	(14.96)	(12.61)
Percent of population Hispanic	0.058**	0.066**	0.043**	0.041**	0.015**	0.025**
	(12.67)	(12.84)	(14.53)	(12.29)	(8.15)	(11.84)
Percent ownership rate	0.058**	0.082**	0.028**	0.043**	0.031**	0.040**
	(17.40)	(25.42)	(12.80)	(19.74)	(21.68)	(29.67)

(continued)

TABLE 6.10 (continued)

	Subprime loans/100 units		Subprime purchases/100 units		Subprime refinances/100 units	
	(1)	(2)	(3)	(4)	(5)	(6)
Percent unemployed	0.19**	—	0.11**	—	0.09**	—
	(5.17)		(4.38)		(5.56)	
HPI appreciation in previous year	0.26**	—	0.14**	—	0.12**	—
	(25.27)		(20.53)		(29.76)	
Lagged permits in United States/100 units	0.83**	—	0.56**	—	0.28**	—
	(20.47)		(19.59)		(18.14)	
Constant	−10.13**	−10.32**	−5.60**	−5.72**	−4.57**	−4.65**
	(−22.49)	(−25.95)	(−18.70)	(−21.45)	(−24.93)	(−27.61)
MSA fixed effects	No	Yes	No	Yes	No	Yes
Observations	15,281	15,611	15,281	15,611	15,281	15,611
R-squared value	0.45	0.58	0.37	0.49	0.48	0.63
Mean of dependent variable	5.38		2.84		2.54	

NOTES: Dependent variable: higher-priced subprime loans as a percentage of total housing units in 2000. Observations are zip codes. The sample is restricted to first-lien mortgages on properties located in an MSA that are not backed by manufactured housing or by buildings with more than four units. Higher-priced are mortgages in the HMDA data with an APR of 3 or more percentage points above Treasury securities. For the specifications without MSA fixed effects, we drop 330 zip codes with missing unemployment rate or permit data. HPI = house price index; MSA = metropolitan statistical area; ** = statistically significant at the .05 level. T-statistics are shown in parentheses.

TABLE 6.11 Incidence of HMDA HUD Subprime Originations in MSA Zip Codes, 2005

	Subprime loans/100 units		Subprime purchases/100 units		Subprime refinances/100 units	
	(1)	(2)	(3)	(4)	(5)	(6)
Income in bottom quintile	1.39**	−0.53**	0.48**	−0.45**	0.92**	−0.08
	(10.67)	(−4.21)	(6.03)	(−6.02)	(15.26)	(−1.33)
Income in second quintile	0.77**	−0.63**	0.21**	−0.51**	0.56**	−0.11**
	(8.46)	(−6.35)	(3.87)	(−8.70)	(12.51)	(−2.41)
Income in third quintile	0.47**	−0.54**	0.11**	−0.41**	0.36**	−0.13**
	(5.52)	(−6.04)	(2.25)	(−7.69)	(8.54)	(−3.14)
Income in fourth quintile	0.15**	−0.40**	0.04	−0.25**	0.11**	−0.15**
	(2.21)	(−5.80)	(1.01)	(−6.07)	(3.30)	(−4.45)
Percent with low VantageScore	−0.04**	0.03**	−0.02**	0.02**	−0.02**	0.01**
	(−5.75)	(3.58)	(−5.42)	(3.42)	(−5.24)	(3.34)
Percent with mid-VantageScore	0.35**	0.49**	0.17**	0.25**	0.18**	0.24**
	(19.58)	(27.15)	(16.63)	(23.23)	(19.16)	(26.46)
Percent of population black	0.06**	0.04**	0.03**	0.02**	0.03**	0.03**
	(16.56)	(12.47)	(13.94)	(8.22)	(15.77)	(14.14)
Percent of population Hispanic	0.06**	0.06**	0.04**	0.04**	0.02**	0.03**
	(15.18)	(15.91)	(16.61)	(15.02)	(11.63)	(14.66)
Percent ownership rate	0.04**	0.06**	0.02**	0.03**	0.03**	0.03**
	(15.50)	(24.28)	(10.02)	(17.98)	(19.74)	(28.05)

(continued)

TABLE 6.11 (continued)

	Subprime loans/100 units		Subprime purchases/100 units		Subprime refinances/100 units	
	(1)	(2)	(3)	(4)	(5)	(6)
Percent unemployed	0.17**	—	0.09**	—	0.08**	—
	(5.44)		(4.81)		(5.50)	
HPI appreciation in previous year	0.23**	—	0.10**	—	0.13**	—
	(28.97)		(22.23)		(34.05)	
Lagged permits in United States/100 units	0.52**	—	0.31**	—	0.21**	—
	(18.11)		(17.74)		(16.52)	
Constant	-7.37**	-7.71**	-3.45**	-3.76**	-3.92**	-3.95**
	(-21.07)	(-25.89)	(-16.73)	(-21.40)	(-23.46)	(-26.84)
MSA fixed effects	No	Yes	No	Yes	No	Yes
Observations	15,281	15,611	15,281	15,611	15,281	15,611
R-squared value	0.48	0.62	0.39	0.54	0.50	0.65
Mean of dependent variable	3.88		1.72		2.15	

NOTES: Dependent variable: HUD subprime loans as a percentage of total housing units in 2000. Observations are zip codes. The sample is restricted to first-lien mortgages on properties located in an MSA that are not backed by manufactured housing or by buildings with more than four units. HMDA HUD subprime are loans on the HMDA data originated by lenders on the HUD subprime lender list. For the specifications without MSA fixed effects, we drop 330 zip codes with missing unemployment rate or permit data. HPI = house price index; MSA = metropolitan statistical area; ** = statistically significant at the .05 level. T-statistics are shown in parentheses.

larger than those in table 6.8. Indeed, most of the coefficients are somewhat larger in the first column of table 6.10 than in that column in table 6.8. Smaller differences persist. For example, higher-priced loans are slightly overrepresented over the securitized subprime loans in the middle credit score category, but are relatively less prevalent in zip codes with higher black and Hispanic populations. This latter result suggests that studies based on the LP data might show a larger incidence of subprime lending in minority neighborhoods than studies based on the higher-priced data. Higher-priced loans are also somewhat less represented in locations with higher unemployment rates and higher past home price appreciation.

We show regressions with the HUD measure of subprime lenders in table 6.11. The mean number of loans originated by HUD subprime lenders is 3.93, about 8 percent more overall than in LP. Thus, coefficients in table 6.11 would be only slightly larger than those in table 6.8 if the measures of lending were closely comparable. In the first column, the only appreciable differences are that HUD subprime lenders seem more likely to lend in lower-income zip codes and less likely to lend in the worst credit score districts. Given the correlation between these two measures, such offsetting changes may well be due to random variation. Coefficients on other variables are quite similar.

Regressions with LP Originations in Relation to All HMDA Originations

Finally, we consider how our results would differ if we normalized LP subprime originations by all HMDA originations in 2005 (table 6.12).[11] The demographic factors associated with subprime originations are consistent with the earlier regressions: zip codes with more residents who are low-income, minorities, owner-occupants, or unemployed, or who have poor credit, have more subprime originations. Adjusting for the fact that subprime mortgages are about 7.5 times more prevalent as a share of loan originations than of housing units, the magnitudes of the coefficients are about the same as in earlier regressions.

However, home price appreciation and construction permits play a small role in these regressions. A one standard deviation increase in home price appreciation is associated with a 5 percent increase in subprime originations as a

---

11. We get similar results when we use HMDA higher-priced originations relative to all HMDA originations and HUD lender originations relative to all HMDA originations as the dependent variables in these regressions.

TABLE 6.12 Incidence of LP Subprime Originations in MSA Zip Codes, 2005

	Subprime loans/ 100 total loans		Subprime purchases/ 100 total loans		Subprime refinances/ 100 total loans	
	(1)	(2)	(3)	(4)	(5)	(6)
Median income is in bottom quintile	5.64**	3.16**	0.88**	0.20	4.75**	2.96**
	(19.29)	(10.81)	(5.49)	(1.21)	(25.62)	(16.17)
Median income is in second quintile	3.40**	1.60**	0.41**	−0.27**	3.00**	1.87**
	(15.70)	(6.88)	(3.50)	(−2.00)	(20.59)	(12.86)
Median income is in third quintile	2.38**	1.03**	0.38**	−0.11	2.00**	1.15**
	(12.74)	(5.42)	(3.76)	(−1.05)	(16.25)	(9.73)
Median income is in fourth quintile	1.36**	0.62**	0.39**	0.09	0.96**	0.53**
	(8.73)	(4.15)	(4.52)	(1.06)	(9.41)	(5.67)
Percent with low VantageScore	0.44**	0.51**	0.26**	0.29**	0.18**	0.22**
	(25.78)	(27.17)	(24.37)	(24.18)	(18.66)	(21.00)
Percent with mid-VantageScore	−0.09**	0.14**	−0.07**	0.02	−0.02	0.12**
	(−1.98)	(3.38)	(−2.69)	(0.82)	(−0.62)	(4.93)
Percent of population black	0.18**	0.20**	0.05**	0.05**	0.13**	0.15**
	(18.75)	(21.62)	(9.37)	(8.36)	(22.94)	(29.43)

	(1)	(2)	(3)	(4)	(5)	(6)
Percent of population Hispanic	0.09**	0.08**	0.06**	0.02**	0.04**	0.06**
	(14.77)	(11.67)	(14.78)	(6.15)	(9.59)	(11.92)
Percent ownership rate	0.11**	0.12**	0.04**	0.04**	0.07**	0.08**
	(19.96)	(23.19)	(11.38)	(14.02)	(20.88)	(23.52)
Percent unemployed	0.67**	—	0.23**	—	0.45**	—
	(9.17)	—	(5.57)	—	(10.26)	—
HPI appreciation in previous year	0.21**	—	−0.01	—	0.21**	—
	(17.55)	—	(−1.01)	—	(26.44)	—
Lagged permits in United States/100 units	0.14**	—	0.28**	—	−0.14**	—
	(2.78)	—	(10.22)	—	(−4.65)	—
Constant	−9.49**	−8.252**	−3.53**	−3.521**	−5.96**	−4.730**
	(−14.28)	(−14.68)	(−9.32)	(−10.44)	(−14.39)	(−13.28)
MSA fixed effects	No	Yes	No	Yes	No	Yes
Observations	15,281	15,611	15,281	15,611	15,281	15,611
R-squared value	0.37	0.43	0.35	0.42	0.33	0.40
Mean of dependent variable	27.95		10.61		17.33	

NOTES: Dependent variable: LP subprime originations as a percent of all HMDA originations in 2005. Observations are zip codes. The sample is restricted to first-lien mortgages on properties located in an MSA that are not backed by manufactured housing or by buildings with more than four units. LP subprime denotes loans that were packaged into subprime mortgage pools. For the specifications without MSA fixed effects, we drop 330 zip codes with missing unemployment rate or permit data. HPI = house price index; MSA = metropolitan statistical area; ** = statistically significant at the .05 level. T-statistics are shown in parentheses.

share of all originations, as opposed to a 39 percent increase as a share of housing units. Likewise, a one standard deviation increase in housing permits is associated with a less than 1 percent increase in subprime originations relative to all originations, as opposed to a 21 percent increase relative to housing units. When we break out purchases and refinances separately, home price appreciation is positively associated only with refinances, whereas permits are positively associated only with purchase mortgages. We observed a similar but less dramatic pattern in the housing units specifications.

These regression results are consistent with our earlier conclusion, based on tables 6.3–6.6, that subprime originations as a share of housing units appear to be more prominent in hot housing markets, whereas subprime originations as a share of all originations appear to be more prominent in depressed housing markets. In areas with hot housing markets, both prime and subprime originations may be elevated, and so subprime mortgages are high in relation to housing units but not necessarily in relation to originations. However, subprime originations may also appear high in relation to housing units in hot housing markets because our 2000 measure of housing units understates, by a greater degree, the true 2005 level.

Conclusions and Future Research

We explore a number of thought-provoking patterns in the geographic dispersion of subprime lending. Subprime originations appear to be heavily concentrated in fast-growing parts of the country with considerable new construction, such as Florida, California, Nevada, and the Washington, DC area. These locations saw home prices rise at faster-than-average rates relative to their own history and relative to the rest of the country. However, this link between construction, home prices, and subprime lending is not universal, as other markets with high home price growth, such as the Northeast, did not see especially high rates of subprime usage. Subprime loans were also heavily concentrated in zip codes with more residents in the moderate credit score category and more black and Hispanic residents. Areas with lower income and higher unemployment had more subprime lending, but these associations are smaller in magnitude.

The measure that provides the most reliable estimate of subprime originations appears to differ over time. From the 1990s through the early 2000s, most subprime loans were originated by subprime specialists, and fewer of these loans were securitized. For these years, the HUD measure appears to gauge subprime originations most reliably. Later, more subprime loans were originated by lenders that traditionally operated in the prime market, and more of these loans were securitized. For this period, the LP data may be the best choice. At the moment, both the HUD lender and the LP measures are likely to miss large shares of subprime originations—the LP data because securitization of subprime loans has dried up, and the HUD measure because many subprime specialists have gone out of business. For the time being, the HMDA higher-priced measure may provide the most comprehensive coverage.

Our results provide only hints of answers to many of the most important questions about the subprime crisis, leaving much room for future research. We find that subprime originations are more prevalent in black and Hispanic zip codes, but we do not, at this point, have data that allow us to confidently determine why that occurred. Some previous work has suggested that minorities have been underserved by mortgage markets in the past and are more likely to be credit constrained (Charles and Hurst, 2002; Gabriel and Rosenthal, 2005; Ladd, 1998). To the extent that subprime loans provided credit to underserved areas, either to obtain cash back on homes or to purchase new homes, such credit may have been a positive development for some borrowers. However, it is also possible that subprime loans were substituted for conventional loans, leaving some minority borrowers with higher-cost credit than they might have otherwise received. Disentangling these two effects is an important task for future studies.

The link between subprime lending and new construction and home price appreciation is also intriguing. Although we do not make any causal claim in this chapter, Mian and Sufi (2008) suggest that greater securitized subprime usage leads to home price appreciation. Mayer and Sinai (2007) find a correlation between subprime lending and higher price-to-rent ratios. However, neither analysis fully explains the puzzle of some MSAs having high subprime concentrations, such as Las Vegas and Miami, where both new construction and home prices rose rapidly, while other MSAs with high subprime concentrations, such as Houston and Atlanta, saw high construction but not high rates of home price appreciation.

Finally, unlike previous studies, we focus on subprime originations as a share of housing units, not of total mortgage originations. Economically stressed states such as Michigan and Ohio had low rates of subprime lending in relation to the number of housing units, but high rates in relation to the number of originations. This finding suggests that the relatively small volume of lending that occurred in these states was disproportionately subprime. It is also consistent with our regression result that subprime originations were more prevalent in areas with higher unemployment rates. However, it does not resolve the question of whether subprime mortgages provided valuable credit to credit-constrained households in these areas or actually amplified the existing economic stress.

APPENDIX: MERGING CENSUS TRACT AND ZIP CODE DATA

This appendix describes how we merged tract-level data from HMDA and the census to zip code–level data from LP.

We based the merge on a zip code tabulation area (ZCTA) to census tract crosswalk from the Missouri Census Data Center (http://mcdc2.missouri .edu/websas/geocorr2k.html). ZCTAs are generalized representations of zip codes developed by the U.S. Bureau of the Census to facilitate census tract–zip code matches. Each ZCTA is composed of the census blocks (subunits of census tracts) that correspond to a given zip code. If a census block spans zip codes, some residents of that block may be assigned to the wrong zip code. The file also excludes zip codes created after January 2000 as well as changes made to zip code boundaries after that date. We use the ZCTA tabulation designed for the 2000 census.

To carry out this merge, we aggregated the relevant HMDA variables to the census tract level, and then merged on the ZCTA definitions for each tract. If a census tract corresponded to more than one ZCTA, we created one observation for each census tract–ZCTA pair. For each observation, we also included a weight, provided by the Missouri Census Data Center, that indicates what share of households in a given tract lived in each ZCTA. Using this weight, we aggregated the census tracts to the ZCTA level, and merged on the zip code–level LP data by the ZCTA variable. Because HMDA data are comprehensive only for counties within MSAs, we dropped zip codes that straddled MSA lines or lay entirely outside of an MSA.

We calculated the census-tract-level variables that are percentage variables (such as the percent of residents with low VantageScores) at the zip code level once we created the final data set. That is, we aggregated the number of residents with low VantageScores and the number of total residents to the zip code level, and then calculated the share. We believe that this procedure is more robust to outliers than calculating these percentage variables at the census tract level and then aggregating to the zip code level.

REFERENCES

Avery, Robert, Kenneth Brevoort, and Glenn Canner. 2007a. "The 2006 HMDA Data." *Federal Reserve Bulletin* 93: A73–A109.

———. 2007b. "Opportunities and Issues in Using HMDA Data." *Journal of Real Estate Research* 29(4): 351–379.

Avery, Robert, Glenn Canner, and Robert Cook. 2005. "New Information Reported Under HMDA and Its Application in Fair Lending Enforcement." *Federal Reserve Bulletin* 91: 344–394.

Bostic, Raphael, Kathleen Engel, Patricia McCoy, Anthony Pennington-Cross, and Susan Wachter. 2008. "State and Local Anti–Predatory Lending Laws: The Effect of Legal Enforcement Mechanisms." *Journal of Economics and Business* 60(1–2): 47–66.

Brooks, Rick, and Constance Mitchell Ford. 2007. "The United States of Subprime." *Wall Street Journal*, October 11, A1. http://online.wsj.com/article/SB1192059255 19455321.html.

Brooks, Rick, and Ruth Simon. 2007. "Subprime Debacle Traps Even Very Credit-Worthy." *Wall Street Journal*, December 3, A1. http://online.wsj.com/article/SB119662974358911035.html.

Calem, Paul, Kevin Gillen, and Susan Wachter. 2004. "The Neighborhood Distribution of Subprime Mortgage Lending." *Journal of Real Estate Finance and Economics* 29(4): 393–410.

Center for Responsible Lending. 2006. "Unfair Lending: The Effect of Race and Ethnicity on the Price of Subprime Mortgages." May.

Charles, Kerwin Kofi, and Erik Hurst. 2002. "The Transition to Home Ownership and the Black-White Wealth Gap." *Review of Economics and Statistics* 84(2): 281–297.

Consumer Federation of America. 2006. "Subprime Locations: Patterns of Geographic Disparity in Subprime Lending." September.

Demyanyk, Yuliya, and Otto Van Hemert. 2008. "Understanding the Subprime Mortgage Crisis." Social Science Research Network Working Paper.

Gabriel, Stuart, and Stuart Rosenthal. 2005. "Homeownership in the 1980s and 1990s: Aggregate Trends and Racial Gaps." *Journal of Urban Economics* 57(1): 101–127.

Gerardi, Kristopher, Adam Hale Shapiro, and Paul S. Willen. 2007. "Subprime Outcomes: Risky Mortgages, Homeownership Experiences, and Foreclosures." Federal Reserve Bank of Boston Working Paper No. 07-15.

Inside Mortgage Finance. 2006. *The 2006 Mortgage Market Statistical Annual.* Bethesda, MD: Inside Mortgage Finance Publications.

Keys, Benjamin J., Tanmoy K. Mukherjee, Amit Seru, and Vikrant Vig. 2008. "Did Securitization Lead to Lax Screening? Evidence from Subprime Loans." Social Science Research Network Working Paper.

Ladd, Helen. 1998. "Evidence on Discrimination in Credit Markets." *Journal of Economic Perspectives* 1 (Spring): 223–234.

Mayer, Christopher, and Todd Sinai. 2007. "Housing and Behavioral Finance." Paper presented at the Federal Reserve Bank of Boston Conference "Implications of Behavioral Economics on Economic Policy."

Mian, Atif, and Amir Sufi. 2008. "The Consequences of Mortgage Credit Expansion: Evidence from the 2007 Mortgage Default Crisis." Social Science Research Network Working Paper.

Pennington-Cross, Anthony, and Giang Ho. 2006. "The Termination of Subprime Hybrid and Fixed Rate Mortgages." Federal Reserve Bank of St. Louis Working Paper 2006-042A.

Scheessele, Randall. 2002. "Black and White Disparities in Subprime Mortgage Refinance Lending." Housing Finance Policy Working Paper Series, HF-014. Washington, DC: U.S. Department of Housing and Urban Development.

U.S. Department of Housing and Urban Development. 2000. *Unequal Burden: Income and Racial Disparities in Subprime Lending in America.* http://www.huduser.org/publications/fairhsg/unequal.html.

C. F. SIRMANS AND KERRY D. VANDELL

It is a basic tenet of policy analysis that in order to prescribe an appropriate set of policies responsive to an identified policy issue, one must first be able to define the issue. Such has been the problem with analysis of the recent credit crisis that has gripped the capital markets in the United States and spread internationally. "Subprime" mortgages frequently have been blamed in the press, and have pervaded public consciousness, as being the prime cause of the recent rapid run-up in house prices, as well as the ensuing "bust" (already in excess of 30 percent in some jurisdictions) and a spike in defaults.

Chris Mayer and Karen Pence make one of the first serious attempts at trying to address a major omission in the search for a policy solution to this crisis: not only do we not know where subprime loans have been made and who has gotten them or why, we do not even know what a subprime loan is. Mayer and Pence consider several alternatives and settle on the Department of Housing and Urban Development's (HUD's) survey of loans made by subprime lenders and reported in the Home Mortgage Disclosure Act (HMDA) as the most complete estimate of the population of subprime loans over the period of the rapid spread of alternative private mortgage products—from the late 1990s to 2007. They recognize that this may include some loans that are actually prime, but made by subprime lenders, and that it may exclude some subprime loans made by prime lenders. Nonetheless, they consider it to be the best estimate available, representing about 12 percent of total HMDA loans made between 1998 and 2005, with slightly more used for refinancing (about 13 percent) than for purchase (about 10 percent). They decide to use the metric of subprime loans per 100 housing units, rather than subprime loans per total loans made, as the basis for measuring subprime origination density, because they assert that the availability of subprime loans may affect the decision to take out a loan as well as the decision of what type of loan to choose. Only first-lien mortgages that originated in zip codes within metropolitan statistical areas (MSAs) in the 48 contiguous states and Washington, DC are included in the sample, excluding manufactured home loans and those written on properties with five or more units. Loans below $25,000 are also dropped because they are likely junior liens that have been miscoded.

Next, the authors turn to the geographic dispersion of subprime lending. They find concentrations especially pronounced in the fastest-growing MSAs in the West and South, with fewer in the Midwest and Northeast, with the exceptions of certain cities in these areas such as Washington, DC, Chicago, and Providence. The exurbs and fastest-growing affordable first-time home-buyer communities on the fringes of these metropolitan areas—including Riverside County and the fringes of the San Francisco Bay Area, as well as suburban areas of other cities, such as Boston—saw the most use of subprime mortgages. Only in a few central cities, such as Atlanta, Houston, and Chicago, was subprime lending very apparent. Stagnant industrial areas in the Midwest, such as Cleveland and Detroit, saw little concentration of subprime lending (based on the number of housing units), even though they saw high rates of default on such loans. Clearly, there was a disconnect between viewing subprime lending on the basis of total housing units versus the number of totals loans made.

First, we comment on the definitional aspects of Mayer and Pence's analysis, its scope, and their basic observations of the volume, purpose, and location of lending according to their definitions. Then we examine their regression analysis, which seeks to isolate various correlates with subprime lending activity.

Although we applaud their rigorous definitional criteria, empirical analysis, and interpretation of the results, we have two primary concerns with the Mayer-Pence analysis as it stands. First, their primary reliance on the number of housing units as the normalization standard for subprime presence is flawed in a couple of ways, to a degree that renders its selection questionable.

The first of these flaws is the fact that the denominator is the number of housing units, not the number of owner-occupied housing units. This clearly biases the results toward underestimation of subprime impact in largely renter-occupied areas, as rental stock would not generally be considered relevant for consideration, hence should be excluded from the analysis.[1]

The second flaw is already recognized by the authors: the use of a per-housing-unit denominator tends to bias the apparent density of subprime loan activity upward in high-growth areas with high house price appreciation, as compared with a per-loan originated denominator.

To decide on the proper basis for normalizing subprime loan origination activity, one must recognize that the ultimate question is the extent to which

---

1. There are two conditions that would cause an exception to this statement. The first is that, at the margin, subprime lending could encourage rental stock to become owner-occupied. However, most of the evidence points to the fact that the preponderance of the new home ownership in the subprime market was generated through new construction and not conversion of an existing unit from rental occupancy to ownership. The second condition is that investor loans could be intended to make units available for rental occupancy as well as home ownership through "flipping." However, it is not clear that the HUD data from subprime lenders includes investor (i.e., non–owner-occupant) loans. Thus, the preponderance of evidence suggests that Mayer and Pence should have excluded the existing rental stock from the per-housing-unit denominator.

the availability of subprime lending made a difference in the market. This difference could reference any of several conditions: the level of home ownership, price changes (up or down), default rates, and so forth. Thus, the appropriate denominator would depend on the dimension of housing market impact in which policy makers are interested.

In the case of changes in home ownership and house prices, we would argue that the most appropriate denominator is per loan origination for the purpose of purchase and owner occupancy (for home ownership) or purchase and either owner or renter occupancy (for house prices). Changes in the level of home ownership and house prices come exclusively from actual sales that establish comparables for use in estimating future house price levels. Subprime lending for the purpose of cash-out or lowering the interest rate or monthly payment provides greater consumption and investment potential to the household but does not directly influence house prices or the level of home ownership. Default rates are a somewhat different matter, however, in that the contemporaneous loan-to-value ratio (LTV) is the dominant variable, and this could be exacerbated through refinancing as well as purchase. Thus, if one is interested in addressing the causes of increased default rates, the most appropriate denominator may be per total loan origination for all purposes.

The second primary concern has to do with Mayer and Pence's narrow (if carefully drawn) perception of "subprime" as the appropriate indicator of credit newly available to households that would otherwise have been excluded from (or forced to pay significantly more for) it. As indicated before, they confine their sample to HUD-reported first-lien mortgages only. Thus, their sample would omit many of the other novel private-market instruments introduced during the early 2000s that may not be subprime in the sense of making credit available to lower-credit-quality borrowers, but that may still affect the availability or cost of credit otherwise unavailable to borrowers for the purpose of purchase or refinancing. These include such novelties as Alt-As (sometimes called no-docs or low-docs), option-ARMs, teaser-rate ARMs, interest-only (IO) mortgages, 2-28s, high loan-to-value ratio loans (HLTVs, sometimes called 125s), and others. Furthermore, by considering only first-lien mortgages, they miss another set of loan structures that make use of structured finance vehicles, including second and (sometimes) third liens. An example is the 80-10-10 arrangement, which substituted subordinate liens for private mortgage insurance (PMI) and could even require no down payment. To examine fully the anatomy of the impact of the new array of alternative mortgage designs on the housing and mortgage markets, one must move beyond the subprime, however the term is defined, to explore in much greater detail the full spectrum of products available on the market.

Next, we turn our attention to the regression results reported in the chapter. What variables are correlated with the higher subprime loan shares? What are the implications of observed variations in subprime lending? Does the analysis reveal potential benefits (or costs) of subprime lending that might have policy implications?

To examine these questions, the authors estimate a series of cross-sectional regression models to examine the correlation between various measures of subprime lending at the MSA zip code level (a total sample of about 15,000 geographic areas) and a set of independent variables representing various characteristics of the zip codes. Three measures of subprime lending are used as the dependent variable: the number of LoanPerformance subprime mortgages, HMDA high-cost loans, and mortgages by HUD-reported subprime loans in HMDA per 100 housing units based on the 2000 census. In addition, analysis is done on the pooled sample as well as on disaggregated samples consisting of purchase loans and refinancings. As a further robustness check, Mayer and Pence estimate the regressions with and without MSA fixed effects. The results are not qualitatively different across purpose of the loan or with the fixed effects.

The independent variables used include the percentage minority, a measure of credit score, the level of unemployment, the amount of new construction, and house price appreciation trends. The summary statistics for their sample, reported in table 6.7, appear to be reasonable. As might be expected, zip codes exhibit skewness in the percentage minority. The other variables are consistent with national averages.

What do we learn from their regressions? First, the proportion of subprime mortgages goes up with increases in the percentage minority. Second, the proportion of subprime mortgages is higher in zip codes with mid-level credit scores. Third, zip codes in the bottom of the income distribution have the highest proportion of subprime mortgages. Fourth, higher unemployment rates result in a greater proportion of subprime mortgages. Fifth, zip codes with high (past) house price appreciation have a greater proportion of subprime mortgages. Sixth, higher proportions of subprime loans are in zip codes with higher construction activity.

What are some implications of their analysis for policy decisions related to the subprime "problem"? As Mayer and Pence note, the positive correlation with the unemployment rate suggests that subprime loans are an additional source of credit when economic conditions turn down and thus may offer some advantages in terms of stabilizing declining housing markets. The positive correlation with construction suggests that subprime lending probably contributed to the housing boom. It is interesting to note that potential policies leading to higher credit scores would significantly reduce the proportion of subprime mortgages. Mayer and Pence's results also suggest that policies that make it more difficult to originate subprime mortgages may limit the effects these mortgages could have in stabilizing declining local markets.

Clearly, understanding the what, who, and where aspects of the subprime mortgage market are important. Subprime mortgages represent a critical segment of the overall housing finance system and serve a major role in making home ownership, and its accompanying social benefits, possible for underserved households. Policies about subprime underwriting will have substantial benefits if implemented correctly and potentially harmful effects if not carefully analyzed. In spite of our suggestions for refinement of their analysis, however, we commend Chris Mayer and Karen Spence for their careful initiation of an important line of investigation that can have significant implications for mortgage credit policy.

7

Government-Sponsored Enterprises, the Community Reinvestment Act, and Home Ownership in Targeted Underserved Neighborhoods

STUART A. GABRIEL
STUART S. ROSENTHAL

Efforts to expand access to mortgage credit and to increase home ownership have dominated U.S. federal housing policy for much of the last
20 years. In support of those objectives, the Clinton administration in
1994 called for the Department of Housing and Urban Development (HUD)
to create programs designed to increase home ownership, especially among
minorities and low-income families.[1] In 2002, the Bush administration
called for a sharp increase in minority home ownership by 2010.[2] These policy goals went hand in hand with long-standing efforts to expand access to
mortgage credit among disadvantaged segments of society. The 1977 Community Reinvestment Act (CRA) targets regulated financial institutions and
mandates increased mortgage lending in underserved areas; the 1992 Federal Housing Enterprise Financial Safety and Soundness Act, often referred
to as the GSE Act (GSEA), targets the giant secondary-market institutions,
Fannie Mae, and Freddie Mac, and mandates increased purchases of con-

Funding for this project from the National Association of Realtors is greatly appreciated. We thank Bill Apgar, Paul Bishop, Glenn Canner, Larry Jones, John Quigley, and an anonymous referee for helpful comments. Any errors are our own.

1. See http://www.pragueinstitute.org/housing_us.htm for the full text of, and related commentary to,
President Bill Clinton's 1994 letter to HUD Secretary Henry Cisneros.

2. See http://www.whitehouse.gov/news/releases/2002/06/20020618-1.html for the full text of President
George W. Bush's remarks.

forming loans in underserved communities. Although these federal government efforts to promote increased access to mortgage credit and home ownership have been prominent, it is far less apparent what effect these initiatives have actually had on access to credit and home ownership. This chapter seeks to fill part of that gap.

On the surface, there is every reason to anticipate that the CRA and GSEA would increase lending and home ownership in targeted, underserved tracts: the CRA mandates that primary lenders provide additional credit to such communities, and Fannie Mae and Freddie Mac are obliged to securitize more loans in those areas. However, the intended beneficial effects of the government-sponsored enterprise (GSE) and CRA legislation in underserved communities may be partly offset for a variety of reasons. For example, with less than perfectly elastic credit supply, efforts to increase loan originations in one market segment (e.g., conforming versus nonconforming) would imply reduced lending activity in the alternate market segment. In addition, GSE loan purchase activity may be partly offset by crowd-out of unsubsidized private-entity loan purchases in the secondary market (as shown in Gabriel and Rosenthal, 2007a).[3] Using a regression discontinuity approach, we compare mortgage lending activity and home ownership rates in census tracts just above and below the GSEA and CRA "underserved" income cutoffs. Our focus on census tracts close to the income cutoffs dictated by the GSEA and CRA legislation helps control for unobserved factors that may obscure the impact of these policies. A long list of census tract socioeconomic attributes and county fixed effects are also included in the regression models to further control for the influence of unobserved effects.

Our priors are influenced by the institutional detail of the GSEA and CRA programs, along with potential substitution between markets. With regard to GSEA effects, it is important to emphasize that the GSEs are obliged to purchase a disproportionate number of conventional, conforming loans in underserved tracts. Those loan purchases must conform to GSEA underwriting requirements and must not exceed loan size limitations set forth by the regulator. If the number of loans supplied to the secondary mortgage market is less than perfectly elastic, it is possible that GSEA efforts to acquire greater numbers of conforming loans could encourage primary lenders to originate conforming size loans at the expense of nonconforming mortgages. This suggests

---

3. If GSEA purchase activity is fully offset by crowd-out of non-GSEA private-sector secondary-market purchases, then GSEA regulations would have no effect on loan supply in either the conforming or nonconforming market segments. Gabriel and Rosenthal (2007a) find evidence of such effects in 2004. But in 1994, 1996, 1998, 2000, and 2002, there is evidence of only partial crowd-out; this is consistent with the idea that GSEA activities affected credit supplies in those years.

that some of the increased activity in the conforming sector in response to the purchase goals set forth in the GSEA could be partly offset by declines in non-conforming loan activity.[4] This is one reason why GSE regulations may have a limited effect on home ownership rates in targeted, underserved census tracts. A second reason, noted above, is that some portion of the GSEA purchase activity in targeted underserved tracts could be offset through the crowd-out of loan purchases by unsubsidized private-sector secondary-market entities.

The anticipated possible effects of CRA legislation are different. The CRA mandates increased lending activity by regulated financial institutions in targeted zones, but does not impose restrictions on the size or type of loans originated. The expansion in supply of local credit resulting from the CRA will tend to lower the local cost of borrowing. At the margin, this could encourage individuals who would have secured loans in the absence of the program to obtain larger loans. In this case, the CRA could increase loan activity in the nonconforming segment and decrease activity in the conforming segment while having little impact on home ownership. It is also possible that the reduced cost of credit resulting from the CRA could encourage some renters to secure loans and switch to home ownership. In this case, the CRA could have a positive impact on conforming-loan-size lending activity and should increase home ownership.

We test for these effects using Home Mortgage Disclosure Act (HMDA) data from 2000 in conjunction with U.S. Bureau of the Census tract information from 1990 and 2000. From HMDA, we measure the number of conforming and nonconforming loan size applications and originations in a census tract, as well as the GSEA share of mortgage loans purchased in the tract. From the census tract data, we obtain information on tract home ownership rates, as well as a host of socioeconomic tract attributes in both 1990 and 2000. Our key dependent variables are the number of applications and originations for conforming and nonconforming sized loans at the census tract level. We also examine impacts on the sum of conforming and nonconforming activity. In addition, we examine impacts on the difference in home ownership rates between 1990 and 2000. In all of these regressions, our unit of observation is the census tract.

To isolate the GSEA and CRA effects, we first estimate our models using the full sample of census tracts regardless of income, controlling for tract socioeconomic status (SES) attributes and county fixed effects. Results from these models are compared to samples that restrict the census tracts to those

---

4. Note that increased secondary-market demand for conforming sized loans causes the price of conforming loans to increase relative to that of nonconforming mortgages. Primary lenders will likely then respond by making conforming loans more affordable, and this will induce some loan applicants to substitute conforming for nonconforming sized loans.

within 10 percent of the GSEA and CRA income cutoffs and to those within 5 percent of the cutoffs.

Our results have important implications for the assessment of GSEA and CRA policies. With respect to GSEA effects, we find essentially no evidence that designating a tract as underserved increases either lending activity or home ownership in the community. This finding is consistent with the possibility that GSEA activity may be offset by various forms of crowd-out among loan size segments of the market (i.e., conforming versus nonconforming) or private secondary-market loan purchases (as examined by Gabriel and Rosenthal, 2007a). We also cannot rule out the possibility that unobserved factors may account for our limited evidence of positive GSEA effects. In contrast, we do find evidence of a positive impact the CRA has on nonconforming mortgage lending. This result is robust to sample composition and model specification. We do not detect reliable evidence of a CRA impact on lending activity in the conforming sector. Together, these patterns suggest that the CRA expands the supply of mortgage credit in targeted tracts and may also draw some local renters into home ownership. Consistent with that possibility, our estimates indicate a small positive CRA effect on local home ownership rates. Nevertheless, on balance, the lack of more compelling evidence of GSEA and CRA effects on mortgage lending and home ownership rates among targeted underserved tracts is striking and warrants further attention in the context of recent debate regarding the federal policy emphasis on home ownership and the future of the GSEs.

The plan for the remainder of the chapter is as follows. The following section provides further context by briefly describing the institutional features of the CRA and GSEA policies. It also reviews previous literature on the impact of these programs. The section after that describes the data and sample designs central to the research approach, followed by a presentation of the estimates of our various models and then the conclusion to the chapter.

BACKGROUND

Institutional Context

As already noted, as a matter of long-standing policy the U.S. government has sought to aggressively increase the flow of mortgage capital to lower-income, minority, and underserved communities. Central to these efforts have been the passage of the 1977 CRA and the 1992 GSEA. These acts form the cornerstone of government efforts to enhance the availability of credit and the attainment of home ownership among targeted households and zones. The government regulation operates on two margins, focusing both on the origination of loans by financial institutions in the primary market (CRA) and the purchase of loans by government-sponsored enterprises in the secondary market (GSEA). This section provides a brief overview of these policies.

The CRA directs the federal banking regulatory agencies to evaluate the extent to which federally insured banking institutions meet the credit needs of all communities in their service areas, including lower-income areas, while maintaining safe and sound operations.[5] The legislation derived, in part, from concerns that banking institutions were engaged in "redlining," a practice by which lenders fail to seek out lending opportunities in minority and lower-income neighborhoods. In the context of federal bank examinations, the CRA instructs regulators to consider the institution's CRA performance when reviewing applications for merger, acquisition, or other structural change. Among other tests, CRA examinations of banking institutions scrutinize the geographic distribution of lending activities. These examinations compare the proportion of loans extended within the institution's CRA "assessment area" as compared to the proportion of loans extended outside of its assessment area.[6] CRA examinations also take note of the distribution of neighborhood income status associated with loans issued to different locations within a financial institution's assessment area. For this portion of the exam, lending in low-to-moderate-income neighborhoods receives particular weight.[7]

An important feature of the CRA that we draw upon in the empirical work to follow is the policy-specific definition of a low-income neighborhood. For these purposes, the CRA defines low-to-moderate-income neighborhoods as census tracts that have a median family income of less than 80 percent of the median family income in the metropolitan area in which the census tract is located (Federal Reserve System, 1990).[8] Regulatory agencies use this definition

---

5. The federal agencies that have regulatory authority under the CRA include the Board of Governors of the Federal Reserve System, the Office of the Comptroller of the Currency, the Federal Deposit Insurance Corporation, and the Office of Thrift Supervision.

6. Banking institutions specify their CRA assessment area as the set of locations in which the institution operates branches and conducts much of its lending activity. Definitions of CRA assessment areas must be approved by the federal regulatory agencies and are used by examiners during CRA evaluations. See Board of Governors of the Federal Reserve System (2000) for further details.

7. The CRA also requires examiners to take note of the distribution of borrower income for loans issued to families within an institution's assessment area.

8. To assess depository-institution performance, the CRA requires specific tests of lending, investment, and service activities. Also assessed are the institution's product offerings and business strategy, its capacities and constraints, its past performance, the performance of similarly situated lenders, and information and public commentary contained in the institution's public CRA file. When assessing lending activities, the CRA considers the geographic distribution of lending, the distribution of lending across different borrower groups, community development lending, and other innovative lending practices consistent with the larger CRA goals.

in CRA performance evaluations of lending activity in targeted locations. These evaluations take account of differences in lending activity inside and outside of targeted tracts within a given metropolitan area. To the extent that the CRA motivates lenders to extend credit to low-income areas, CRA-targeted census tracts should exhibit disproportionate lending activity and higher rates of home ownership when compared to tracts just above the CRA income cut-off. This idea forms the basis for part of the empirical work to follow. Moreover, because regulators typically use data from the HMDA to conduct CRA examinations, evidence of elevated lending activity should be evident in these data.[9] Partly for that reason, we use HMDA data for the analysis later in the chapter.

The secondary market for mortgages long has been dominated by Fannie Mae and Freddie Mac. These two giant GSEs have accounted for the majority of conventional, conforming home mortgage purchases. Fannie Mae and Freddie Mac are federally chartered private corporations. Given their federal charters, market participants came to view the debt securities of these entities as implicitly guaranteed by the full faith and credit of the U.S. government. This implicit guarantee gave Fannie and Freddie access to the capital markets at a cost of credit substantially below that of private participants in the secondary market. In exchange for this benefit, government charters obliged Fannie and Freddie to pay particular attention to the enhancement of mortgage liquidity among lower-income and minority families and neighborhoods. These goals were reaffirmed and strengthened by the GSE Act of 1992. The GSE Act increased the level of support that Fannie Mae and Freddie Mac were required to provide to lower-income and minority communities. In so doing, the act also authorized HUD to establish "affordable housing goals" for the federally chartered secondary-market institutions.[10]

Like the CRA, the GSEA targets underserved communities and individuals for extra support. In the case of the GSEA, this is accomplished by requiring that the share of conventional, conforming loans purchased by Fannie Mae and Freddie Mac attain a set of minimum thresholds, or goals, specified by HUD. These goals include loans to lower-income borrowers (the "low-moderate income" goal), loans to borrowers residing in lower-income communities, loans to borrowers in "high-minority" neighborhoods (jointly, the "geographically

---

9. As noted above, the CRA pertains to the lending activities in designated assessment areas of federally insured banking institutions, including commercial banks and savings associations. It is important to note, however, that in recent years substantial growth in lending activity has occurred among institutions not covered by the CRA, as well as by CRA institutions outside their assessment areas.

10. Although the housing GSEs (Fannie Mae and Freddie Mac) were established to provide liquidity to mortgage markets and to mitigate severe cyclical fluctuations in housing, those entities are intended as well to support the provision of affordable housing and the attainment of home ownership in lower-income and minority communities.

targeted" or "underserved areas" goal), and loans to very-low-income borrowers and low-income borrowers living in low-income areas (the "special affordable" goal).[11] The goals are potentially overlapping in the sense that a single loan can potentially count toward GSE credit for multiple goal categories.

Table 7.1 describes HUD goals for GSE purchase activity since 1994. Observe that the goals have changed over time and, in general, have become more stringent. The most recent set of goals, specified in November 2004, have governed purchase activity since 2005. With these most recent guidelines, the low- and moderate-income goal was set at 54 percent of total GSE purchases, the geographically targeted goal at 38.5 percent, and the special affordable goal at 24 percent.

TABLE 7.1   HUD-Specified Affordable Housing Loan Purchase Goals

	Low- and moderate-income goals	Underserved neighborhoods	Special affordable goal
1994–1995	30	30	—[a]
1996	40	21	12
1997–2000	42	24	14
2001–2004	50	31	20
2005–2008	52–56	37–39	22–27

NOTES: All figures are percentages of the total number of units associated with the mortgages purchased by each GSE. During 1994 and 1995, underserved neighborhoods were defined differently than they would be under the current definition. The percentage thresholds for 1996–2000 were published on 1 December 1995; those for 2001–2003 were published on 31 October 2000; and those for 2005–2008 were published on 2 November 2004. According to HUD, the increase in the underserved neighborhoods goal (from 31 percent in 2001–2004 to 37 percent in 2005–2008) largely reflects adjustments in the 2000 census data, whereby the 2001–2004 goal of 31 percent would have been equivalent to 36 percent under the current definition. HUD used the 1990 census data to create housing goals prior to 2005, and used the 2000 census data to create goals for 2005–2008.

[a] The special affordable goal in 1994–1995 was specified in dollar amounts rather than as a percentage of loans purchased.

SOURCES: U.S. Department of Housing and Urban Development (1995, 2000, 2004).

---

11. The GSEA defines lower-income borrowers (for purposes of the low-moderate income goal) as those having incomes that are less than the metropolitan-area median income. Under the geographically targeted goal, lower-income neighborhoods are defined as those having a median income that is less than 90 percent of the area median income and high-minority neighborhoods are defined as those having a minority population that is at least 30 percent of the total population and a median income of less than 120 percent of the area median. For the special affordable goal, very-low-income borrowers are those with incomes of less than 60 percent of the area median income. The special affordable goal also includes borrowers living in low-income areas with incomes of less than 80 percent of the area median income.

An important feature of these goals that we draw on in the empirical work to follow is the policy-specific definition of an "underserved" neighborhood. For these purposes, the GSEA defines underserved neighborhoods as census tracts that meet one of the following conditions: (1) the tract's average income is below 90 percent of its metropolitan statistical area (MSA) median income; or (2) the tract's average income is below 120 percent of its MSA median income, and the tract's population is more than 30 percent black and Hispanic. If either of these conditions is met, the GSEA deems a given census tract as underserved, and Fannie and Freddie receive credit toward their geographic purchase goals for purchases in such communities. It should also be noted that for years before 2003, 1990 MSA and tract attributes (e.g., income and racial composition) are used to determine underserved status on the basis of 1990 census tract geographic boundaries. Beginning with 2003, those benchmarks were shifted to year-2000 values and census tract geography.

To confirm that the mandated GSE goals are associated with increased GSE loan purchases in underserved communities, table 7.2 presents results from an illustrative regression. Using census tract HMDA data from 2000, we form the ratio of GSE purchases to all secondary-market purchases for all conforming and nonconforming loans in the conventional home purchase segment of the mortgage market. This measure is then regressed on the census tract GSE underserved status and MSA fixed effects. Observe that the coefficient on the tract's underserved status is 0.091. This indicates that the GSE share of secondary-market purchases is 9.1 percent higher in underserved tracts than in tracts not subject to GSE purchase requirements. This confirms what

TABLE 7.2   Impact of GSE Underserved
Status on GSE Purchase Share

GSE underserved tract	0.09128
	(57.34)
Constant	0.49213
	(541.58)
Observations	50,104
MSA fixed effects	330
R-squared value within	0.0620
R-squared value between	0.1181
R-squared value overall	0.0417

NOTES: GSE purchase share equals GSE purchases of
conforming and nonconforming loans divided by all
purchases of conforming and nonconforming loans.
Absolute values of t-ratios are in parentheses.
MSA = metropolitan statistical area.

has been documented elsewhere in the literature: the GSEs respond to their mandated purchase goals by increasing their level of activity in underserved communities.[12]

In combination with the CRA, the GSE loan purchase goals represent a remarkable degree of government intervention in the allocation of mortgage credit. Ours, of course, is not the first study to consider the impact of these important programs. We review briefly some of the existing literature below. Although much has been learned from various studies to date, we believe that fundamental gaps remain in our understanding of how these programs have affected access to credit and home ownership.

Previous Studies of CRA and GSE Policy Effects

A number of studies have sought to document financial-institution response to CRA or GSE regulatory goals.[13] Of those studies that have focused on financial institution responses, Avery, Bostic, and Canner (2005) find a limited increase in the percentage of institutions engaged in community lending activities as a result of the CRA. Other researchers, including Schwartz (1998) and Bostic and Robinson (2003), indicate increased levels of CRA-qualified lending among financial institutions that are bound by CRA agreements, which typically include pledges to extend loans in targeted communities. Apgar and Duda (2003) compare CRA-eligible lending to minorities among CRA-regulated and non-CRA lenders; results of that study suggest elevated loan origination shares among CRA-regulated lenders.[14] In that same study, Apgar and Duda suggest that the impact of the CRA on mortgage loan originations may have attenuated over the course of the 1990s.[15]

---

12. See also Gabriel and Rosenthal (2007a) for further discussion of the extent to which the GSEs adhere to their purchase goals.

13. See, for example, Apgar and Duda (2003); Avery, Bostic, and Canner (2005); Bostic and Robinson (2003); Bunce (2002); Bunce and Scheessele (1996); Gabriel and Rosenthal (2007a); Manchester (1998); Manchester, Neal, and Bunce (1998); and Schwartz (1998).

14. For whites, the difference was minimal, but for blacks, assessment area lenders had CRA-eligible shares that were 17 percentage points (38 percent) higher than shares for lenders outside assessment areas and 20 percentage points (48 percent) higher than shares for non-CRA lenders. For Hispanics, the CRA-eligible share for assessment area lenders was 13 percentage points (28 percent) higher than that for lenders outside the assessment area, and 16 percentage points (39 percent) higher than that for non-CRA lenders.

15. According to Apgar and Duda (2003), the number of home purchase loans made by CRA-regulated institutions in their assessment areas as a share of all home purchase loans declined from 36.1 percent to 29.5 percent between 1993 and 2000. The decline in the CRA share of loan originations could owe to a variety of factors associated with evolution in the mortgage industry, including, notably, the rise of secondary-market and mortgage banking operations and the related reduction in share of loan originations funded by retail deposits. By 1997, mortgage companies accounted for 56 percent of one-to-four-family mortgage loan originations, with commercial banks and thrift institutions accounting for only 25 percent and 18 percent of loan originations, respectively.

Other recent studies have similarly sought to evaluate the GSEs' response to the loan purchase goals associated with the 1992 legislation. Bunce and Scheessele (1996), Bunce (2002), and others provide evidence that in the years following enactment of the 1992 GSEA, the GSEs increased the proportion of loan purchases from targeted populations. Between 1992 and 1995, for example, Fannie Mae doubled the share of loan purchases from lower-income borrowers while Freddie Mac increased its share by roughly 50 percent. Manchester (1998) documents that in 1995, Fannie Mae and Freddie Mac both surpassed the affordable loan purchase housing goals established by HUD. Manchester, Neal, and Bunce (1998) reach similar conclusions.[16] More recently, Gabriel and Rosenthal (2007a) demonstrate that on controlling for the size of the local market for conforming loans, the GSEs are much more active in underserved communities targeted by the 1992 GSEA. Collectively, these studies provide evidence that the GSEs have largely met the loan purchase targets imposed by the regulatory authorities.

In comparison to the many studies that have examined financial institution response to the CRA and GSEA, few studies have sought to identify the impact of those acts on local mortgage and housing market outcomes, including home ownership (e.g., Bradbury, Case, and Dunham, 1989). A recent exception is Avery, Calem, and Canner (2003). That study analyzes the effects of CRA on changes in tract-level vacancy rates, crime rates, owner-occupied units, and home ownership rates over the decade of the 1990s. To identify CRA effects, the paper compares neighborhood outcome measures among census tracts just below and above the relative income threshold used to distinguish CRA-eligible tracts.[17] As suggested by the authors, results of the analysis are mixed and difficult to interpret. This could be consistent with the lack of a clear-cut relationship between changes in the neighborhood measures and the CRA.[18] But this result could also reflect challenges in specifying a model that adequately strips away confounding factors that tend to obscure the potential impact of the CRA.

---

16. See also Listokin and Wyly (2000); Myers (2002); Case, Gillen, and Wachter (2002); and Freeman and Galster (2004) for related discussions.

17. In the Avery, Calem, and Canner (2003) analysis, regression equations are estimated for changes over the 1990s in neighborhood outcomes among a sample of tracts within the range of 10 percentage points above 80 percent of MSA median income threshold for CRA eligibility. The authors then apply the models to predict changes in outcomes in census tracts that have relative median incomes between 70 percent and 80 percent and calculate residuals and determine their statistical significance. They then test for any relationship between regression residuals and various measures of CRA-related activity.

18. Results were not robust to a reversal of procedure whereby the CRA-eligible cohort was used to predict outcomes for the not-CRA-eligible cohort.

212 | Stuart A. Gabriel and Stuart S. Rosenthal

In an analogous fashion, Bostic and Gabriel (2006) assess the effects of the GSE loan purchase goals on changes in home ownership among California communities that are the focus of the 1992 GSEA. The study adopts a methodology similar to that of Avery, Calem, and Canner (2003), but focuses on outcomes among a sample of tracts within 10 percentage points of the 90 percent of MSA median income threshold established by the GSE legislation.[19] Results of the study provide little evidence that GSE loan purchase goals elevate home ownership in targeted tracts despite other evidence (e.g., Gabriel and Rosenthal, 2007b) that suggests that a more active secondary mortgage market does expand the supply of mortgage credit.[20]

Ambrose and Thibodeau (2004) consider the degree to which the frequency of underserved tracts within an MSA affects the number of mortgage originations in the metropolitan area (including purchase and refinance loans that do and do not conform to GSE underwriting requirements). They conclude that for the years between 1995 and 1999, only in 1998 did GSE activity increase originations. An and Bostic (2008) restrict their attention to census tracts in 1996 and 2000 that are just below and just above 90 percent of an MSA's median income, which is the cutoff used to define underserved tracts for purposes of the GSE purchase targets. The authors conclude that GSE purchases reduce subprime and Federal Housing Administration (FHA) originations in underserved tracts close to the target cutoff.

The studies above have added considerably to our understanding of the impact of CRA and GSE regulations on access to mortgage credit and home ownership. Nevertheless, taken as a whole, prior studies do not provide a unified, integrated assessment of the effects of CRA and GSE regulatory goals on access to mortgage credit and home ownership. This chapter attempts to make progress in that direction.

---

19. Additional tests evaluated the interactive effects of GSE geographic targeting of tracts with those tracts ranked highly in terms of the proportion of borrowers qualifying for the low-moderate income and special affordable GSE housing goals. Also, the analysis sought to assess the robustness of estimation results across local housing markets.

20. Among other analyses, An, Bostic, Deng, and Gabriel (2007) expand on tests undertaken by Bostic and Gabriel (2006). Using a two-stage approach, the authors first estimate models of GSE purchase intensity (defined as the proportion of mortgage loans in the tract that were purchased by the GSEs), controlling for the GSE housing goals; predicted values of GSE purchase intensity are then used as regressors in analyses of changes in tract housing market conditions. Results of that analysis show that GSE purchase intensity increased significantly in tracts targeted under the geographically targeted goal, suggesting that the GSEs responded affirmatively to incentives established through the affordable housing goals. Further, increases in GSE purchase intensity are associated with declines in neighborhood vacancy rates and increases in median home values.

DATA AND SAMPLE DESIGN

Data

The data used for the analysis were the year-2000 files of the HMDA and census tract information from the 1990 and 2000 decennial census. All the data were coded to year-2000 census tract boundaries to ensure geographic comparability over time. The HMDA data derive from individual loan records as initially reported by regulated financial institutions. These data were cleaned and aggregated to the census tract level, after which they were merged with the decennial census tract information.

As described at the beginning of this chapter, our primary empirical approach is to use a regression discontinuity design that compares borrowing activity and home ownership rates in census tracts just above and below the CRA and GSE income cutoffs. Identification in this model is based on the idea that the CRA and GSE regulation results in policy-induced discrete changes in mortgage supply and related activity as one crosses the income threshold used to define an underserved census tract. In contrast, demand for mortgage debt and lender perceptions of borrower creditworthiness likely vary in a smooth, continuous fashion with income and other socioeconomic factors. In addition, recall from table 7.1 and the prior discussion that GSE loan purchase requirements include goals that target loans issued to borrowers of low-income status as well as loans originated in targeted underserved tracts. Partly for that reason, the GSEs seek out opportunities to purchase loans in all tracts that include low-income families, not just those that meet the definition of being underserved. Accordingly, to isolate the impact of designating a census tract as underserved, it is essential to include additional controls in the model that allow for socioeconomic factors that may drive local supply and demand for mortgage credit or attract GSE attention for reasons unrelated to CRA and GSE targeting of underserved communities.[21] With this in mind, our models are specified as follows.

Except where noted, all of the regression models include a large number of year-1990 and year-2000 census tract socioeconomic attributes. Most importantly, from each of these years, controls include tract average income,

---

21. Note that tracts above the GSE underserved income cutoff, for example, could still include many low-income individuals that correspond to the category of low-moderate income or special affordable goals. To isolate the effect of tract underserved status, therefore, it is necessary to control for the presence of low-income households regardless of whether a tract is designated underserved. The extensive set of tract socioeconomic indicators described herein address this need while also controlling for more fundamental socioeconomic drivers of the demand and supply for mortgage credit.

average income squared, average income cubed, and average income to the fourth power. Also included in the models are the 1990 and 2000 tract unemployment rate, poverty rate, and percent of households that are headed by a single female with children; the percent of the population that is Hispanic and the percent that is black; the average age of the population and the percent that is male; the percent of the adult population with no high school, with some high school, with a high school degree, or with some college; the average age of homes, the percent of homes that are single-family dwellings, and the population density. Finally, all the models also include controls for the 1990 home ownership rate and fixed effects for roughly 700 to 850 counties.

Two remaining control variables complete the specification of our models and are central to our empirical work. A tract was coded as GSE underserved if it met one of the following conditions: (1) the tract's average income was below 90 percent of its MSA median income in 1990; or (2) the tract's average income was below 120 percent of its MSA median income in 1990 and the tract's 1990 population was more than 30 percent black and Hispanic. If either of these conditions was met, GSE underserved tract status was set equal to 1. If neither condition was met, the variable was set equal to 0. This coding is consistent with the definition of underserved tracts as laid out in the federal regulation.

A tract is also coded as meeting CRA definitions of low-income, and thus eligible for CRA credit, if the tract's 1990 average income was less than 80 percent of MSA median income. In this case, the CRA variable was coded as 1 and 0, otherwise. This definition is also consistent with federal guidelines governing the identification of CRA-eligible tracts.

Comparing these two definitions for GSE underserved tract status and CRA tract status, it is apparent that there are three groups of census tracts in the population. The first group includes tracts that are neither underserved nor subject to CRA regulations. These tracts have an average income above 90 percent of the area median income (AMI), except for high-minority tracts with an average income above 120 percent of the AMI. The second set of census tracts are those between the CRA and GSE underserved income cutoffs. This includes tracts with an average income between 80 and 90 percent of the AMI (except for the high-minority tracts with an average income that may extend up to 120 percent of the AMI). These tracts are subject to GSE purchase requirements but are not subject to CRA origination goals. The third set of census tracts are those with an average 1990 income below 80 percent of the AMI. These tracts are subject to both GSE purchase requirements and CRA.

Mortgage activity is measured using HMDA data. As will be apparent, much of our analysis focuses on two key dependent variables: the number of loan applications and the number of loan originations. These variables are measured separately for loans below the GSE conforming loan size limit for a given metropolitan area (referred to as "conforming" loans) and for loans in excess of the conforming loan size limits (referred to as "nonconforming" loans). We also estimate models that add together activity from the conforming and nonconforming sectors.

For all the samples used in the analysis, mortgage variables are drawn only from HMDA records pertaining to conventional home purchase loans. HMDA loan records for which the type or purpose of the loan could not be determined were dropped from the samples. In addition, throughout the analysis, we include only census tracts in MSAs as defined in the 2000 U.S. Census.

Sample Design

Before proceeding to the empirical results, it is useful to highlight additional features of the samples used to estimate the models and the specifications of the models themselves. As will become apparent, all the regressions were estimated twice, first including the GSE underserved census tract dummy variable as a control, and a second time replacing that variable with the CRA census tract indicator. In each case, regressions were run for six different dependent variables: the number of applications for conforming sized conventional home purchase loans, the number of originations for conforming sized conventional home purchase loans, their analogues for nonconforming sized loans, the sum of these variables between the conforming and nonconforming sectors, and the difference in home ownership rates between 2000 and 1990.

Each of these regressions was estimated separately over three different samples in order to apply successively tighter filters as part of the regression discontinuity approach. The first sample includes all census tracts in identified MSAs, regardless of tract income. The second sample includes only tracts for which the average income is within 10 percent of the cutoff associated with the GSE or CRA underserved income definitions. The third sample includes only tracts for which average income is within 5 percent of the income cutoff for the policy in question.

In defining these samples, it is worth reiterating that the GSE definition of an underserved tract is one whose average income is below 90 percent of the AMI or below 120 percent of the AMI with a minority population share in excess of 30 percent. The CRA definition of underserved, in contrast, is 80 percent of the AMI. This implies that the "all-tract" sample effectively mixes three different types of tracts relative to the GSE and CRA goals: tracts with income above both the GSE and CRA income limits, tracts with income between the two income limits and for which only GSE goals apply, and tracts with income below the CRA limit and for which both the CRA and GSE goals apply. This mixing of tract types potentially obscures the influence of CRA and GSE policy effects. For the CRA analysis, for example, the CRA dummy variable effectively compares tracts subject to both CRA and GSE goals to a blend of two types of tracts—those that are subject to GSE goals and those that are not.

In contrast, the 5 percent and 10 percent window samples provide a sharper comparison. When focusing on GSE effects, the 5 percent and 10 percent window samples exclude any tracts subject to CRA targeting. For this sample, the GSE underserved dummy variable highlights effects in GSE-targeted tracts relative to those not targeted by the GSEA. Analogously, when focusing on CRA effects, the 5 percent and 10 percent window samples exclude all tracts not subject to GSE goals. In these instances, the CRA dummy variable highlights activity in CRA-targeted tracts relative to those not directly subject to the CRA, bearing in mind that all of the sample tracts are subject to GSE purchase priorities.

Given these features of the different samples, it seems likely that the 5 percent and 10 percent window samples are likely to provide a more accurate assessment of GSE and CRA policy effects. In part, this is because these samples provide a sharper delineation of tract type as just described. In addition, narrowing the sample by income type is likely to further control for unobserved effects not captured directly by the SES variables and fixed effects included in the models. Of course, against those benefits must be weighed a significant disadvantage of the more refined samples: as the sample focus is narrowed, the number of tracts in the sample is correspondingly reduced, and this makes it more difficult to obtain precise estimates, all else being equal. Tables 7.3 and 7.4 indicate the sample sizes associated with each of the different regressions. For the all-census tract models, sample size is just over 50,000. With a 10 percent window restriction, sample size is reduced to roughly 8,000 to 10,000 tracts, depending on the policy in question. With a 5 percent window restriction, sample size is further reduced to roughly 4,000 to 5,000, depending on the policy in question. Although the restricted samples are clearly much smaller, they still contain thousands of census tracts. For that reason, on balance, we believe that these restricted samples yield more reliable results.

TABLE 7.3 Impact of GSE Underserved Census Tract Status

	Dependent variables		
	Applications for conventional home purchase loans	Originations for conventional home purchase loans	Change in home ownership rate, 2000–1990
All census tracts			
Conforming mortgages	−2.216	−0.1105	
(Observations: 50,402 tracts in 853 counties)	(2.01)	(0.15)	
Nonconforming mortgages	0.6476	0.4663	
(Observations: 50,374 tracts in 853 counties)	(2.21)	(2.34)	
Conforming + nonconforming mortgages	−1.527	0.3699	
(Observations: 50,370 tracts in 853 counties)	(1.24)	(0.44)	
All households			−0.0002
(Observations: 50,341 tracts in 853 counties)			(0.23)
Tracts within 10% of underserved border			
Conforming mortgages	−4.826	−2.606	
(Observations: 10,052 tracts in 741 counties)	(1.91)	(1.51)	
Nonconforming mortgages	−1.286	−0.8894	
(Observations: 10,048 tracts in 741 counties)	(1.73)	(1.88)	
Conforming + nonconforming mortgages	−6.144	−3.517	
(Observations: 10,048 tracts in 741 counties)	(2.15)	(1.81)	
All households			−0.0009
(Observations: 10,079 tracts in 741 counties)			(0.46)
Tracts within 5% of underserved border			
Conforming mortgages	−2.429	−1.831	
(Observations: 5,057 tracts in 652 counties)	(0.77)	(0.85)	
Nonconforming mortgages	−1.906	−1.394	
(Observations: 5,055 tracts in 652 counties)	(1.82)	(2.09)	

(*continued*)

TABLE 7.3 *(continued)*

	Dependent variables		
	Applications for conventional home purchase loans	Originations for conventional home purchase loans	Change in home ownership rate, 2000–1990
Conforming + nonconforming mortgages	−4.368	−3.256	
(Observations: 5,055 tracts in 652 counties)	(1.21)	(1.32)	
All households			0.0015
(Observations: 5,076 tracts in 652 counties)			(0.62)

NOTES: Absolute values of t-ratios based on robust standard errors are in parentheses. All models include the following census tract control variables from both 1990 and 2000: average income, average income squared, average income cubed, and average income to the fourth power; unemployment rate, poverty rate, and percent of households headed by a single female with children; percent of population that is Hispanic and percent that is black; average age of population and percent of population that is male; percent of adult population with no high school, with some high school, with a high school degree, or with some college; average age of homes, percent of single-family homes, and population density. All the models also include the 1990 home ownership rate and county fixed effects. To conserve space, estimates from these control measures are not reported.

RESULTS

Socioeconomic Controls

As noted earlier, a very long list of tract socioeconomic characteristics are included in the regressions to ensure that we adequately control for the influence of underlying drivers of demand and supply for mortgage credit apart from the influence of the GSE and CRA policy goals. In total, 37 socioeconomic variables are included in the models, in addition to fixed effects, for roughly 700 to 850 counties. This very large number of control variables requires that we be parsimonious in presentation. Partly for that reason, and also because of the reduced form nature of the socioeconomic controls, we do not discuss the coefficients on those variables. Instead, it is sufficient to note that many of the socioeconomic controls from both 1990 and 2000 are significant predictors of mortgage activity and changes in home ownership rates, as would be anticipated. As an illustrative example, we report the complete regression results for the origination regressions that examine CRA effects in all three samples already described here. Those estimates are provided in appendix

TABLE 7.4   Impact of CRA Census Tract Status

	Dependent variables		
	Applications for conventional home purchase loans	Originations for conventional home purchase loans	Change in home ownership rate, 2000–1990
All census tracts			
Conforming mortgages	0.1387	1.386	
(Observations: 50,402	(0.14)	(2.27)	
tracts in 853 counties)			
Nonconforming mortgages	1.243	0.8896	
(Observations: 50,374	(5.11)	(5.39)	
tracts in 853 counties)			
Conforming + nonconforming	1.392	2.289	
mortgages			
(Observations: 50,370	(1.25)	(3.38)	
tracts in 853 counties)			
All households			−0.0038
(Observations: 50,341			(3.56)
tracts in 853 counties)			
Tracts within 10% of CRA border			
Conforming mortgages	−1.397	−0.4674	
(Observations: 8,322	(0.81)	(0.48)	
tracts in 794 counties)			
Nonconforming mortgages	0.7344	0.4742	
(Observations: 8,320	(1.99)	(2.03)	
tracts in 794 counties)			
Conforming + nonconforming	−0.6534	0.0201	
mortgages			
(Observations: 8,320	(0.35)	(0.02)	
tracts in 794 counties)			
All households			0.0035
(Observations: 8,283 tracts in			(2.11)
794 counties)			
Tracts within 5% of CRA border			
Conforming mortgages	−0.1460	0.6270	
(Observations: 4,191 tracts in	(0.06)	(0.48)	
699 counties)			
Nonconforming mortgages	0.7251	0.4851	
(Observations: 4,190 tracts in	(1.49)	(1.57)	
699 counties)			

(continued)

TABLE 7.4 *(continued)*

	Dependent variables		
	Applications for conventional home purchase loans	Originations for conventional home purchase loans	Change in home ownership rate, 2000–1990
Conforming + nonconforming mortgages	0.5539	1.097	
(Observations: 4,190 tracts in 699 counties)	(0.22)	(0.76)	
All households			0.0024
(Observations: 4,175 tracts in 699 counties)			(1.08)

NOTES: Absolute values of t-ratios based on robust standard errors are in parentheses. All models include the following census tract control variables from both 1990 and 2000: average income, average income squared, average income cubed, and average income to the fourth power; unemployment rate, poverty rate, and percent of households headed by a single female with children; percent of population that is Hispanic and percent that is black; average age of population and percent population that is male; percent of adult population with no high school, with some high school, with a high school degree, or with some college; average age of homes, percent of single-family homes, and population density. All the models also include the 1990 home ownership rate and county fixed effects. To conserve space, estimates from these control measures are not reported. CRA = Community Reinvestment Act.

table 7A.1. To conserve space, the complete results from the other regressions are not reported. This leaves us free to focus here on the coefficients on GSE underserved tract status and CRA tract status, which are the coefficients of primary interest.

GSE and CRA Effects

Tables 7.3 and 7.4 summarize the core results of the chapter and are presented in a manner intended to facilitate comparisons across model and sample designs. Table 7.3 presents the coefficients on GSE underserved tract status from the various regressions, and table 7.4 presents the analogous set of coefficients on CRA tract status. It is important to note that each coefficient in these tables is taken from a separate regression as described above. In addition, robust standard errors were used in calculating the t-ratios reported in parentheses.

Consider first the impact of GSE underserved tract status as described by the results summarized in table 7.3. When using the complete sample of all census tracts in MSAs, the impact of GSE underserved status on the sum of conforming and nonconforming loan activity is not significant, both for applications and originations. In addition, GSE underserved status has no discernible effect on originations for conforming mortgages, but there is evidence of a negative and significant impact on applications. In the nonconforming sector, GSE underserved tract status has a modest positive and significant effect on both applications and originations. This pattern of results is difficult to explain from an economic standpoint because GSE underserved status would seem more likely to boost local activity in the conforming sector of the market at the expense of the nonconforming sector, not the reverse. Observe also that underserved tract status has no impact on the change in home ownership during the decade of the 1990s: the coefficient is −0.0002 with a t-ratio of 0.23. Given this mix of results, we view the full sample results with caution.

Consider next the 5 percent and 10 percent window sample estimates in table 7.3. As noted above, these samples are much smaller, but, we hope, still large enough to yield reliable results. They are also cleaner in their composition. Bearing this in mind, note that the estimated impact of GSE underserved tract status on lending activity is negative. This holds for the nonconforming sector, the conforming sector, and the sum of the two sectors. Many of the estimates are also either significant or nearly so. An important exception is the estimated GSE effect on conforming loan activity in the 5 percent sample: those estimates (for applications and originations) are quite a bit smaller in magnitude than for the 10 percent sample and have t-ratios below 1. Whereas a negative impact of GSE activity on the nonconforming sector could occur if borrowers shift from nonconforming to smaller conforming sized loans, that would tend to be associated with a positive GSE effect on the conforming sector. The lack of evidence of a positive impact of underserved status on conforming loan activity is therefore important. In addition, notice that for both the 5 percent and 10 percent window samples, the estimated effect on the change in home ownership in the 1990s is very small, not significant, and fails to indicate a compelling positive effect of GSE underserved status.

Two possible explanations may contribute to the lack of a coherent and positive impact of GSE underserved status in the three samples, especially with respect to conforming loan size activity and home ownership. The first is that despite the long list of control variables and the sharp focus of the window sample design, we cannot rule out the possibility that all of the models in table 7.3 may suffer from some degree of unobserved effects that bias our estimates. This could account for the negative sign on the GSE effects in the conforming segment of the market, given the inherent tendency of lower-income areas to display less mortgage activity. At the same time, we note again that the estimated impacts in the conforming sector are not generally significant, and especially so in the 5 percent sample. In addition, the estimated impacts on home ownership are tiny and positive in the 5 percent sample. A second explanation is that the GSE goals may simply have little positive effect on conforming mortgage lending activity and home ownership, and as a result, any positive impacts are swamped by downward bias from unobserved factors. In this context, one reason why GSE underserved status may have little impact on conforming loan activity would be if GSE purchases crowd out unsubsidized private-sector purchase activity (e.g., Gabriel and Rosenthal, 2007a). Such crowd-out effects could mitigate the impact of GSE tract status on originations and home ownership.

Table 7.4 presents corresponding results for the impact of a census tract's CRA status. For the full sample, the CRA has a generally positive and significant impact on lending activity in both the conforming and nonconforming segments of the market. That same result is apparent in the combined measure of conforming plus nonconforming loans. This is possible to the extent that the CRA encourages existing homeowners to obtain larger loans, and also encourages some renters to become homeowners (and likely obtain smaller, conforming sized loans). Note, however, that the estimated impact of the CRA on home ownership in the 1990s was negative and significant—the coefficient is -0.0038 with a t-ratio of 3.56. It is difficult to provide an economic rationale for this result, as the CRA almost certainly works to expand mortgage supply and, if anything, should increase home ownership. Instead, once again, despite the extensive set of SES controls and county fixed effects, we cannot rule out the possibility that unobserved factors may contaminate our estimates of CRA policy effects in the full sample models.

Focusing on the 5 percent and 10 percent window sample models yields more encouraging results. Note first that for both samples, CRA effects on conforming loan activity are generally negative or not significant. In contrast, CRA status has a positive and significant effect on nonconforming loan applications and originations. This is plausible given the nature of the CRA's goals. In addition, observe that the estimated effect of CRA tract status on nonconforming loan activity is remarkably similar for both samples: in both cases, the estimated impact on applications is roughly 0.7 loans per tract whereas the estimated effect on originations is roughly 0.5 loans per tract. Moreover, these estimates are significant, or nearly so. These estimates are also close to their analogues obtained for the full sample (all-tract) model. It is also apparent that for the 10 percent window sample, CRA tract status has a positive and significant impact on home ownership: the coefficient is 0.0035 with a t-ratio of

2.11. For the 5 percent sample, the corresponding coefficient is smaller and loses significance — 0.0024 with a t-ratio of 1.08.[22]

Summarizing the CRA effects, we find robust evidence of the CRA's having a positive and significant impact on nonconforming loan activity: this pattern is evident in each of the three samples. In the restricted samples we tend to see either negative or zero impact on the conforming sector, but in all cases the estimates are insignificant. In the 10 percent window sample, the CRA has a positive and significant impact on home ownership; that effect is slightly smaller in magnitude and loses significance in the 5 percent window sample, but remains positive.

Overall, we interpret these results as follows. From a conceptual standpoint, the CRA should have an unambiguous positive impact on the local supply of mortgage credit and home ownership. The robust evidence of a positive CRA effect on nonconforming loan activity is consistent with that prior. The same is true for the significant impact on home ownership in the 10 percent sample, although the estimate loses significance in the smaller 5 percent sample. Moreover, it is possible that the CRA could elevate lending in the nonconforming sector without having a positive impact on the conforming segment; this would occur if the CRA encourages some borrowers to substitute larger, nonconforming loans for smaller, conforming sized loans. On balance, therefore, the patterns in table 7.4 suggest that the CRA has indeed contributed to an expansion in the supply of mortgage credit in targeted census tracts.

Alternative Specifications

A number of alternative model specifications were also used to assess the impact of GSE and CRA underserved status on local mortgage activity and home ownership. We briefly note these models here and highlight any differences from the estimates reported in tables 7.3 and 7.4. In most instances, those differences were small, and in no case did the overall qualitative nature of the results change. For that reason, we do not table out the estimates from these alternative models.

Our first alternative was to experiment with a less nonlinear set of controls for tract income. We did this out of concern that there may be a high degree of collinearity in our key regressors and that this could make identification

---

22. Observe also that for the pooled sample of conforming plus nonconforming loans, all estimated CRA tract coefficients in the 5 percent and 10 percent samples are insignificant. Given the robust and significant impact of CRA tract status on nonconforming loan activity, this result highlights the importance of not treating all loan size segments of the market as if they were alike.

more difficult. Accordingly, all of the regressions in tables 7.3 and 7.4 were reestimated omitting average income cubed and average income to the fourth power from both 1990 and 2000. This change had little impact on the 10 percent and 5 percent window samples for both the GSE and CRA effects. The full sample (all-tract) models were affected in that the coefficients on conforming and nonconforming loan activity took on a different pattern of signs. However, we do not view those results as being reliable in comparison to the restricted window samples.

We also considered the possibility that the long list of socioeconomic controls could contribute to excessive collinearity that would obscure identification, especially in the smaller 5 percent and 10 percent window samples. To address that concern, we reran the regressions in tables 7.3 and 7.4 two additional times. In the first instance, we omitted all the 1990 socioeconomic control measures except for the tract income terms. In the second instance, we omitted all socioeconomic controls from both 1990 and 2000 except for the tract income terms. In both cases, restricting the set of control variables tended to cause the estimated impact of GSE and CRA tract status to have a more negative impact on lending activity and home ownership. Given that mortgage activity and home ownership are less prevalent in lower income communities, these results suggest that insufficient controls were included in the above models to address underlying fundamental determinants of mortgage demand and supply, as well as of home ownership.

Based on these alternative models, we believe that the most reliable specifications are those reported in tables 7.3 and 7.4 for the 5 percent and 10 percent window samples and which include the full set of tract income and socioeconomic controls from both 1990 and 2000. Those controls work to eliminate more traditional drivers of mortgage demand and supply, as well as of home ownership. For the GSE analysis, they also help to address possible confounding effects of the low-moderate income and special affordable goals, as described in table 7.1 and discussed earlier in the chapter.

CONCLUSION

Together, the CRA and GSEA have been a centerpiece to U.S. government efforts to expand access to mortgage credit and home ownership in targeted, underserved neighborhoods. We empirically assess these efforts by applying a regression discontinuity design to HMDA data from 2000 along with county fixed effects and an extensive set of control measures based on 1990 and 2000 census tract attributes. Based on a variety of models and specifications, we find no evidence of a positive impact of GSE underserved tract status on lending activity in the conforming sector or on local home ownership rates, although underserved status does appear to have a negative impact on lending in the nonconforming sector. These patterns could be consistent with GSE crowd-out of unsubsidized private-sector secondary-market activity (e.g., Gabriel and Rosenthal, 2007a). Negative impacts on the nonconforming sized sector also suggest that pressure on the GSEs to secure greater numbers of conforming sized loans creates competition for scarce capital and reduces nonconforming loan activity. At the same time, we cannot rule out the possibility that unobserved tract-specific factors may be biasing our estimates downward, given the inherent tendency of lower-income tracts to exhibit less mortgage lending activity and home ownership. In contrast, as largely anticipated, we do find robust evidence that the CRA increases mortgage lending activity in the nonconforming segment of the mortgage market. In addition, evidence also indicates that the CRA has had a small, positive impact on local home ownership rates. These patterns are consistent with conceptual arguments that the CRA should unambiguously expand the local supply of mortgage credit in targeted areas.

Overall, the policy implications from our results are mixed. The absence of a compelling positive GSE impact on conforming mortgage lending activity and home ownership in targeted, underserved tracts is striking, given HUD-specified goals that mandate high shares of GSE purchases in such communities. The evidence of positive CRA effects in targeted low-income tracts is more in keeping with the policy goals of the CRA, but even here the estimated patterns are not as pronounced as policy makers may have anticipated. These are issues that clearly warrant further discussion in the context of ongoing policy debate regarding the future of the GSEs.

APPENDIX

TABLE 7A.1 Impact of CRA Census Tract Status on Nonconforming Originations

	All census tracts		Tracts within 10% of CRA border		Tracts within 5% of CRA border	
	Coefficient	t-ratio	Coefficient	t-ratio	Coefficient	t-ratio
CRA tract status	0.8896	5.39	0.4742	2.03	0.4851	1.57
Average income in 2000	−2.576E-01	−6.67	−1.539E+00	−4.78	−2.314E+00	−3.47
Average income^2 in 2000	4.515E-03	11.85	2.759E-02	4.14	4.155E-02	2.91
Average income^3 in 2000	−1.340E-05	−11.96	−1.774E-04	−3.16	−2.768E-04	−2.22
Average income^4 in 2000	9.840E-09	11.53	3.770E-07	2.37	6.110E-07	1.66
Unemployment rate in 2000	−7.5533	−5.82	−4.3364	−2.58	−6.2319	−2.38
Poverty rate in 2000	0.8298	0.65	−3.7112	−2.16	−2.9218	−1.06
Percent female with child in 2000	5.3818	7.27	0.4670	0.48	−0.5528	−0.32
Percent Hispanic in 2000	−11.5865	−10.60	−0.9866	−0.61	1.0510	0.42
Percent black in 2000	−1.0282	−1.40	−1.8204	−1.13	−0.1322	−0.09
Average age in 2000	−0.2699	−8.03	−0.0295	−0.73	0.0087	0.18
Percent male in 2000	11.7811	5.12	1.9501	0.64	−3.3498	−0.79
Percent no high school in 2000	−20.2002	−9.96	−13.8766	−4.24	−9.2066	−1.92
Percent some high school in 2000	−10.2525	−5.60	−10.9373	−3.58	−9.4013	−1.96
Percent high school in 2000	−16.0942	−9.52	−11.5952	−4.29	−10.3909	−2.30
Percent some college in 2000	−26.7849	−11.70	−12.3333	−3.47	−7.5702	−1.33
Average age of homes in 2000	−0.2858	−11.67	−0.0622	−2.01	−0.0805	−1.68
Percent single-family homes in 2000	0.8714	1.00	0.4369	0.34	2.6488	1.24
Population density in 2000	−2.060E-05	−0.69	2.020E-05	0.54	1.079E-04	2.01
Average income in 1990	−2.252E-01	−3.77	8.902E-01	1.00	−1.513E-03	0.00

Average income^2 in 1990	4.209E-03	5.81	-2.873E-02	-1.31	-1.517E-02	-0.41
Average income^3 in 1990	-1.850E-05	-6.04	3.775E-04	1.68	3.201E-04	0.88
Average income^4 in 1990	2.340E-08	5.71	-1.580E-06	-2.00	-1.580E-06	-1.26
Unemployment rate in 1990	-0.9778	-0.54	3.0268	0.74	5.7464	0.85
Poverty rate in 1990	2.1567	1.67	-0.9077	-0.46	-1.9190	-0.59
Percent female with child in 1990	5.0537	6.43	2.3014	2.06	1.7025	0.95
Percent Hispanic in 1990	4.7139	4.11	2.5756	1.30	-0.6060	-0.19
Percent black in 1990	-2.8630	-3.81	0.1039	0.06	-1.6568	-1.01
Average age in 1990	0.2167	6.88	0.0074	0.17	-0.0169	-0.27
Percent male in 1990	-2.7723	-1.01	-2.3336	-0.65	-1.1713	-0.21
Percent no high school in 1990	16.8378	7.80	5.8442	1.90	2.1472	0.42
Percent some high school in 1990	19.1781	9.59	3.9533	1.26	0.8470	0.16
Percent high school in 1990	16.7020	9.14	4.7290	1.62	1.1557	0.25
Percent some college in 1990	23.1562	8.64	4.4021	1.25	6.6141	1.23
Average age of homes in 1990	0.1532	6.34	0.0433	1.51	0.0517	1.16
Percent single-family homes in 1990	-1.4074	-1.40	-0.7564	-0.52	-2.6371	-1.03
Population density in 1990	0.0001	2.00	0.0000	0.25	-0.0001	-1.52
1990 home ownership rate	3.3189	4.45	2.2600	2.03	3.3991	1.70
Observations	50,374		8,320		4,190	
County fixed effects	853		794		699	
R-squared value (overall)	0.3794		0.2677		0.2673	

NOTES: t-ratios are calculated using robust standard errors. CRA = Community Reinvestment Act.

REFERENCES

Ambrose, Brent W., and Thomas G. Thibodeau. 2004. "Have the GSE Affordable Housing Goals Increased the Supply of Mortgage Credit?" *Regional Science and Urban Economics* 34(3): 263–273.

An, Xudong, and Raphael W. Bostic. 2008. "GSE Activity, FHA Feedback, and Implications for the Efficacy of the Affordable Housing Goals." *Journal of Real Estate Finance and Economics* 36(2): 207–231.

An, Xudong, Raphael W. Bostic, Yongheng Deng, and Stuart A. Gabriel. 2007. "GSE Loan Purchases, the FHA, and Housing Outcomes in Targeted, Low-Income Neighborhoods." Brookings-Wharton Papers on Urban Affairs. Washington, DC: The Brookings Institution.

Apgar, William C., and Mark Duda. 2003. "The Twenty-Fifth Anniversary of the Community Reinvestment Act: Past Accomplishments and Future Regulatory Challenges." *FRBNY Economic Policy Review* (June): 169–191.

Avery, Robert B., Raphael W. Bostic, and Glenn B. Canner. 2005. "Assessing the Necessity and Efficiency of the Community Reinvestment Act." *Housing Policy Debate* 16(1): 143–172.

Avery, Robert B., Paul S. Calem, and Glenn B. Canner. 2003. "The Effects of the Community Reinvestment Act on Local Communities." Proceedings of "Seeds of Growth: Sustainable Community Development: What Works, What Doesn't, and Why," conference sponsored by the Federal Reserve System. http://www.chicagofed.org/cedric/files/2003_conf_paper_session5_canner.pdf.

Board of Governors of the Federal Reserve System. 2000. "The Performance and Profitability of CRA Related Lending." Report to Congress, July.

Bostic, Raphael, and Stuart Gabriel. 2006. "Do the GSEs Matter to Lower-Income Housing Markets?" *Journal of Urban Economics* 59: 458–479.

Bostic, Raphael, and Breck L. Robinson. 2003. "Do CRA Agreements Increase Lending?" *Real Estate Economics* 31(1): 23–51.

Bradbury, Katherine, Karl Case, and Constance Dunham. 1989. "Geographic Patterns of Mortgage Lending in Boston: 1982–1987." *New England Economic Review* (September/October): 3–30.

Bunce, Harold. 2002. "The GSEs Funding of Affordable Loans: A 2000 Update." Housing Finance Working Paper Series HF-013. Washington, DC: U.S. Department of Housing and Urban Development.

Bunce, Harold, and Randall Scheessele. 1996. "The GSEs Funding of Affordable Loans." Housing Finance Working Paper Series HF-001. Washington, DC: U.S. Department of Housing and Urban Development.

Case, Bradford, Kevin Gillen, and Susan M. Wachter. 2002. "Spatial Variation in GSE Mortgage Purchase Activity." *Cityscape* 6(1): 9–84.

Federal Reserve System. 1990. "Community Reinvestment (Regulation BB)." 60 *Federal Register* 22190, 12 CFR Part 288 (May 4).

Freeman, Lance, and George Galster. 2004. "The Impact of Secondary Mortgage Market and GSE Purchases on Underserved Neighborhood Housing Markets: A Cleveland Case Study." Report to the U.S. Department of Housing and Urban Development.

Gabriel, Stuart, and Stuart S. Rosenthal. 2007a. "HUD Purchase Goals and Crowd Out: Do the GSEs Expand the Supply of Mortgage Credit?" Working Paper 2007-15, Ziman Center for Real Estate, University of California, Los Angeles.

———. 2007b. "Secondary Markets, Risk, and Access to Credit: Evidence from the Mortgage Market." Working Paper 2007-02, Ziman Center for Real Estate, University of California, Los Angeles.

Listokin, David, and Elvin K. Wyly. 2000. "Making New Mortgage Markets: Case Studies of Institutions, Home Buyers, and Communities." *Housing Policy Debate* 11(3): 575–644.

Manchester, Paul. 1998. "Characteristics of Mortgages Purchased by Fannie Mae and Freddie Mac, 1996–97 Update." Housing Finance Working Paper Series HF-006. Washington, DC: U.S. Department of Housing and Urban Development.

Manchester, Paul B., Sue Neal, and Harold Bunce. 1998. "Characteristics of Mortgages Purchased by Fannie Mae and Freddie Mac, 1993–1995." Housing Finance Working Paper Series HF-003. Washington, DC: U.S. Department of Housing and Urban Development.

Myers, Samuel L. 2002. "Government-Sponsored Enterprise Secondary Market Decisions: Effects on Racial Disparities in Home Mortgage Loan Rejection Rates." *Cityscape* 6(1): 85–113.

Schwartz, Alex. 1998. "From Confrontation to Collaboration? Banks, Community Groups, and the Implementation of Community Reinvestment Agreements." *Housing Policy Debate* 9(3): 631–662.

U.S. Department of Housing and Urban Development. 1995. "The Secretary of HUD's Regulation of the Federal National Mortgage Association and the Federal Home Loan Mortgage Corporation; Final Rule." 60 *Federal Register* 61846, 24 CFR Part 81 (December 1).

———. 2000. "HUD's Regulation of the Federal National Mortgage Association (Fannie Mae) and the Federal Home Loan Mortgage Corporation (Freddie Mac); Final Rule." 65 *Federal Register* 65043, 24 CFR Part 81 (October 31).

———. 2004. "HUD's Housing Goals for the Federal National Mortgage Association (Fannie Mae) and the Federal Home Loan Mortgage Corporation (Freddie Mac) for the Years 2005–2008 and Amendments to HUD's Regulation of Fannie Mae and Freddie Mac; Final Rule." 69 *Federal Register* 63579, 24 CFR Part 81 (November 2).

Commentary

LAWRENCE D. JONES

The Community Reinvestment Act (CRA) of 1977 and the Federal Housing Enterprise Financial Safety and Soundness Act, often referred to as the GSE Act of 1992 (GSEA), include provisions intended to improve access to mortgage credit by households and communities that are perceived to be underserved. The CRA requires regulators to assess the extent to which their federally insured institutions are meeting the credit demands of those in low-income and minority neighborhoods in particular. The GSEA requires Freddie Mac and Fannie Mae to ensure that specific percentages of their secondary-market purchases consist of loans made to lower-income and minority communities and borrowers. The purpose of the chapter by Stuart Gabriel and Stuart Rosenthal is to measure the extent to which the objectives of these legislative initiatives have been met in the form of increases in mortgage lending and home ownership rates in targeted communities.

The empirical strategy Gabriel and Rosenthal follow is to perform ordinary least squares estimations to capture the effect of government-sponsored enterprise (GSE) underserved status and CRA-eligible status on mortgage lending activity and the log change in home ownership rates for metropolitan statistical area (MSA) census tracts. Data on mortgage loan applications and originations come from the Home Mortgage Disclosure Act (HMDA) database for the year 2000 and are aggregated to census tract level. To control for other factors affecting the demand and supply of mortgage credit and the home ownership decision, a number of variables capturing the socioeconomic characteristics of census tracts are included as explanatory variables in the regressions, along with MSA fixed effects. The socioeconomic attributes and home ownership rates are drawn from 1990 and 2000 census files.

Separate regressions are estimated to capture the GSEA and CRA tract effects. Also, because the authors believe it is important to recognize that conforming and nonconforming loans are substitutes at the margin, separate estimations are performed for each of these loan types. Their distinction between conforming and nonconforming is based solely on loan size. In an attempt to further control for unobservable factors that may affect mortgage loan activity and home ownership decisions, estimates are also performed on restricted samples that contain only tracts that fall under GSEA (CRA) status or are in the neighborhood of the income or minority cutoffs that define GSEA (CRA) tracts. In the GSEA estimations, these restricted samples exclude all tracts subject to the CRA, whereas all tracts in the CRA restricted samples are tracts that have GSE status. To explain mortgage loan activity, the authors run separate estimates for loan applications and originations.

This interesting chapter addresses highly relevant issues that are important for policy formulation. I like the focus on assessing the impact of the GSEA and CRA on the ultimate goal of increasing home ownership in the targeted communities. Integrating the HMDA data with census tract data allows the authors to realize the strengths of both data sources. The decisions they make in specification and sample design are reasonable within the data limits that create some difficulty in distinguishing CRA from GSEA effects.

The reservations I have with the chapter reside mostly with the authors' working hypotheses, and consequently in determining how some of their empirical results should be interpreted. These issues go especially to the key question of how lending activity that is generated by lenders and the GSEs as a result of complying with legislative requirements affects home ownership decisions. I find that understanding how the authors' expectations are formulated is made difficult by the absence of a theoretical model from which their hypotheses can be derived.

For the mortgage activity regressions in which the explanatory variable is the dummy GSE status, the authors expect that GSE purchase activity will result in an expansion of conforming loan originations and likely reduce the number of nonconforming loans made. This is a plausible hypothesis, and the empirical results for the full sample do corroborate this expectation. What is difficult to understand is their prior belief that these lending results will have an ambiguous effect on home ownership in the targeted areas. They perceive that the potential reduction in nonconforming lending may offset the expansion in the supply of conforming loans and the presumed reduction in the cost of conforming loans. I would think that increases in ownership rates over the 1990s would have been driven primarily by younger households making their initial rent-to-own transition and that the financing used in most of these cases would have been conforming sized loans. There are reasons why GSE purchase activity might not have translated into increased ownership rates in targeted communities, but I have difficulty understanding the authors' explanation of why GSE status fails to have a positive effect on the change in ownership rates in their empirical results.

In the chapter, CRA lending requirements are treated as being in effect for any census tract with median family income at less than 80 percent of median income in the MSA in which the tract is located. Here the authors' hypothesis is that because the institutions covered by the CRA can make loans of all sizes, households are induced to choose larger loans than they would have without the CRA requirements. I can understand how the CRA requirements could induce larger conforming loans, but I am puzzled by the authors' expectation that households in these low-income communities will have a significant incentive to move to nonconforming sized loans. The authors' hypothesis is confirmed by the empirical results, but it is not clear why this result occurs. Even more puzzling is the authors' expectation that this lending effect of CRA status will have a positive impact on home ownership. In one of the restricted samples in the CRA estimations, they do find a positive effect on the change in home ownership over the decade, but given their view that the primary effect of CRA lending is in inducing a shift from conforming to nonconforming loans, it is not clear how CRA status could positively affect home ownership while GSE status does not.

It would also help readers to understand the context in which the authors' prior beliefs are being formulated if some descriptive statistics were provided. In particular, it would be helpful to provide the number of conforming and nonconforming loans that exist in each of the five samples used in the mortgage activity regressions. In order to have a base case for comparison, it would be useful to show the same loan breakdown for a sixth sample of census tracts, including only tracts that are not classified as either GSEA underserved or CRA status.

The authors do not explain why they choose to estimate the impact of GSEA and CRA status on both mortgage loan applications and originations. In effect, they treat these simply as alternative ways of measuring mortgage lending activity. However, in my mind, their choice raises questions about how the demand for loans may be resolved differently in different types of census tracts. The HMDA file provides detailed classifications of what happens to loan applications, including loan denials. It would be helpful to have evidence on how lenders disposed of applications in each of the six samples.

8

Siting, Spillovers, and Segregation: A Reexamination of the Low-Income Housing Tax Credit Program

INGRID GOULD ELLEN
KATHERINE M. O'REGAN
IOAN VOICU

M any economists and policy analysts have criticized place-based housing programs as being inefficient (Case, 1991). The basic charge is that place-based housing programs distort housing choices, including the choice of neighborhood location. Myriad accounts document how federal housing programs—and the public housing program in particular—have helped concentrate poverty over the years (Carter, Schill, and Wachter, 1998; Hirsch, 1983). Through encouraging large-scale public housing developments that almost exclusively house very-low-income tenants and allowing these developments to be sited almost exclusively in very-low-income neighborhoods, federal housing policy generally has steered subsidized tenants to extremely low-income and high-poverty communities. Yet some community development advocates have countered that well-designed, subsidized housing investments can generate positive neighborhood spillovers and thereby help to revitalize distressed, high-poverty areas. Thus, there may be a trade-off in building low-income units in low-income areas—specifically, although building subsidized housing in high-poverty neighborhoods may

We are very grateful to Keren Horn for exceptional research assistance. We would also like to thank our discussants, Dan McMillen and Tsur Somerville, who provided excellent feedback, and to acknowledge the many comments we received from other participants at the Housing and the Built Environment conference as well as from researchers and students at New York University's Furman Center. We especially want to thank the editors of this book for their extremely helpful suggestions. The views expressed in this chapter are those of the authors alone and do not necessarily reflect those of the Office of the Comptroller of the Currency or the Department of the Treasury.

heighten the concentration of the poor initially, it may also contribute to improvements in these neighborhoods and thereby lessen poverty concentration over time.

This debate is currently playing out in the context of the Low-Income Housing Tax Credit (LIHTC) program, which has become the largest source of support for subsidized housing production in the country and now houses a larger population than public housing (Schwartz, 2006). As of the end of 2005, the LIHTC program had allocated $7.5 billion in federal tax credits and supported the development of more than 1.5 million units (Danter Company, 2007). A growing number of advocates and observers worry that the LIHTC program, by failing to monitor the siting of developments and, more directly, by giving priority to developers building housing in high-poverty areas, is furthering poverty and racial concentration. Yet, many community development organizations see the tax credit program as a central tool in their efforts to revitalize these high-poverty, urban neighborhoods. In this chapter, we try to inject some empirical evidence into this debate by examining the extent to which the tax credit program may have contributed to poverty concentration as well as to neighborhood revitalization.

We offer three different forms of empirical evidence. First, and most simply, we describe the siting patterns of LIHTC developments to examine whether tax credit units are disproportionately being constructed in high-poverty neighborhoods and therefore potentially exacerbating poverty concentration, at least in the short term. Second, we examine whether there is any evidence that the construction of new LIHTC developments is triggering improvements in high-poverty neighborhoods. We present some suggestive evidence on the link between the number of tax credit units built in a neighborhood and changes in poverty rates and, using property-level sales data in New York City, explore effects on surrounding property values. Finally, we explore the extent to which the use of tax credits in a metropolitan area is correlated with changes in poverty concentration and segregation.

In brief, we find little evidence that the program is exacerbating poverty concentration, at least on average. Of course, LIHTC activity may be heightening poverty concentration in particular metropolitan areas. We find some suggestive evidence that this could be true in areas in which the bulk of LIHTC units are constructed in high-poverty neighborhoods. But even here, depending on the local investment strategy, the story might be more nuanced, at least in some circumstances. The results from New York City suggest that the siting of tax credit units in low-income, urban neighborhoods can encourage community improvement, at least when it is part of an explicit revitalization effort.

It is worth underscoring that this chapter does not address the more general question of the merits of production programs in relation to alternatives. The LIHTC program is likely here to stay, at least for a while. Rather, we explore one particular facet of the tax credit program—its siting in neighborhoods and the resulting effects on both segregation and neighborhood spillovers.

THE LIHTC PROGRAM

Established in 1987, the Low-Income Housing Tax Credit program has now become the primary source of support for creating place-based, affordable rental housing in the United States. The LIHTC program was created as part of the Tax Reform Act of 1986, which simultaneously eliminated an array of more general real estate and housing tax benefits. The result is a much more narrow tax benefit, limited to the acquisition, construction, or rehabilitation of affordable rental housing. Established for a three-year period at its start, Section 42 of the Internal Revenue Code was made permanent in 1993.

Unlike receipt of many other tax credits, receipt of the LIHTC is not automatic. Recipients must apply for a limited pool of credits that are allocated annually to states on the basis of state population. At the program's start, the state per capita allocation was set at $1.25. This amount was increased to $1.75 in 2002, and has been adjusted for inflation thereafter, reaching $1.95 in 2007.[1] Each annual allocation authorizes a 10-year stream of tax credits, reaching over $670 million for 2006. Table 8.1 shows the annual number of units placed in service between 1987 and 2003, with well over a million units of low-income housing produced by 2003.

States are permitted to issue these credits to developers to support qualified, low-income rental housing projects. A project can qualify through either of two income criteria for occupants: at least 20 percent of households have incomes below 50 percent of the area median income (AMI); or at least 40 percent of households have incomes below 60 percent of the AMI.[2] Projects must meet these requirements for a minimum of 15 years to qualify for the 10-year stream of tax credits. In practice, the vast majority of LIHTC projects contain only low-income units. The last column of table 8.1 shows that since 1993, more than 90 percent of units in tax credit projects qualified as affordable,

---

1. In 2001, a state minimum credit of $2 million (indexed for inflation) was adopted; this increased tax credits above the per capita rate for 13 states with smaller populations.

2. Although the credit sets a minimum share of units within developments that are deemed affordable, the amount of tax credits available for a project increases with the share of units that are affordable.

TABLE 8.1 LIHTC Units Placed in Service by Year

Year LIHTC unit placed in service	Total LIHTC units	Total low-income LIHTC units	LIHTC units that are low-income (percent)
1987	25,445	21,947	86.25
1988	57,533	51,279	89.13
1989	69,668	59,649	85.62
1990	47,992	38,966	81.19
1991	48,196	40,574	84.19
1992	51,186	45,937	89.75
1993	62,815	57,124	90.94
1994	62,905	60,338	95.92
1995	79,262	73,892	93.23
1996	82,482	76,705	93.00
1997	87,273	79,838	91.48
1998	93,706	86,129	91.91
1999	107,750	97,853	90.81
2000	99,034	90,468	91.35
2001	100,812	93,052	92.30
2002	99,854	92,639	92.77
2003	112,478	101,966	90.65
Total	1, 288,391	1,168,356	90.65

NOTE: LIHTC = Low-Income Housing Tax Credit.

SOURCE: Authors' analysis of data from the HUD Low-Income Housing Tax Credit Database, http://www.huduser.org/datasets/lihtc.html.

low-income units (that is, owners guaranteed that rent levels would be set to be affordable to households earning 60 percent of the area median income or less).[3]

The amount of tax credits awarded to a project also depends on the nature of the housing (acquired, constructed, or rehabilitated), the presence of federally subsidized loans, and total eligible development costs.[4] As noted previously, projects located in high-poverty neighborhoods (qualified census tracts, or QCTs) receive a 30 percent bonus. A similar bonus is available to projects located in Difficult Development Areas (DDAs), which are counties or metropolitan areas in which construction, land, and utility costs are high in relation to area income.[5]

---

3. Total LIHTC units are all units in buildings that receive LIHTC credits, regardless of rent restrictions. Total low-income LIHTC units are those meeting the income and rent requirements.

4. For a good overview of program details, see Schwartz (2006).

5. The 30 percent increase is not additive. Projects located in QCTs within DDAs receive a 30 percent increase in credits, total.

The LIHTC is also different from other tax credits in that it is effectively administered at the state level. Under the LIHTC program, each state must designate a specific agency to allocate tax credits, most typically the state Housing Finance Agencies (HFAs).[6] The explicit intent of this structure is to have the LIHTC tailored to state and local conditions.[7] These allocating agencies determine the priorities for the LIHTC program, and also award credits. They are required to submit yearly qualified allocation plans (QAPs) that relate the priorities for use of LIHTC credits to local housing conditions and needs. These plans generally provide concrete guidance to developers on the specific state priorities, including selection criteria when awarding tax credits. There are many common criteria shared across allocating agencies that reflect federal requirements, such as reasonable development costs, serving the lowest-income households, and using the minimum amount of tax credit financing feasible. There are also variations across states, such as set-asides for developments in rural areas, and priority points for geographic areas within the state with greatest need (based on low vacancy rates, high rents, or both). As the competition for credits has increased, these criteria are likely to play a greater role in the final distribution of tax credit projects.[8]

This variation in state priorities might translate into differences in likely impacts on poverty segregation. To get a sense of the variation across states in their use of LIHTC credits, we examined data on each state's allocations over the 1990s, as reported to the National Council of State Housing Agencies (NCSHA).[9] We found large variations in three dimensions of LIHTC allocations that could affect poverty segregation: who is served, where the housing is located, and developer mission (nonprofit status). Although the states reported allocating, on average, just over 22 percent of tax credits to QCTs, this nine-year average varied from a minimum of zero to a high of 80 percent. Sixty-four percent of state allocations were reportedly supporting units targeted at the highest eligible income category (51 percent to 60 percent of AMI), ranging from a low of 23 percent to a high of 92 percent. On average, approximately

---

6. There are 59 allocating agencies because several states have multiple allocating agencies and two territories are allocating agencies (Puerto Rico and the Virgin Islands). See www.huduser.org.

7. These agencies typically have a range of housing-related responsibilities beyond issuing debt. The majority of allocating agencies also administer Section 8 project-based and voucher programs, and have some responsibility for state-level programs (including state tax credits for about 15 HFAs).

8. LIHTC projects that are 50 percent financed through tax-exempt bonds can automatically qualify for LIHTC credits of 4 percent. Although these credits must meet all LIHTC restrictions, such developments do not go through the competitive process set forth in QAPs, so would not necessarily be affected by state priorities. These tax credits do not count toward the state yearly per capita cap.

9. NCSHA publishes an annual fact book that is based on self-reported data for all allocating agencies. These data are based on allocations, not completed projects, and are not verified independently. They are, however, available for purchase. Our numbers are based on reports from 1992 to 2000.

36 percent of allocations were made to nonprofits over this period, ranging from 0 percent to 69 percent. Federal legislation requires a 10 percent set-aside for nonprofits, but approximately six states typically did not meet this standard in each year.

Although the LIHTC is a critical component of our national affordable housing policy, we actually have quite limited information on its performance. As a tax credit program, direct outlays are not recorded or monitored each year and federal oversight is the responsibility of the Internal Revenue Service (IRS), a federal agency that does not administer programs and has no responsibility for housing.[10]

Why Might LIHTC Investments Affect the Segregation of Poor Households?

The most obvious and direct way in which LIHTC investments might further poverty segregation is the siting of developments. A growing number of fair-housing advocates are worried that these siting decisions are furthering racial and economic segregation by locating a disproportionate share of tax credit developments in high-poverty neighborhoods. They point to program provisions that actually provide higher tax credit amounts to projects developed in "qualified census tracts," defined as neighborhoods where at least 50 percent of the households have incomes below 60 percent of their metropolitan area's median family income.[11] Moreover, in 2000, Congress modified the program to require states and localities to give a preference to projects located in qualified census tracts "that contribute to a concerted community revitalization plan" (Orfield, 2005).[12] Many advocates see these preferences as antithetical to the goal of poverty deconcentration, as they encourage developers to use the tax credits (and thus build subsidized housing) in high-poverty areas (Orfield, 2005).[13]

---

10. State allocating agencies are required to submit data to the IRS. As tax-related documents, these data are not available for analysis.

11. There was no debate in either the House of Representatives or the Senate regarding the QCT provision (Orfield, 2005).

12. In 2000, the definition of QCT was also altered so that localities could use a 25 percent poverty threshold instead to define QCTs. On average, the two thresholds are roughly equivalent.

13. Many advocates have also argued that the LIHTC program should be bound by the same siting guidelines adopted by HUD in the 1970s to minimize the concentration of poor and minority households (Poverty and Race Research Action Council, 2004; Roisman, 2000). Specifically, following the mandate legislated in the Civil Rights Act of 1968 that the federal government must administer its housing programs in a way that "affirmatively furthers" fair housing goals, HUD issued siting guidelines in the 1970s that discouraged local housing authorities from locating new assisted housing in neighborhoods with high concentrations of poor and minority households.

Although it is surely worth questioning why an explicit preference for lower-income areas is warranted, its existence does not prove that states and localities are in fact allocating credits disproportionately to QCTs. Baum-Snow and Marion (2007) show that at the margin tax credit developments are being sited in QCTs, but this does not suggest that most LIHTC units are located in QCTs, nor does it preclude the possibility that many are being constructed in higher-income communities.[14] Although Congress now requires states and localities to give preference to projects located in qualified census tracts, it is only one of a set of preferences that states and localities use in allocating their tax credits. And although developers receive higher credit amounts when building in high-poverty neighborhoods, they may have other reasons to build in higher-income areas.[15]

It is worth underscoring that in considering potential impacts of siting on poverty segregation, the key question is whether tax credit projects are located in neighborhoods with higher poverty than the neighborhoods LIHTC households would live in, absent the opportunity to live in a subsidized, tax credit unit. Evidence from the Moving to Opportunity (MTO) program, a national demonstration that offered housing vouchers to families living in public housing, reminds us that even with portable rent subsidies, poor households tend to live in fairly high-poverty communities.

Consider a simple numerical example. Assume a city has five neighborhoods of 1,000 people each, one of which is 60 percent poor, one of which is 10 percent poor, and three of which have no poor residents. Although 14 percent of the city's population is poor overall, the average poor resident lives in a neighborhood where 53 percent of the population is poor. This is the weighted average of the 60 percent poor neighborhood in which 600 poor residents live and the 10 percent poor neighborhood in which 100 poor residents live. (This weighted average is also described as an isolation index of 0.53.[16]) By contrast, the average nonpoor resident lives in a neighborhood with only a 7.7 percent poverty rate.

---

14. The authors show that a significantly greater share of rental units are subsidized through the LIHTC in tracts that are just above the QCT threshold (those in which between 50 percent and 51 percent of households earn less than 60 percent of the area median income) as compared to tracts that are just slightly below the threshold (those in which between 49 percent and 50 percent of households earn less than 60 percent of the median income).

15. Because developers are permitted to convert units to market-rate status after 15 or 30 years, they may wish to build in neighborhoods where they think the market will be stronger. Moreover, developers may have an easier time building tax credit housing in higher-income areas than other forms of subsidized housing. Politically, tax credit housing may face fewer "not in my backyard" (NIMBY) barriers than publicly owned and other HUD-administered housing, precisely because it is viewed as being more independent of government regulation (Freeman, 2004).

16. See the section on the construction of LIHTC units and segregation, later in this chapter, for a full discussion of this index.

Now imagine that a developer builds a set of LIHTC units that house 300 poor residents (and no nonpoor residents). If the units are built in the high-poverty area of this city — the neighborhood that is initially 60 percent poor — poverty concentration will increase, and the isolation index will rise to 0.63.[17] If those units are instead spread evenly across the neighborhoods that initially have no poor residents, the poverty isolation index will fall to 0.40. Finally, consider a third alternative, placing the LIHTC units in the census tract that is originally 10 percent poor, an exposure to poverty that is higher than the typical nonpoor person faces but lower than that faced by the average poor person. In this case, the isolation index will fall to 0.48.[18]

There are two caveats to this simple example, however, or reasons why building a disproportionate share of LIHTC units in high-poverty neighborhoods may not necessarily exacerbate the isolation of the poor, at least in the long run. First, many LIHTC residents may not be poor. There is unfortunately no public source of information about tenant incomes in the tax credit program, but some tax credit developments include market-rate units, and the few studies that examine the characteristics of qualifying, low-income LIHTC tenants suggest that their incomes are higher, on average, than the incomes of tenants living in other forms of federally subsidized housing (Buron et al., 2000; McClure, 2006). The program guidelines allow for tenants to earn up to 60 percent of an area's median income, and LIHTC developments tend to charge rents that are close to the maximum allowed by the program (McClure, 2006).[19] This is not to say that no LIHTC tenants are poor. Many tax credit tenants also receive Section 8 vouchers, which allow them to afford the tax credit rents (General Accounting Office, 1997). One study estimates that approximately 40 percent of LIHTC tenants have incomes below 30 percent of median income, which is approximately equal to the poverty line in the average metropolitan area (Buron et al., 2000).[20]

A second reason why building tax credit developments in low-income areas may not further segregation is that the housing investments supported by tax

---

17. This is assuming that there is no growth in the population of nonpoor residents in the city. The same result, although less dramatic, would hold if we assumed the nonpoor population rose so that the city population remained 14 percent poor overall.

18. To be precise, the isolation index will fall if the neighborhood poverty rate where the LIHTC units are placed (as calculated after any additional poor move in) is lower than the neighborhood poverty rate the average poor person experienced ex ante.

19. Analyzing rents from a large sample of LIHTC developments, Cummings and DiPasquale (1999) find that in 1996, only one-third of qualifying renter households could have paid the median LIHTC rent without spending more than 30 percent of their income.

20. The study also finds that a majority of LIHTC tenants have incomes below 50 percent of median income.

credits may help improve distressed neighborhoods and make them more appealing to higher-income households by removing blight, building attractive new housing, repopulating a community, inviting other investment and improvements, or some combination of all of these (Baum-Snow and Marion, 2007; Eriksen and Rosenthal, 2007; Schwartz et al., 2006). When the public housing program was first established, such neighborhood benefits were a key justification, and there was considerable optimism that the program's investments would help revitalize distressed areas and even increase property values (Fisher, 1959). Although such optimism about the potential of public housing to revitalize communities has clearly waned, many advocates maintain that the LIHTC program has helped to further neighborhood revitalization in many low-income areas.

It is also possible that LIHTC investments discourage unsubsidized, private development in the local market. Eriksen and Rosenthal (2007) provide some evidence suggesting that this may occur. We do not investigate the possibility of crowd-out in this chapter.

SITING OF LIHTC UNITS

Table 8.2 shows the distribution of low-income tax credit units built in low- and high-poverty census tracts during the 1980s, the 1990s, and between 2000 and 2003.[21] As shown in the fourth column, during the 1980s, 9 percent of tax credit units were built in high-poverty census tracts (those with poverty rates of at least 40 percent at the start of the decade). This share rose in the 1990s, to 12.2 percent, and then fell back again to 8.5 percent after 2000.[22]

To some extent, these shifts may be driven by changes over time in the proportion of all census tracts that qualify as high-poverty tracts.[23] The final column of table 8.2 thus shows the ratio of the share of tax credit units located in high-poverty tracts in an MSA to the share of all housing units located in high-poverty tracts in the same MSA. For each of the three periods, LIHTC units are approximately three times more likely to be located in high-poverty tracts, as compared to all housing units. There is little change over time in this ratio; we see no increase in the 1990s, nor any change after the 2000 amendment that required states and localities to give preference to LIHTC developments located in QCTs.

---

21. The distributions are largely unchanged when we exclude older units.
22. These figures are consistent with past studies (see Newman and Schnare, 1997).
23. In our sample, 2.9 percent of all housing units were located in high-poverty tracts in 1980, 4 percent in 1990, and 2.8 percent in 2000.

TABLE 8.2   Distribution of Low-Income LIHTC Units by Neighborhood Poverty Level

	Percent of low-income LIHTC units built in tracts with:				Percent of low-income LIHTC units built in:	
	10% poor or lower (low poverty)	10–30% poor	30–40% poor	40% poor or higher (high poverty)	Low-poverty tracts/% all units built in low-poverty tracts	High-poverty tracts/% all units built in high-poverty tracts
U.S. total						
1980s	32.0	44.9	14.0	9.0	0.54	3.10
1990s	36.4	40.4	11.0	12.2	0.62	3.05
2000s	34.2	44.2	13.1	8.5	0.59	3.04
Northeast						
1980s	25.6	45.1	21.4	8.0	0.41	2.07
1990s	31.0	32.1	14.7	22.2	0.46	6.39
2000s	25.9	36.8	21.0	16.3	0.42	4.62
Midwest						
1980s	35.5	39.0	8.0	17.5	0.52	6.37
1990s	41.8	31.4	11.6	15.2	0.67	2.96
2000s	38.8	36.2	12.3	12.7	0.58	5.06
South						
1980s	33.7	46.6	14.3	5.4	0.65	1.42
1990s	35.4	45.5	9.9	9.2	0.69	1.82
2000s	36.5	45.9	12.3	5.3	0.69	1.77
West						
1980s	30.6	50.2	14.9	4.3	0.53	5.17
1990s	35.2	48.7	9.3	6.8	0.63	3.50
2000s	32.1	50.4	10.8	6.8	0.60	3.15
Large MSAs (over 1 million)						
1980s	27.7	43.8	16.5	12.0	0.44	3.61
1990s	33.8	38.2	13.0	14.9	0.54	3.84
2000s	33.7	42.5	13.4	10.4	0.55	3.84
Midsized MSAs (between 250,000 and 1 million)						
1980s	39.0	43.0	11.1	6.9	0.67	3.02
1990s	39.3	42.5	9.2	8.9	0.68	2.38
2000s	34.9	46.8	12.5	5.8	0.61	2.06
Small MSAs (less than 250,000)						
1980s	30.3	55.6	11.5	2.6	0.63	0.97
1990s	39.0	43.7	7.1	10.2	0.89	1.95
2000s	35.4	47.7	12.8	4.1	0.74	1.29

NOTES: LIHTC = Low-Income Housing Tax Credit; MSAs = metropolitan statistical areas.

SOURCE: Authors' analysis of decennial Census data (http://factfinder.census.gov) linked with data from HUD's Low-Income Housing Tax Credit Database, http://www.huduser.org/datasets/lihtc.html.

Table 8.2 also shows that about one-third of LIHTC units are located in low-poverty census tracts (tracts with poverty rates of less than 10 percent), a finding consistent with that of other work (see, e.g., Khadduri, Buron, and Climaco, 2006; McClure, 2006). This proportion appears to have increased slightly during the 1990s and then decreased (even more slightly) after 2000.

A key question is how these distributions compare to those of other subsidized housing programs. LIHTC units are far less likely to be located in high-poverty neighborhoods than are public housing units.[24] As compared to those of voucher holders, LIHTC units are somewhat more likely to be located in high-poverty tracts, although they are also more likely to be located in low-poverty areas (McClure, 2006).[25] Consider that even among the members of the MTO experimental group, who were given vouchers that they had to use in low-poverty census tracts for at least one year, only 13 percent of them were living in low-poverty census tracts a few years after receipt of their voucher (Orr et al., 2003), as compared to roughly one-third of LIHTC tenants.

Perhaps the most critical question, however, is how the location of tax credit units compares to that of other poor and low-income households? Has the typical LIHTC unit been constructed in a neighborhood that is more or less poor than the typical neighborhood lived in by other poor households? To answer this question, we compare the average poverty rate of the neighborhoods lived in by poor residents in 1990 to the average poverty rate of the neighborhoods where LIHTC units were built during the 1990s. We find that in 1990 the typical poor resident of a metropolitan area lived in a neighborhood that was 23.4 percent poor. The typical tax credit unit built during the 1990s, meanwhile, was constructed in a census tract in which the poverty rate was 4.5 percentage points lower, 18.9 percent. At first blush, then, these siting patterns show no clear push toward increased concentration or segregation of the poor.

It is worth underscoring that these national averages conceal a great deal of variation across states and metropolitan areas. The LIHTC program is essentially state run, so states have wide latitude to make different choices about where to allocate their tax credits. The regional differences shown in table 8.2 are fairly striking. LIHTC units are far more likely to be located in high-poverty neighborhoods in the Northeast and Midwest and far less likely to be located in high-poverty neighborhoods in the South. And this is not

---

24. See Cummings and Dipasquale (1999), Newman and Schnare (1997), and Rohe and Freeman (2001).

25. The greater share of LIHTC units in low-poverty neighborhoods appears to be driven in large part by the suburban LIHTC units, half of which have been built in low-poverty census tracts (McClure, 2006).

simply due to differences in the share of high-poverty neighborhoods across regions (see the final column). Similarly, the table shows that LIHTC units are far more likely to be located in high-poverty neighborhoods in larger metropolitan areas.[26] Indeed, in New York City, the typical LIHTC unit built in the 1990s was located in a neighborhood with virtually the identical poverty rate as the typical neighborhood lived in by poor residents of the city in 1990 (30.8 percent). As noted previously, the ultimate effect of such decisions to target LIHTC developments to poor neighborhoods depends to a large degree on whether there are positive spillovers from the investments, the question to which we turn next.

SPILLOVERS

Although siting low-income units in low-income areas may further segregation in the short run, such subsidized housing investments can potentially help to revitalize low-income areas over the longer run. Some prior research has found evidence of such neighborhood spillovers, as measured by increases in the value of neighboring properties (Pedone, Remch, and Case, 1983; Schwartz et al., 2006). [27] But much of the research is mixed and suffers from data limitations in identifying causal relationships. It is fair to say that many are now skeptical that such spillover effects are significant.

A few recent papers examine the spillover effects of the LIHTC program in particular. Green, Malpezzi, and Seah (2002) use data on home sales in one city and three counties in Wisconsin to examine the association between proximity to LIHTC developments and home values. The results are mixed. They find no effect in two counties, small negative impacts in the third, and positive effects in their one city.[28]

Baum-Snow and Marion (2007) explore the impacts of the completion of LIHTC developments on median income levels and turnover rates in surrounding neighborhoods. They rely on tract-level decennial census data to estimate their models. Recognizing that developers may choose to build in gentrifying neighborhoods, they cleverly exploit the QCT eligibility cutoff to

---

26. In 40 metropolitan areas, a majority of tax credit units built in the 1990s were located in tracts with poverty rates of 30 percent or more.

27. In their careful study, Santiago, Galster, and Tatian (2001) also find that scattered-site public housing can deliver neighborhood benefits, but their results are more mixed.

28. Green, Malpezzi, and Seah (2002) estimate a repeat sales model and utilize an interesting gravity measure of distance to LIHTC development sites. But because they do not have access to project completion dates, their coefficients on distance cannot be interpreted as impact measures.

undertake a regression discontinuity analysis that helps to correct for any potential endogeneity from siting decisions. They find that LIHTC developments depress median neighborhood incomes and increase turnover in owner-occupied units within three kilometers. As they note, however, their approach allows them to estimate the impacts of LIHTC developments on moderately poor neighborhoods that are near the border of the QCT threshold, and their results may not be generalizable to higher-poverty areas. Another issue is that the authors use decennial census data, which means that they are restricted to census geographies and must rely on 10-year changes. Given the small size of these LIHTC developments (roughly 70 units, on average), it is also worth questioning whether they could generate effects that extend out to three kilometers.

Eriksen and Rosenthal (2007) offer another interesting analysis of the neighborhood impacts of LIHTC developments on unsubsidized construction and self-reported rents and home values in surrounding neighborhoods. Using decennial census data, they find that LIHTC developments have a modest positive amenity effect in nearby low-income areas but a negative "stigma" effect in nearby higher-income areas. They also argue that the LIHTC developments crowd out unsubsidized, private development.

Our first test for spillovers is fairly straightforward, using decennial census data to estimate a very simple, reduced form regression showing the association between the number of LIHTC units built in a census tract during the 1990s and the change in the poverty rate in that tract during the 1990s. Specifically, we estimate the following model:

$$\Delta Poverty_{ij} = \alpha + \beta X_{ij} + \mu_j + \varepsilon_{ij} \qquad (8.1)$$

where $\Delta Poverty_{ij}$ is the change in the poverty rate in census tract i in metropolitan area j between 1990 and 2000, X_{ij} is a vector of tract level demographic and housing characteristics in 1990 (population, racial composition, proportion of foreign-born residents, poverty rate, proportion with college degrees, home ownership rate, the proportion of the housing stock that is very old, and the proportion that was built in the past five years), and μ_j is a vector of MSA fixed effects.

Table 8.3 shows the results of this simple model. The first column shows that when considering the full set of metropolitan tracts, we find that the completion of more LIHTC units in a tract during the 1990s is associated with increases in the poverty rate during the decade. Given that the poverty rate among the population living in LIHTC developments is clearly higher than the poverty rate of the typical census tract in a metropolitan area, this result is unsurprising.

TABLE 8.3 Regression Results: Change in Tract Poverty Rate, 1990–2000

	Sample: all metro tracts	Sample: high-poverty tracts[a]	Sample: moderate/low-poverty tracts[b]
Intercept	0.1020***	0.2519***	0.0932***
	(.0084)	(0.0385)	(0.0084)
Number of LIHTC	0.0449***	−0.0431	0.0609***
units built/1,000,	(.0045)	(.0293)	(0.0043)
1990–2000			
Tract population/	0.0006***	0.0096***	0.0000
1,000, 1990	(.0001)	(.0013)	(0.0001)
Percent black, 1990	.0483***	0.0091	0.0533***
	(.0013)	(0.0109)	(0.0013)
Percent Hispanic,	0.0202***	−0.0384**	0.0368***
1990	(0.0024)	(0.0172)	(0.0029)
Percent foreign-	0.0426***	−0.0664**	0.0533***
born, 1990	(0.0036)	(0.0285)	(0.0036)
Percent college	−0.0368***	−0.0135	−0.0446***
graduates, 1990	(0.0018)	(0.0273)	(0.0015)
Poverty rate, 1990	−0.3754***	−0.446***	−0.4281***
	(0.0032)	(0.0247)	(0.0060)
Home ownership	−0.0839***	−0.181***	−0.0706***
rate, 1990	(0.0014)	(0.0166)	(0.0013)
Percent of housing	−0.0217***	−0.0162	−0.0206***
units built in past	(0.0019)	(0.036)	(0.0016)
five years			
Percent of housing units	0.0072	−0.0287***	0.0124***
over 40 years old	(0.0012)	(0.0105)	(0.0011)
N	50,185	2,614	40,258
MSA fixed effects	Yes	Yes	Yes

NOTES: We estimated these regressions using clustered standard errors and results were essentially unchanged. Standard errors are in parentheses. [a] = Census tracts with 1990 poverty rate of at least 40%. [b] = Census tracts with 1990 poverty rate of less than 20%. ** = statistically significant at the .05 level; *** = statistically significant at the .01 level. MSA = metropolitan statistical area.

SOURCE: Authors' analysis of decennial Census data (http://factfinder.census.gov) linked with data from HUD's Low-Income Housing Tax Credit Database, http://www.huduser.org/datasets/lihtc.html.

Of greater interest, perhaps, is what happens to the poverty rate when LIHTC units are placed in poorer tracts. The results in the second column speak to this question. Here, the sample includes only census tracts with poverty rates of at least 40 percent in 1990. With this higher-poverty sample, the coefficient on the number of tax credit units becomes negative and is almost statistically significant at the 10 percent level. In other words, the construction of tax credit units in high-poverty tracts is, if anything, associated with reductions in poverty. By way of contrast, the final column presents results when the sample is limited to tracts with poverty rates of less than 20 percent. The coefficient on the number of tax credit units is significantly positive. This contrast is consistent with Eriksen and Rosenthal (2007) and suggests caution in generalizing findings from the impacts of LIHTC units in moderately poor areas to those in higher-poverty tracts.

Of course, there are many weaknesses in this simple analysis. The selection of where to locate tax credit units is clearly endogenous, in ways that could either make impacts appear more negative (if placed in neighborhoods with increasing poverty rates) or overstate positive changes (if placed in neighborhoods that are improving).

In this regard, we believe our second empirical strategy, which uses property-level data, is more persuasive. Using property-level sales data from New York City, we estimate the spillover effects of LIHTC developments on surrounding property values, building on our earlier work on the neighborhood impacts of a broader set of city- and federally-assisted housing developments (Ellen et al., 2007; Schwartz et al., 2006). The strength of these data is that they offer far more variation over time and space. Of course, the weakness of our approach is that we study only the impacts of tax credits in a single jurisdiction.

In some ways, however, New York City is an ideal place in which to explore spillovers in poor neighborhoods, as it clearly allocated its tax credits with an eye toward revitalizing high-poverty areas.[29] The city used its tax credits in large part to support its Ten-Year Capital Plan for Housing, which aimed to build or rehabilitate housing on the city-owned sites that had been taken through tax foreclosure during the late 1970s. These city-owned properties were located in many of the city's poorest areas, and an explicit aim of the plan was neighborhood revitalization.[30] As shown in table 8.4, 44 percent of the LIHTC units placed in service in the city during the 1990s were built in high-poverty neighborhoods during the 1990s, as compared to just 12 percent nationally. Figure 8.1 presents a map showing the distribution of LIHTC developments in New York City as of 2003. It shows clearly that LIHTC activity has been concentrated in some of the highest-poverty neighborhoods in the city.

---

29. New York City is unusual in that it directly allocates tax credits.

30. A document produced by the Department of Housing Preservation and Development (HPD) early in the Ten-Year Capital Plan for Housing demonstrates the focus on neighborhood revitalization: "We're creating more than just apartments—we're re-creating neighborhoods. We're revitalizing parts of the city that over the past two decades have been decimated by disinvestment, abandonment, and arson" (New York City, Department of Housing Preservation and Development, 1989).

TABLE 8.4 Distribution of LIHTC Units in New York City

	Percent of LIHTC units built in tracts with:			
	10% poor or lower (low poverty)	10–30% poor	30–40% poor	40% poor or higher (high poverty)
1980s	0.0	48.5	19.4	32.1
1990s	10.4	25.4	20.7	43.6
Post-2000	6.9	19.9	31.0	42.3

NOTE: LIHTC = Low-Income Housing Tax Credit.

SOURCE: Authors' analysis of decennial Census data (http://factfinder.census.gov) linked with data from HUD's Low-Income Housing Tax Credit Database, http://www.huduser.org/datasets/lihtc.html.

To estimate impact on neighborhood, we use data on sales prices for all apartment buildings, condominium apartments, and single-family homes selling in the city between 1980 and 2005.[31] Our final sample includes 501,898 property sales, spread across 1,896 census tracts. We obtain characteristics of these properties from the Real Property Assessment Data file, a data set collected for the purposes of computing property tax assessments.

We link these sales data to data describing all 42,077 housing units constructed or rehabilitated through the LIHTC program between 1987 and 2003, obtained from HUD User and the Local Initiatives Support Corporation (LISC). For each LIHTC project, this data set indicates its precise location (address), the year of completion, and the number of total and low-income units that were built or rehabilitated. We also secured address-specific data on all other types of federally and city-subsidized housing developments from HUD User, the New York City Housing Authority (NYCHA), and New York City's Department of Housing Preservation and Development (HPD).[32]

We use Geographic Information Systems (GIS) software to identify whether property sales are in the vicinity of subsidized housing sites. Specifically, we measure the distance from each property sale to all subsidized housing sites and, from these distance measures, create a set of variables that identify properties within 1,000 feet of housing investments of different types.[33]

---

31. We limited the analysis to properties that are located within the 52 community districts (of the total 59) where LIHTC units were developed. Note that sales of cooperative apartments are excluded from the data set because they are not considered to be sales of real property.

32. See Ellen et al. (2007) for a detailed description of these data sets.

33. We used a "cross-walk" data file (the "Geosupport File" from the New York City Department of City Planning, http://www.nyc.gov/html/dcp/pdf/bytes/geosupport.pdf) to link each tax lot to an x,y coordinate (i.e., latitude, longitude using the U.S. State Plane 1927 projection). Using this method, we are able to assign x,y coordinates and other geographic variables to more than 98 percent of the sales. For federal housing units, we used a coordinate conversion software (PROLAT) to convert the latitude and longitude coordinates — available from HUD — into x,y coordinates.

FIGURE 8.1 Location of LIHTC Developments in New York City

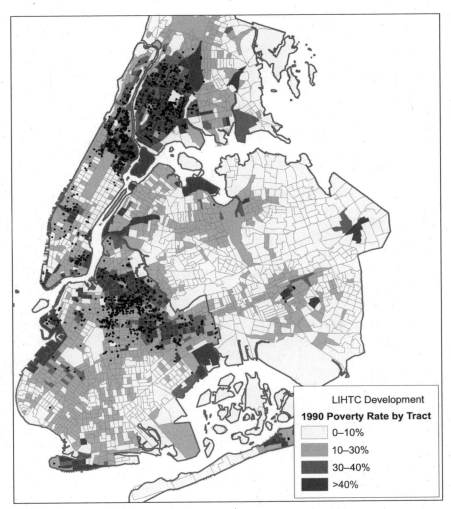

We use these data to estimate a hedonic regression model that explains the sales price of a property as a function of its structural characteristics (such as lot size and age of the building), its neighborhood surroundings, and its proximity to subsidized housing. We can then compare the prices of properties that are within 1,000 feet of LIHTC sites to prices of comparable properties that are outside this 1,000-foot ring but still located in the same neighborhood. We examine whether the magnitude of this difference changes after the LIHTC housing units are completed.

Specifically, our regression model is as follows:

$$
\begin{aligned}
\ln P_{icdt} = {} & \alpha + \beta X_{it} + \delta_c W_c + \gamma^{LIHTC} R_{it}^{LIHTC} \\
& + \theta R_{it}^{LIHTC} D_i + \gamma^o R_{it}^o + \rho_{dt} I_{dt} + \varepsilon_{it},
\end{aligned}
\tag{8.2}
$$

where $\ln P_{icdt}$ is the log of the sales price per unit of property i in census tract c, in community district d, and in quarter t, X_{it} is a vector of property-related characteristics (including age and structural characteristics), W_c are a series of census tract fixed effects, R_{it} are vectors of ring variables (described below), and I_{dt} are a series of dummy variables indicating the quarter and community district of the sale.[34] The coefficients to be estimated are α, β, δ, γ, θ and ρ, and ε is an error term.[35]

The property-related characteristics, X_{it}, include structural characteristics of the properties, including building age, square footage, the number of buildings on the lot, and a set of dummy variables distinguishing 18 different building classifications, such as "single-family detached," "two-family home," and so on. To control for unobserved, time-invariant features of different neighborhoods, we include census tract fixed effects (W_c). To control for broader trends in housing appreciation, we include a series of community district-specific, time dummies, I_{dt} (one for each quarter in each year of the study period) for each of the 52 community districts used in the analysis. (A joint test of significance of census tract specific time dummies indicated that they contributed little explanatory power over the community district time dummy variables.)

The ring variables (R_{it}^{LIHTC}) capture the impact of proximity to LIHTC housing units.[36] To be specific, "In Ring" is a dummy variable that takes a value of one if the property is located within 1,000 feet of a site on which there is, or

---

34. New York City is divided into a total of 59 community districts, each of which has a Community Board whose members are appointed by the Borough President and by the City Council members who represent the district. The typical community district houses roughly 30 times as many people as the average census tract in the city.

35. Note that there might be spatial autocorrelation in the errors. Unfortunately, the large sample size makes the use of more rigorous methods of addressing possible spatial correlation computationally prohibitively demanding. Indeed, to our knowledge, there is no publicly available statistical software that can effectively perform tests and corrections for spatial autocorrelation for sample sizes as large as ours. However, our use of census tract fixed effects alleviates this problem, by removing potential spatial correlation between properties located in different tracts.

36. We also include similar sets of ring variables (R_{it}^o) that control for proximity to other types of subsidized housing, as it is possible that the location of these other types of units is correlated with that of the LIHTC units on which we focus. These include housing created or rehabilitated through other federal programs (such as Section 236, public housing, Section 8, and Section 202), and through programs sponsored by the city under the Ten-Year Capital Plan for Housing.

will be, at least one LIHTC unit.[37] Thus, "In Ring" captures baseline differences in sales prices of properties located within a 1,000-foot ring of LIHTC sites and those outside. Because the baseline of property values may also be associated with the size of the site,[38] we also include number of LIHTC units to be built within 1,000 feet of the sold property, and its square.

A "Post Ring" dummy variable takes a value of one if the sale is within the ring of some number of completed LIHTC units; its coefficient provides the simplest impact estimate.[39] We also include the number of completed units within the ring of the sale (and its square), to estimate the marginal effects of additional subsidized units. Finally, we include a "Tpost" variable (and its square) that equals the number of years between the date of sale and the project completion date for properties in the 1,000-foot ring and that allows the impact to vary over time.[40]

Interactions between distance, D_i, and the set of ring variables R_{it}^{LIHTC} permit us to estimate a pre-project distance gradient within the 1,000-foot ring, plus a post completion distance gradient (again within the ring) and allow this gradient to change over time post completion. In addition, by interacting distance with Tpost and number of units, we explore how that gradient changes over time and with project scale.

As noted by Baum-Snow and Marion (2007), it is possible that the locations of LIHTC developments were related in some systematic way to preexisting trends, not just levels, in housing prices. In choosing sites for new housing, for instance, developers might have aimed to pick neighborhoods with growth potential. If so, then what we interpret as positive LIHTC effects might simply be a continuation of these prior trends.

To help mitigate concerns about such selection bias, we also estimated a specification that includes controls for trends in the relative price of housing in the vicinity of subsidized housing sites before the construction of the housing. This specification differs from equation 8.2 mainly in that here we add a ring-specific time trend that measures the overall price trend in the ring (not simply the trend after completion). This variable is defined in much the same way as Tpost, except that it also applies to properties sold before project

---

37. New York City blocks are typically between 250 and 500 feet long. Thus, the 1,000-foot ring allows for impacts extending two to four blocks away from the housing investment.

38. We expect that larger projects may have been systematically sited in more distressed locations than smaller projects. This is a likely scenario, given that the extent of blight to be removed is larger in more dilapidated neighborhoods.

39. If a sale was within 1,000 feet of more than one project, we use the completion date of the first completed project.

40. Tpost equals 1/365 if a sale is located within the ring of an LIHTC development and occurs the day after its completion; it equals one if the sale occurs one year after completion; and so on.

completion. For example, if a property is sold exactly two years before completion, the trend takes the value of -2.

Table 8.5 shows summary statistics for our sales sample. Panel A shows the location and structural characteristics of sales properties, and panel B shows their prices over time. The first column of panel A shows the characteristics of our full sample of property sales; the second column shows the characteristics of sales located within 1,000 feet of an LIHTC site, before or after completion. As shown, most sales were located in Brooklyn and Queens, largely because those boroughs are dominated by small properties, which sell more frequently than apartment buildings. More than two-thirds of all buildings sold were either one- or two-family homes, and three-quarters were single-family homes, two-family homes, or small apartments. Approximately one-third of the transacting properties had garages and more than three quarters were built before World War II.

The second column of panel A reveals some systematic differences between properties located close to LIHTC sites and those that are not. Properties located within the 1,000-foot ring are far more likely to be in Brooklyn and Manhattan and far less likely to be in Staten Island and Queens. Properties in the 1,000-foot ring are also much older, much less likely to be single-family homes, more likely to be walk-up apartments, and, consistent with these differences, much less likely to have garages.

Panel B shows that in 1980, per unit sales prices for buildings located within 1,000 feet of a future LIHTC site were, on average, 44 percent lower than the prices of buildings located outside the 1,000-foot rings. These projects, in other words, were clearly located in neighborhoods with depressed housing prices. Yet, the table also shows that the differential has fallen over time, starting from 1987 (perhaps not coincidentally, the year when the first LIHTC units were completed). By 2005, properties sold within 1,000 feet of an LIHTC site were, on average, only 20 percent lower than the mean price outside the rings.

Table 8.6 shows our baseline regression results for the property value model. The negative and significant coefficient on InRing shows that LIHTC developments in New York City have typically been built on highly distressed sites within lower-income areas. Before LIHTC projects are built, we find that properties located within 1,000 feet of a (future) LIHTC housing site sold for significantly less than comparable properties located outside the 1,000-foot ring. As expected, the price discount diminishes with distance from the site. Estimated sales prices right next to a site that will ultimately hold an average-sized LIHTC project (64 units) are initially 13.4 percent lower than those in the surrounding neighborhood. At a distance of 1,000 feet from such a site, baseline prices are about 2.1 percent lower than those in the surrounding area. The price discount is somewhat larger for larger sites.

TABLE 8.5   Characteristics of Residential Properties Sold

	A. Location and structural characteristics	
	Percentage of all sales	Percentage of sales within 1,000 feet of LIHTC sites
Borough		
Manhattan	11.2	29.5
Bronx	9.5	13.8
Brooklyn	33.0	52.0
Queens	36.8	2.4
Staten Island	9.5	2.2
Building class		
Single-family detached	24.2	5.4
Single-family attached	12.9	4.9
Two-family	32.1	27.5
Walk-up apartments	15.2	33.4
Elevator apartments	0.8	2.1
Loft buildings	0.1	0.2
Condominiums	12.0	21.7
Mixed-use, multifamily (includes store or office plus residential units)	2.9	5.1
Other structural characteristics		
Built pre–World War II	75.3	87.2
Garage	34.3	7.6
Corner location	8.5	6.7
Major alteration prior to sale	1.4	3.4
N	501,898	87,406

	B. Prices in rings and outside the rings, by year		
	Average per unit price (in 2005 $)		Prices in rings relative to prices outside the rings (percent)
Year	in 1,000-foot ring	outside 1,000-foot ring	
1980	59,531	107,273	−44.5
1981	64,964	109,634	−40.7
1982	62,131	109,031	−43.0
1983	68,779	121,406	−43.3
1984	66,517	140,634	−52.7
1985	73,252	170,629	−57.1
1986	108,286	224,822	−51.8
1987	190,335	275,241	−30.8
1988	278,842	308,256	−9.5
1989	250,869	286,289	−12.4

(*continued*)

TABLE 8.5 (continued)

	B. Prices in rings and outside the rings, by year		
	Average per unit price (in 2005 $)		Prices in rings relative to prices outside the rings (percent)
Year	in 1,000-foot ring	outside 1,000-foot ring	
1990	211,516	258,758	−18.3
1991	190,715	242,023	−21.2
1992	157,288	219,901	−28.5
1993	149,026	219,560	−32.1
1994	152,923	208,023	−26.5
1995	159,513	206,257	−22.7
1996	164,532	206,365	−20.3
1997	187,023	213,285	−12.3
1998	180,692	227,572	−20.6
1999	167,304	244,846	−31.7
2000	197,431	250,850	−21.3
2001	200,462	251,331	−20.2
2002	251,814	297,192	−15.3
2003	258,993	319,752	−19.0
2004	288,014	360,240	−20.0
2005	314,610	393,453	−20.0
1980–2005	192,477	232,709	−17.3

NOTES: Universe = all sales in community districts with LIHTC projects. LIHTC = Low-Income Housing Tax Credit.

SOURCE: Authors' analysis of sales and property characteristics data from the New York City Department of Finance, confidentially maintained at New York University's Furman Center.

As for effects, the coefficients on Post Ring and Number of Units show that on average, the construction of LIHTC housing units in New York City generated positive and statistically significant external benefits to the surrounding neighborhood.[41] We estimate that the completion of an average-size project in our sample (64 units) increases the relative value of properties that are 100 feet away from the site by 5.7 percentage points.[42] In other words, after the completion of an average-size LIHTC development, the gap between prices of homes that are 100 feet away from the project site and prices of homes in the same neighborhood but more than 1,000 feet away from the development shrinks from 13.4 percent to 7.7 percent. That is, the impact of a project on

---

41. Note that our results may not be inconsistent with Baum-Snow and Marion (2007), as they examine spillovers over a much larger radius, and as noted below, we find that effects diminish with distance from the site.

42. Adjacent properties are defined as those that are 100 feet away from the LIHTC site.

TABLE 8.6 Regression of Spillover Effects on Property Values in New York City

LIHTC	
In ring	−0.1276***
	(0.0066)
In ring*D	1.1E-04***
	(8.1E-06)
Number of units ever completed	−3.0E-04***
	(4.0E-05)
Number of units ever completed^2	1.2E-07***
	(3.1E-08)
Number of units ever completed*D	2.2E-07***
	(4.5E-08)
Post ring	0.0497***
	(0.0101)
Post ring*D	1.5E-05
	(1.3E-05)
Number of units at the time of sale	1.2E-04**
	(5.4E-05)
Number of units at the time of sale^2	3.6E-08
	(5.1E-08)
Number of units at the time of sale*D	−3.8E-07***
	(6.4E-08)
TPost	0.0071***
	(0.0018)
TPost^2	8.8E-05
	(9.1E-05)
TPost*D	−1.3E-05***
	(1.6E-06)
Other federal programs	
In ring	−0.0462***
	(0.0050)
Post ring	0.0042
	(0.0052)
Number of units at the time of sale	−7.9E-05***
	(5.0E-06)
TPost	8.6E-04***
	(1.1E-04)
New York City Ten-Year Capital Plan for Housing,	
new construction, and rehabilitation of vacant buildings	
In ring	−0.0596***
	(0.0026)
Post ring	0.0385***
	(0.0032)

(*continued*)

TABLE 8.6 *(continued)*

Number of units at the time of sale	1.3E-05
	(1.6E-05)
TPost	0.0036***
	(3.3E-04)
New York City Ten-Year Capital Plan for Housing	
and rehabilitation of occupied buildings	
In ring	−0.0481***
	(0.0019)
Post ring	0.0147***
	(0.0019)
Number of units at the time of sale	2.5E-05***
	(5.0E-06)
TPost	0.0026***
	(2.0E-04)
Characteristics of properties sold	
Odd shape	2.3E-02***
	(1.6E-03)
Garage	0.0324***
	(0.0012)
Extension	0.0257***
	(0.0017)
Corner	0.0381***
	(0.0016)
Major alteration before sale	0.0623***
	(0.0041)
Major alteration missing before sale	0.1544***
	(0.0101)
Age of unit	−0.0065***
	(9.5E-05)
Age of unit^2	4.4E-05***
	(8.4E-07)
Age of unit missing	−0.1048***
	(0.0037)
Log square feet per unit	0.4860***
	(0.0015)
Number of buildings on same lot	−9.2E-04
	(0.0018)
Includes commercial space ·	0.0158***
	(0.0027)
Square feet missing	3.2534***
	(0.0153)
Condo and square feet missing	0.2468***
	(0.0090)
Single-family detached	0.0966***
	(0.0017)

TABLE 8.6 *(continued)*

Two-family home	−0.3064***
	(0.0016)
Three-family home	−0.5398***
	(0.0023)
Four-family home	−0.6940***
	(0.0036)
Five- or six-family home	−1.1183***
	(0.0038)
More than six families, no elevator	−1.4634***
	(0.0039)
Walk-up, units not specified	−1.2604***
	(0.0043)
Elevator apartment building, cooperatives	−1.6151***
	(0.0313)
Elevator apartment building, not cooperatives	−1.4682***
	(0.0060)
Loft building	−0.6590***
	(0.0208)
Condominium, single-family attached	−0.2276***
	(0.0095)
Condominium, walk-up apartments	−0.2921***
	(0.0047)
Condominium, elevator building	−0.4184***
	(0.0046)
Condominium, miscellaneous	−0.1444***
	(0.0284)
Multiuse, single-family with store	−0.0358***
	(0.0065)
Multiuse, two-family with store	−0.4234***
	(0.0046)
Multiuse, three-family with store	−0.6669***
	(0.0084)
Multiuse, four or more family with store	−0.8351***
	(0.0060)
N	501,898
R-squared value	0.8567

NOTES: The regression includes census tract and community district-quarter dummies. Standard errors are in parentheses. ** = statistically significant at the .05 level; *** = statistically significant at the .01 level.
LIHTC = Low-Income Housing Tax Credit.

adjacent properties is estimated to be 5.7 percentage points (i.e., 13.4–7.7). These positive impacts grow over time, so that five years after completion, the estimated impact rises to 8.8 percentage points.

As expected, effects decline with distance from the LIHTC development. For example, effects for properties located 500 feet away from the site are 5.3 percentage points immediately after completion and 6 percentage points five years after completion. Also as expected, building more units appears to bring a greater benefit, although this marginal effect declines as the number of units and the distance from the project site increase. For example, the estimated impact of a 100-unit project, 100 feet away from the project site and immediately after completion, is 6.0 percentage points (as compared to 5.7 percentage points for a 64-unit development). As shown in table 8.6, we find that other subsidized units built and rehabilitated through the city's Ten-Year Capital Plan for Housing generated positive spillover effects on neighborhoods as well.

As noted, we also estimated a specification that includes controls for trends in the relative price of housing in the vicinity of subsidized housing sites prior to the completion of the housing. Controlling for these prior trends lowers the magnitude of estimated effects slightly, but the main findings are not affected.

We next explore the extent to which the effects of LIHTC projects vary with income levels in a neighborhood. We test for heterogeneity in effects between low- and middle-income areas by including interactions among all of our variables and a dummy variable indicating neighborhood income level.[43] Following Schwartz et al. (2006), we identify two submarkets—defined by community districts—based on household income information from the 1990 decennial census: the low-income submarket consists of community districts with an average household income of less than 80 percent of the MSA mean household income, and the middle-income submarket includes all the remaining districts.[44] Although we find no difference in the impact of smaller projects across the two types of neighborhoods, our results suggest that larger projects generate larger spillover benefits in lower-income areas.[45] We recognize these findings are for one jurisdiction only, but find this compelling evidence that LIHTC developments can provide positive spillovers in poor neighborhoods. Whether they generally do deliver such spillovers requires more comprehensive analysis.

---

43. In earlier models, an F-test rejected the hypothesis that the coefficients on property characteristics are similar across neighborhoods.

44. To create submarkets, we matched census-tract-level data to community districts. The threshold used to distinguish the two submarkets is $39,037, or 80 percent of the MSA mean household income in 1990.

45. The table is available from the authors on request.

The Construction of LIHTC Units and Segregation

As noted, our key interest is the ultimate impact of the tax credit units on segregation patterns, whether through moving poor households to poorer (or less poor) neighborhoods, moving nonpoor households into different neighborhoods, generating spillover effects in the surrounding neighborhoods, or some combination of all three. To answer this question, we build on the work of Bendernagel et al. (2007), to examine whether the completion of a greater number of LIHTC units in a metropolitan area is associated with higher levels of poverty segregation or isolation. For this analysis, we rely on a panel of 258 metropolitan areas, from 1980 through 2000. Our primary data on metropolitan area characteristics come from the decennial census in 1980, 1990, and 2000. Our data on LIHTC units placed in service come from HUD's low-income tax credit database, which describes the location of LIHTC units placed in service between 1987 and 2003. We limit our analysis to tax credit units built between 1987 and 1999.

We estimate a series of simple models of MSA poverty segregation, as follows:

$$PovSeg_{it} = \alpha + \beta X_{it} + \gamma LIHTC_{it} + \eta MSA_i \\ + \theta REGION^*YEAR_t + \varepsilon \tag{8.3}$$

where X_{it} is a vector of metropolitan-level characteristics found relevant in previous research[46] and $LIHTC_{it}$ is the total number of LIHTC units per capita as of year t in MSA_i. We also include MSA fixed effects and region-specific year dummies, to help control for time-invariant metropolitan-area characteristics as well as geographically varying time effects. Because we might expect differences in siting policies across areas (specifically the degree to which lower-income areas are targeted) to shape how tax credit production affected segregation, we also estimate models in which we include an interaction variable between $LIHTC_{it}$ and the proportion of tax credit units in that metropolitan area that were placed in QCTs in that decade.

For our dependent variable, we employ two measures of segregation, both of which are widely used in the literature on segregation, and each of which captures a different dimension of segregation.[47] The first, the dissimilarity index,

---

46. For example, see Jargowsky (1996) and Watson (2006).
47. For overviews of the issues and measures, see James and Taeuber (1985), Taeuber and Taeuber (1965), and White (1987).

is the most widely used measure to capture the unevenness of a population's distribution. A dichotomous index, it captures the extent to which two groups (in this case, poor and nonpoor) sort differently across neighborhoods within a metropolitan area. Although this measure has its weaknesses (James and Taeuber, 1985; Reardon and Firebaugh, 2002), it has been used extensively in both the residential and school segregation literatures, and has general intuitive appeal. Here, the index can be interpreted as the share of poor residents that would have to be redistributed in order for poor and nonpoor to have the identical distributions. Thus, when there is no segregation, the index is zero, and with complete segregation, it equals one. (See the appendix for a mathematical presentation of both indices.)

The second index we use is the isolation index, mentioned previously, which captures the extent to which poor people live in census tracts with other poor people. The isolation index is equivalent to the tract poverty rate experienced by the average poor person in an MSA. Although the dissimilarity and isolation indices are clearly related, prior work has shown that they are far from perfectly correlated.[48] The dissimilarity index corresponds to the maximum vertical distance between the segregation equivalent of the Lorenz curve and the 45-degree line, and is thus insensitive to changes that do not affect this distance (Duncan and Duncan, 1955). For example, a residential change that does not entail moving a nonpoor person to a poorer-than-average neighborhood, or moving a poor person to a less-poor-than-average neighborhood, will have no effect on the index. Thus, if the LIHTC increases poverty concentration by moving poor households from poor neighborhoods to even poorer neighborhoods, this would not be captured in the dissimilarity index. Hence, it is important that we consider more than one measure of segregation.

One potential limitation of both indices is the exclusive focus on people below the poverty threshold. Although this focus on the poor is consistent with past research and policy debates, the LIHTC program (and other federal housing programs) serves populations that can earn incomes above the federal poverty line (which is approximately 30 percent of the AMI, on average). As explained above, the cutoffs used for the LIHTC program are 50 percent or 60 percent of the AMI. To examine the locational outcomes of this broader population, we estimate a second version of each of our two indices that measures segregation between households earning incomes that are less than 150 percent of the poverty line and those earning more. Because an income that

---

48. Particularly relevant here is the fact that changes in these measures are not highly correlated over time.

is 150 percent of the poverty line corresponds roughly to 50 percent of the AMI, on average, potential residents of LIHTC housing should earn less than 150 percent of the poverty line.[49]

Table 8.7 shows regression results for the poor/nonpoor dissimilarity index and the poor isolation index. In each case, the second model adds an interaction term between the number of per capita LIHTC units and the share of those units placed in QCTs in that decade in that metropolitan area.

The coefficients on the metropolitan-area controls are mostly as expected. As for the coefficient on the number of per capita LIHTC units, it is negative in all four models, and statistically significant in both of the isolation models, suggesting that the poor are actually less isolated in the metropolitan areas where more LIHTC units have been built.[50] Although the magnitude of the negative association is quite small, it clearly suggests that the LIHTC program is not adding to poverty concentration, as many advocates fear. Moreover, the coefficient on the interaction between the number of per capita LIHTC units and the share that are placed in QCTs in that decade in that metropolitan area is insignificant in both models.

These results still leave open the possibility that the program is exacerbating the isolation of near-poor tenants. To address this question more directly, we estimate the same regressions on the segregation and isolation of residents who earn up to 150 percent of the poverty line. The results of these models are presented in table 8.8. The coefficients on the metropolitan-area characteristics change somewhat, given that we are now explaining the spatial distribution of a different population. We once again find that all four coefficients on the per capita tax credit units are negative, although none reaches conventional levels of statistical significance here. One difference here is that the coefficient on our interaction term is now positive and larger than its standard error, suggesting that the negative association between tax credit units and segregation may be diminished in metropolitan areas that allocate a greater share of LIHTC units to QCTs. Although the coefficient on this interaction term does not reach conventional levels of statistical significance, we have run alternative specifications in which it does.

---

49. Because of the poverty-ratio cutoffs recorded in the census, we cannot pick a ratio of 1.67, which might more closely correspond to 50 percent of the AMI (on average). The next poverty-ratio cutoff is 1.99, above 60 percent of the AMI. And as noted earlier, most residents receiving tax credits probably earn less than 50 percent of AMI.

50. It is worth noting that, in separate work, we have examined factors associated with neighborhood economic gains (increased tract mean income) over the 1990s (Ellen and O'Regan, 2008). Controlling for a variety of metropolitan and tract level characteristics, we found low-income tracts were more likely to experience such gains in metropolitan areas where more LIHTC units were placed in service (per capita). Obviously, such evidence is only suggestive, but it is consistent with the findings in this chapter.

TABLE 8.7 Regression Results: Segregation of the Poor

	Dependent variable = dissimilarity index		Dependent variable = isolation index	
	Model 1	Model 2	Model 1	Model 2
Intercept	.0463	.0526	.4194***	.4234***
	(.1596)	(.1596)	(.0789)	(.0788)
Per capita LIHTC units	−2.3905	−1.5483	−2.0962***	−1.5667*
	(1.4687)	(1.6490)	(.0726)	(.8145)
Poverty rate	−.0124	−.0133	1.0742***	1.0736***
	(.1070)	(.1070)	(.0529)	(.0529)
Percent college graduate	.0391	.0384	−.1905***	−.1909***
	(.0820)	(.0820)	(.0405)	(.0405)
Log population	.0315**	.0309**	−.0139**	−.01429**
	(.0139)	(.0139)	(.0069)	(.0069)
Percent black	.2333*	.2324*	−.2779***	−.2785***
	(.1235)	(.1235)	(.0611)	(.0610)
Percent Hispanic	−.0794	−.069	−.2049***	−.1983***
	(.0898)	(.0902)	(.0444)	(.0446)
Percent foreign-born	−.1886**	−.1958**	−.0966**	−.1011**
	(.0940)	(.0942)	(.0465)	(.0465)
Percent under 18 years of age	.1752	.1778	.1365*	.1381*
	(.1462)	(.1462)	(.0723)	(.0722)
Percent over 65 years of age	−.4927***	−.4967***	−.5374***	−.5399***
	(.1743)	(.1743)	(.0862)	(.0861)
Percent working in manufacturing	.0386	.0288	−.0545	−.0607*
	(.0730)	(.0735)	(.0361)	(.0363)
Per capita LIHTC units * % in QCTs		−4.3626		−2.7432
		(3.8880)		(1.9205)
R-squared value	0.914	0.914	0.982	0.982
Number of MSAs	258	258	258	258
Number of years	3	3	3	3
MSA fixed effects	yes	yes	yes	yes
Region* year fixed effects	yes	yes	yes	yes

NOTES: Standard errors are in parentheses. * = statistically significant at the .10 level; ** = statistically significant at the .05 level; *** = statistically significant at the .01 level. LIHTC = Low-Income Housing Tax Credit; QCTs = qualified census tracts; MSAs = metropolitan statistical areas.

SOURCE: Authors' analysis of decennial Census data (http://factfinder.census.gov) linked with data from HUD's Low-Income Housing Tax Credit Database, http://www.huduser.org/datasets/lihtc.html.

TABLE 8.8   Regression Results: Segregation of the Near Poor (Those Earning up to 150 Percent of Poverty)

	Dependent variable = dissimilarity index		Dependent variable = isolation index	
	Model 1	Model 2	Model 1	Model 2
Intercept	.1383	.1377	.0746***	.7413***
	(.1702)	(.1704)	(.1317)	(.1318)
Per capita LIHTC units	−1.9004	−1.9723	−1.4718	−2.0821
	(1.5664)	(1.7610)	(1.2124)	(1.3617)
Poverty rate	.1190	.1190	1.2295***	1.2302***
	(.1142)	(.1143)	(.0884)	(.0884)
Percent college graduate	.1601*	.1601*	−.2658***	−.2653***
	(.0874)	(.0875)	(.0677)	(.0677)
Log population	.0176	.0177	−.0325***	−.0320***
	(.0148)	(.0148)	(.0115)	(.0115)
Percent black	.1196	.1197	−.3927***	−.3920***
	(.1318)	(.1319)	(.1020)	(.1020)
Percent Hispanic	.0399	.0390	−.0499	−.0575
	(.0958)	(.0964)	(.0741)	(.0745)
Percent foreign-born	−.1227	−.1221	−.0772	−.0719
	(.1003)	(.1006)	(.0776)	(.0778)
Percent under18 years of age	.0550	−.0548	.0317	−.0299
	(.1560)	(.1561)	(.1207)	(.1207)
Percent over 65 years of age	−.3374*	−.3371*	−.3950***	−.3921***
	(.1859)	(.1861)	(.1439)	(.1439)
Percent working in	.0253	.0261	−.1533**	−.1462**
manufacturing	(.0779)	(.0785)	(.0603)	(.0607)
Per capita LIHTC units*		.3724		3.1612
% in QCTs		(4.1519)		(3.2106)
R-squared value	0.890	0.890	0.958	0.958
Number of MSAs	258	258	258	258
Number of years	3	3	3	3
MSA fixed effects	yes	yes	yes	yes
Region* year fixed effects	yes	yes	yes	yes

NOTES: Standard errors are in parentheses. * = statistically significant at the .10 level; ** = statistically significant at the .05 level; *** = statistically significant at the .01 level. LIHTC = Low-Income Housing Tax Credit; QCTs = qualified census tracts; MSAs = metropolitan statistical areas.

SOURCE: Authors' analysis of decennial Census data (http://factfinder.census.gov) linked with data from HUD's Low-Income Housing Tax Credit Database, http://www.huduser.org/datasets/lihtc.html.

Conclusion

Although there may be other serious concerns about the tax credit program, such as its high cost and its potential to crowd out unsubsidized development (see, e.g., Eriksen and Rosenthal, 2007), there is little evidence that the program is exacerbating the concentration of poverty, as many advocates fear. Indeed, a quick comparison with the voucher program suggests that the LIHTC program is doing a better job, on average, at getting low-income households into low-poverty neighborhoods.

It is worth emphasizing that these are average results; in some areas, tax credit developments are heavily concentrated in high-poverty neighborhoods. But even in these areas, we do not find evidence that these investments are associated with increases in poverty concentration. Moreover, the results from New York City suggest that the siting of tax credit units in higher-poverty, urban neighborhoods can encourage community revitalization, at least when it is part of an explicit revitalization effort.

In short, criticism of the LIHTC that focuses on the possible negative spatial effects seems poorly aimed. That said, even if building LIHTC units in QCTs can help revitalize them in some circumstances, it is hard to justify the current statutory preference for qualified census tracts. Although it is possible that these tax credit units help revitalize the QCTs, it seems more sensible to give states leeway to decide how they will use their tax credits—whether to provide opportunities in low-poverty areas or as a tool to help revitalize lower-income communities.

Appendix: Segregation and Exposure Measures

Dissimilarity Index (D)

The index between demographic group j (e.g., nonpoor) and k (e.g., poor) is calculated as follows:

$$D = \frac{1}{2} \sum_i^M \left| \frac{N_{ki}}{N_k} - \frac{N_{ji}}{N_j} \right|$$

where
N_{ji}, N_{ki} = the number of people of group j, k in census tract i, M tracts in total
N_j, N_k = the number of people of group j, k in aggregate

Isolation Index (I)

The isolation index of group k (e.g., poor) is:

$$_k I_k = \sum_i^M \left| \frac{N_{ki}}{N_k} * \frac{N_{ki}}{N_i} \right|$$

where
N_{ki} = the number of people of group k in tract i, M tracts in total
N_k = the number of people of group k in aggregate

REFERENCES

Baum-Snow, Nathaniel, and Justin Marion. 2007. "The Effects of Low Income Housing Developments on Neighborhoods." Working Paper 2007-5, Department of Economics, Brown University. http://www.brown.edu/Departments/Economics/Papers/2007/2007-5_paper.pdf.

Bendernagel, Jimmy, Michael Berne, Peter Madden, Keren Mertens, and Kim Romano. 2007. "To What Extent Do Low Income Housing Tax Credits Influence Economic Segregation Patterns?" New York University, Robert F. Wagner Research Capstone. Final Paper.

Buron, Larry, Sandra Nolden, Kathleen Heintz, and Julie Stewart. 2000. "Assessment of the Economic and Social Characteristics of LIHTC Residents and Neighborhoods." Washington, DC: U.S. Department of Housing and Urban Development.

Carter, William H., Michael H. Schill, and Susan M. Wachter. 1998. "Polarisation, Public Housing, and Racial Minorities in U.S. Cities." *Urban Studies* 35(10): 1889–1911.

Case, Karl E. 1991. "Investors, Developers, and Supply-Side Subsidies: How Much Is Enough?" *Housing Policy Debate* 2(2): 341–356.

Cummings, Jean, and Denise DiPasquale. 1999. "The Low-Income Housing Tax Credit Program: An Analysis of the First Ten Years." *Housing Policy Debate* 10(2): 251–307.

Danter Company. 2007. "Statistical Overview of the LIHTC Program, 1987 to 2005." http://www.danter.com/TAXCREDIT/stats.htm.

Duncan, Otis, and Beverley Duncan. 1955. "A Methodological Analysis of Segregation Indices." *American Sociological Review* 20: 210–217.

Ellen, Ingrid Gould, and Katherine O'Regan. 2008. "Exploring Changes in Low-Income Neighborhoods in the 1990s." Paper presented at the Federal Reserve Bank of Philadelphia Conference "Reinventing Older Communities: How Does Place Matter?" March 26–28.

Ellen, Ingrid Gould, Michael Schill, Amy Schwartz, and Ioan Voicu. 2007. "Does Federally-Subsidized Rental Housing Depress Property Values?" *Journal of Policy Analysis and Management* 26(2): 257–280.

Eriksen, Michael D., and Stuart S. Rosenthal. 2007. "Crowd Out, Stigma, and the Effect of Place-Based Subsidized Rental Housing." Mimeo. http://student.maxwell .syr.edu/meriksen/Crowd%20Out%20and%20Stigma.pdf.

Fisher, R. M. 1959. *Twenty Years of Public Housing*. New York: Harper & Brothers.

Freeman, Lance. 2004. "Siting Affordable Housing: Location and Neighborhood Trends of Low Income Housing Tax Credit Developments in the 1990's." Washington, DC: The Brookings Institution, Census 2000 Survey Series.

General Accounting Office. 1997. "Tax Credits: Opportunities to Improve Oversight of the Low-Income Housing Program." GGD/RCED-97-55. Washington, DC: General Accounting Office.

Green, Richard K., Stephen Malpezzi, and Kiat-Ying Seah. 2002. "Low Income Housing Tax Credit Housing Developments and Property Values." Wisconsin Center for Real Estate Working Paper 02-10.

Hirsch, Arnold. 1983. *Making the Second Ghetto: Race and Housing in Chicago, 1940–1960*. New York: Cambridge University Press.

James, David R., and Karl E. Taeuber. 1985. "Measures of Segregation." In Nancy Tuma, ed., *Sociological Methodology*, 1–32. San Francisco: Jossey-Bass.

Jargowsky, Paul. 1996. "Take the Money and Run: Economic Segregation in U.S. Metropolitan Areas." *American Sociological Review* 61: 984–998.

Khadduri, Jill, Larry Buron, and Clarissa Climaco. 2006. "Are States Using the Low Income Housing Tax Credit to Enable Families with Children to Live in Low Poverty and Racial Integrated Neighborhoods?" Cambridge, MA: Abt Associates. http://www.prrac.org/pdf/LIHTC_report_2006.pdf.

McClure, Kirk. 2006. "The Low-Income Housing Tax Credit Program Goes Mainstream and Moves to the Suburbs." *Housing Policy Debate* 17(3): 419–446.

Newman, Sandra, and Ann Schnare. 1997. ". . . And a Suitable Living Environment: The Failure of Housing Programs to Deliver on Neighborhood Quality." *Housing Policy Debate* 8(4): 703–741.

New York City, Department of Housing Preservation and Development. 1989. *The 10 Year Plan*. New York: Author.

Orfield, Myron. 2005. "Racial Integration and Community Revitalization: Applying the Fair Housing Act to the Low Income Housing Tax Credit." *Vanderbilt Law Review* 58: 1747–1805.

Orr, Larry, Judith Feins, Robin Jacob, Erik Beecroft, Lisa Sanbonmatsu, Lawrence Katz, Jeffrey Liebman, and Jeffrey Kling. 2003. *Moving to Opportunity: Interim Impacts Evaluation*. Washington, DC: U.S. Department of Housing and Urban Development.

Pedone, Carla, Patricia Remch, and Karl E. Case. 1983. *The Urban Homesteading Program: An Assessment of Its Impact on Demonstration Neighborhoods, 1977–1979*. Cambridge, MA: Urban Systems, Research and Engineering.

Poverty and Race Research Action Council (PRRAC). 2004. "Civil Rights Mandates in the Low Income Housing Tax Credit Program." http://www.prrac.org/pdf/ crmandates.pdf.

Reardon, Sean F., and Glenn Firebaugh. 2002. "Measures of Multi-Group Segregation." *Sociological Methodology* 32(1): 33–67.

Rohe, William M., and Lance Freeman. 2001. "Assisted Housing and Residential Segregation: The Role of Race and Ethnicity in the Siting of Assisted Housing Developments." *Journal of the American Planning Association* 67(3) (Summer): 279–292.

Roisman, Florence. 2000. "Poverty, Discrimination and the Low Income Housing Tax Credit Program." Washington, DC: Memo prepared for the meeting of the Loose Association of Legal Services Housing Advocates and Clients. http://indylaw.indiana.edu/instructors/roisman/lihtcmemo.pdf.

Santiago, Anna M., George C. Galster, and Peter Tatian. 2001. "Assessing the Property Value Impacts of the Dispersed Housing Subsidy Program in Denver." *Journal of Policy Analysis and Management* 20(1): 65–88.

Schwartz, Alex. 2006. *Housing Policy in the United States: An Introduction.* New York: Routledge, Taylor and Francis.

Schwartz, Amy Ellen, Ingrid Gould Ellen, Ioan Voicu, and Michael H. Schill. 2006. "The External Effects of Subsidized Housing." *Regional Science and Urban Economics* 36: 679–707.

Taeuber, Karl E., and Alma F. Taeuber. 1965. *Negroes in Cities: Residential Segregation and Neighborhood Change.* Chicago: Aldine.

Watson, Tara. 2006. "Metropolitan Growth, Inequality, and Neighborhood Segregation by Income." *Brookings-Wharton Papers on Urban Affairs* 2006: 1–52. http://muse.jhu.edu/journals/urb/.

White, Michael J. 1987. *American Neighborhoods and Residential Differentiation.* New York: Russell Sage Foundation.

Commentary

Daniel P. McMillen

Since its inception in 1987, and through the end of 2005, the Low-Income Housing Tax Credit (LIHTC) program has subsidized the construction of more than 1.5 million housing units. Many of these units are built in low-income areas that have not witnessed new building in years. Although it might be expected that a program subsidizing the construction of affordable rental housing in economically distressed areas would be welcomed by community development advocates, the program has generated a surprising amount of criticism. One of the potential benefits of the program—providing low-income households with affordable new housing in their current neighborhoods—may also reinforce the spatial concentration of poverty. According to this view, the LIHTC program runs the danger of repeating the harm caused by the large-scale public housing developments of the 1950s, which met a pressing need at the time by helping to create the social problems of the future.

Ingrid Gould Ellen, Katherine O'Regan, and Ioan Voicu's work provides a welcome perspective on the LIHTC program's potential for either reinforcing or counteracting the spatial concentration of poverty. Using data on the number of low-income tax credit units built in high-poverty census tracts since the 1980s, they find that about 10 percent of LIHTC units are built in high-poverty tracts and about a third of the units are built in low-poverty tracts. They then calculate dissimilarity and isolation indices for 258 metropolitan areas. These indices measure the spatial concentration of households in poverty within an urban area. The empirical question is whether the existence of a higher number of LIHTC units per capita leads to a greater concentration of poverty. If units constructed under the LIHTC program are concentrated in low-income neighborhoods, then urban areas with more LIHTC units per capita may have higher values for the dissimilarity and isolation indices after controlling for population and other metropolitan-area characteristics. If anything, the opposite turns out to be true. The results suggest that the LIHTC program is associated, on average, with lower levels of isolation and segregation of the near poor. Overall, the results suggest that the LIHTC program has little effect on the general spatial concentration of poverty because units are being built in both low-poverty and high-poverty neighborhoods.

Data for New York City put these numbers in some perspective. According to data from the U.S. Bureau of the Census, New York City had slightly more than 8 million residents in 2000, with an average of 2.65 residents per housing unit. During the 1990s, about 132,000 new housing units were built in New York City. New construction thus represents 4.37 percent of the 2000 housing stock, or enough to hold about 350,000 residents if the new housing units generally have the same number of residents as the average for the city. In 2000, 20.84 percent of the city's residents were classified by the census as living in poverty. The segregation index for poverty calculated using data for New York census tracts is 0.336 and the isolation index is 0.296. How much could 132,000 new housing units alter these values?

As an extreme, suppose that all 132,000 new units are built for low-income households, and suppose that new housing construction brings 350,000 new residents to New York, all of whom are classified as living in poverty. If these new residents are allocated to census tracts according to each tract's current share of the poverty-level population, the value of the dissimilarity index does not change, whereas the isolation index increases by 0.037, to a value of 0.333. The poor are more isolated than before because there is a higher probability that a randomly drawn resident of a census tract will also be poor; the dissimilarity index, however, does not change, because each census tract has exactly the same proportion of the city's low-income residents as before.

The results are different if the 350,000 new residents are allocated to census tracts according to each tract's current share of the population that is not living in poverty. In this case, the dissimilarity index falls by 0.058, to a new value of 0.278, whereas the isolation index rises slightly to 0.305 (a change of 0.010). Across the full United States, the dissimilarity index for black households relative to white households is 60.3, and the comparable index for Asian households is 41.2—a much, much larger difference than is capable of being generated by an extreme case in which all new construction in New York City is devoted to low-income households and with the construction concentrated in high-income census tracts.[1] Indeed, in a more reasonable case in which only 20 percent of the new construction is allocated to low-income households, with the new units instead concentrated in high-income neighborhoods, the dissimilarity index declines by only 0.014, whereas the change in the isolation index is only −0.007.

The point is that there is not enough new construction in large metropolitan areas to have significant effects on the overall spatial concentration of poverty. The number of people living in poverty is too large, and the number of new units being constructed is too small.

---

1. The source for the U.S. figures is http://www.censusscope.org/us/s40/p75000/chart_dissimilarity.html. Other calculations are my own, made using data from the U.S. Bureau of the Census.

Although the LIHTC program is unlikely to have much effect on the overall level of poverty concentration, it can have very significant effects on smaller areas. Also, adding more low-income units to an area that is already economically distressed has the potential to perpetuate a cycle of poverty. On the other hand, building new units in wealthy areas for households living in poverty may help the poor immensely and have little or no effect on existing residents. Indeed, the authors' regression results for New York City suggest that the construction of LIHTC units increased prices in surrounding neighborhoods. The chapter offers a welcome dose of objectivity to an important issue that too often is influenced more by anecdotal than empirical evidence.

9

Measuring Land Use Regulations and Their Effects in the Housing Market

JOHN M. QUIGLEY
STEVEN RAPHAEL
LARRY A. ROSENTHAL

L and use regulation—the power of local governments to control residential development within their boundaries—is ubiquitous across American cities and metropolitan areas. Regulations range from limits on residential densities to prescriptions concerning building design, construction, and the aesthetics of urban and suburban neighborhoods. Aside from setting requirements for permits and limits on new construction, localities may require developers to participate in public hearings. Regulations frequently require analysis of the environmental and fiscal effects of proposed projects.

The application of these regulations affects the pattern and pace of development, the price of land and housing, the demographic character of local communities, the economic and ethnic composition of neighborhoods and cities, and the rents and selling prices of residences. Specific rules are, for the most part, locally enacted and controlled, and they may be adopted for a variety of reasons. Study of the attributes of regulation and its administration must take place at the level of the jurisdiction. Yet, outside of particular enactments and decisions, the details of regulations are nowhere compiled systematically. The ways in which the regulations are actually applied and enforced are rarely

We are grateful for the comments of Edward Glaeser, Richard Green, and Stephen Malpezzi. This research was funded by the MacArthur Foundation. Additional resources were provided by the Berkeley Program on Housing and Urban Policy. We are grateful for the support and assistance of Paul Campos of the Home Builders Association of Northern California, Joan Douglas of the Bay Area Chapter of the Association of Environmental Professionals, and Erika Poethig of the MacArthur Foundation. Expert research assistance has been provided by Corie Calfee, Paavo Monkkonen, and Joseph Wright.

measured, in part because of the complexity and unpredictability of such processes. For this reason, estimates of the impact of local regulations on housing
outcomes have been quite mixed (Quigley and Rosenthal, 2005).

This chapter assembles data on the local regulation of housing and its administration for the separate jurisdictions in one large metropolitan housing
market. We conduct this study in California, a state known for its high home
prices, stringent regulation of residential development, and rare "as of right"
entitlements of land. Hence, we do not expect our findings to reflect typical
conditions around the country. We focus on the San Francisco Bay Area,
renowned for its restrictive regulatory environment. The Bay Area comprises
nine counties within the 11-county San Francisco Consolidated Statistical
Area (CSA). San Francisco is the fifth-largest CSA in the United States, with
a population of 7.1 million people in 2000.

We analyze raw data on land use regulation and administration from five
independent sources compiled at various times over the past 18 years. First,
we utilize data from three independent surveys of building officials in this
metropolitan region, conducted in 1992, 1998, and 2007. We also report systematic information from the developers who must contend with local entitlement processes, and we incorporate their perspectives and interpretations
into the description. Finally, we utilize survey information obtained from
members of the professional association of environmental consultants who
facilitate the permitting process in the region.[1]

We begin with a brief description of the San Francisco Bay Area and its
regulatory environment, and we include information placing California into
a national perspective. The next section introduces the surveys and instruments used to compile information on land use regulatory processes, and is
followed by a section that presents descriptive statistics and introduces the indexes of regulation we derive from them. Before the concluding section, we
describe relationships among the different measures of regulation and relate
these measures to observable outcomes in housing prices and rents.

THE BAY AREA'S REGULATORY ENVIRONMENT

The San Francisco Bay Area is composed of 101 local political jurisdictions (called "cities" under the California constitution) and nine county

---

1. All data analyzed in this chapter are available for download at http://urbanpolicy.berkeley.edu. Details, definitions, and data collection methods may be found in Calfee et al. (2007), available at the same
Web site.

governments.[2] One jurisdiction, San Francisco, features a consolidated city and county government. Each of the cities is empowered to adopt and administer its own land use regulations; counties regulate land only within the unincorporated areas lying outside cities. There are thus 109 Bay Area jurisdictions with direct authority to facilitate or inhibit growth and development. Although the unincorporated land areas of Bay Area counties greatly exceed the combined acreage of their cities, more than 90 percent of the Bay Area's population lives in the latter. Figure 9.1 indicates the land use boundaries within the region. For each jurisdiction, we compile information from the surveys of local regulation described in the survey results section herein.

We analyze linkages among the residential builders who apply for construction permits, the governing land use authorities, and housing outcomes. We recognize that, in the Bay Area and elsewhere in California, the sphere of policies influencing the pace and nature of housing development extends well beyond how permits are granted and denied in individualized proceedings. For example, a long-established state system governs the adoption and review of general plans issued by land use jurisdictions. These plans must include housing "elements" detailing how local governments offer to accommodate allocated proportions of housing growth. The housing elements are reviewed, by the state government in Sacramento, to determine whether local regulation allows construction of a sufficient number of units affordable to lower-income households.[3]

Developers and others can sue land use authorities to insure that statewide planning standards for allowing residential development are observed. However, this litigation is largely procedural rather than substantive, and remedies typically involve paper-trail planning revisions rather than the issuance of permits for specific projects (Calavita, Grimes, and Mallach, 1998). This distinguishes the California land use system from other states like New Jersey, which have made use of a more forceful "builder's remedy" to overcome obstacles to building. In California, local evaluation of building-permit applications is

---

2. Two outlying counties to the south (Santa Cruz and San Benito), included within the federally defined 11-county Bay Area CSA, are both excluded from the regional Association of Bay Area Governments (belonging instead to the Association of Monterey Bay Area Governments). Our analysis here includes the nine counties physically bordering the San Francisco Bay: Alameda, Contra Costa, Marin, Napa, San Francisco, San Mateo, Santa Clara, Solano, and Sonoma.

3. As of mid-May 2008, 84 percent of the 109 Bay Area jurisdictions we study here were deemed by the California Department of Housing and Community Development (HCD) to be in full compliance with state housing-element law. A statewide report showing the compliance status of each city and county is regularly updated and made downloadable via HCD's Web site at http://www.hcd.ca.gov/hpd/hrc/plan/he/status.pdf.

FIGURE 9.1 Cities and Counties of the San Francisco Bay Area

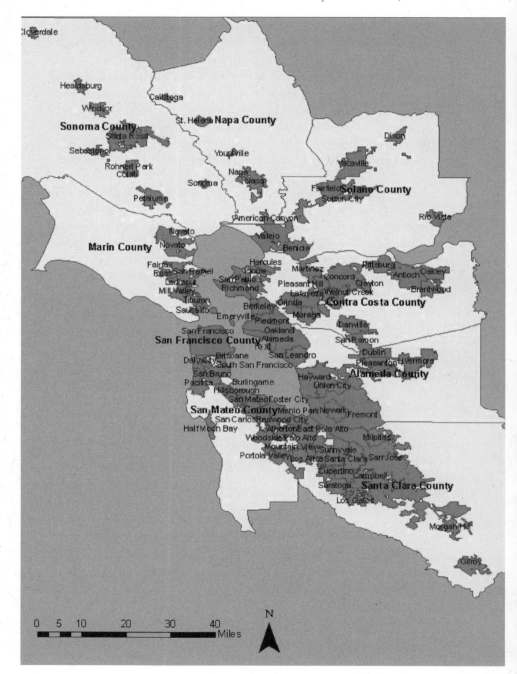

viewed as discretionary rather than ministerial, and considerable deference is paid by the courts and other bodies to decisions of local regulators.

In addition, a variety of state and regional bodies exert influence over the Bay Area's transportation expenditures, air quality management, water supply and quality, earthquake and fire safety, and other policies affecting land. These entities represent a measure of local-government collaboration on these subjects. However, there is no mechanism coordinating regional decisions concerning housing supply, job creation, or economic development more broadly. Local government retains its primacy concerning what gets built, where, and when. In a metropolitan area with more than 100 authorities, this means that land administration may vary greatly, and that the real costs and time burdens of entitling land can be fragmented, opaque, and unpredictable. These conditions bedevil measurement of regulatory conditions. Further, because permit decisions not "as of right" are essentially discretionary acts on the part of regulators, developers bear the risk that review standards may vary greatly from place to place and may fluctuate even during the pendency of a single project proposal.

Two additional, state-level regimes bear mention. First, the California Environmental Quality Act[4] (CEQA) requires localized assessment of all projects involving discretionary agency approval. The measurement of environmental impact adds cost and complexity to the enforcement of traditional zoning and growth control regimes. Planners report that CEQA undermines traditional zoning and planning approaches for locating residential projects (Landis et al., 2006). Enacted by the California legislature in 1970, CEQA ostensibly imposes uniform requirements across jurisdictions, but in practice the stringency of environmental review is quite idiosyncratic.

Second, in 1977 the state enacted a Permit Streamlining Act[5] to address excessive cost and delay in local land use decisions. The goal of the law was to rationalize land use decision making and to make it more transparent and predictable for both developers and project opponents. Despite these efforts and subsequent reform attempts, residential permit review remains time consuming and expensive in a state infamous for its high-cost real estate markets.

In combination, these factors create an environment of extensive regulation of development at the state and local level. The figures that follow depict these conditions and place them into national context. Figures 9.2 and 9.3, based on the Census Public Use Micro Samples for 1990 and 2000, show that California jurisdictions adopting greater numbers of growth control measures

---

4. California Public Resources Code, §21000 et seq.
5. California Government Code, §65920 et seq.

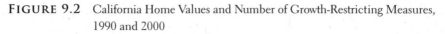

FIGURE 9.2 California Home Values and Number of Growth-Restricting Measures, 1990 and 2000

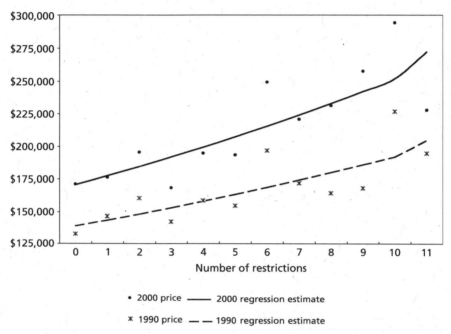

SOURCE: Quigley and Raphael (2004).

tend to have higher house prices and rent levels (Quigley and Raphael, 2004). Figure 9.4 compares the link between land use restrictions and the prices of houses in California relative to conditions elsewhere around the country. The figure matches metropolitan statistical area–level (MSA-level) house prices reported in the 1990 census with an index of land use regulation based on data from a national survey of local building and planning officials (Malpezzi, 1996). Compared to metropolitan areas in other regions, California's urban centers feature real estate markets that are both expensive and inhospitable toward new residential projects.

The economics of land use suggests a variety of motivations for stringent development controls exercised by local government, motivations not always mutually exclusive.[6] Regulation may be motivated by both budgetary

---

6. For further discussion on the imposition of stringent land controls, see, e.g., Fischel (1985), Mills and Oates (1975), Pogodzinski (1995), Quigley and Rosenthal (2005), and Rolleston (1987).

FIGURE 9.3   California Rents and Number of Growth-Restricting Measures, 1990 and 2000

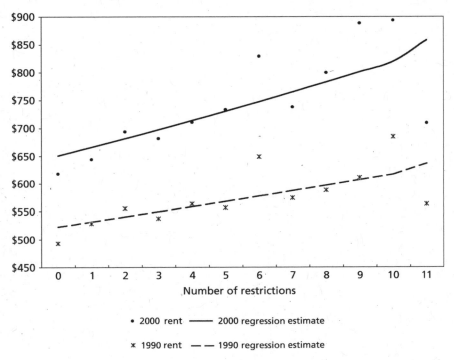

• 2000 rent ⸺ 2000 regression estimate

✕ 1990 rent ⸺ ⸺ 1990 regression estimate

SOURCE: Quigley and Raphael (2004).

facts and subjective perceptions. Purposes may include maintenance of fiscal balance, protection of amenities, maximization of private land values, preservation of neighborhood aesthetics, and even certain forms of social exclusionism.

As will be described in greater detail below, our analytical approach recognizes that community features and housing market outcomes may be jointly determined. Moreover, our survey and our regulatory index include factors relating to local political attitudes toward growth. However, we do not specifically attempt to isolate the socioeconomic factors underlying patterns of regulatory stringency in the Bay Area. Rather, we mean to improve on the measurement of regulation utilizing a multifaceted strategy, incorporating the experiences of those working in the regulated sector, and then to evaluate how well observed levels of restrictiveness correlate with prices and rents.

FIGURE 9.4 Housing Prices and Regulation, U.S. Metropolitan Areas, 1990

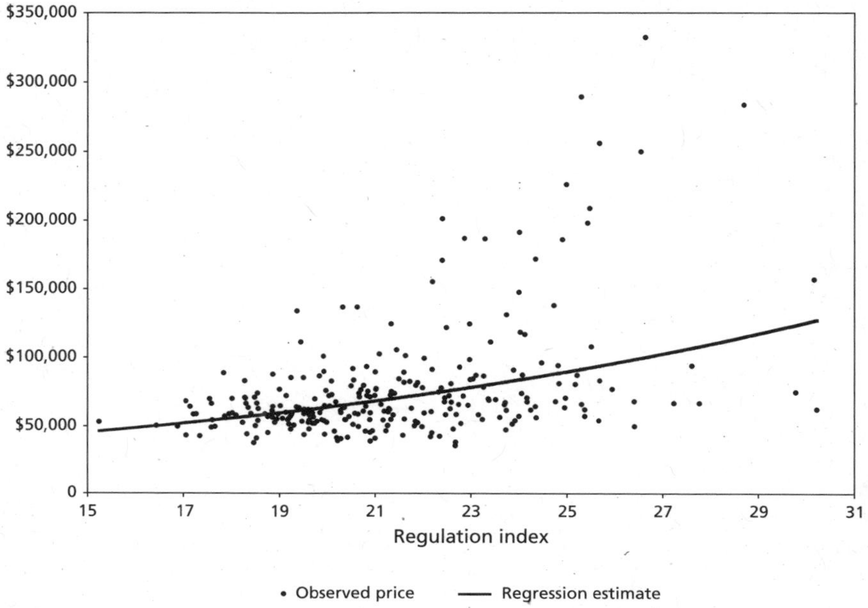

• Observed price   —— Regression estimate

SOURCE: Stephen Malpezzi, personal communication.

THE SURVEY INSTRUMENTS

Data on land use regulation typically focus on enactments by category, frequency, and timing; this approach has clear shortcomings. Indeed, the enactment of rules may reflect concurrent political conditions in some very general way. But the rules may reveal little about how the business of regulation is actually conducted. One city may have 20 quite restrictive-looking enactments that are rarely enforced; another may have only one or two, regularly used as the basis for denying a majority of permit applications. Accordingly, our survey of building officials supplements simple enactment data by asking specifically about implementation effects such as cost, delay, and likelihood of permit approval. We also surveyed developers and their environmental consultants to provide context and perspective concerning the application of local standards to actual residential projects. The first survey of growth control measures in California that we draw on was undertaken by Glickfield and Levine in 1988, reported in a Lincoln Institute monograph (Glickfield and Levine, 1992) and then expanded and updated in 1992 (Levine, 1999). In 1998, the California Department of Housing and Community Development (HCD) administered a second, parallel instrument to update the Glickfield and Levine (1992) survey. The HCD survey collected information about growth control measures enacted between 1995 and 1998.[7] Supplementing these prior efforts (which already included Bay Area jurisdictions), we conducted a third survey in 2007, covering regulation of land use by political jurisdictions in the Bay Area specifically. The current survey was modeled on one originally designed by Anita Summers and her colleagues at the Wharton School, administered to a national sample of political jurisdictions in 1990. The Summers survey instrument was updated in 2005 and again administered intensively in Philadelphia as well as in several other metropolitan regions (see Gyourko, Saiz, and Summers, 2008).[8]

Our online survey of builders and developers asked them to report experiences at the project level regarding permit applications in various jurisdictions. This survey was undertaken with the cooperation and assistance of the Home Builders Association of Northern California (HBANC). HBANC is a nonprofit association with a membership of about 1,000 firms representing developers, builders, and the construction trades. Our builder survey yielded information on 62 projects in 33 jurisdictions in the San Francisco Bay Area.

Finally, we undertook an additional online survey, fielded to members of the Bay Area Chapter of the National Association of Environmental Professionals (BAC/NAEP). BAC/NAEP members serve as consultants to governments and firms in the land use approval process mandated by CEQA. We obtained responses from environmental consultants relating to 27 projects in 14 different jurisdictions. The survey of CEQA consultants excluded BAC/NAEP members who work solely as employees of or as contractors to the local governments surveyed in our poll of building officials.

---

7. This latter survey, combined with the previous Glickfield and Levine survey, formed the basis for recent analyses of local growth control and growth management programs by John Landis and his associates (Landis, 2000, 2006; Landis, Deng, and Reilly, 2002).

8. The results of the original Summers survey of local officials were analyzed in Summers, Cheshire, and Senn (1993). Subsequently, that survey formed the basis for a series of extensions by Stephen Malpezzi and his associates (Green, Malpezzi, and Mayo, 2005; Malpezzi, 1996; Malpezzi and Green, 1996) analyzing national land use patterns. A revised version was subsequently administered to all jurisdictions in the greater Philadelphia region, now the seventh largest CSA in the United States (Gyourko and Summers, 2006). Our response rate, 79 percent, is somewhat higher than the 64 percent response rate obtained by Summers in Philadelphia using a similar instrument.

Survey Results

The Glickfield and Levine and HCD Surveys

The Glickfield and Levine 1992 survey and the HCD 1998 survey were devoted entirely to issues of growth regulation and management. The four categories of enactments covered by these early surveys are (1) growth control (e.g., limits on residential permits, restrictions on annexation); (2) growth management (e.g., adequate public facilities ordinances, urban limit lines); (3) zoning changes (e.g., up- and down-zoning, prescribed floor-area ratios); and (4) related growth control measures (e.g., fees and exactions, supermajority voting requirements for zoning changes and specified planning decisions).

As reported elsewhere (e.g., Quigley and Raphael, 2005), California jurisdictions adopted many restrictive land use and growth control measures during the 1990s, with substantial growth in the use of adequate public facility ordinances, provisions for growth management in town plans, and urban limit lines. Three indexes of the stringency of growth control, derived from the earlier surveys, are reported in figure 9.5. The restrictiveness indexes are counts of the number of restrictive adoptions reported by survey respondents, computed from the 1992 and 1998 surveys of California building and planning officials. The hospitality index measures the receptiveness of local jurisdictions to development.[9]

The 2007 Survey and the Berkeley Land Use Regulation Index (BLURI)

Our 2007 survey of local building officials asked about a variety of factors affecting housing development. Duration, timing, and specific regulations were addressed. The more recent survey also asked about political influence, project approval procedures, delays, inclusionary zoning, and open space. Survey responses were obtained from 86 jurisdictions. Our survey instrument, based on the Summers/Wharton survey and then adapted for California, is available online at http://urbanpolicy.berkeley.edu.

THE BLURI AND ITS COMPONENTS

Using the responses to the 2007 survey, we develop an index, the Berkeley Land Use Regulation Index (BLURI), comprising 10 separate measures of

---

9. These indexes are described in greater detail by Landis (2000) and Rosenthal (2000).

FIGURE 9.5   Indexes of Growth Management for the San Francisco Bay Area

Restrictiveness index, 1992

Hospitality index, 1992

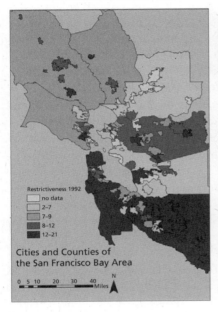

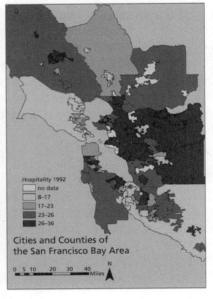

Restrictiveness index, 1998

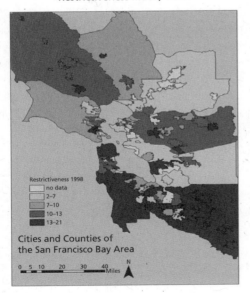

distinct aspects of local practice: political influence, project approvals, zoning change, development caps, density restrictions, open space requirements, infrastructure improvement obligations, inclusionary housing, project approval delays, and permit approval rates. Some key components of the BLURI are noted later, together with details on their calculation.[10] For the Political Influence Index, we aggregate responses to questions concerning the involvement of different actors in permit decisions and the importance of various influences on residential development. The separate panels of table 9.1 summarize the responses to these questions for the Bay Area governments and report a composite index of political influence. The underlying survey items address, in detail, formal and informal actions, attitudes among various constituencies, and specific features of the entitlement process. Interestingly, the city of Berkeley ranks in the middle of the political influence distribution, as do diverse, mixed-income places like San Jose and Vallejo. Jurisdictions reporting strong political influence in these processes include unincorporated Marin County, the city of Richmond, and the city and county of San Francisco.

Project Approvals/Zoning Change. To describe the approval process for new development projects, respondents were asked to note which particular reviews are required when no zoning change is sought. These reviews may be mandated by the planning commission, the city council or board of supervisors, a landmark or historical department, fire department, health department, parking or transportation authority, a provision of CEQA, a growth management analysis, or some other procedure. The index is constructed as the sum of 11 dichotomous variables. Survey responses indicate that small towns like Piedmont and Larkspur have relatively few regulatory layers in the governance of permit applications. Larger city governments like San Francisco and Berkeley, among others, have the greatest number of project approval participants and processes, among our respondent jurisdictions.

Zoning-change requests may trigger reviews by a variety of local bodies. The survey asked respondents to report additional approvals necessary when applicants require variances, conditional use permits, and the like. Table 9.2 reports the kinds of reviews and their frequencies across Bay Area jurisdictions

---

10. More extensive analyses, as well as histograms of each component, are reported in a longer narrative downloadable via http://urbanpolicy.berkeley.edu. In the text here, we report on indexes of political influence, project approvals, zoning change, and caps on units and densities. Appendix tables 9A.2, 9A.3, and 9A.4 provide information on the indexes describing open space dedications, infrastructure obligations, inclusionary housing, and permit delays and approval rates.

TABLE 9.1 BLURI: Political Influence Index (Observations in 86 Bay Area Jurisdictions)

Involvement in residential development	Mean	Standard deviation
Local elected officials	4.5	0.90
Neighbors/community pressure	4.1	0.97
State legislature	1.9	1.03
Courts and litigation	1.8	0.93
Ballot measures	1.9	1.24
Organized labor	1.6	0.99
Planning/zoning staff	4.8	0.57
Environmental advocates	3.0	1.20

Factors affecting development of single-family housing

	Mean	Standard deviation
Supply of developable land	4.7	0.84
Density restrictions	3.3	1.41
Infrastructure requirements	2.8	1.36
Local fiscal conditions	2.4	1.18
Inclusionary housing ordinances	2.3	1.10
Parking requirements	2.4	1.29
School crowding	1.9	1.06
CEQA review	2.7	1.33
Density bonuses	1.7	0.79
Citizens' attitudes on growth	3.4	1.23
Elected officials' positions on growth	3.5	1.26
Mixed-use requirements	2.0	1.16
Impact fees/exactions	2.5	1.17
Duration of entitlement process	2.7	1.17

Factors affecting development of multifamily housing

	Mean	Standard deviation
Supply of developable land	4.5	0.92
Density restrictions	3.4	1.40
Infrastructure requirements	2.9	1.30
Local fiscal conditions	2.4	1.16
Inclusionary housing ordinances	2.6	1.27
Parking requirements	2.9	1.28
School crowding	1.9	1.05
CEQA review	2.8	1.17
Density bonuses	2.2	1.07
Citizens' attitudes on growth	3.6	1.21
Elected officials' positions on growth	3.8	1.14
Mixed-use requirements	2.6	1.29
Impact fees/exactions	2.7	1.20
Duration of entitlement process	2.9	1.22
Political Influence Index Score	**98.63**	**23.56**

NOTES: Scores range from 1 (not involved) to 5 (very involved). CEQA = California Environmental Quality Act.

TABLE 9.2 BLURI: Project Approval and Zoning Change Indexes (Observations in 86 Bay Area Jurisdictions)

	Frequency	
Required reviews (1 = yes)	For project approval and issuance of building permit	For projects requiring zoning change
Planning commission	65	80
City council (or board of supervisors)	19	82
Landmarks/historical commission	14	1
Architectural/design review	51	10
Building department	72	45
Fire department	71	63
Health department	23	65
Parking/transportation	23	24
CEQA review	68	26
Growth management analysis	12	73
Other	20	17
	Mean	**Standard deviation**
Project Approval Index Score	5.01	2.13
Zoning Change Index Score	5.74	2.41

NOTES: Scores range from 1 (not involved) to 5 (very involved). CEQA = California Environmental Quality Act.

for both the Project Approval and Zoning Change Indexes. The table also summarizes each of the parallel indexes generated.

Development Caps and Density Restrictions. We also asked local officials whether their jurisdictions had adopted limits on the number of permits issued. Gauged to cover numerical or proportional growth, such caps may govern single-family housing, multifamily housing, or the residential population itself. The caps subindex is the sum of five dichotomous variables.

Respondents were also asked if their jurisdiction imposes minimum lot sizes and, if so, at what levels. An index of density restrictions was created by summing four dichotomous variables specifying separate, minimum-lot-size categories. The great majority of responding jurisdictions report no caps at all; outlying areas like Cotati and Petaluma in Sonoma County, and Gilroy and Morgan Hill in Santa Clara County, are among those experimenting with such restrictions. Density restrictions of various types are more prevalent, particularly in county unincorporated areas and a number of suburban enclaves.

TABLE 9.3   BLURI: Development Caps and Density Restrictions
Indexes (Observations in 86 Bay Area Jurisdictions)

Development caps (1 = yes)	Frequency
Single-family home permits	14
Multifamily permits	13
New single-family housing	10
New multifamily housing	10
Population growth	4

Density restrictions (1 = yes)	Frequency
Minimum lot size less than .5 acres	73
Minimum lot size between .5 and 1 acres	31
Minimum lot size between 1 and 2 acres	26
Minimum lot size 2 or more acres	20

	Mean	Standard deviation
Development Caps Index Score	0.59	1.26
Density Restrictions Index Score	1.69	1.34

NOTE: Scores range from 1 (not involved) to 5 (very involved).

Table 9.3 reports the frequencies of responses concerning items underlying both the Development Caps and Density Restrictions Indexes.

COMBINING THE SUBINDEXES

For the analysis of regulatory impact, we develop a single indicator, the BLURI, summarizing restrictiveness in each Bay Area jurisdiction. The 10 subindexes described here and in appendix table 9A.1 are combined by standardization and aggregation. Each component is normalized to a mean of zero and a standard deviation of one, so that different metrics are accorded equal weight in aggregation. Two techniques are used to aggregate the 10 components: a simple summation and a factor extraction. Standard principal-components analysis, applied to the 10 elements, produces a single factor that explains 76 percent of the covariances among the original variables. Moreover, the second factor generated by this method has an eigenvalue of less than one, suggesting that a single factor is sufficient to explain the variability of the underlying data. The simple correlation between the scores of the single factor extracted from the 10 indexes and the sum of the subindexes is 0.79. Table 9.4 reports the correlations among the values of the 10 standardized subindexes and two BLURIs constructed from the

TABLE 9.4 Correlation Matrix of BLURI Subindexes and BLURI Values

	Political influence	Project approvals	Zoning changes	Development caps	Density	Open space	Infrastructure improvements	Inclusionary housing	Approval delays	Rate of approval	BLURI I	BLURI II
Political influence	1.00											
Project approvals	0.11	1.00										
Zoning changes	0.06	0.72	1.00									
Development caps	0.17	0.01	0.19	1.00								
Density	−0.07	0.04	0.13	0.22	1.00							
Open space	0.08	0.29	0.20	0.01	0.04	1.00						
Infrastructure improvements	−0.04	0.07	0.09	0.02	0.10	0.19	1.00					
Inclusionary housing	0.19	0.20	0.15	−0.03	−0.20	−0.04	−0.13	1.00				
Approval delays	0.20	0.02	0.16	0.33	0.14	0.03	−0.02	0.04	1.00			
Rate of approval	−0.12	−0.16	−0.20	−0.07	−0.30	−0.12	−0.09	−0.18	0.07	1.00		
BLURI I	0.23	0.87	0.90	0.26	0.23	0.36	0.14	0.23	0.22	−0.37	1.00	
BLURI II	0.41	0.59	0.64	0.48	0.29	0.43	0.31	0.26	0.51	−0.04	0.79	1.00

NOTES: BLURI I is computed by factor analysis using the first principal factor of the covariance among the 10 subindexes. BLURI II is computed as the simple sum of values of the 10 subindexes.

FIGURE 9.6   Scatterplot: BLURI Factor Scores by Raw Sum of Indexes (N = 86)

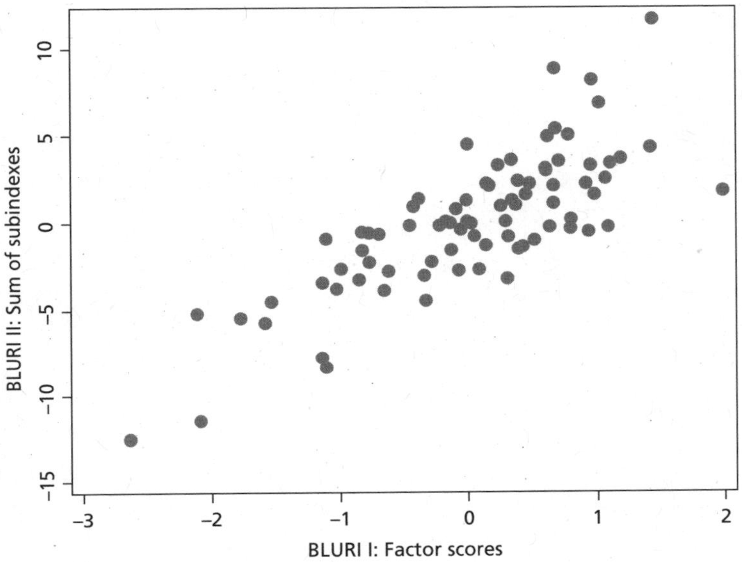

BLURI II: Sum of subindexes

BLURI I: Factor scores

NOTE: BLURI = Berkeley Land Use Regulation Index.

underlying data.[11] Appendix table 9A.1 reports factor loadings and correlations between the 10 subindexes and the composite BLURI level.

A scatterplot of the factor scores and the sum of the standardized values of the 10 subindexes is shown in figure 9.6. Remarkably, the complexity of the 10 underlying measurements can be summarized very well by either a single factor or by the sum of the underlying subindexes. Figure 9.7 reports the two BLURIs of land use restrictiveness in the San Francisco Bay Area.

Surveys of Bay Area Developers and Environmental Professionals

Respondents completing our 2007 developer survey provided information on a total of 62 projects located in 33 land use jurisdictions in the Bay Area.

---

11. We impute missing data points when aggregating the subindexes; otherwise, missing data for one component value would make the values of the other subindexes unusable. Data were missing from one jurisdiction for the Project Approval Index, from 15 jurisdictions for the Approval Delay Index, and from 20 jurisdictions on the Rate of Approval Index. Values for missing data points are imputed using the "impute" command (in Stata 9.0), which uses a multivariate regression to predict the missing values.

FIGURE 9.7   BLURI for the San Francisco Bay Area

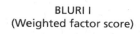

BLURI I
(Weighted factor score)

BLURI II
(Simple sum)

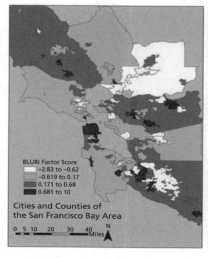 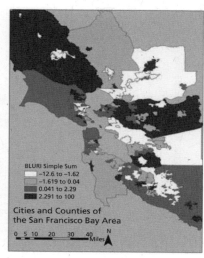

NOTE: BLURI = Berkeley Land Use Regulation Index.

For each project, respondents identified the product type, size, and other characteristics. They also estimated an inherent *ex ante* entitlement risk for the project and its level of controversy. Developers then provided three summary measures describing each specific project: (1) the total time for the completion of the permit-review process; (2) the all-inclusive cost of securing the entitlement; and (3) the perceived accuracy of their initial estimates of the time that would be required to secure entitlements.

In a format similar to that used for our developer survey, environmental consultants answered a series of questions about recent development projects on which they served as hired experts. Responses cover 27 projects in 14 jurisdictions. In addition to questions about project characteristics, such as the type of development and the number of units, two sets of questions were asked about the environmental aspects of the process. The first set of items identified total cost, time, and related components of local review. Consultants responding to the survey also evaluated regulatory reasonableness, transparency, and other local conditions. Like the developers, these respondents also rated the perceived level of controversy and ex ante entitlement risk for particular projects. Beyond these factors, we asked how consultants rated the degree of environmental mitigation required, given the nature, design, and location of the project in question.

TABLE 9.5 Selected Project Level Indicators by Product Type (Survey of Developers)

Indicator	Single-family homes (37 projects)		Attached, mixed-use, and planned unit (25 projects)	
	Mean	Standard deviation	Mean	Standard deviation
Number of units	121	173	331	219
Controversy level (1–3)	1.57	0.55	2.04	0.89
Entitlement risk (1–5)	2.70	0.91	3.08	1.15
Number of special permits	2.03	1.40	2.60	1.47
Entitlement cost ($ millions)	1.31	1.88	2.34	3.34
Entitlement cost per unit	$22,620	$30,760	$9,070	$13,250
Time (years)	2.46	1.25	2.04	1.24
Accuracy (years)	1.25	0.88	0.72	0.85

Table 9.5 summarizes developer responses separately for single-family housing developments and for all other projects (i.e., apartments, condominiums, mixed-use, and planned-unit developments). As indicated in the table, developments of single-family housing in our sample involved fewer units—121 units on average, as opposed to 331 units for other developments. The level of controversy ex ante was considered substantially lower for single-family developments, averaging 1.6 on a scale of 1 to 3.[12] By comparison, other projects averaged 2.0 in terms of controversy. The ex ante entitlement risk was an average of 2.7, on a scale of 1 ("very low risk") to 5 ("very high risk") for single-family projects; in comparison, other projects scored an average of 3.1. Single-family projects also required fewer special permits for construction than other projects did.

When builders were asked to estimate "the all-inclusive cost of the entire entitlement process," responses averaged $1.3 million for single-family developments of varying sizes, and about $22,600 per new dwelling unit. Entitlement costs for other types of development, which tended to be significantly larger and more complex, averaged $2.3 million per project, or about $9,100 per dwelling unit. The single-family entitlement process averaged delays of almost two-and-a-half years, as opposed to delays of about two years for non-single-family construction.[13]

---

12. The survey item asked respondents to rate project controversy as "standard," "mildly controversial," or "pushing the envelope." These levels were given coded values from one to three, respectively.

13. These averages, and those in tables 9.6 and 9.7, conceal a great amount of variation. Our longer narrative describing this study, downloadable via http://urbanpolicy.berkeley.edu, presents frequency distributions for out-of-pocket costs associated with the entitlement process, total per-unit costs, time to entitlement, and accuracy of initial entitlement time estimates, all broken out by development type.

TABLE 9.6   Selected Project Level Indicators by Controversy Level (Survey of Developers)

Indicator	"Standard" projects (26 projects)		Mildly controversial and pushing the envelope (36 projects)	
	Mean	Standard deviation	Mean	Standard deviation
Number of units	175	184	227	239
Entitlement risk (1–5)	2.31	0.93	3.25	0.91
Number of special permits	1.65	1.02	2.69	1.56
Entitlement cost ($ millions)	1.41	2.01	1.98	2.98
Entitlement cost per unit	$18,870	$28,930	$15,740	$23,630
Time (years)	2.00	1.20	2.52	1.26
Accuracy (years)	0.92	0.78	1.12	0.98

Table 9.6 reports the same selected indicators of projects, entitlement delays, and costs by the level of ex ante controversy of the project. As expected, larger projects tended to be viewed as more controversial, as did those exhibiting greater entitlement risk or requiring special permits. Less controversial projects required about $1.4 million in entitlement costs, or about $8,000 per dwelling unit. More controversial projects required about $1.9 million in out-of-pocket costs, or about 10 percent more per dwelling unit produced. On average, more controversial projects took 25 percent longer—about six months—to receive permission to build.

Tables 9.7 and 9.8 present results from our survey of environmental professionals. Table 9.7 indicates that non-single-family projects tend to be much larger, averaging 271 units (nearly 200 units more than single-family developments, on average). The level of controversy tends to be lower for single-family projects, averaging 1.69 on the previously defined scale. For multifamily housing, the controversy level is 2.14, on average. Similarly, the level of entitlement risk for single-family homes is lower, although it is only about 5 percent less than for multifamily and other housing.

Indicators of delay and mitigation were only slightly lower for single-family housing developments than for multifamily housing and mixed use, although costs and the length of time for the environmental review process were higher. On a scale of 1 to 4, where 1 is "none" and 4 is "very high," single-family homes experienced an average delay of 2.6, whereas the average delay for non-single-family projects was 2.9. On the same scale of 1 to 4, developers of single-family projects were required to undertake a very similar

TABLE 9.7   Selected Project Level Indicators by Product Type (Survey of Environmental Professionals)

Indicator	Single-family homes (13 projects)		Apartments, condominiums, mixed-use, and other (14 projects)	
	Mean	Standard deviation	Mean	Standard deviation
Number of units	74.46	79.19	270.93	277.88
Controversy level (1–3)	1.69	0.75	2.14	0.66
Entitlement risk (1–5)	2.85	1.14	3.00	0.68
Number of drivers of risk	1.62	1.45	2.79	1.63
Delays (1–4)	2.63	1.29	2.93	0.73
Mitigation (1–4)	2.50	1.00	2.64	0.84
Time (years)	2.27	1.62	1.93	0.62
Entitlement cost	$110,300	$138,380	$301,150	$315,060
Entitlement cost per unit	$8,140	$20,650	$2,990	$6,650

TABLE 9.8   Selected Project Level Indicators by Controversy Level (Survey of Environmental Professionals)

Indicator	Standard projects (8 projects)		Mildly controversial and pushing the envelope (19 projects)	
	Mean	Standard deviation	Mean	Standard deviation
Number of units	135.38	200.46	193.58	240.24
Entitlement risk (1–5)	2.25	0.89	3.21	0.79
Number of drivers of risk	1.25	1.16	2.63	1.64
Delays (1–4)	2.33	1.03	2.95	0.97
Mitigation (1–4)	1.86	0.69	2.84	0.83
Time (years)	1.33	0.68	2.32	1.18
Entitlement cost	$40,190	$51,140	$285,120	$283,560
Entitlement cost per unit	$1,250	$2,160	$7,040	$17,250

level of environmental mitigation, rating an average of 2.5, whereas non-single-family projects were rated 2.6, on average. As with the developer survey, overall costs were much higher for multifamily and mixed-use projects, but per-unit costs and the time required for completion of the review process were not. On average, single-family projects took 2.3 years and multifamily and mixed-use projects took only 1.9 years. The costs for environmental review averaged $8,000 for each single-family unit built, as opposed to $3,000 for multifamily and mixed-use development.

Table 9.8 compares the average value of "standard" projects with those considered more controversial by the respondents. Similar to developers' experiences, the more controversial projects described by environmental professionals had more units, took more time to secure entitlements, had a higher overall cost, and had a higher cost per dwelling unit. For example, for the average "mildly controversial" or "pushing-the-envelope" project, the entitlement process took one year longer than for the average "standard" project. The unit cost of securing permits for the average standard project was less than one-fifth that of an average controversial project. Additionally, on the scale of 1 to 4, where 1 is "none" and 4 is "very high," more controversial projects had higher levels of delay than standard projects. Similarly, developers of more controversial projects ultimately faced more extensive legal obligations to mitigate environmental impact.

Land Use Restrictiveness, Prices, and Rents

Finally, we explore the relationship between these regulation measures and the cost of housing—monthly rents and the prices of owner-occupied homes—using the Public Use Micro Sample (PUMS) for the San Francisco Bay Area from the 2000 census. The census micro data provide a rich description of the hedonic characteristics of housing—numbers of rooms and bedrooms, structure types, year built, and quality of kitchen and bath. Dwelling units are identified geographically by Public Use Microdata Area (PUMA), not city or civil division. We allocate observations on dwellings by PUMA to cities in the Bay Area by proportional representation, using the geographical correlation engine developed at the University of Missouri.[14] This technique essentially weights observations from those PUMAs that contain more than one city or that cross city boundaries, in proportion to dwellings in those cities as a fraction of all dwellings in the PUMA.

To address the joint determination of regulation and housing market outcomes, we use preexisting measures of the political predisposition in each city, and more recent plebiscites showing citizen attitudes toward housing bond issuance, as instruments for the index of regulatory restrictiveness. In general,

---

14. This allocation mechanism is identical to that used in Quigley and Raphael (2005) (see footnote 2) to allocate observations in the 1990 and 2000 PUMS to California land use jurisdictions.

our instrumental variable (IV) estimates are similar to those generated by the ordinary least squares (OLS) models. Finally, to account for unmeasured spatial and civic factors, we include in these models indicator variables identifying jurisdictions that are "coastal" (bordering the San Francisco Bay or Pacific Ocean) and those that are counties governing unincorporated land outside chartered and incorporated California cities.

Table 9.9 presents the results of a series of regressions of housing value on the hedonic characteristics of individual owner-occupied dwellings and the measure of regulatory stringency developed in this research. The basic hedonic

TABLE 9.9 Regulatory Restrictions and the Value of Owner-Occupied Housing

	Ordinary least squares		Instrumental variable[a]	
	(1)	(2)	(3)	(4)
Number of rooms	0.155	0.155	0.155	0.156
	(76.32)	(78.65)	(75.82)	(78.17)
Number of bedrooms	0.032	0.015	0.029	0.009
	(9.21)	(4.56)	(8.35)	(2.65)
Age	0.002	0.001	0.002	0.001
	(17.86)	(4.32)	(19.07)	(4.78)
Complete kitchen	−0.210	−0.203	−0.209	−0.200
(1 = no)	(−3.04)	(−2.99)	(−3.03)	(−2.94)
Complete plumbing	−0.121	−0.107	−0.125	−0.111
(1 = no)	(−2.6)	(−2.35)	(−2.72)	(−2.45)
County dummy	−0.111	0.318	−0.098	0.321
	(−21.5)	(39.86)	(−18.74)	(40.74)
Coastal	−0.032	−0.166	−0.056	−0.194
	(−7.31)	(−37.82)	(−11.58)	(−40.60)
Log basic jobs		0.245		0.277
		(93.06)		(89.86)
Log developable land		−0.051		−0.039
		(−37.15)		(−26.54)
BLURI	0.012	0.022	0.038	0.053
	(23.42)	(40.59)	(28.67)	(35.53)
	[1.51]	[2.51]	[1.27]	[1.33]
R-squared	0.38	0.42	0.37	0.40
R-squared first stage			0.18	0.24

NOTES: Dependent variable in logarithms. All models include dummy variables for 10 structure types (e.g., condominium, single-detached), persons per room, and a constant term. BLURI = Berkeley Land Use Regulation Index.

[a] Instruments include the percent of votes: favoring Proposition 13 (1976); for Reagan (1980); and favoring housing bond propositions 46 and 1C (2002 and 2006, respectively).

model is identical to that used by Quigley and Raphael (2004, 2005). These regressions are based on the 62,905 owner-occupied dwellings in the San Francisco Bay Area reflected in the 2000 PUMS. The hedonic characteristics alone explain about 38 percent of the variance in the log of house values. This fraction increases to 42 percent when variables measuring changes in the nearby location of basic employment and the amount of vacant land are added to the model. The variable measuring restrictive regulation has a coefficient between 0.01 and 0.02 and a computed t-ratio above 20. When the models are estimated by instrumental variables using political preferences expressed well before the 2000 U.S. Census (e.g., the percent voting for Ronald Reagan in 1980), the coefficient on regulatory stringency is substantially larger.

Of course, large t-ratios computed for the regulatory measure are misleading, because the sample for these statistical models includes only about 80 different jurisdictions enacting land use regulations in the Bay Area. However, when the standard errors are appropriately grouped by jurisdiction, the t-ratio in the OLS model, including measures of jobs and developable land, remains statistically significant. The clustered t-ratios are reported in square brackets in the table.

Table 9.10 reports a comparable analysis based on the 38,184 rental units sampled in the 2000 census. The hedonic models explain a smaller fraction of the variance in log rents, only about 17 percent when job growth and developable land are included as variables.[15] The coefficient on the measure of regulatory stringency is again larger when the models are estimated by instrumental variables. To a greater extent than was true for the home value models already reported here, these coefficients are statistically significant when the standard errors are grouped appropriately.

A more detailed analysis of the influence of individual components of the constructed BLURI measure on house prices suggests that rents and house values are particularly sensitive to the complexity of the approvals process for new housing developments. Additional review requirements significantly add to the costs of navigating the entitlements process and increase the expense and delay in getting projects built. Table 9.11 summarizes this relationship. The table reports the results when our earlier price and rent models are reestimated using the project approvals subindex (PAI) and the political influence subindex (PI) instead of the broader BLURI of which they are part. The spec-

---

15. The differences in the explanatory power of the models for owner-occupied and rental dwellings may arise from less price variation among rental units (see Capozza, Green, and Hendershott, 1996).

TABLE 9.10 Regulatory Restrictions and Monthly Rents

	Ordinary least squares		Instrumental variable[a]	
	(1)	(2)	(3)	(4)
Number of rooms	0.050	0.052	0.047	0.050
	(16.78)	(17.86)	(15.62)	(16.46)
Number of bedrooms	0.093	0.088	0.096	0.090
	(19.67)	(18.96)	(19.97)	(18.80)
Age	−0.002	−0.003	−0.003	−0.003
	(−17.30)	(−20.43)	(−19.79)	(−23.99)
Complete kitchen	−0.157	−0.148	−0.177	−0.171
(1 = no)	(−6.31)	(−5.92)	(−6.88)	(−6.53)
Complete plumbing	−0.269	−0.267	−0.281	−0.282
(1 = no)	(−9.43)	(−9.36)	(−9.53)	(−9.48)
County dummy	−0.077	0.181	−0.065	0.222
	(−13.31)	(20.51)	(−11.08)	(23.31)
Coastal	−0.021	−0.108	−0.065	−0.176
	(−4.51)	(−22.93)	(−11.85)	(−29.45)
Log basic jobs		0.164		0.210
		(55.43)		(59.20)
Log developable land		−0.023		−0.017
		(−15.74)		(−10.84)
BLURI	0.009	0.014	0.046	0.060
	(14.91)	(23.44)	(30.79)	(36.83)
	[1.92]	[4.04]	[2.46]	[2.26]
R-squared value	0.15	0.17	0.10	0.10
R-squared first stage			0.17	0.19

NOTES: Dependent variable in logarithms. All models include dummy variables for 10 structure types (e.g., condominium, single-detached), persons per room, and a constant term. BLURI = Berkeley Land Use Regulation Index.

[a] Instruments include the percent of votes: favoring Proposition 13 (1976); voting for Reagan (1980); and favoring housing bond propositions 46 and 1C (2002 and 2006, respectively).

ification does not appear sensitive to using the raw PAI or PI composites or their logarithms, as reflected in the table.

The results suggest that the number of approvals required to authorize additions to the housing supply has a large effect upon the housing prices in a jurisdiction. These coefficients are statistically significant and economically important. The OLS models suggest that the addition of one required review to the development process is associated with price increases of about 4 percent. In terms of relative magnitudes, the PAI reported in table 9.2 has a mean of 5 reviews and a standard deviation of 2.13.

TABLE 9.11 Project Approvals Index, Political Influence Index, and House Values

	Ordinary least squares		Instrumental variable[a]	
	(1)	(2)	(3)	(4)
Project approval index	0.041	0.043	0.254	0.293
	(46.29)	(49.38)	(52.49)	(53.99)
	[2.99].	[3.90]	[2.46]	[2.25]
Log (project approval)	0.173	0.171	1.455	1.544
	(48.31)	(50.71)	(56.67)	(61.76)
	[2.52]	[3.32]	[2.22]	[2.32]
Political influence index	0.001	0.004	0.018	0.022
	(7.94)	(37.96)	(64.16)	(66.56)
	[0.46]	[2.48]	[3.04]	[3.06]
Log (political influence)	0.052	0.344	1.645	1.912
	(5.71)	(35.55)	(63.44)	(66.22)
	[0.32]	[2.18]	[2.59]	[2.74]

NOTES: Dependent variable in logarithms. All specifications are the same as those reported in tables 9.9 and 9.10. Columns (2) and (4) include the variables measuring growth in basic jobs and the amount of developable land.

[a] Instruments include the percent of votes: favoring Proposition 13 (1976); voting for Reagan (1980); and favoring housing bond propositions 46 and 1C (2002 and 2006, respectively).

House values and rents are both significantly affected by the composite index of regulatory stringency, whereas key components like political influence and project approvals and their logarithms appear to affect home values to a greater extent than they do rents.

CONCLUSION

This chapter presents a description of land use regulation in the San Francisco Bay Area, a region containing more than 100 independent regulatory authorities, and one in which housing prices have tripled since 1995 (and doubled since 1999).[16] We compare the results from our 2007 survey of government building officials with prior surveys conducted in the 1990s. We also compare these results with surveys of developers and land use intermediaries in the Bay Area, finding that regulatory stringency is consistently associated with higher costs for construction, longer delays in completing projects, and greater uncertainty about the elapsed time to completion of residential developments.

---

16. See http://www.ofheo.gov/hpi_download.aspx.

We find strong evidence that regulatory restrictiveness leads to higher house prices and higher rents in the jurisdictions imposing the regulations. These effects are quite large. An increase of one standard deviation in the number of governmental reviews required to authorize residential development (i.e., from a mean of five required agency reviews, to a total of seven) is associated with an 8 percent increase in the average prices of single-family housing in the existing stock. Regulation clearly seems profitable to the owners of existing housing.

APPENDIX

TABLE 9A.1 Factor Loadings and Correlations Between Subindexes and BLURI I

Subindexes	Factor loading	Correlation with factor score
Political influence	0.197	0.225
Project approvals	0.756	0.866
Zoning changes	0.788	0.902
Development caps	0.229	0.262
Density restrictions	0.199	0.228
Open space restrictions	0.314	0.359
Infrastructure improvements	0.126	0.145
Inclusionary housing	0.202	0.231
Approval of delays	0.195	0.223
Rate of approvals	−0.319	−0.366

TABLE 9A.2 BLURI: Open Space, Infrastructure Improvement, and Inclusionary Housing Indexes (Observations in 86 Bay Area Jurisdictions)

Measure	Frequency		
	Open space	Infrastructure improvements	Inclusionary housing
No restrictions	10	3	13
In lieu fees option	47	55	54
Restrictions	29	28	19
		Mean	Standard deviation
Open Space Index Score		0.71	0.32
Infrastructure Improvements Index Score		0.75	0.23
Inclusionary Housing Index Score		0.64	0.32

TABLE 9A.3 BLURI: Approval Delay Index (Observations in 79 Bay Area Jurisdictions)

	Estimated delay in months		
Type of project	No zoning change	Zoning change	Subdivision
1–4 single-family units	7	10	NA
5–49 single-family units	15	15	15
≥ 50 single-family units	17	17	18
Multifamily units	14	14	14
Median	13	14	17

	Mean	Standard deviation
Approval Delay Index Score	12.66	7.32

TABLE 9A.4 BLURI: Rate of Approval Index (Observations in 69 Bay Area Jurisdictions)

Type of project	Mean applications	Mean approvals
Zoning change	72	32
Subdivision applications	8	4

	Mean	Standard deviation
Rate of Approval Index Score	0.74	0.30

REFERENCES

Calavita, Nico, Kenneth Grimes, and Allan Mallach. 1998. "Inclusionary Zoning in California and New Jersey: A Comparative Analysis." *Housing Policy Debate* 8(1): 109–142.

Calfee, Corie, Paavo Monkkonen, John M. Quigley, Steven Raphael, Larry A. Rosenthal, and Joseph Wright. 2007. "Measuring Land Use Regulation: A Report to the MacArthur Foundation." Berkeley, CA: Berkeley Program on Housing and Urban Policy, P07-002[2], August.

Capozza, Dennis, Richard K. Green, and Patric Hendershott. 1996. "Taxes, Mortgage Borrowing, and Residential Land Prices." In Henry Aaron and William Gale, eds., *The Economic Effects of Fundamental Tax Reform*, 171–210. Washington, DC: Brookings Institution Press.

Fischel, William A. 1985. *The Economics of Zoning Laws: A Property Rights Approach to American Land Use Controls*. Baltimore: Johns Hopkins University Press.

Glickfield, Madelyn, and Ned Levine. 1992. *Regional Growth, Local Reaction: The Enactment and Effects of Local Growth Control and Management Measures in California.* Cambridge, MA: Lincoln Institute of Land Policy.

Green, Richard K., Stephen Malpezzi, and Stephen K. Mayo. 2005. "Metropolitan-Specific Estimates of the Price Elasticity of Supply of Housing and Their Sources." *American Economic Review* 95(2): 334–339.

Gyourko, Joseph E., Albert Saiz, and Anita A. Summers. 2008. "A New Measure of the Local Regulatory Environment for Housing Markets: Wharton Residential Land Use Regulatory Index." *Urban Studies* 45(3): 693–729.

Gyourko, Joseph E., and Anita A. Summers. 2006. "Residential Land Use Regulation in the Philadelphia MSA." Zell/Lurie Real Estate Center Working Paper No. 560.

Landis, John D. 2000. "Raising the Roof: California Housing Development Projections and Constraints, 1997–2020." Sacramento: California Department of Housing and Community Development (Statewide Housing Plan Update), May.

———. 2006. "Growth Management Revisited: Efficacy, Price Effects, and Displacement." *Journal of the American Planning Association* 72(4): 411–430.

Landis, John D., Lan Deng, and Michael Reilly. 2002. "Growth Management Revisited." IURD Working Paper No. 2002-02, University of California, Berkeley.

Landis, John D., Heather Hood, Guangyu Li, Thomas Rogers, and Charles Warren. 2006. "The Future of Infill Housing in California: Opportunities, Potential, and Feasibility." *Housing Policy Debate* 17(4): 681–726.

Levine, Ned. 1999. "The Effects of Local Growth Controls on Regional Housing Production and Population Redistribution in California." *Urban Studies* 36(12): 2047–2068.

Malpezzi, Stephen. 1996. "Housing Prices, Externalities, and Regulation in U.S. Metropolitan Areas." *Journal of Housing Research* 7(2): 209–241.

Malpezzi, Stephen, and Richard K. Green. 1996. "What Has Happened to the Bottom of the US Housing Market?" *Urban Studies* 33(10): 1807–1820.

Mills, Edwin S., and Wallace E. Oates, eds. 1975. *Fiscal Zoning and Land Use Controls.* Lexington, MA: D. C. Heath.

Pogodzinski, J. M. 1995. "A Public Choice Perspective on Zoning and Growth Controls: NIMBYism, the Tiebout Mechanism, and Local Democracy." In J. M. Pogodzinski, ed., *Readings in Public Policy*, 145–180. Cambridge, MA: Blackwell.

Quigley, John M., and Steven Raphael. 2004. "Regulation and the High Cost of Housing in California." Working Paper No. W04-008, Berkeley Program on Housing and Urban Policy.

———. 2005. "Regulation and the High Cost of Housing in California." *American Economic Review* 95(2): 323–329.

Quigley, John M., and Larry A. Rosenthal. 2005. "The Effects of Land Use Regulation on the Price of Housing: What Do We Know? What Can We Learn?" *Cityscape* 8(1): 69–138.

Rolleston, Barbara Sherman. 1987. "Determinants of Restrictive Suburban Zoning: An Empirical Analysis." *Journal of Urban Economics* 21(1): 1–21.

Rosenthal, Larry A. 2000. "Long Division: California's Land Use Reform Policy and the Pursuit of Residential Integration." Unpublished PhD thesis, University of California, Berkeley, Goldman School of Public Policy.

Summers, Anita A., Paul C. Cheshire, and Lanfranco Senn, eds. 1993. *Urban Change in the United States and Western Europe*. Washington, DC: The Urban Institute.

Commentary

RICHARD K. GREEN

John Quigley, Steven Raphael, and Larry Rosenthal have written a chapter that is remarkable for its painstaking development of data characterizing land use regulation in the San Francisco Bay Area.[1] As such, it provides many important stylized facts about land markets in the Bay Area; it also argues that it finds that more stringent land use regulation is (not surprisingly) associated with higher home prices. The work will doubtless be useful to those studying land use regulation in the future. I, for one, found it interesting and astonishing that so many communities in the San Francisco Bay Area have a minimum lot size requirement of two acres. Given how valuable land is in the Bay Area, one would think the economic pressure to subdivide would overcome the political pressure not to do so. My guess is that many scholars and policy makers will refer to the Berkeley Land Use Regulation Index (BLURI) in the years to come.

SOME COMMENTS ON THE BROAD RESULTS

The first thing that is striking about empirical results is that the impact of layering land use regulations seems to have grown across time. In both figures 9.2 and 9.3, the slope of the relationship between the number of regulations and price or rent was steeper in 2000 than in 1990. This suggests that perhaps "unwritten" regulations are becoming increasingly important and are interacting with the written regulations.

Also striking is that the home price regressions perform much better than the rent regressions: the R-square on the home price regressions is around .4, whereas on the rent regressions it is around .1 to .15. This may be because there is less variation in rent than in prices across jurisdictions. The fact that rents have relatively low variation, whereas prices have much variation, implies that rent-to-price ratios must vary within the San Francisco Bay Area. To understand how this can happen, consider a simple version of the user cost model of housing:

$$\frac{\text{Rent}}{\text{Value}} = (1 - \tau_y)\text{r} + (1 - \tau_y)\tau_p + \text{m} - \pi$$

---

1. The only similarly thorough study I can think of is Schuetz and White's (1993) piece on land use regulation in the Milwaukee metropolitan area.

where τ_y = marginal income tax rate, r = before-tax cost of capital, τ_p = property tax rate, m = maintenance + depreciation + amortized transaction costs, and π = expected growth in rents.

Capozza, Green, and Hendershott (1996) show that cross-metropolitan variations in rent-to-price ratios can largely be explained by variations in the after-tax cost of capital across metropolitan areas, along with differences in property tax rates. In the San Francisco Bay Area context, property tax rates probably do not vary very much across communities (because of Proposition 13), but marginal federal and state tax rates may vary quite a lot, because incomes almost always vary a lot.[2] Local income measures are not included in the rent or price regressions. If the BLURI is correlated with per capita income, its significance in explaining home prices may reflect this correlation.

Beyond differences in taxes, differences in rent-to-price ratios may reflect differences in discount rates and in expected rent growth. Whether it is one or the other is important. Lower discount rates reflect lower expected risk; households who live in heavily regulated places may perceive that their risk is lower, and therefore are willing to pay more. If this is the case, it is not entirely clear that land use regulation is inefficient. On the other hand, if regulations are simply making land market inelastic, expectations about rent growth will be pushed upward, because increased future demand will be absorbed in higher rents rather than in greater supply. This is almost certainly not a welfare-improving result.

One final point on welfare: one of the arguments for land use regulation is that it increases the amenity value of jurisdictions—that it makes places more pleasant for day-to-day life. If this is in fact the case, the increased value should show up in differences in rents.

Some Cautions on the Bottom-Line Results

As I already noted, the BLURI is exceptionally useful, and I hope policy makers will consult with it in the future. That said, the index does not do a particularly good job of predicting either rents or prices. In four out of eight regressions, the adjusted t-statistics on the BLURI coefficient are less than 1.96, and in three regressions, they fail even the 90 percent confidence test of being different from zero. Making the result even less impressive is the fact that as an index, the BLURI is basically gathering numerous explanatory variables into one variable, which should make its coefficient estimate sharper.

---

2. In 2000, Atherton had a per capita income of $112,408, whereas Oakland's per capita income was $21,936. See U.S Bureau of the Census (2000).

This is not to say that land use regulation does not matter. It may be the case that most jurisdictions in the San Francisco Bay Area are above the threshold where it does matter, and that the variation—once regulation exceeds a certain threshold—does not make much difference. Perhaps we may look forward to future work in which researchers use Quigley, Raphael, and Rosenthal's techniques in a market that has a wider variety of land use regulatory schemes.

REFERENCES

Capozza, Dennis, Richard K. Green, and Patric Hendershott. 1996. "Taxes, Mortgage Borrowing and Residential Land Prices." In Henry Aaron and William Gale, eds., *The Economic Effects of Fundamental Tax Reform*, 171–198. Washington, DC: Brookings Institution Press.

Schuetz, Mary Kay, and Sammis B. White. 1993. "Identifying and Mitigating Local Regulatory Barriers to Affordable Housing in Waukesha County, WI." Working Paper, University of Wisconsin–Milwaukee.

U.S. Bureau of the Census. 2000. Census 2000, Summary File 3 Data, Per Capita Personal Income, 1999. http://factfinder.census.gov.

Commentary

STEPHEN MALPEZZI

Over the past two decades, there has been an increasing focus on supply-side issues in housing and other real estate markets. The regulation of land use and development is by no means the only supply-side issue—the roles of geography and natural constraint, labor and materials markets, and the "industrial organization" of the housing market come to mind—but regulatory issues are important and, at least in principle, more within human control than, say, the geographic challenges created by the existence of San Francisco Bay or Mount Davidson.

In this careful and well-constructed chapter, John Quigley, Steven Raphael, and Larry Rosenthal have made a valuable contribution to the growing literature on the measurement of development regulation and its effects on housing markets. One way much of this recent empirical research can be roughly categorized is between studies that measure the stringency of regulation across metropolitan areas (or less often, across states or countries). Such studies (for example, Glaeser, Gyourko, and Saks, 2006; Green, Malpezzi, and Mayo, 2005; Gyourko, Saiz, and Summers, 2008; Hwang and Quigley, 2006; Linneman et al., 1990; Mayer and Somerville, 2000; Quigley and Raphael, 2005; Quigley, Raphael, and Rosenthal, 2004; and many studies surveyed in the excellent review by Quigley and Rosenthal, 2005) take advantage of the substantial variation in regulatory regimes across U.S. metropolitan areas, and have the further advantage of giving us a big-picture view of a large number of the United States' diverse local housing markets. But among other shortcomings of such studies is the fact that all of us who engage in them are aware of the problematic maintained assumption that we can neglect within-metropolitan variation in regulatory regimes; Keith Ihlanfeldt (2007) provides a good example of such a critique. Studies that examine one or a few regulating jurisdictions, such as early studies by George Peterson (1974) and later work by Henry Pollakowski and Susan Wachter (1990) and Richard Green (1999), not only address but actually take advantage of the richness of within-market variation, but corresponding questions can be raised about their generalizability.

Although this chapter is a study of a single metropolitan area, in many respects it contributes to both strands of research. By using an index that is constructed in a manner broadly similar to those of the cross-metro studies, the authors undertake a within-market analysis that can be more directly compared to cross-market literature. One of their important findings is a validation of the critique that cross-market studies lose something by aggregating local regulating jurisdictions to a single metropolitan average. Another finding is that these results from the cross-metro studies and the within-metro study are qualitatively similar: more stringent regulations drive up housing costs within, as well as across, metropolitan areas.

There are other advantages of Quigley, Raphael, and Rosenthal's approach. Many of us would also express a prior belief that cross-metro differences in "average" regulatory environments might not provide an especially reliable guide to effects of a marginal change in actual regulations in a single jurisdiction; and real-world regulatory changes usually follow that path, rather than a large change in a wide range of regulations across many jurisdictions within a metropolitan area.

Quigley, Raphael, and Rosenthal also make some important contributions to our thinking about how to design regulatory surveys and how to construct indices from their results. Here I point out just three: (1) their care in reporting separately (as well as in aggregates) the responses of different actors in the development process (developers, government, and environmental officials); (2) their integration of the "usual suspects," such as growth management rules and density restrictions, with attitudinal and political questions; and (3) their construction of different aggregates for different development types (e.g., single-family versus multifamily).

I would also point out that their chapter is very much an investment. There is much inertia in regulatory environments. We now have a baseline of regulation for a wide range of San Francisco jurisdictions circa 2007. How will housing prices and development activity evolve going forward from this baseline? As we enter a period of price volatility after the recent long run-up and the subprime crisis, will we find (à la Malpezzi and Wachter, 2005) that more stringently regulated markets face a different risk-return tradeoff than more elastic markets? I expect there will be many fruitful follow-up studies by the present and other authors of the Bay Area, now that Quigley, Raphael, and Rosenthal have armed us with these indices.

There are too many interesting specific results in the chapter to review in detail here, but let me mention just a few. The usual ordinary least squares (OLS) regression of house prices or rents on regulatory indices raises suspicion that perhaps regulations are partly a response to past price changes (which in turn affect today's levels). Quigley, Raphael, and Rosenthal thus present both OLS and Instrumental Variables (IV) results that can mitigate the effects of this endogeneity. We carried out a similar cross-metro exercise in Malpezzi, Chun, and Green

(1998); we found that the IV results were qualitatively similar but smaller in magnitude and with smaller t-statistics. Quigley, Raphael, and Rosenthal find that their IV results are stronger and more precise. The Malpezzi, Chun, and Green results suggest that the main bias in OLS estimation of house price models with regulation on the right-hand side is related to endogeneity of the regulatory measure; the Quigley, Raphael, and Rosenthal results (and a similar result for Florida cities, found in Ihlandfeldt, 2007) suggest that measurement error might dominate. How this issue shakes out in other markets is a question for future work, and how much it might depend on a superior IV first stage by Quigley, Raphael, and Rosenthal are among the questions it would be interesting to answer. In fact, this suggests a follow-up chapter that brings the determinants of this regulatory stringency to center stage, à la Ortalo-Magné and Prat (2006).

Much remains to be done in this area. Most regulatory stringency measures are one-off designs.[1] Thus, studies are limited to cross-sectional experimental designs or to panel data on house prices, and other variables are related to a single cross-section of regulatory measures. Full cost-benefit analysis of land use regulation would extend the current studies of regulatory effects on house prices, rents, and construction activity to a wider range of possible cost and benefit measures — e.g., commuting patterns, environmental outcomes, and so forth.[2] And to date, most studies of these supply-side issues have focused on housing; extensions to office, retail, industrial, and other nonresidential real estate are naturals.

REFERENCES

Fischel, William A. 1990. *Do Growth Controls Matter? A Review of Empirical Evidence on the Effectiveness and Efficiency of Local Government Land Use Regulation*. Cambridge, MA: Lincoln Institute of Land Policy.

Glaeser, Edward L., Joseph Gyourko, and Raven Saks. 2006. "Urban Growth and Housing Supply." *Journal of Economic Geography* 6(1) (January): 71–89.

---

1. Many, although not all, measures have been influenced or derived from questionnaires developed by Anita Summers and her Wharton associates (Linneman and Summers; Gyourko, Saiz, and Summers). Even the two surveys fielded by the Wharton teams are not completely compatible. Both survey efforts initially attempted to collect information within, as well as across, metropolitan areas; but despite the substantial effort they made, they found it difficult to collect sufficient information to present reliable within-metro indices. Over the past several years, the U.S. Department of Housing and Urban Development (HUD) has undertaken preliminary planning for a larger, government-sponsored effort collecting regulatory information across a wide range of markets, which could conceivably break through this barrier. As of this writing, it is unclear whether HUD will in fact fully undertake that effort.

2. The point is cogently made in Fischel (1990). See also Peterson (1974) and Malpezzi (1996).

Green, Richard K. 1999. "Land Use Regulation and the Price of Housing in a Suburban Wisconsin County." *Journal of Housing Economics* 8(2) (June): 233–248.

Green, Richard K., Stephen Malpezzi, and Stephen K. Mayo. 2005. "Metropolitan-Specific Estimates of the Price Elasticity of Supply of Housing, and Their Sources." *American Economic Review: Papers and Proceedings* 95(2) (May): 334–339.

Gyourko, Joseph, Albert Saiz, and Anita Summers. 2008. "A New Measure of the Local Regulatory Environment for Housing Markets: The Wharton Residential Land Use Regulatory Index." *Urban Studies* 45(3) (March): 693–729.

Hwang, Ming, and John M. Quigley. 2006. "Economic Fundamentals in Local Housing Markets: Evidence from U.S. Metropolitan Regions." *Journal of Regional Science* 46(3) (August): 425–453.

Ihlanfeldt, Keith R. 2007. "The Effect of Land Use Regulation on Housing and Land Prices." *Journal of Urban Economics* 61(3) (May): 420–435.

Linneman, Peter, Anita Summers, Nancy Brooks, and Henry Buist. 1990. "The State of Local Growth Management." Wharton Real Estate Working Paper No. 81, November.

Malpezzi, Stephen. 1996. "Housing Prices, Externalities, and Regulation in U.S. Metropolitan Areas." *Journal of Housing Research* 7(2): 209–241.

Malpezzi, Stephen, Gregory Chun, and Richard Green. 1998. "New Place to Place Housing Price Indexes for U.S. Metropolitan Areas, and Their Determinants: An Application of Housing Indicators." *Real Estate Economics* 26(2) (Summer): 235–275.

Malpezzi, Stephen, and Susan Wachter. 2005. "The Role of Speculation in Real Estate Cycles." *Journal of Real Estate Literature* 13(2): 143–166.

Mayer, Christopher J., and Tsuriel C. Somerville. 2000. "Land Use Regulation and New Construction." *Regional Science and Urban Economics* 30(6) (December): 639–662.

Ortalo-Magné, François, and Andrea Prat. 2006. "The Political Economy of Housing Supply." Working Paper, University of Wisconsin, Center for Real Estate.

Peterson, George E. 1974. "The Influence of Zoning Regulations on Land and Housing Prices." Working Paper No. 1207-24, Urban Institute.

Pollakowski, Henry O., and Susan M. Wachter. 1990. "The Effects of Land Use Constraints on Housing Prices." *Land Economics* 66(3) (August): 315–324.

Quigley, John M., and Steven Raphael. 2005. "Regulation and the High Cost of Housing in California." *American Economic Association Papers and Proceedings* 95(2) (May): 323–328.

Quigley, John M., Steven Raphael, and Larry A. Rosenthal. 2004. "Local Land Use Controls and Demographic Outcomes in a Booming Economy." *Urban Studies* 41(2) (February): 389–421.

Quigley, John M., and Larry Rosenthal. 2005. "The Effects of Land-Use Regulation on the Price of Housing: What Do We Know? What Can We Learn?" *Cityscape* 8(1): 191–214.

10

Do Real Estate Agents Compete on Price? Evidence from Seven Metropolitan Areas

ANN B. SCHNARE
ROBERT KULICK

The extent of competition in the real estate brokerage industry has been the subject of much debate among scholars, policy makers, and the popular press over the past few years. Critics have claimed that "traditional" full-service brokers have restricted competition from discount and limited-service providers in order to maintain artificially high commission rates.[1] Other analysts have countered that the brokerage industry is highly competitive, and that the emergence of alternative service offerings has given home buyers and sellers more information and more choices than ever before.[2] Despite the intensity of the debate, relatively little is known about the current structure of commission rates or the extent to which they vary in ways that are consistent with price competition.

This chapter uses Multiple Listing Service (MLS) data from seven metropolitan areas to examine variations in buy-side commission rates within markets, across markets, and over time. Unless otherwise noted, the time frame for the analysis is the seven-and-one-half-year period from January 2000 to June 2007. This period encompassed an unprecedented housing boom, as well as a pronounced market downturn that began in mid- to late 2005. It also witnessed the explosion of the Internet and the widespread adoption of other

This analysis is part of a larger study of the real estate brokerage industry prepared for the National Association of Realtors. The authors would like to thank Richard Green, Frank Nothalf, John Quigley, and Susan Wachter for their helpful comments.

1. See, for example, Hahn, Litan, and Gurman (2006); Woodall and Brobeck (2006).
2. See National Association of Realtors (2005); Sawyer (2005); Zumpano, Elder, and Crellin (1993).

technologies that have dramatically transformed the operations of the real estate brokerage industry.

The chapter has been organized into five sections. The section that immediately follows presents an overview of the real estate brokerage industry and the issues that have been raised by the industry's critics. This is followed by a section that summarizes what is currently known about the level and structure of commission rates. The next section describes recent trends in commission rates in the selected metropolitan areas. The section on regression analysis presents a series of regression equations that attempt to identify factors that are related to observed variations in commission rates, and is followed by a conclusion.

OVERVIEW OF THE INDUSTRY AND THE ISSUES

The real estate brokerage industry comprises real estate brokers, their sales agents (real estate "agents"), and real estate firms. Although both brokers and agents must be licensed by the state—and although the majority of brokers serve in a sales capacity—only licensed real estate brokers can execute, or "broker," a sale. In 2006, there were roughly 600,000 real estate brokers, 1.5 million real estate agents, and 98,000 real estate firms actively engaged in the brokerage industry.[3]

Barriers to entry in the real estate industry are extremely low. Licensing requirements vary from state to state, but many require fewer than 60 hours of professional course work to receive a sales agent's license, and not all require a high school diploma or general equivalency diploma (GED).[4] Because it is relatively easy to obtain a real estate license, the number of active real estate agents is particularly sensitive to market conditions. A booming market typically attracts relatively large numbers of newly minted (or previously inactive) sales agents, whereas a declining market typically drives them out.

Although the industry has experienced some consolidation in recent years, the number of regional or national brokerage firms generally is relatively small. In 2007, for example, only 17 percent of all Realtors worked for a regional or national firm.[5] The majority of real estate brokerages are local

---

3. Association of Real Estate License Law Officials (2006), Licensees/Registrant Counts. The data are limited to state-licensed brokers and agents who are actively engaged in the real estate industry.

4. Real Trends (2006), 129. Although the list of states is not exhaustive, Vermont (0 hours), Massachusetts (24 hours), Kansas (30 hours), and California (36 hours) have the lowest requirements, while Kentucky (96 hours), Ohio (120 hours), Colorado (168 hours), and Texas (210 hours) have the highest.

5. National Association of Realtors (2007), exhibit 3-1.

companies that operate out of a single office and concentrate on relatively small geographic areas. Although many have affiliated with a national franchise, most franchise firms are independently owned and operated, and there are often multiple franchise holders within a given market. In 2005, the median residential real estate brokerage firm had eight real estate licensees, primarily working on a commission basis.[6]

The Role of Multiple Listing Services

One reason the brokerage industry continues to have large numbers of small local firms is the information sharing that occurs through local MLSs. MLSs are regional databases that are primarily owned and operated by local real estate boards. The MLS was created more than 100 years ago to enable brokers to share their listings with other brokers in order to facilitate sales. Listings were once distributed in printed form, but the more than 900 MLSs in operation today maintain sophisticated electronic databases with detailed information on the properties available for sale within a particular region or housing market.

The cooperative relationships created through local MLSs help smaller firms and newer agents compete by providing access to all MLS listings. Once a listing is entered into the MLS, it is generally available to any licensed broker who joins the MLS, regardless of the size of her company or the number of listings that she may have. In some cases, brokers must join the local Realtor association to participate, but membership fees are relatively modest and any licensed broker can join. The cooperative arrangement facilitated through an MLS benefits sellers and buyers alike. Sellers benefit by getting increased exposure for their homes. Buyers benefit by having a single source of information on the properties available for sale.

Although participation in the MLS is restricted to licensed brokers, most MLSs now maintain public Web sites or send a subset of listing information to third-party aggregators, such as Realtor.com.[7] In addition, many brokers display their own listings on their company Web sites, along with the listings of other brokers.[8] The impact of displaying MLS listings on the Internet should not be underestimated. In the past, real estate agents served as gatekeepers to information on the homes that were available for sale. Although

---

6. National Association of Realtors (2006), exhibit 1-10.

7. NAR has developed policies related to Internet listing displays that govern the 900 multiple listing services that are owned and operated by Realtor organizations. See Realtor.org.

8. NAR has an Internet Data Exchange (IDX) policy under which brokers exchange consent to display each other's listings on the Internet. See Realtor.org.

homes were advertised through newspapers, yard signs, and other means, prospective home buyers needed to use a real estate agent to identify MLS listings. Today, more than 90 percent of the properties for sale are posted on a public Web site.[9]

The "Apparent Paradox"

Even the industry's most ardent critics acknowledge that there is an apparent contradiction between the objective characteristics of the brokerage industry and their claims that the industry acts as a noncompetitive price "cartel." On the surface, at least, the industry has every marker of a highly competitive market—low barriers to entry, limited economies of scale, relatively little market concentration, and information sharing arrangements made possible through local MLSs. Any of these characteristics would make efforts to maintain a rigid structure of fees exceedingly difficult. Established firms might attempt to collude on price and keep "mavericks" out of the industry, but new agents attempting to capture market share through lower fees would inevitably undermine their efforts and the cartel would collapse.

Critics have offered a number of explanations for why they believe a noncompetitive pricing structure could persist over time. Most of these explanations revolve around the role of local MLSs. For example, critics have argued that the cooperative nature of the MLS discourages participants from effectively going against the norm.[10] Because agents must rely on other agents for the majority of their sales, they might be reluctant to behave in ways that would be perceived to be a threat to the collective interests of the group. A 1983 report by the Federal Trade Commission (FTC) put it this way: "Individual brokers, we hypothesize, police the system by withholding cooperation in selling listings which carry a lower than customary 'split' or commission. In doing so, they engage both in typical profit-maximizing (refusing to sell their services for less than the going rate) and also prevent a collective lowering of commissions generally. This, we believe is exacerbated by the fact that the inherent economies connected with information exchanges almost always requires a firm to be a member if it is to cooperate effectively."[11]

However, as Zumpano notes, policy changes by the National Association of Realtors (NAR) have made it difficult, if not impossible, to detect price

---

9. Unpublished data obtained from the National Association of Realtors.
10. For example, see Hahn, Litan, and Gurman (2006); Nagel (2006); Woodall and Brobeck (2006).
11. U.S. Federal Trade Commission (1983), 37.

concessions by MLS participants.[12] Although the MLS originally posted data on the entire commission, only the amount that is offered to the cooperating broker (i.e., the buy-side agent) is now typically displayed. This policy was enacted by the NAR in 1980 to prevent a "conscious parallelism" in the establishment of fees.

Critics have also claimed that the collective members of an MLS act in ways that disadvantage—or even exclude—alternative service providers from full participation in the system. For example, most have alleged that "full-service" agents steer their clients away from listings offered by discount brokers and generally "disparage" the services that such agents provide.[13] However, it is difficult to see how such behavior would protect the status quo over an extended period. As the great majority of real estate agents are independent contractors who depend on commissions to earn a living, it is likely that some agents would be willing to go against the "collective will" in order to gain a sale. Again, the argument comes down to the interdependency of the brokerage function and the presumed effect it could have on the behavior of real estate agents. Critics contend that the incentives are sufficiently strong to maintain collusive behavior over time, but other observers are skeptical.

More recently, critics have focused on issues related to Internet access, and have claimed that full-service providers and local MLSs have colluded to prevent the listings of alternative service providers from being displayed on public Web sites. Because large numbers of consumers now use the Internet to search for homes, such behavior could presumably put alternative service providers at a disadvantage, as their listings would effectively be "hidden" from prospective home buyers. To address these concerns, NAR recently adopted a policy that requires that MLSs that operate a public Web site or send their listings to an aggregator make *all* of their listings available.[14] However, even if one believes that limited access to public Web sites has restricted the growth of alternative service models, it is difficult to see how such policies or practices could have prevented full-service real estate agents from actively competing on price.

Finally, critics have argued that local real estate commissions and several state legislatures have adopted policies specifically designed to maintain the status quo.[15] For example, a number of states have imposed minimum service requirements for licensed agents, and some state legislatures or real estate

---

12. Zumpano (2002).
13. For example, see Hahn, Litan, and Gurman (2006); Nagel (2006); Woodall and Brobeck (2006).
14. The exception is for listings that identify the address of the property and display a for-sale-by-owner sign. See *Realties*, January 2007.
15. For example, see Hahn, Litan, and Gurman (2006).

commissions have prohibited agents from offering rebates.[16] Although local real estate boards contend that such policies are designed to protect consumers, critics have argued that they are intended to limit the growth of limited-service brokers and maintain and protect commission rates that are artificially high.

In the end, the arguments largely come down to a series of assertions that the industry behaves in ways that protect the status quo and prevents real estate agents from competing on price. The remainder of this report presents data that can be used to examine the case from a more analytic perspective. At the outset, however, it is important to understand what one might expect to see in a market where agents compete on price in addition to quality of service.

What Would a Competitive Market Look Like?

A recent paper by Lawrence White lays out the conditions he would expect to see in a more competitive market.[17] Among other things, he identified declining commission rates, a variety of service offerings at varying prices, an embrace of Internet-driven technologies to buy and sell homes, commission rates that react to changes in housing prices, and further industry consolidation. White bases much of his analysis on the recent history of the securities industry. Although many industry experts would disagree with this analogy— i.e., the buying and selling of a home is fundamentally different from the purchase or sale of common stock—there is probably more agreement on his other statements regarding the expected behavior of commission rates.

For example, most observers would expect to see declining commission rates, particularly in light of the dramatic run-up in housing prices that occurred in the past few years and the efficiency gains that have been generated by consumers' increasing use of the Internet in searching for homes.[18] In fact, as shown by Hsieh and Moretti (2002), if housing units and real estate agents were homogeneous, under perfect competition a 1 percent increase in housing prices would lead to a 1 percent decrease in commission rates; commission rates would be fixed in (real) dollar terms because the marginal cost of selling an expensive and inexpensive home would be the same. The expected relationship between housing prices and commission levels under more realistic

---

16. The laws are described in a U.S. Department of Justice Web site. See http://www.usdoj.gov/atr/public/real_estate/states_map.htm.
17. See White (2006).
18. Ibid.

assumptions regarding the heterogeneity of the housing stock and the supply of real estate agents is more difficult to determine. For example, one could argue that more expensive homes require a higher level of service or that the demand for real estate services among their owners is less sensitive to price.[19] However, such factors should have less effect on the relationship between commission rates and housing prices that is observed over time. Although the value of a real estate agent's services may vary with the housing cycle (see below), the elasticities produced by a time series analysis should be closer to -1 than a cross-sectional analysis might suggest.

One would also expect to see at least some variation in commission rates within a particular market at a particular time. Although price variation would not be expected in markets with homogeneous products and services, housing is by its very nature heterogeneous, and real estate agents are not perfect substitutes for one another. As a result, commission rates in a competitive market should be related to the value added by the agent and her firm, and to the expected degree of difficulty in selling a particular home. By extension, one might also expect to see more variation of commission rates in markets where the housing stock is more heterogeneous—for example, markets with a well-defined urban core—and less variation in markets where both housing units and neighborhoods are viewed as more interchangeable. Indeed, most critics—including the Federal Trade Commission—have tended to view a "clustering" of commission rates as prima facie evidence that the industry does not compete on price.

Finally, one would expect to see commission rates respond to underlying changes in market demand and supply. Sirmans and Turnbull (1997) argue that a competitive brokerage market will promote trends in commission rates that are counter-cyclical to the housing market. In general, an excess demand for housing (i.e., a sellers' market) should trigger a decline in commission rates because homes are easier to sell and relatively low barriers to entry lead to a dramatic increase in the supply of agents. On the other hand, an excess supply of housing (i.e., a buyers' market) should cause commission rates to rise because homes are more difficult to sell and "marginal" brokers leave the industry, thereby reducing pressures on commission rates. Based on their analysis of Baton Rouge between 1985 and 1992, Sirmans and Turnbull conclude that the industry does in fact compete on price.

But regardless of their particular perspective on the industry, most observers appear to agree that variations in commission rates within markets, across markets, and over time can reveal a great deal about the competitive nature of the

---

19. See Hsieh and Moretti (2002).

real estate brokerage market. For example, if one believes that the market competes on price, commission rates should vary in ways that reflect

- the value added by the real estate agent and the firm;
- the overall strength of the housing market;
- the heterogeneity of the housing stock;
- trends in production costs; and
- the supply of real estate agents.

On the other hand, if one believes that the market operates on a "fixed commission" basis, few if any of these relationships would be observed. Although there might be some variation in rates—for example, the industry could have an explicit or implicit "schedule" that is based on the price of the home—differences would be minimal, uniformly applied, and bear little, if any relationship to objective measures of "value added."

THE EXISTING EVIDENCE

A recent paper by John Weicher reviewed the existing evidence on the structure and level of real estate brokerage commissions.[20] Although most of the studies were theoretical, four were empirical analyses of commission rates in local housing markets.[21] However, all but one of the studies examined transactions that were more than 20 years old, and the latest was for 1992. In addition, as Weicher notes, although each study found that commission rates were lower for higher-priced homes and newly constructed units, the impact of other variables was either not considered or the findings were inconsistent. As a result, Weicher concluded that the existing evidence is inconclusive and that additional research is required to address the issue of price competition.

In addition to these local studies, Weicher examined national trends in commission rates based on annual surveys, conducted by Real Trends, of the "Top 500" real estate brokerage firms. The Real Trends data are proprietary, but Weicher was able to construct a partial time series using citations from a variety of published sources. Table 10.1 presents Weicher's original compilations, updated to reflect newly released estimates of average commission rates in 2006.[22]

---

20. See Weicher (2006).
21. See Carney (1982); Goolsby and Childs (1988); Larsen and Park (1989); and Sirmans, Turnbull, and Benjamin (1991).
22. 2006 rate reported by Harney (2007).

TABLE 10.1   Trends in Average Commission Rates

Year	Average commission rate (percent)	Average existing home price	Average total commission	Average real commission (2006 $)
1991	6.1	$128,400	$7,832	$11,593
1992	—	—	—	—
1993	—	—	—	—
1994	—	—	—	—
1995	5.98	$139,100	$8,750	$11,575
1996	—	—	—	—
1997	—	—	—	—
1998	5.5	$159,000	$9,656	$11,943
1999	—	—	—	—
2000	5.48	$176,200	$9,656	$11,305
2001	5.4	$185,300	$10,006	$11,390
2002	5.1	$199,200	$10,159	$11,384
2003	5.1	$215,000	$10,965	$12,014
2004	5.1	$236,000	$12,067	$12,878
2006	5.2	$268,200	$13,946	$13,946

SOURCE: Weicher (2006), 140, updated to 2006.

Although Weicher (2006) argues that the Real Trends' data are likely to be biased downward, the data nevertheless suggest that average commission rates have fallen significantly over time, from 6.1 percent in 1991 to 5.2 percent in 2006. The data also suggest that total commissions (in real dollars) were relatively constant until the recent housing boom (2003), a pattern that suggests that the average elasticity of commission rates to real housing prices was relatively close to −1 for much of the period. Finally, the data suggest that commission rates began to rise in 2006—a development that could reflect the recent weakening of the housing market and the greater value added by real estate agents. Each of these patterns is broadly consistent with price competition.

Surveys of real estate agents and recent home sellers also provide anecdotal evidence on the extent to which agents compete on price. According to a recent industry survey by Inman News, about 54 percent of real estate agents reported that their average *gross* commission was about the same as it was five years ago, and only 26 percent said it was higher.[23] When asked to identify the factor that had had the greatest impact on their commission rate in the previous year, 67 percent responded "competition from agents offering discounts" as opposed to "more agents" (33 percent), "savvy sellers" (20 percent),

---

23. See Inman News (2006).

or the "Web" (13 percent).[24] The Inman survey also suggests that individual agents have a fair amount of discretion in setting their commission rates. Only 27 percent reported that their broker required a commission level or range in order to list a home.[25]

A recent Real Trends study, *The Consumer Tsunami* (2006), also examined agents' perceptions on price competition within the industry. In general, the findings are consistent with the Inman Report. Among other things, the study found that 62 percent of sales professionals now feel pressure to negotiate their commission. It also found that the vast majority of real estate agents (81 percent) attributed this growing pressure to competition from other agents, as opposed to consumer resistance or the emergence of discount realty firms. Like the Inman study, the Real Trends survey asked agents about their ability to negotiate sales commissions. Although the numbers (and questions) were somewhat different, the findings are reasonably consistent. Fifty-one percent of the agents interviewed in the Real Trends survey said they had an ability to negotiate their commissions, 30 percent said their company determined the rate they charged, and 12 percent said they did not negotiate on fee even though their company allowed it.[26]

Finally, a 2007 NAR survey of recent home buyers and sellers asked sellers if they had negotiated the fee or commission for selling their home with their real estate agent (see table 10.2). The survey found that about 70 percent of recent sellers negotiated the sales commission with their real estate agent.

TABLE 10.2 Negotiation of the Agent's Commission or Fee

Percent of sellers who responded in the following way:	
Real estate agent brought up the topic	39
Client brought up the topic and the real estate agent was willing to negotiate the commission or fee	31
Client brought up the topic and the real estate agent was *not* willing to negotiate the commission or fee	9
Client did know that commissions and fees were negotiable but did not bring up the topic	9
Client did *not* know that commissions and fees were negotiable	13

NOTE: Percentages do not add up to 100 due to rounding.
SOURCE: National Association of Realtors, 2007 Survey of Recent Home Buyers and Sellers.

24. Ibid., 47.
25. Ibid., 28.
26. Real Trends (2006), 134.

Commission Rates in Selected Metropolitan Areas

To get a better understanding of the current level and structure of real estate commissions, we analyzed MLS data in seven metropolitan areas: Baltimore, Chicago, Dallas–Fort Worth, Kansas City, Miami–Fort Lauderdale, Orange County–Los Angeles, and Washington, DC. In most of the markets, a single MLS covered the entire metropolitan area (and typically, the surrounding rural areas as well). In these instances, we limited the analysis to the officially designated metropolitan statistical area (MSA.) However, both Los Angeles and Miami–Fort Lauderdale have more than one MLS in their areas. In Miami–Fort Lauderdale, we obtained data from the three largest MLSs. Although the data do not represent a 100 percent count of all transactions, they cover the majority of listings in every county. In Los Angeles, we obtained data for Orange County in its entirety, and parts of Southeast Los Angeles. As the data exclude significant portions of Los Angeles, we have referred to the area as "Orange County–Los Angeles."

In general, the time frame for our analysis is the seven-and-one-half-year period between January 2000 and June 2007. However, the commission data for Kansas City and Miami–Ft. Lauderdale go back only to 2002 and 2005, respectively. Although this is a relatively minor limitation for Kansas City, our analysis for Miami–Fort Lauderdale is primarily restricted to behavior in a market downturn.[27]

The Selected Markets

Although the sample was not designed to be representative in a statistical sense, the selected metropolitan areas represent a range of market conditions and types. Table 10.3 presents median sales price data for the selected metropolitan areas and the United States as a whole, based on the NAR Survey of Existing Home Sales. The different markets have been ranked in descending order on the basis of their five-year average annual house price appreciation (HPA) rates through June 2007. In addition to the median sales price in June 2007, the exhibit shows the average annual (compounded) change in the median sales price over different periods of time.

---

27. We have some information on commission rates in the Miami–Fort Lauderdale area in the first half of 2005, when the market was still extremely strong. However, the sample for this period is very small because information on commission rates was just being added to the archived data. As a result, findings for this period may not be representative of broader trends.

TABLE 10.3   House Price Appreciation in Selected Metropolitan Areas

	Median sale price: June 2007	Compound annual increase (percent)			
		1 year	3 years	5 years	10 years
Orange County–Los Angeles	$588,100	4.0	14.3	17.6	13.2
Miami–Fort Lauderdale	$375,600	−1.9	13.7	16.8	12.5
Baltimore	$284,200	3.5	13.3	15.0	11.4
Washington, DC	$431,700	−0.8	12.8	14.4	10.5
Chicago	$274,500	1.4	6.5	7.3	6.5
Kansas City	$153,700	−1.6	1.6	2.5	4.2
Dallas–Fort Worth	$149,400	0.0	2.7	2.4	3.5
United States	$220,300	−1.9	5.9	6.6	5.9

SOURCE: National Association of Realtors, Survey of Existing Home Sales. The data for Los Angeles cover the entire metropolitan area, not just Orange County.

House price appreciation slowed in each of the seven markets between 2005 and 2007, and three of the markets—Kansas City, Miami–Fort Lauderdale, and Washington, DC—experienced net declines in their median sales price.[28] However, the markets behaved very differently before this time:

- Four of the markets—Baltimore, Orange County–Los Angeles, Miami–Fort Lauderdale, and Washington, DC—had among the highest HPA rates in the country, placing them in the top 20 percent of all metropolitan areas.
- Two of the markets—Dallas–Fort Worth and Kansas City—had HPA rates that were relatively low by national standards, placing them in the lower 20 percent of all metropolitan areas.
- The seventh market—Chicago—had an HPA rate that more or less tracked the national average.

The areas also represent a range of legal and regulatory regimes (see table 10.4). Three of the markets—Chicago, Kansas City, and Dallas–Fort Worth— are in states with minimum service requirements. In addition, Kansas City is subject to state laws that prohibit buyer rebates.

---

28. These results are generally consistent with the S&P/Case-Shiller Home Price Index. However, the Case-Shiller Home Price Index also shows declines in Chicago and Los Angeles.

TABLE 10.4 Applicable State Laws

	Minimum service requirements	Consumer rebates prohibited
Baltimore	No	No
Chicago	Yes	No
Dallas–Fort Worth	Yes	No
Kansas City		
Kansas	No	Yes
Missouri	Yes	Yes
Miami–Fort Lauderdale	No	No
Orange County–Los Angeles	No	No
Washington, DC	No	No

SOURCE: http://www.usdoj.gov/atr/public/real_estate/states_map.htm.

The Commission Data

Ideally, one would base the analysis on the total commission paid at closing. However, the MLS data show only the "buy side" of the total commission, i.e., the commission that is offered to the agent who produces a buyer for the property. Presumably, one could estimate total commissions by simply doubling the buy-side agent's fee (or by applying some other multiple that reflects the typical "split" within the area). However, this approach would be inappropriate with many nontraditional brokerage models. For example, sellers using a limited or flat-fee service may nevertheless offer a "market" commission rate to the buy-side agent. Likewise, buyers using a "rebate" broker will receive part of the sales commission when the property is sold.[29] The net result is that the commission data presented here will tend to overstate total commission levels and understate their variation. As a result, the analysis should represent a relatively conservative view of the extent of price competition within the industry.

Market Trends

Figure 10.1 presents NAR data on housing trends in each of the seven markets from the first quarter of 2000 through the second quarter of 2007, including (1) the quarterly HPA rate (measured by the percent change in median sales price of an existing home over the same quarter of the previous year); (2) the quarterly change in sales volume (measured by the percent change in the

---

29. In addition, actual commission rates tend to be lower and show more variability than quoted rates, as they are sometimes renegotiated at the time of sale to facilitate the deal. See Weicher (2006), 127.

FIGURE 10.1 Housing Market Trends in Selected Markets

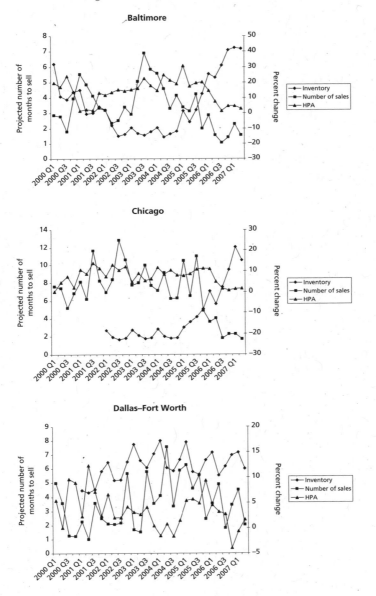

(continued)

FIGURE 10.1 *(continued)*

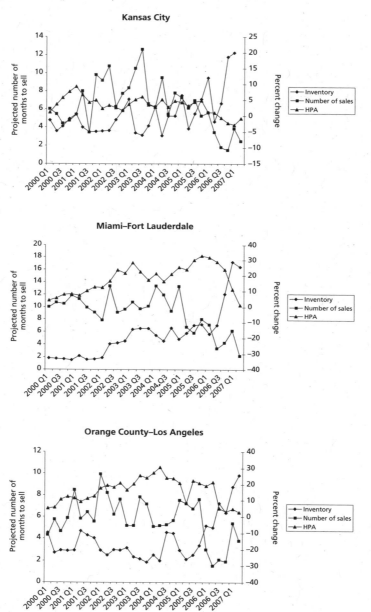

(continued)

FIGURE 10.1 *(continued)*

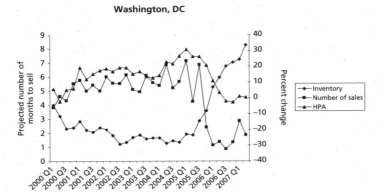

Washington, DC

NOTES: Percent change is measured year over year. HPA = house price appreciation.
SOURCE: National Association of Realtors.

number of units sold over the same quarter of the previous year); and (3) the size of the unsold housing inventory (measured in terms of the projected number of months required to sell). In the case of Orange County–Los Angeles, the data refer to the entire metropolitan area.

The trends depicted in the chart once again illustrate both the differences and the similarities across the seven markets. The four "boom" markets— Baltimore, Orange County–Los Angeles, Miami–Fort Lauderdale, and Washington, DC—experienced a surge in sales activities and housing prices at the beginning of the decade, followed by a dramatic softening of the market. Although the markets reached their peaks at somewhat different periods of time— Los Angeles was the earliest, and Miami–Fort Lauderdale was the latest—all four markets were clearly on the decline by late 2005. House prices stagnated or declined; home sales dropped below the levels observed in earlier years; and inventories rose significantly.

The general patterns observed in Chicago are similar to those observed in the so-called boom markets, but much less pronounced. While the market clearly softened in 2006 and 2007, the slowdown was not as severe as that observed in the formerly high-growth areas.

The two other markets—Dallas–Fort Worth and Kansas City—experienced much more stable housing conditions over the decade. HPA rates in both markets were anemic by national standards, growing at roughly the rate of inflation. Although Kansas City experienced rising inventories and declining sales volumes and housing prices in 2006 and 2007, conditions in Dallas–Fort Worth remained more or less flat.

FIGURE 10.2 Average Quarterly Buy-Side Commission Rates, 2000–2007

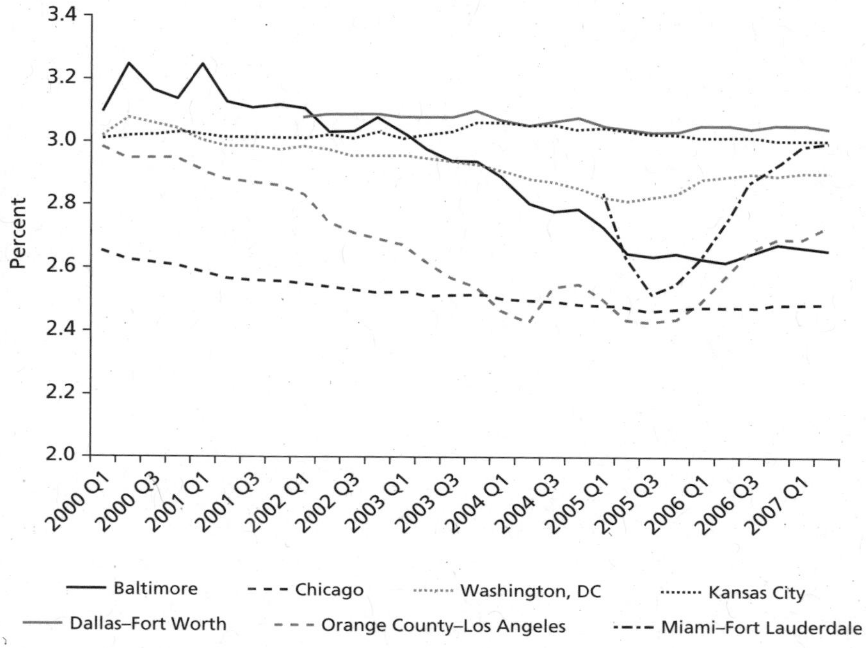

Baltimore — Chicago - - - Washington, DC ········· Kansas City ·········
Dallas–Fort Worth —— Orange County–Los Angeles - - - Miami–Fort Lauderdale -··-

SOURCE: Multiple Listing Service.

Trends in Average Commission Rates

Figure 10.2 shows trends in the average buy-side commission rate in each of the seven markets between 2000 and 2007.[30] As noted earlier, while five of the sites had data going back to 2000, information on commission rates in Kansas City and Miami–Fort Lauderdale goes back only to 2002 and 2005, respectively.

As shown in the chart, commission rates clearly varied across markets and over time. Interestingly, commission rates in Chicago were consistently lower than they were in the other markets despite the fact that Illinois law requires that agents provide a minimum level of service. Although rates were higher in the two other markets that are subject to similar restrictions—Dallas–Fort Worth and Kansas City—the differences more likely reflect the

---

30. Commission data are typically entered by the listing agent and not validated in any way. As a result, the data presented here have been subject to routine cleaning procedures to eliminate obvious outliers (e.g., zero values, values above 5) and to correct for differences in format (e.g., values between 0.01 and 0.05 were multiplied by 100).

characteristics of these housing markets than the impact of their regulatory regimes.

The data also reveal a strong countercyclical relationship between trends in commission rates and the strength of the local housing market. In general, markets that experienced the greatest swings in housing conditions also experienced the greatest movements in buy-side commission rates.

- Four of the markets—Baltimore, Orange County–Los Angeles, Miami–Fort Lauderdale, and Washington, DC—experienced some of the most rapid HPA rates in the country between 2000 and 2005, followed by pronounced market declines. These same markets also exhibited the most dramatic movements in commission rates. When the markets were hot, commission rates declined significantly. When the markets began to cool, commission rates leveled off and then began to rise.[31] This countercycle behavior is consistent with a competitive model of the brokerage market, and most likely reflects the increased value added by real estate brokers in a declining market (and the greater ease of selling a home when the market is strong).

- Commission rates in the Chicago market also followed a cyclical pattern, although the changes were much less pronounced. Again, this pattern is consistent with the trends that were observed in the housing market. HPA rates in the Chicago metropolitan area were relatively moderate over the period, placing it close to the national average. And although the Chicago market also softened in 2005, the downturn was not as pronounced.

- The last two of the markets in our sample—Dallas–Fort Worth and Kansas City—had some of the lowest HPA rates in the country between 2000 and 2007, placing them in the bottom 20 percent of all housing markets. Market conditions were relatively stable over most of the period, although house price appreciation slowed in the second half of 2006. Not surprisingly, commission rates in these markets displayed relatively little cyclical behavior. Although rates in Kansas City appear to be trending downward, buy-side commission rates in Dallas–Fort Worth were virtually the same in 2000 as they were in 2007.

---

31. The commission data for Miami–Fort Lauderdale go back only to 2005 and, as a result, primarily pertain to behavior in a market downturn. Although commission rates appear to have fallen in the first two quarters of 2005 (when the market was booming), the sample size for this period is relatively small (presumably because the commission data were just being added to the archived databases). However, beginning in mid-2005, commission rates in Miami–Fort Lauderdale began to rise dramatically (as did the coverage of the commission data). In fact, the upward trend in Miami–Fort Lauderdale was more pronounced than it was in the other areas.

This general finding that commission rates are relatively stable in stable markets—and countercyclical in more volatile markets—is consistent with a model of the real estate brokerage industry in which brokers compete on price as well as service.

The relationship between house price appreciation and the cumulative change in commission rates is further illustrated by the graphs in figure 10.3. In the more rapidly appreciating markets—for example, Orange County–Los Angeles—cumulative changes in the average commission rate were almost mirror images of trends in the HPA rate. However, in more stable markets— for example, Dallas–Fort Worth and Kansas City—trends in both the commission rate and house price appreciation were relatively flat.

Variation in Commission Rates Within Markets

Figure 10.4 shows the underlying distributions of commission rates at two points in time: 2000 (or the earliest available date) and 2007. In both years, there was a fair amount of variation in commission rates within each market. The data also illustrate the dramatic shifts that took place in several of the markets. Although the data for Miami–Fort Lauderdale go back only to 2005, the distributions of commission rates for most of the other markets clearly shifted downward. For example,

- in Orange County–Los Angeles, the share of listings offering a 3 percent commission rate to the buyer's agent fell from 79 percent in the first of quarter 2000 to 37 percent in the second quarter of 2007, whereas the share offering 2.5 percent rose from 17 percent to 52 percent;
- in Baltimore, the share offering 3 percent fell from 70 percent to 27 percent, whereas the share of 2.5 percent rose from 6 percent to 65 percent;
- in Washington, DC, the share offering 3 percent fell from 91 percent to 76 percent, whereas the share offering 2.5 percent rose from 3 percent to 20 percent;
- in Chicago—which had the lowest commission rates in the sample—the share offering 3 percent fell from 25 percent to 6 percent, whereas the share offering 2 percent rose from 3 percent to 12 percent; and
- in Kansas City—which had the highest commission rates in the sample—the share offering 3.5 percent fell from 20 percent in 2002 (the earliest available data) to 7 percent in 2007, whereas the share offering 3 percent rose from 71 percent to 83 percent.

In contrast to the other markets, commission rates in the Dallas–Fort Worth area showed remarkably little change. In fact, the distribution of rates in 2000 is nearly identical to the rates observed in 2007.

FIGURE 10.3 HPA Versus Commission Trends by MSA

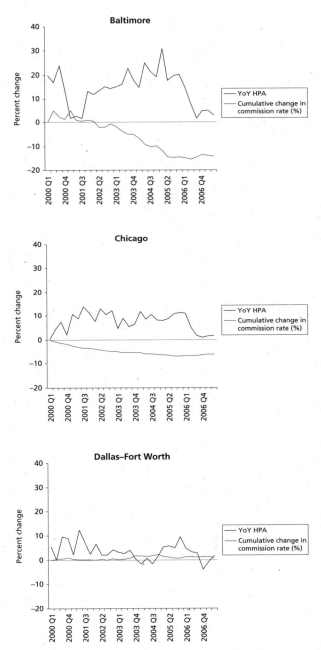

(*continued*)

FIGURE 10.3 *(continued)*

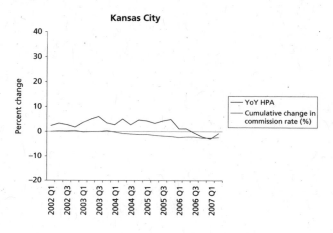

Kansas City

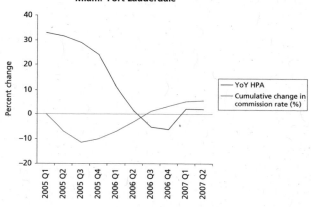

Miami–Fort Lauderdale

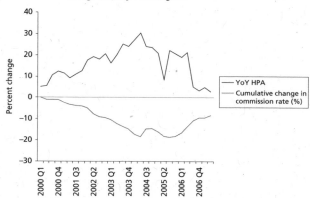

Orange County–Los Angeles

(continued)

FIGURE 10.3 *(continued)*

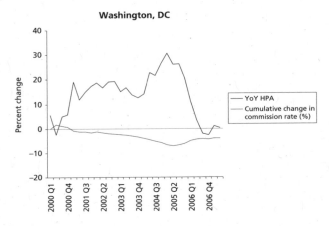

NOTES: YoY = year over year; HPA = house price appreciation.
SOURCE: Multiple Listing Service, NAR Survey of Existing Home Sales.

Table 10.5 compares the means and standard deviations of buy-side commission rates at three points in time: 2000, 2005, and 2007. As noted earlier, average commission rates declined significantly in the markets that experienced a housing boom between 2000 and 2005. As shown in table 10.5, these same markets also experienced a significant increase in the underlying variation in commission rates over the same period.

In 2000, the standard deviation of the commission rate was about 8 or 9 percent of the sample mean in most of the markets. (The one exception was the Washington, DC area, where the standard deviation in commission rates was only about 5 percent of the sample mean). However, between 2000 and 2005, the variance in commission rates increased significantly in the three most rapidly appreciating areas (Orange County–Los Angeles, Washington, DC, and Baltimore), whereas the variance in the more stable markets (Chicago, Kansas City, and Dallas–Fort Worth) actually declined. As a result, in 2005 the standard deviation ranged from 11 percent to 13 percent of the sample mean in the three rapidly appreciating markets, as opposed to about 8 percent in Chicago and Kansas City and only about 4 percent in Dallas–Fort Worth. Although the data for Miami–Fort Lauderdale go back only to 2005, commission rates in this area exhibited a much higher degree of variation than they did in the other markets in both 2005 and 2007.

Theory would predict that the areas with the most heterogeneous housing stock would show the greatest variation in commission rates. It is difficult to

FIGURE 10.4 Distribution of Commission Rates, 2000 and 2007

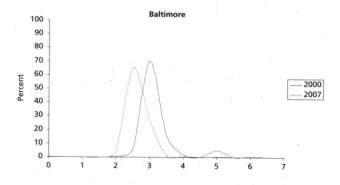

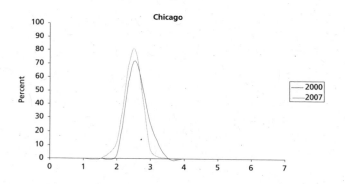

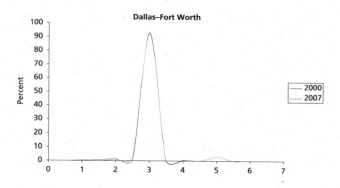

(*continued*)

FIGURE 10.4 *(continued)*

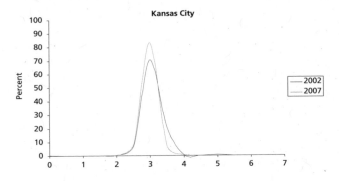

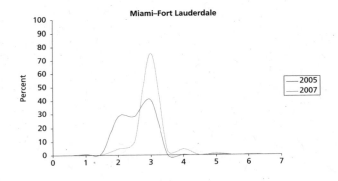

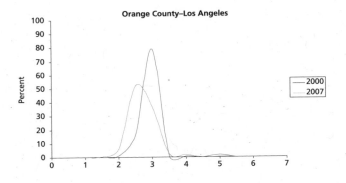

(continued)

FIGURE 10.4 *(continued)*

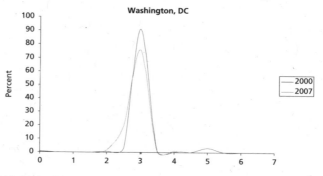

SOURCE: Multiple Listing Service.

TABLE 10.5 Means and Standard Deviations of Buy-Side Commissions, Selected Years

	2000		2005		2007	
	Mean	Standard deviation	Mean	Standard deviation	Mean	Standard deviation
Orange County–Los Angeles	2.92	0.230	2.45	0.321	2.70	0.365
Washington, DC	2.99	0.158	2.82	0.312	2.90	0.269
Miami–Fort Lauderdale	NA	NA	2.55	0.482	3.00	0.506
Baltimore	3.07	0.291	2.62	0.318	2.65	0.297
Chicago	2.63	0.248	2.47	0.193	2.49	0.209
Dallas–Fort Worth	2.96	0.230	2.99	0.147	2.98	0.163
Kansas City	3.07	0.272	3.01	0.232	3.00	0.227

NOTES: Year 2000 data for Miami–Fort Lauderdale not available. Year 2000 data for Kansas City are for 2002.
SOURCE: MLS data.

establish causality, but the patterns revealed in the different markets are at least broadly consistent with these hypotheses. For example, one could reasonably argue that the relatively high standard deviations that characterize Miami–Fort Lauderdale and Orange County–Los Angeles reflect the fact that both markets have unique geographic features that make housing units imperfect substitutes for one another. On the other hand, the relatively low standard deviations that are observed in Dallas–Fort Worth and the two midwestern markets may simply reflect their relatively homogeneous housing stocks.

One might also expect that the variation in commission rates would be more pronounced in areas with more variation in the level or quality of services provided by real estate agents. Again, the data are broadly consistent with this hypothesis. In particular, one could reasonably argue that the increased variation in commission rates that was observed in the more rapidly appreciating markets reflects the surge of inexperienced agents (and the growth of alternative service models) that generally accompanied the housing boom. However, this same line of reasoning would lead one to expect a subsequent tightening of rates when the market turned. Although this appeared to have happened in Washington, DC and Baltimore, standard deviations have continued to rise in both Miami–Fort Lauderdale and Orange County–Los Angeles.

THE REGRESSION ANALYSIS

To explore these dynamics in more detail, we estimated a series of regression models based on the buy-side commission rates that were observed in each of the markets between 2000 (or the earliest available date) and June 2007. The regression analysis was designed to test the extent to which variations in commission rates are generally consistent with price competition. The counter-cyclical patterns identified from the previous charts—i.e., declining rates in strong markets and increasing rates in weakening markets—would certainly support this hypothesis. However, we wanted to see if we could identify other factors that could help to explain the observed variation.

Table 10.6 summarizes the regression results for every market. The dependent variable in each equation was the percent commission fee that was offered to the buy-side agent.[32] The independent variables included a variety of demand- and supply-side factors thought to influence commission rates:

- the property's list price (expressed as a natural log);
- the average annual number of completed sides of the listing agent (a proxy for the agent's skills and experience);
- the average annual number of completed sides of the listing agent's office (a proxy for the company's local brand);
- an indicator for limited-service listing agents;
- indicators for new homes at different stages of the housing cycle;
- the annualized HPA rate in the quarter the property was listed (as measured by the change in the median sales price of an existing home); and
- the total number of active real estate agents in the quarter in which the property was listed (active agents had at least one listing or sale).

---

32. Because of suspected data errors, the sample was limited to observations with a reported buy-side commission rate of between 1.0 percent and 5.0 percent and a list price of between $30,000 and $3,000,000. It also excluded flat-fee commissions, which were a negligible portion of the sample.

TABLE 10.6 Summary of Regression Results

	Baltimore		Chicago		Dallas–Fort Worth	
	Coefficient	Z-statistic	Coefficient	T-statistic	Coefficient	T-statistic
LN list price	−0.16623	−89.3	−0.048118	−159.4	−0.09031	−118.1
New construction (2006–2007)	0.15467	30.1	0.025568	14.8	−0.00756	−5.1
New construction (2000–2005)	−0.06027	−18.3	−0.009967	−6.4	−0.04133	−45.0
Agent sides	0.00132	49.6	0.000813	83.1	0.00148	80.0
Office sides	0.00020	66.8	0.000052	80.9	0.00003	24.7
House price appreciation	−0.28232	−32.1	−0.283309	−51.9	−0.06754	−4.9
Supply of agents	−0.00003	−23.6	0.000004	32.0	−0.00001	−8.8
Limited service	−0.03617	−3.7	N/A	N/A	−0.05253	−32.6
FSBO	−0.00978	−1.1	N/A	N/A	N/A	N/A
Quarter	−0.01082	−45.8	−0.006379	−113.8	0.00453	16.8
R-squared value	.2798		.0996		.0466	
Number of observations	393,514		1,426,968		838,501	

	Kansas City		Orange County–Los Angeles		Miami–Fort Lauderdale	
	Coefficient	T-statistic	Coefficient	T-statistic	Coefficient	T-statistic
LN list price	−0.060147	−42.9	−0.06730	−70.6	0.06459	33.2
New construction (2006–2007)	−0.029187	−11.8	0.11427	11.0	0.18362	10.1
New construction (2000–2005)	−0.120018	−72.9	0.02672	4.0	0.18677	6.2
Agent sides	0.001218	20.2	0.00063	22.9	0.00044	5.0
Office sides	0.000026	11.6	0.00015	71.4	0.00033	14.5
House price appreciation	0.257124	6.6	−1.15872	−182.1	−0.11959	−5.7
Supply of agents	−0.000001	−0.8	−0.00002	−58.7	−0.00002	−8.7
Limited service	−0.020793	−2.6	−0.07085	−14.9	N/A	N/A
FSBO	N/A	N/A	N/A	N/A	N/A	N/A
Quarter	−0.004453	−19.0	−0.00517	−44.0	0.06554	55.0
R-squared value	.0844		.2012		.1440	
Number of observations	221,482		591,466		119,854	

(continued)

TABLE 10.6 (*continued*)

	Washington, DC	
	Coefficient	Z-statistic
LN list price	−0.03079	−35.8
New construction (2006–2007)	0.05588	26.9
New construction (2000–2005)	−0.03235	−24.1
Agent sides	0.00059	46.6
Office sides	0.00005	38.6
House price appreciation	−0.33191	−88.0
Supply of agents	−0.00001	−19.9
Limited service	−0.10526	−28.1
FSBO	−0.02041	−10.3
Quarter	−0.00361	−35.2
R-squared value	.1330	
Number of observations	820,702	

NOTES: LN = natural log; FSBO = for sale by owner.
SOURCE: Authors' analysis of MLS data.

We also included a continuous measure of time based on the quarter in which the property was listed, as well as dummy variables identifying the county in which the property was located. To simplify the presentation, county fixed effects are not reported here.

As the supply of real estate agents is likely to be endogenous (i.e., jointly determined) with the commission rate, we used a two-stage least squares regression procedure in most markets.[33] In particular, we regressed the number of active real estate agents in a given quarter on the area's total population, unemployment rate, and number of home sales. We then used the regression estimates to create an instrumental variable for the supply of real estate agents that was included in the regressions for the commission rate. In general, the parameters derived from the two-stage regressions are very similar to those produced through ordinary least squares (OLS).

The commission rate and the property's list price may also be jointly determined. In Washington, DC and Baltimore, we were able to control for this effect by estimating three-stage regressions. In addition to an instrument for

---

33. We also applied a robust standard error correction procedure to control for heteroskedastisticity in the error term.

the supply of real estate agents (described earlier), we used the property's physical attributes (i.e., square feet of living space, number of bedrooms, number of bathrooms, and number of garages) to serve as an instrument for the property's list price. Again, the resulting parameters are very similar to those derived using OLS regressions. Although we did not have the necessary data to derive three-stage regression estimates in the other markets, based on the results for Washington, DC and Baltimore, we believe that any resulting bias would be minimal.

The results presented in Table 10.6 represent either the two- or three-stage regression estimates, depending on the market. The OLS estimates for each market, along with variable means and standard deviations, are presented in appendix table 10A.1. In general, the regressions yielded roughly comparable results in each of the markets. Although some variables did not have the expected signs in certain markets, these exceptions primarily occurred in markets where both housing markets and commission rates were relatively stable over the period. Overall, the models worked relatively well in the markets that experienced the greatest movements in commission rates—Baltimore, Orange County–Los Angeles, and Washington, DC—and not as well in Dallas–Fort Worth and Kansas.

List Price

Like previous studies, our analysis finds a strong inverse relationship between the list price of the property and the buy-side commission rate in most of the markets. (Similar results were found when we used the property's actual sales price.) Because list price is expressed as a natural log, our analysis also suggests that the marginal impact on commission rates declines with increasing values.[34] The one exception to this pattern was in Miami–Fort Lauderdale, where commission rates generally increased with the value of the property. This counterintuitive finding was quite robust. A positive relationship was also observed when we restricted the sample to single-family homes (i.e., excluding condominiums), less expensive properties (i.e., under $1 million), or a single year (i.e., 2006). Although we will examine estimated elasticities in a later section, this tapering of commission rates is generally consistent with some degree of price competition.[35]

---

34. We tested a variety of functional forms in our initial regressions. In general, the results were robust, i.e., the particular specification did not affect the overall conclusions.

35. See White (2006). However, Weicher argues that such a pattern may simply reflect a uniform pricing strategy. See Weicher (2006), 138.

New Construction

Previous studies have also found that commission rates are lower for newly constructed homes, a pattern that has been attributed to the greater sophistication and market power of home builders as compared to individual property owners. However, our preliminary analysis of the data revealed marked differences in the patterns observed in different stages of the real estate cycle. To capture these differences, we created two interaction terms: the first identifies newly constructed homes placed on the market between 2000 and 2005; the second identifies newly constructed homes listed in 2006 or 2007. In three of the markets—Baltimore, Chicago, and Washington, DC—commission rates on newly constructed homes were consistently lower than the rates on resale properties for homes that were listed between 2000 and 2005, but significantly higher than resale properties in 2006 and 2007. In Dallas–Fort Worth and Kansas City, commission rates on newly constructed homes were lower in both periods, but the discount was significantly reduced in 2006 and 2007. In Orange County–Los Angeles, newly constructed homes had higher commission rates both before and after the market downturn, but the size of the premium increased. Thus, regardless of the relationship to resale units, the relative commission rate on newly constructed homes appears to have risen in each of these markets in recent years.[36] One plausible explanation for these changing relationships is the recent weakening of the housing market, which has caused builders' inventories to rise. Although most home sellers can delay the sale of their homes until more favorable conditions return, this is not the case for home builders, who may offer higher commissions to buyers' agents in an attempt to move their growing inventories.

Service Offerings

The commission rates offered to buyers' agents also appear to vary with the level of services provided by the listing agent.[37] In general, the indicator for limited-service providers had a significant negative effect in all six markets.

---

36. In Miami–Fort Lauderdale, new homes had higher commission rates in both periods, but the estimated coefficient were about the same. However, there were relatively few observations for the pre-2006 data.

37. Three of the seven markets (Dallas–Fort Worth, Kansas City, and Orange County–Los Angeles) had a specific indicator that identified listings posted by a "limited service agent." In Washington, DC and Baltimore—which share the same MLSs—no specific indicator was available, although we could identify such transactions through an optional comment field and through a separate indicator that primarily captures FSBO transactions. The MLS in Chicago did not identify agents who provided limited service.

On the surface, at least, these findings would tend to refute the claim that limited-service providers must offer higher buy-side rates to get agents to show their properties. In the two markets where we were able to identify "for sale by owner (FSBO)" properties, the results were much the same. In both Washington, DC and Baltimore, FSBO listings offered buy-side agents somewhat lower commission rates, although the coefficient in Baltimore was not statistically significant.

Characteristics of the Listing Agent

More experienced agents should be able to command higher fees in a competitive market. To measure the experience of the listing agent—and capture differences in the quality of the services provided—we created a variable that measured the agent's average annual number of completed "sides" from 2000 (or the earliest available date) to 2007. Our regression analysis found that commission rates in every market rose with increases in the listing agent's total sales volume. This finding suggests that top producers are able to command higher rates than less experienced agents, which translates into higher buy-side fees.

Characteristics of the Brokerage Firm

A similar effect is observed for firm size, measured by the average annual number of sides that were executed by the listing agent's office from 2000 (or the earliest available date) through 2007.[38] In general, commission rates rose with increases in the company's overall sales activity, a premium that most likely reflects the underlying value of a well-established local brand. Again, such differentials are consistent with a model of price competition, with the most successful brokerages demanding and receiving higher fees.

House Price Appreciation Rate

A competitive analysis of the brokerage industry also suggests that commission rates will vary with the strength of the housing market. Although the raw

---

38. Most of the MLSs that participated in the study were either unwilling or unable to provide information on the agent's company. However, it is not obvious whether sides by company would be a better indicator of local presence than sides by office.

data are certainly consistent with this hypothesis, we wanted to test the extent to which observed variations could be directly linked to an objective indicator of market strength. To do this, we included a variable that measured the annualized quarterly house price appreciation rate in the month in which the property was listed.[39] In a competitive market, when the housing market is relatively weak and house price appreciation is relatively low, newly listed homes will be more difficult to sell and agents should be able to command a higher fee. With the exception of Kansas City, the regression results confirm these expectations. All else equal, commission rates tended to be higher when house price appreciation was weak. This pattern most likely reflects a premium attached to the services of real estate professionals when properties become more difficult to sell, and captures the countercyclical effect that one would expect to see in a competitive market.

Market Supply

We also included a variable designed to capture cyclical swings in the supply of real estate brokers. In particular, we calculated the number of real estate agents who were active in each quarter; our definition of "active" was based on whether or not an agent had at least one completed side or sale. Past research has shown that the supply of real estate agents generally rises in an up market (because of low barriers to entry) and declines when the market weakens (as marginal agents leave). Although our supply-side measure is admittedly crude, we nevertheless found a strong, inverse relationship between the number of active real estate agents and buy-side commission rates in five of the markets. The two exceptions were Kansas City, where the variable had the expected negative sign but was insignificant, and Chicago, where the sign was both positive and statistically significant.

Secular Trends

In addition to cyclical measures of the strength of the housing market and the supply of real estate agents, we included a continuous time variable (ranging from 1 to 30, reflecting the quarter in which the property was listed) to capture secular trends. In general, we found evidence of a secular decline in

---

39. In earlier regressions, we also included the "average number of days on the market" for properties that sold in the month in which the home was listed, as well as an NAR estimate of the size of the unsold inventory. As these variables were highly correlated with the HPA rate, only the latter is presented here.

commission rates in six of the seven markets. The one exception was Dallas–Fort Worth, where the trend appeared to be in the opposite direction.[40]

Geographic Submarkets

Finally, we included county fixed effects to account for differences in the demand and supply of housing and real estate agents that are not captured by the other variables. In general, we found that the underlying patterns differed from market to market. These findings reinforce the notion that real estate markets are inherently local, and that significant differences can arise even within a metropolitan area.

ESTIMATED ELASTICITY OF COMMISSION RATE TO HOUSING PRICES

As noted earlier, under certain assumptions regarding the homogeneity of the housing stock and real estate agents, the elasticity of commission rates to housing prices over time would be expected to be close to −1. Although our analysis combines cross-sectional and time-series data, higher elasticities (in absolute terms) would presumably be consistent with a higher degree of price competition.

The first column of table 10.7 presents the estimated price elasticities that were derived from our regression models.[41] Miami–Fort Lauderdale again has the puzzling result that commission rates are higher for higher-priced properties. However, the estimated elasticities in the other sites are extremely low, ranging from −0.015 in Washington, DC to −0.07 in Baltimore. It is likely that the time-sensitive variables (e.g., quarterly fixed effects) are capturing some of the impact of rising housing prices. As a result, we ran a second set of regressions that excluded the time-sensitive variables, but retained the variables capturing list price, agent sales, office sales, service type (i.e., limited, FSBO), and fixed county effects. The resulting elasticity estimates are presented in the second column of table 10.7. As shown, eliminating variables that may be correlated with

---

40. We also estimated an alternative set of regression equations that replaced the three variables designed to capture changing market conditions—house price appreciation, supply of real estate agents and the secular trend—with quarterly dummies reflecting the time that the property was listed. The coefficients of these dummies reflect the same cyclical patterns described in our discussions of figure 10.2.

41. To test the impact of dropping the time-sensitive variables, the elasticities presented in table 10.7 are from the OLS regressions. However, they are very similar to the ones produced using two- or three-staged least squares. We evaluate the elasticities at the means of the independent variables in the form $d(\ln y)/d(\ln x)$.

TABLE 10.7 Estimated Elasticity of Commission Rate to Housing Prices

	Regression-based estimates		Estimates based on changes in means
	Full regression	Excluding time-sensitive variables	
Baltimore	−.070	−.103	−0.178
Chicago	−.019	−.025	−0.168
Dallas–Fort Worth	−.030	−.030	+0.220
Kansas City	−.020	−.030	−0.632
Miami–Fort Lauderdale	.023	.026	NA
Orange County–Los Angeles	−.026	−.065	−0.158
Washington, DC	−.015	−.028	−0.062

SOURCE: Authors' calculations based on MLS data.

rising housing prices (and land values) generally produces higher elasticity estimates (in absolute terms), but they remain relatively low. However, this may again be the result of combining time series and cross-sectional data.

A third approach for estimating elasticities in a given market was to simply take the ratio of the observed percent change in the average commission rate to the observed percent change in real housing prices. Changes in real housing prices were measured by NAR median sales price data, adjusted by either the local (or regional) Consumer Price Index (CPI).[42] To control for cyclical swings in the housing market, the estimates are based on the relationships observed between 2000 and 2005, when housing markets were strong.[43] The results of these calculations are presented in column 3 of the table.

In general, the estimated elasticities are considerably higher (in absolute terms) than those produced by our regression analysis, but still well below the theoretical target of −1. The relatively high ratios for Dallas–Fort Worth and Kansas City should probably be discounted, since neither commission rates nor housing prices changed much in these areas. Baltimore, Chicago, and Orange County–Los Angeles had elasticities of about −0.16 percent to −0.18 percent, whereas the estimate for Washington, DC was only −0.06 percent. Although difficult to interpret, the lower value for Washington, DC could conceivably reflect its relatively large and heterogeneous housing mar-

42. We obtained similar results when the Case-Shiller Home Price Index was used in the markets where it was available.

43. Commission rates generally began to rise when house price appreciation slowed, not when housing prices actually declined. As a result, basing the elasticities on the longer period produces somewhat lower rates in most of the markets.

ket, which includes outlying rural areas, rapidly growing outer suburbs, and a well-established urban core.

CONCLUSIONS

The beginning of the chapter identified a number of factors that one might expect to see if real estate agents compete on price. These include: declining commission rates; a countercyclical relationship between commission rates and the strength of the housing market; and a positive relationship between commission rates, the experience of the real estate agent, and the value-added of her firm. Most of these patterns are evident in the markets examined here. Although the specific results vary from market to market, the regression analysis suggests that commission rates vary in ways that are both predictable and consistent with market-driven pricing.

Undoubtedly, some will look at the evidence presented here and conclude that the variation in commission rates is not enough to justify a conclusion that the brokerage market is "fully" competitive. Commission rates are sensitive to housing prices, but they are clearly not nearly as sensitive as a stylized economic model would suggest. At a minimum, however, our results appear to challenge the basic notion of a "fixed commission" world. Although additional research will be required to get a better understanding of the patterns reported here, commission rates clearly vary within markets, across markets, and over time.

APPENDIX

TABLE 10A.1 OLS Regressions (County Fixed Effects Not Shown)

	Baltimore			
	Coefficient	T-statistic	Mean	Standard deviation
LN list price	−0.19871	−172.7	12.26977	.747492
New construction (2006–2007)	0.16448	32.4	.0177961	.1322097
New construction (2000–2005)	−0.05337	−16.7	.0482016	.2141922
Agent sides	0.00133	49.9	20.22029	24.96822
Office sides	0.00020	68.0	279.618	226.562
House price appreciation	−0.28331	−32.7	.1377377	.0780662
Supply of agents	−0.00004	−36.9	6,643.884	1,501.295

(continued)

	Baltimore			
	Coefficient	T-statistic	Mean	Standard deviation
Limited service	−0.03241	−3.3	.0044141	.0662918
FSBO	−0.01289	−1.5	.005644	.0749145
Quarter	−0.01074	−63.5	16.97802	8.760402
Constant	5.648275	411.9	—	—
R-squared value			.2882	
Observations			393,514	

	Chicago			
	Coefficient	T-statistic	Mean	Standard deviation
LN list price	−0.048195	−159.70	12.40193	.6108526
New construction (2006–2007)	0.025637	14.87	.0084858	.0917269
New construction (2000–2005)	−0.009168	−5.87	.0100815	.0998994
Agent sides	0.000809	82.64	13.75693	20.19317
Office sides	0.000052	80.60	282.0246	235.0972
House price appreciation	−0.336783	−69.61	.07558	.0382029
Supply of agents	0.000002	30.64	16,474.3	4,553.269
Quarter	−0.005513	−162.26	16.24186	8.552508
Constant	3.155898	820.28	—	—
R-squared value			.1003	
Observations			1,426,968	

	Dallas–Fort Worth			
	Coefficient	T-statistic	Mean	Standard deviation
LN list price	−0.090427	−118.29	11.98201	.6430982
New construction (2006–2007)	−0.007827	−5.30	.0501884	.2183336
New construction (2000–2005)	−0.040506	−44.32	.1259056	.3317432
Agent sides	0.001484	80.03	29.34406	35.20051
Office sides	0.000034	24.46	337.7075	269.2789
House price appreciation	−0.111264	−8.36	.0305251	.0324288
Supply of agents	0.000000	0.79	11,662.82	1,994.518
Limited service	−0.053020	−32.84	.0441264	.2053759
Constant	4.03552	398.57	—	—
R-squared value			.0469	
Observations			838,501	

(continued)

TABLE 10A.1   *(continued)*

	Kansas City			
	Coefficient	T-statistic	Mean	Standard deviation
LN list price	−0.060132	−42.89	11.96745	.5823745
New construction (2006–2007)	−0.029108	−11.77	.0589122	.2354609
New construction (2000–2005)	−0.120077	−72.93	.1520891	.3591081
Agent sides	0.001218	20.21	17.79152	26.21345
Office sides	0.000026	11.58	400.7942	282.3474
House price appreciation	0.269544	7.20	.0232369	.0247129
Supply of agents	−0.000002	−1.69	7,077.874	969.6795
Limited service	−0.020753	−2.59	.0051426	.0715277
Quarter	−0.004345	−21.37	12.47237	6.435646
Constant	3.808601	217.60	—	—
R-squared value			.0844	
Observations			221,482	

	Miami–Fort Lauderdale			
	Coefficient	T-statistic	Mean	Standard deviation
LN list price	0.063257	32.68	12.70294	.6767263
New construction (2006–2007)	0.186485	10.20	.0089359	.0941068
New construction (2000–2005)	0.170053	5.64	.0022694	.0475846
Agent sides	0.000446	5.08	11.30278	18.3981
Office sides	0.000327	14.60	48.52918	61.85609
House price appreciation	−0.077374	−4.02	.0835699	.1246385
Supply of agents	−0.000035	−40.99	10,367.16	1,627.184
Quarter	0.069286	74.36	6.57087	2.612887
Constant	1.864867	67.28	—	—
R-squared value			.1455	
Observations			119,854	

	Orange County–Los Angeles			
	Coefficient	T-statistic	Mean	Standard deviation
LN list price	−0.07010	−73.98	12.91539	.6306252
New construction (2006–2007)	0.12837	12.37	.0035725	.0596634

(continued)

TABLE 10A.1 (*continued*)

	Orange County–Los Angeles			
	Coefficient	T-statistic	Mean	Standard deviation
New construction (2000–2005)	0.02271	3.36	.005505	.073991
Agent sides	0.00068	24.66	10.74228	19.21954
Office sides	0.00015	72.00	201.2449	209.4882
House price appreciation	−1.18117	−186.92	.1583951	.0758666
Supply of agents	−0.00001	−60.08	13,384.24	4,459.992
Limited service	−0.06523	−13.77	.0177085	.13189
Quarter	−0.00723	−79.62	15.32617	8.647919
Constant	3.970999	336.30	—	—
R-squared value			.2030	
Observations			591,466	

	Washington, DC			
	Coefficient	T-statistic	Mean	Standard deviation
LN list price	−.0430736	−70.57	12.66314	.635766
New construction (2006–2007)	.0588091	28.44	.0243511	.1541368
New construction (2000–2005)	−.0295583	−22.51	.0772132	.2669295
Agent sides	.0005976	47.23	20.73968	26.33238
Office sides	.0000525	38.81	283.5383	236.6662
House price appreciation	−.341391	−96.33	.136406	.0952565
Supply of agents	.000004	−20.83	13,347.11	3,122.619
Limited service	−.1055106	−28.12	.0077592	.087744
FSBO	−.0217767	−10.97	.0299488	.1704461
Quarter	−.0040142	−51.55	17.06663	8.543996
Constant	3.514573	476.47	—	—
R-squared value			.1336	
Observations			820,702	

NOTE: LN = natural log; FSBO = for sale by owner.
SOURCE: Authors' analysis of MLS data.

References

Association of Real Estate License Law Officials (ARELLO). 2006. *Digest of Real Estate License Laws and Current Issues.* Montgomery, AL: ARELLO.

Carney, Michael. 1982. "Costs and Pricing of Home Brokerage Services." *Journal of the American Real Estate and Urban Economics Association Journal* (AREUEA Journal) 10(3): 331–354.

Goolsby, William C., and Barbara J. Childs. 1988. "Brokerage Firm Competition in Real Estate Commission Rates." *Journal of Real Estate Research* 3(2): 11–20.

Hahn, Robert W., Robert E. Litan, and Jesse Gurman. 2006. "Bringing More Competition to Real Estate Brokerage." *Real Estate Law Journal* 35: 86.

Harney, Ken. 2007. "Full Commissions Make a Comeback." *Washington Post*, June 9.

Hsieh, Chang-Tai, and Enrico Moretti. 2002. "Can Free Entry Be Inefficient? Fixed Commissions and Social Waste in the Real Estate Industry." National Bureau of Economic Research Working Paper No. 9208, September.

Inman News. 2006. "The State of Real Estate Commissions: 2006. Inside the Black Box." September 18.

Larsen, James E., and Won J. Park. 1989. "Non-Uniform Percentage Brokerage Commissions and Real Estate Market Performance." *Journal of the American Real Estate and Urban Economics Association Journal* (AREUEA Journal) 17(4): 423–438.

Nagel, Mark S. 2006. "A Critical Assessment of the Standard, Traditional, Residential Real Estate Commission Rate Structure." Working Paper, AEI-Brookings Joint Center for Regulatory Studies, Washington, DC, October.

National Association of Realtors (NAR). 2005. "Structure, Conduct and Performance of the Real Estate Brokerage Industry." Washington, DC: NAR, November.

———. 2006. "Profile of Real Estate Firms: An Industry Overview." Washington, DC: NAR.

———. 2007. "Member Profile." Washington, DC: NAR.

Real Trends. 2006. *The Consumer Tsunami.* Denver, CO: Real Trends, August.

Sawyer, Steve. 2005. "Local Real Estate Competition: Evidence and Insight from an Analysis of 12 Local Markets." Working Paper, Pennsylvania State University, August.

Sirmans, C. F., and Geoffrey K. Turnbull. 1997. "Brokerage Pricing Under Competition." *Journal of Urban Economics* 41: 102–117.

Sirmans, C. F., Geoffrey K. Turnbull, and John D. Benjamin. 1991. "The Markets for Housing and Real Estate Broker Services." *Journal of Housing Economics* 1: 207–217.

U.S. Federal Trade Commission. 1983. "The Residential Real Estate Brokerage Industry." Washington, DC: U.S. Government Printing Office, December.

Weicher, John C. 2006. "The Price of Residential Real Estate Brokerage Services: A Review of the Evidence, Such as It Is." *Real Estate Law Journal* 35: 119–144.

White, Lawrence J. 2006. "The Residential Real Estate Brokerage Industry: What Would More Competition Look Like?" *Real Estate Law Journal* 35: 20–26.

Woodall, Patrick, and Stephen Brobeck. 2006. "How the Real Estate Cartel Harms Consumers and How Consumers Can Protect Themselves." Washington, DC: Consumer Federation of America, June.

Zumpano, Leonard, Harold W. Elder, and Glenn E. Crellin. 1993. "The Market for Residential Brokerage Services: Costs of Production and Economies of Scale." *Journal of Real Estate Finance and Economics* 6: 237–250.

Zumpano, Leonard V. 2002. "The Possible Consequences of Bank Entry into the Real Estate Brokerage Market: What Research Tells Us." *Journal of Real Estate Literature* 10(2): 247.

Part

IV

URBAN FORM

11

The Role of Job Creation and Job Destruction Dynamics

NANCY E. WALLACE
DONALD W. WALLS

I n urban economics, the consensus view concerning the growth-rate dynamics of establishments over the size distribution is that (1) Gibrat's law
holds for establishment growth dynamics;[1] (2) city-industry growth dynamics exhibit substantial mean reversion over the size distribution;[2] and (3) the
growth-rate dynamics of metropolitan statistical areas (MSAs) over the size distribution generally follow Gibrat's law, but the growth-rate dynamics of cities
do not.[3] The empirical support for this consensus often rests on empirical testing strategies that abstract from one or more factors of production because of
the limitations of available date sets. Often the focus has been on the labor factor, abstracting from the effects of capital innovations and the accumulation
rates of physical capital. A common alternative strategy, following the neoclassical growth literature, abstracts from the labor factor and focuses on the accumulation rates of physical capital. Relatively few studies have focused on
possible differences in the growth dynamics of establishments and the size distribution of establishments across narrowly defined industry sectors characterized by production technologies that differ in the relative intensities of the
labor and capital factors (Rossi-Hansberg and Wright, 2007a).

The purpose of this chapter is threefold. First, we introduce a unique
new data set, the National Establishment Time-Series (NETS) database that

---

1. See Lucas (1967, 1978) and Sutton (1997) for an excellent overview.
2. See Dumais, Ellison, and Glaeser (2002), Ellison and Glaeser (1997), Glaeser et al. (1992), and Henderson, Kuncoro, and Turner (1995), among others.
3. See Eeckhout (2004), Gabaix (1999), and Gabaix and Ibragimov (2007), among others.

includes the number of jobs in all firms and establishments in the United States, measured at the eight-digit standard industrial classification for each establishment. The data also include the geographic location of all establishments, both by MSAs and by five-digit Federal Information Processing Standards (FIPS) for state and county codes. The data set allows for a consistent framework in which to analyze the characteristics of job creation and destruction and the size distribution of employment for all U.S. jobs at the level of establishments. We then aggregate this establishment-level employment data into 59 narrowly defined Bureau of Economic Analysis (BEA) sectors for which we have constructed a long panel of the capital-labor factor intensities. Interestingly, we find that, over time, the production technologies defined in terms of capital-labor ratios are quite stable within BEA sectors, but across sectors there is important heterogeneity in these technologies.

Our second purpose is to empirically test two recently proposed explanations for why establishments, or firms, might not exhibit proportionate growth dynamics even though the aggregate economy does. The first of these causal channels is the effects of financial market frictions and the second is the effects of the accumulation of industry-specific human capital. We apply a random-parameters, multilevel econometric specification that allows us to jointly test whether these constraints lead to size dependence of growth and exit rates. We find that BEA sectors characterized by capital-intensive factor structures exhibit mean reversion in job creation and destruction dynamics. In particular, we find that conditioned on the factor market structure of BEA sectors in the U.S. economy, there is a dependence of growth dynamics on establishment size for capital-intensive sectors. Unconditionally, we find that Gibrat's law does apply for the average growth dynamics of job creation and destruction rates over all BEA sectors.

We then extend this analysis to consider briefly the implications of the factor structure of production technology and the availability of financing within industry sectors on the size distribution of establishments and the size distribution of cities that we model as aggregates of our BEA-defined sectors. In this analysis, we again find evidence of violations of proportionate growth in the size distribution of establishments within BEA sectors that are characterized by capital-intensive factor structures. The relationship between capital-intensive production technologies and violations of Gibrat's law for these sectors is not as strongly supported in our analysis of city aggregates. Here, we find Gibrat's law holds for cities overall, although an indirect residual analysis suggests that outlier cities also exhibit higher aggregate capital intensities in production. Solving this puzzle is left to future work.

The chapter is organized as follows. In the next section, we briefly review the literature on the growth and exit dynamics of establishments and cities and discuss the testable null hypotheses that distinguish the various explanations for size dynamics. In the section "Mean Reversion and Size Distribution," we review similar testable null hypotheses that distinguish explanations for the size distribution of establishments and cities. In the section titled "Data," we present the new database that we employ and discuss the dynamics of aggregate job creation and destruction across BEA industrial sectors in the United States. This is followed by "Empirical Tests for Mean Reversion in Establishment Dynamics," in which we develop two empirical specifications to test the null hypotheses identified in the second section for the growth dynamics of establishments. Next, in "Scale and the Size Distribution of Establishments," we report our tests for proportionate growth dynamics, given the observed size distribution of establishments. This is followed by the section "A Remaining Puzzle: The Scale Independence of Geographic Aggregates of BEA Sectors," in which we again test for proportionate growth dynamics for MSA and city aggregates of BEA sectors.

GROWTH AND EXIT DYNAMICS

A number of recent studies have identified channels by which the growth dynamics of establishments, or firms, are related to the size of establishments, or firms. Dunne, Roberts, and Samuelson (1989), Evans (1987), and Henderson (1982) find scale effects in the form of a negative relationship between firm age and size.[4] Models that include inefficiencies in capital markets have shown that firm-specific capital constraints, such as the lack of collateralizable assets on the part of smaller firms, can generate an aggregate dependence between firm size and growth rates (see Albuquerque and Hopenhayn, 2004; Cabral and Mata, 2005; Clementi and Hopenhayn, 2005; and Cooley and Quadrini, 2001). Garicano and Rossi-Hansberg (2004) develop a model in which the distribution of managerial ability in the population leads to size dependence in the growth of firms. Rossi-Hansberg and Wright (2007a) find that if establishment sizes respond monotonically to fluctuations in factor prices and these are, in turn, determined by the stock of human capital, mean reversion in the stock of human capital will lead to mean reversion in establishment sizes. This type of scale dependence would be consistent with mean reversion in factor accumulation, following the general result of neoclassical

---

4. Sutton (1997) provides an excellent overview of similar studies.

growth models, with production functions displaying diminishing marginal returns to capital accumulation (see Lucas, 1967, 1978).

A particularly appealing aspect of the Rossi-Hansberg and Wright (2007a) theory is that it provides a consistent justification for the effects of establishment size on the growth and exit rates of establishments and for the likely scale dependence of the size distribution of establishments. The first testable null hypothesis from this model is that establishment growth and exit rates should decline faster with size in sectors that use human capital less intensively and consequently use physical capital more intensively. The less intensively human capital is used, the faster diminishing returns to scale set in, and the faster the speed of mean reversion occurs. The second testable null hypothesis from their model is that the tails of the size distribution of establishments should be thinner the smaller the human capital share is. If the degree of mean reversion decreases with human capital intensity—similar to the predictions of neoclassical growth models in which the speed of convergence decreases with the physical capital share—then the intensity of physical capital in production should be positively related to the degree of mean reversion in human capital and the observed degree of mean reversion in establishment sizes.

The Rossi-Hansberg and Wright (2007a) predictions are quite different from predictions based on financial constraints as a source of mean reversion. The financial-constraint literature proposes that scale dependence would be more important in industry sectors in which establishments produce output using a physical capital share that is small in relation to the human capital share (see Clementi and Hopenhayn, 2005; Cooley and Quadrini, 2001; and an excellent overview by Cabral and Mata, 2005). This literature develops structural models to motivate the negative correlations that have been found, in an earlier empirical literature, between growth rates, firm size, and firm age (see Evans, 1987; Hall, 1987). The financial-constraint models establish a direct link between the patterns of firm growth and the financial characteristics of firms that are related to size. The Cooley and Quadrini (2001) model is a standard industry dynamics model that includes financial frictions and persistent shocks. The model predicts a simultaneous dependence of industry dynamics on size (conditioning on age) and on age (conditioning on size).

No prior studies have directly tested these two alternative explanations for the size dependence of growth and exit rates of firms or establishments within narrow industry sectors. A key impediment in all of this literature is the difficulty in obtaining comprehensive data sets. For example, data availability has limited the specificity of industry types to only two-digit Standard Industrial Classification (SIC) codes (Rossi-Hansberg and Wright, 2007a) or to a limited number of firm sectors, such as the manufacturing sector (see Dunne,

Roberts, and Samuelson,1989; Evans, 1987; and Hall, 1987). Lack of information on the capital structure of firms has limited the financial-constraints literature to consider only firms that are large enough to issue stock (see Cabral and Mata, 2005). Establishment age is another factor that is often difficult to obtain. Other data problems that have hampered more expansive investigations of these competing theories of growth include issues related to sample truncation and sample selection.

Because city growth rates would be expected to reflect the aggregate establishment size and exit dynamics of the firms that locate within them, there is, not surprisingly, a related literature that considers city growth dynamics. An important regularity found in the empirical literature is that the population growth rates of cities do not depend on city size or rank.[5] Thus, even though there is considerable variance among cities' growth rates within a country, these growth rates appear to vary randomly with size.

MEAN REVERSION AND THE SIZE DISTRIBUTION

The Rossi-Hansberg and Wright (2007a) model predicts that scale dependence in the size distribution of establishments will increase in the intensity of the physical capital factor share within narrowly defined industry sectors because of diminishing returns. Their prediction contrasts with that of Gabaix (1999) and Gabaix and Ibragimov (2007), who have argued that if Gibrat's law characterizes the growth rate of a finite number of establishments, and there exists a lower bound on establishment sizes that converges to zero, then the long-run distribution converges to Zipf's law, or a Pareto distribution that has unbounded support. Rossi-Hansberg and Wright (2007a) show, instead, that for narrow industrial sectors with small physical capital shares, the size distribution of establishments can be close to the Pareto distribution with a shape distribution of one. Because large physical capital shares imply small human capital shares, sectors with large physical capital shares should generate a greater degree of scale dependence in growth rates and in net exit rates and a size distribution of establishments with thinner tails than the Pareto distribution.

The City Size Distribution

A proportionate underlying growth process would be expected to generate an asymptotically lognormal distribution, implying that the empirical distribution

---

5. See Eaton and Eckstein (1997), Eeckhout (2004), Glaeser, Scheinkman, and Schleifer (1995), Krugman (1996), and Overman and Ioannides (2001), among others.

of city population sizes should be observed to be lognormal.[6] However, numerous economic studies have documented Zipf's law, by which the size distribution of a country's largest cities is inversely proportional to population rank.[7] Gabaix (1999) and Gabaix and Ibragimov (2007) show that proportionate growth processes can be consistent with Zipf's law in the upper tail of the population size distribution. Eeckhout (2004) uses U.S. Census data for 2000 to show that the total population distribution for cities is distributed lognormal rather than Pareto. Eeckhout (2004) finds that the existence of the Pareto distribution in the upper tail of the observed population of cities is highly sensitive to the sampling truncation point in the rank size of cities. He provides an empirically testable proposition to determine whether the actual observed city size distribution is converging to the lognormal distribution, which would be expected if growth were proportionate.

Also, no prior studies have attempted to aggregate establishments into their respective cities. As pointed out by Eeckhout (2004), most prior studies of city-level growth rates have focused on aggregate data for the largest 132 cities in the United States. Another advantage of our study is that we consider the role of financial constraints and factor structure regularities on aggregate establishment performance within cities. We are thus able to trace the role of these factors on the aggregate growth rates of cities over time.

DATA

The empirical hypothesis tests that we propose require extensive information on U.S. establishment and city size distributions, as well as information on the capital-labor ratios and the flow of venture capital funding and small-business loans across states and industry sectors. Our unit of analysis is establishments. We follow Rossi-Hansberg and Wright (2007a) and define an "industry" as SICs. In contrast to their study, however, we define industrial sectors at the level of four-digit SIC codes and the geographic identifiers for each establishment are specific to both MSAs and FIPS codes. The only data source with sufficient specificity to provide this level of detail is the NETS historical database. The database consists of 17 annual snapshots of Dun and Bradstreet (D&B) Duns Marketing Information (DMI) files that track more

---

6. See Eeckhout (2004), Gibrat (1931), Kalecki (1945), and Kapteyn (1903).

7. For theoretical and empirical treatments of the Zipf proposition for city size distributions, see Brakman et al. (1999), Dobkins and Ioannides (2000), Eeckhout (2004), Gabaix (1999), Gabaix and Ioannides (2004), Krugman (1996), Reed (2001), Rosen and Resnick (1980), Rossi-Hansberg and Wright (2007b), Soo (2005), and Zipf (1949), among others.

than 32 million establishments between January 1990 and January 2005. The D&B DMI coverage is as close as possible to an annual census of American business.

The establishments are tracked using a unique DUNS number, and each annual establishment record contains information on the number of jobs at the establishment, the number of related establishments in the firm, changes in headquarters or ownership, and the geographic location of the establishment (defined in terms of latitude and longitude, MSA, and FIPS), among many other characteristics. Table 11.1 presents the total size distribution of establishments in the United States for 22 size groupings, from establishments with one employee to establishments with more than 10,000 jobs, over the period from 1990 to 2005. As shown, the total number of establishments has increased over the sample period from slightly over 10.4 million establishments in 1990 to a maximum of 16.5 million establishments in 2004. The relative share of one-job establishments has grown from about 23 percent of total establishments in 1990 to about 36 percent of total establishments in 2005. Table 11.1 clearly indicates that the size distribution of establishments is skewed toward smaller operations. In 2005, 73 percent of the 16.2 million establishments had fewer than five employees. About 85.4 percent of establishments employed 50 or fewer employees, but these accounted for less than one-half of total jobs (48.4 percent). The largest establishments in the database are those with at least 1,000 jobs, and they account for only 0.05 percent of all establishments but represent 13.4 percent of total jobs.

Figure 11.1 illustrates the dynamics of job creation and destruction in the U.S. economy from 1990 to 2005. A net total of more than 19 million new jobs was created during this period. Two important underlying facts should be noted: (1) to produce the observed net change in jobs in the United States, 403 million jobs were either created or destroyed; and (2) on average, about one out of seven establishments contributed to job creation in a given year (14.1 percent). An even smaller number, one out of nine establishments, contributed to job destructions (11.1 percent) over the period. Thus, in aggregate, establishments must create and destroy 21 jobs for every one net new job that survives.

Only a small fraction of existing establishments contribute to the processes of job creation and destruction in any given year. This pattern of job births and deaths is illustrated in figure 11.2. As shown, establishment deaths have been relatively stable until 2004–2005. New establishment births have been the primary driver of net growth. Over the entire period, 73 percent of establishments that created jobs were new establishments (births); however, they accounted for only 58 percent of overall job creations, as they were, on

TABLE 11.1 Summary of the Size Distribution of Establishments

Establishment size	1990	1991	1992	1993	1994	1995	1996	1997
1	2,385,176	2,493,923	2,825,947	2,868,859	3,688,362	3,369,261	4,064,890	4,074,366
2	1,739,039	1,748,666	1,866,629	1,925,338	2,054,364	2,115,552	2,199,342	2,269,086
3	1,758,073	1,805,114	1,860,536	1,999,098	1,817,554	2,111,410	1,975,323	2,155,430
4	855,049	853,266	872,713	907,451	919,061	956,622	936,507	941,854
5	620,908	625,294	648,185	664,001	688,453	706,352	713,033	721,664
6–7	719,725	719,493	746,903	761,278	785,593	802,013	809,262	814,685
8–9	399,027	390,364	399,422	414,671	423,677	436,608	440,116	445,382
10	243,727	255,433	257,532	265,444	280,951	292,494	301,004	312,094
11–13	295,921	285,607	299,846	308,174	316,945	329,200	340,813	349,441
14–16	239,779	243,223	247,095	254,570	265,222	275,776	282,842	292,858
17–21	217,669	219,162	223,307	229,539	238,015	248,514	255,998	264,583
22–29	224,691	215,665	228,268	232,071	237,391	247,740	254,425	264,166
30–39	177,367	177,902	181,818	186,236	191,092	199,347	203,358	210,424
40–59	190,230	190,249	193,672	200,045	204,754	213,402	217,991	225,107
60–99	138,954	138,416	141,097	146,363	149,516	154,682	157,422	163,292
100–199	99,380	99,377	101,822	105,819	108,102	111,457	114,070	118,185
200–499	52,072	51,826	52,247	54,188	54,784	55,950	56,780	58,862
500–999	14,377	14,336	14,416	14,796	14,746	15,015	14,914	15,298
1,000–2,499	7,837	7,791	7,772	7,917	7,969	7,786	7,706	7,815
2,500–4,999	1,814	1,769	1,791	1,866	1,879	1,766	1,716	1,782
5,000–9,999	595	582	578	577	581	569	554	566
10,000+	200	216	220	233	234	216	211	211
Total establishments	10,381,610	10,537,674	11,171,816	11,548,534	12,449,245	12,651,732	13,348,277	13,707,151

	1998	1999	2000	2001	2002	2003	2004	2005
1	4,212,419	4,087,748	4,441,807	5,372,550	4,935,347	5,367,482	5,844,563	5,810,302
2	2,316,890	2,325,326	2,355,072	2,615,704	3,412,800	3,583,083	3,743,079	3,624,628
3	2,078,582	1,948,174	1,856,068	2,032,598	2,075,364	1,936,229	1,512,824	1,507,944
4	935,358	924,964	916,333	928,239	1,003,058	1,015,959	964,992	895,942
5	723,647	730,605	739,333	737,671	725,402	722,852	711,693	703,218
6–7	814,765	815,209	819,113	817,696	804,504	805,705	792,193	798,575
8–9	447,391	448,950	450,268	450,803	447,863	445,136	442,469	435,498
10	316,808	324,108	338,102	341,438	341,763	339,543	336,644	337,825
11–13	354,924	361,128	363,363	367,605	365,641	362,508	359,797	353,189
14–16	297,988	305,228	314,154	318,660	318,378	319,275	316,189	314,936
17–21	270,646	276,850	286,603	290,188	290,706	288,856	285,152	284,600
22–29	269,447	274,397	278,627	282,981	282,301	282,435	281,332	275,126
30–39	214,033	219,264	225,544	230,847	230,938	229,636	226,804	224,885
40–59	230,250	235,280	243,123	248,907	250,630	247,927	246,740	243,203
60–99	167,386	171,133	177,181	181,103	183,263	179,933	177,284	171,308
100–199	121,706	125,079	131,383	136,667	137,347	134,123	130,299	127,405
200–499	60,634	62,355	65,692	68,967	68,697	66,629	63,980	62,864
500–999	15,626	16,105	17,149	18,728	18,093	16,494	15,533	15,027
1,000–2,499	8,091	8,430	8,985	8,859	8,306	7,705	7,266	7,155
2,500–4,999	1,845	1,848	1,965	1,920	1,750	1,643	1,521	1,545
5,000–9,999	585	627	640	608	553	492	473	465
10,000+	205	208	202	195	162	130	116	120
Total establishments	13,859,226	13,663,016	14,030,707	15,452,934	15,902,866	16,353,775	16,460,943	16,195,760

NOTE: This table presents the aggregate composition of jobs in the United States. The row labels are the establishment size categories and each table entry is the number of establishments of that size in the United States for the year reported in the column heading. As shown, there are twenty-two establishment size categories. These categories are defined by the average number of jobs offered by an establishment within a one year interval.

SOURCE: Authors' calculations using the NETS data set.

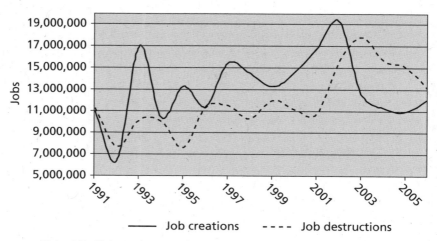

FIGURE 11.1 Total Job Creations and Destructions in the United States, 1990–2005

SOURCE: National Establishment Time-Series database.

FIGURE 11.2 Total Establishment Births and Deaths in the United States, 1990–2005

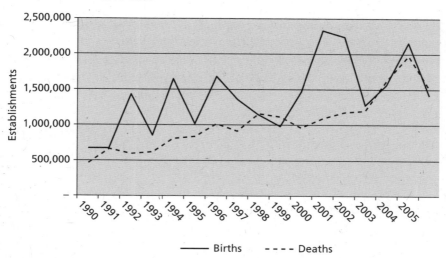

SOURCE: National Establishment Time-Series database.

average, smaller establishments. Deaths among establishments were a slightly less important source of job destructions: 68 percent of establishments destroying jobs died, and they also accounted for a smaller proportion of job destructions (63 percent).

We follow Rossi-Hansberg and Wright (2007a) and focus on the cross-sectional differences in the capital and labor factor structure across industry sectors.[8] In appendix table 11A.1, we list the correspondence between the North American Industry Classification System (NAICS) industry codes, the BEA industry sectors we use to present our results for ease of exposition, and the specific BEA industry codes that we use in all our analyses. Using our eight-digit SIC codes, however, we aggregate up to the BEA's 59 private-industry sectors defined at the four-digit NAICS level. We use the BEA's Current-Cost Net Stock of Private Fixed Assets by Industry national income and product account (NIPA) table 3.1ES as an estimate for industry capital.[9] These estimates incorporate the results from the 2007 annual revision of the national income and product accounts. They reflect new estimates for 2005 and revised estimates for 2004 to 2005. For labor costs, we used the Compensation of Employees by Industry NIPA tables 6.2D and 6.2C.[10]

Our time series of capital-labor ratios for each of the 59 specific BEA industry codes was computed as the ratio, in every year, of the Net Stock of Private Fixed Assets to Total Compensation for each of the BEA industries. To estimate an analogous capital-labor ratio for metropolitan areas, we implicitly assumed constant industry capital-labor ratios across these areas. The variation in metropolitan capital-labor ratios is, thus, a reflection of differing industry mixes across urban areas. Table 11.2 presents summary statistics for the BEA capital-labor ratios for BEA industry sectors.[11] As shown, from 1990 through 2005 there is

---

8. Although our analysis is carried out at the level of BEA industry-specific sectors (roughly four-digit SIC codes), the NETS database allows a cross-walk from eight-digit SIC identifiers for each establishment to the corresponding SIC/NAICS identifiers used by the Bureau of Economic Analysis (BEA) without the usual time series break in 1998 when federal data was transitioned from SIC to NAICS codes. This allowed us to compute industry-specific capital-labor ratios and apply them to establishments at the MSA level.

9. This table is available at http://www.bea.gov/national/FA2004/TableView.asp. Dave Wasshausen of the BEA was especially helpful in providing links to the relevant data and explaining the data's derivation.

10. These tables may be found in section 6, "Income and Employment by Industry," on the BEA Web site http://www.bea.gov/national/nipaweb/SelectTable.asp. George Smith of the BEA provided invaluable insight into the BEA's estimation of compensation and its organization of the data. Because the period 1989 to 1997 was organized around SIC instead of NAICS, we were forced to estimate compensation per employee for our 61 industries. The NIPA total employment data on an NAICS basis, and total compensation at the private-industries level, allowed us to iteratively scale our initial estimates to the total compensation for all industries.

11. Again, these are averages over industry-specific BEA codes and are presented in this format for ease of exposition.

TABLE 11.2 Summary Statistics for the Capital-Labor Ratios by BEA Industry Sectors, 1995–2005

BEA category	Mean	Standard deviation	Minimum	Maximum	BEA category	Mean	Standard deviation	Minimum	Maximum
Accommodation	3.98	0.13	3.74	4.21	Fabricated metal	1.54	0.08	1.39	1.66
Administration, support services	0.42	0.06	0.35	0.51	Federal Reserve, financial intermediation	3.26	0.21	2.93	3.63
Air transportation	5.19	0.81	4.02	6.54	Food service, drinking	1.42	0.07	1.34	1.59
Ambulatory health care services, health care services	0.96	0.12	0.84	1.20	Food, beverage, tobacco	2.68	0.21	2.37	2.92
					Funds, trusts, other	9.92	1.38	7.57	11.90
Amusements, gambling	2.79	0.29	2.50	3.42	Furniture	0.68	0.08	0.59	0.83
Apparel, leather	0.94	0.33	0.56	1.53	Hospitals, nursing care	2.15	0.09	2.00	2.36
Broadcasting, telecommunications	7.31	0.54	6.49	8.67	Information processing	0.59	0.16	0.46	0.88
Chemical products	2.99	0.14	2.81	3.20	Insurance carriers, related	1.20	0.09	1.04	1.33
Computer systems design	0.48	0.08	0.39	0.62	Legal services	0.24	0.01	0.22	0.25
Computers, electronics	1.69	0.35	1.17	2.15	Machinery	1.73	0.28	1.45	2.10
Construction	0.55	0.02	0.51	0.57	Management of companies	2.09	0.17	1.82	2.49
Educational services	2.97	0.17	2.77	3.44	Mining (not oil, gas)	6.92	0.46	6.14	7.73
					Mining support	4.97	0.76	3.48	6.10
Electrical equipment, appliances	1.64	0.07	1.46	1.74	Miscellaneous manufacturing	1.30	0.10	1.13	1.46

Industry				
Motor vehicles	1.23	0.11	1.07	1.44
Movies, recording	1.71	0.21	1.41	2.05
Nonmetallic mineral	2.37	0.17	2.14	2.70
Oil, gas extraction	31.42	6.87	22.05	44.38
Other services	2.13	0.07	2.02	2.26
Other transport	2.74	0.79	1.78	4.32
Other transport equipment	1.48	0.18	1.12	1.69
Paper products	3.28	0.25	2.71	3.62
Performing arts, sports	1.84	0.21	1.59	2.27
Petroleum, coal	8.96	0.86	7.40	10.06
Pipeline transport	16.83	5.83	11.07	28.46
Plastics, rubber	1.75	0.06	1.66	1.86
Primary metals	4.04	0.27	3.57	4.41
Printing, related	1.23	0.11	1.12	1.48
Publishing, software	0.76	0.08	0.64	0.89
Railroad transport	15.81	0.74	14.28	16.78
Real estate leasing, sales	8.47	2.74	4.86	12.07
Real estate	214.71	7.06	204.64	228.46
Retail trade	1.68	0.10	1.60	1.96
Securities, investments	0.75	0.12	0.61	1.00
Services, miscellaneous	0.48	0.08	0.41	0.62
Social assistance	0.59	0.06	0.51	0.73
Textiles	2.31	0.20	2.12	2.78
Transit	3.36	0.17	3.14	3.70
Truck transport	1.13	0.07	1.01	1.25
Utilities	22.29	1.16	20.13	24.14
Warehousing	1.25	0.14	1.11	1.65
Waste management	5.24	0.71	4.37	6.16
Water transport	11.42	0.50	10.53	12.23
Wholesale trade	1.06	0.04	0.99	1.14
Wood products	1.55	0.13	1.41	1.83

NOTES: This table reports the summary statistics for the capital-labor ratios for aggregate BEA categories. The ratios are computed using the BEA's Current-Cost Net Stock of Private Fixed Assets by Industry table (NIPA table 3.1ES) as an estimate for industry capital. For labor costs, we used the Compensation of Employees by Industry NIPA tables 6.2D and 6.2C. BEA = Bureau of Economic Analysis.

SOURCE: Authors' calculations using data from U.S. Department of Commerce, Bureau of Economic Analysis, www.bea.gov/national/nipaweb.

considerable heterogeneity across industry sectors in the average capital-labor ratios. However, there is remarkable stability in these ratios, given the standard deviations and the minimum and maximum values over time within the same industry. The observed modest variation in the industry sector capital-labor ratios over time is consistent with the long-run equilibrium stability of these technological indicators by industry that is assumed in studies such as Rossi-Hansberg and Wright (2007a). The highly capital-intensive industries are commercial real estate, utilities, and oil and gas extraction. Labor-intensive industries include construction, services, and wholesale trade. Manufacturing and transportation industries fall between these extremes.

We construct our measures of the capital market funding constraints using two data sources. Before this study, empirical studies of the financial mechanisms that lead to mean reversion in growth and destruction rates have focused on constraints within firms. These constraints are usually measured for samples of firms that have trading equity and collateral that can be monitored using publicly available information on firm balance sheets (see Albuquerque and Hopenhayn, 2004, Cabral and Mata, 2005, and Clementi and Hopenhayn, 2005). However, as discussed here, the focus of the prior literature on larger firms is likely to introduce significant sample selection biases because most firms in the U.S. economy are small. As small firms do not have trading equity or issue corporate debt, they are systematically ignored in prior studies. The primary funding source for small establishments is small-business loans from commercial banks and, potentially, credit card debt that is not measurable by firms or geography, to our knowledge.

We measure the supply of credit to small establishments using data obtained from the Small Business Administration (SBA). The SBA produces an annual survey of the dollar amount of loans that are smaller than $1 million that were made by Federal Deposit Insurance Corporation (FDIC)–insured commercial banks to small businesses in each state.[12] To compute a comparable small-business lending series across states, we assume that establishments with fewer than 100 jobs within each of the 61 BEA industry sectors are the demanders for these small-business loans within a state. So we computed *small-business loans per capita* (dollars per establishment) for the BEA sectors in each state and then used these to compute business loans per capita for MSAs. Thus, the variation across MSAs in small-business funding reflects both the industrial composition and establishment size distribution of those markets, as well as the total dollar amount of loans available in the respective states.

---

12. These data were obtained from commercial bank call reports as reported by the SBA. See www.sba.gov/advo/research/.

We measure the supply of capital market constraints for larger firms using a measure of the dollar amounts of venture capital expenditure within each state by BEA industry. We obtain these venture capital flows using data on the investment flows of venture capital firms, as reported by Pricewaterhouse-Coopers in their *MoneyTree Report*.[13] These data are available by state-level BEA categories, so we assume that all establishments in each BEA sector have equal access to this source of funding. Using the establishment-level BEA classification in the NETS database, we then compute *per capita venture capital* availability (dollars per establishment) for each BEA sector. As with small-business loans, we use the industrial composition for specific MSAs within a state (along with the BEA-specific per capita venture capital) to compute *per capita venture capital* availability in each MSA.

The upper panel of table 11.3 presents summary statistics for the venture capital flows that are averaged across states with the Census Regional Divisions, for expositional ease. As is clear in the table, there are important cross-sectional differences in the allocation of venture capital dollars by state and Census Division. The largest recipient state, by far, is California, and Massachusetts is a distant second. Some states, such as Alaska, had only one year of venture capital funding flows to establishments within the state. The states in the East South Central and West North and South Central Census divisions have the smallest flows of venture capital to establishments located within those states.[14]

Figure 11.3 presents the venture capital flows again by Census Divisions over time. The figure clearly shows the importance of venture funding capital sources in the U.S. economy during the technology bubble years. Again, the large volumes of capital were concentrated in technology, telecommunications, computers and software, health services, medical devices, biotechnology, and media and entertainment, to the exclusion of other BEA industry sectors. Many of the BEA sectors received zero dollars of venture capital funding over the analysis period. As a result, there is considerable cross-sectional heterogeneity in the capital availability across state-level industry-specific BEA codes.

The lower panel of table 11.3 presents summary statistics for the small-business lending across states within Census Regional Divisions. Here again, there is considerable cross-sectional heterogeneity in the supply of small-business loans in denominations of less than $1 million by state. As shown, there are interesting regional differences between the availability of venture

---

13. The data can be found at www.pwcmoneytree.com.
14. There are also important differences within Census Divisions; however, these do not affect our empirical results because all estimation is carried out using geographic units defined by MSAs and states.

TABLE 11.3 Summary Statistics for Capital Investment Flows by States Within Regional Divisions of the U.S. Census, 1995–2005

Census regional division	Mean	Standard deviation	Maximum	Minimum
State venture capital investments ($)				
East North Central	254,493.09	361,225.96	2,373,727.80	9,103.00
East South Central	129,825.67	178,770.27	793,136.70	850.00
Middle Atlantic	912,373.17	1,249,292.37	6,919,846.90	38,569.90
Mountain	228,044.56	502,509.90	4,206,969.30	133.00
New England	707,362.11	1,514,887.88	10,393,776.60	925.00
Pacific	3,391,715.78	7,589,674.88	43,178,931.40	1,496.00
South Atlantic	358,853.50	446,846.52	2,606,526.40	400.00
West North Central	132,246.17	198,977.89	1,035,139.60	209.20
West South Central	132,015.19	177,712.29	793,136.70	1,250.00
Small-business loans of less than $1 million ($)				
East North Central	8,603,189.54	5,011,659.71	24,873,058.00	2,551,146.00
East South Central	4,672,178.23	3,154,748.73	17,909,928.00	1,711,547.00
Middle Atlantic	8,632,522.70	4,700,201.56	18,633,989.00	1,984,959.00
Mountain	1,420,886.32	1,210,910.83	5,779,335.00	159,781.00
New England	1,083,931.17	1,057,895.63	4,749,010.00	62,988.00
Pacific	5,486,570.07	8,924,837.58	36,112,585.00	218,511.00
South Atlantic	4,656,739.33	5,331,567.11	33,888,566.00	71,539.00
West North Central	2,908,940.03	2,906,901.84	17,536,250.00	397,439.00
West South Central	5,431,547.14	5,053,642.57	20,436,290.00	1,220,941.00

NOTE: The upper panel of the table reports the summary statistics for the aggregate venture capital investments from 1995 through 2005 by Census Regional Divisions. The data were obtained from the *MoneyTree Report* (PricewaterhouseCoopers). The lower panel of the table reports the summary statistics for the loans made by Federal Deposit Insurance Corporation–insured commercial banks to small businesses. These are the total dollar amounts of loans made, in denominations of less than $1 million. The data were obtained from commercial bank call reports, as reported by the Small Business Administration, www.sba.gov/advo/research/.

SOURCE: *MoneyTree Report* (PricewaterhouseCoopers), www.pwcmoneytree.com.

capital and small-business lending across states. In contrast to the prior results, the East North Central Census Division of states is the largest recipient of small-business loans, followed by the Pacific and West South Central Divisions. The East and West South Central also received large funding flows, in contrast to the venture capital results. Figure 11.4 presents the time series dynamics of small-business loan investments. Again, the bulge in loans to small businesses in the late 1990s is apparent; however, it is interesting to note that the growth in lending to small businesses appears to have preceded the growth in venture capital investments in these regions.

FIGURE 11.3 Total Venture Capital Investments by Census Regional Divisions, 1995–2006

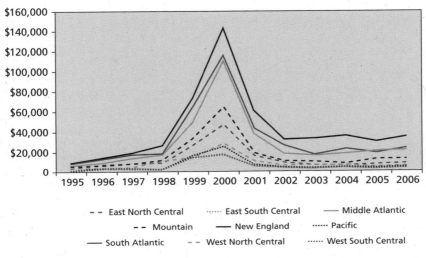

SOURCE: PriceWaterhouseCoopers, *MoneyTree Report*, www.pwcmoneytree.com.

FIGURE 11.4 Total Origination of Small-Business Loans of Less than $1 Million by Census Regional Divisions, 1995–2005

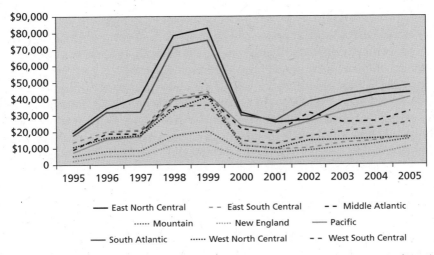

SOURCE: Commercial bank call reports as reported by the Small Business Administration, www.sba.gov/advo/research/.

Together, these graphs suggest that there is an important linkage between small-business loans and venture capital investments, and that in some regions small-business loans may induce subsequent venture capital investments if that capital funding infrastructure exists in a state. Unfortunately, we do not have information on the industry specificity of small-bank lending, so we cannot directly address these timing channels in the following estimation.

EMPIRICAL TESTS FOR MEAN REVERSION IN ESTABLISHMENT DYNAMICS

We first consider whether establishment size affects the creation and destruction rates within BEA sectors, using the Rossi-Hansberg and Wright (2007a) structural specification

$$
\begin{aligned}
\log(Y_{Cj(t)}) = \alpha_{C_j} &+ \gamma_{C_j} \log(X_{j(t)}) \\
&+ \beta_{C_j}(K_{j(t)}/L_{j(t)}) \times \log(X_{j(t)}) + \eta_{Cj(t)},
\end{aligned}
\tag{11.1}
$$

where $Y_{Cj(t)}$ is the log of the establishment creation rate within size categories for the jth industry-specific BEA sector, $Y_{Cj(t)}$ is defined as $(n_{t+1,Cj}/n_{t,Cj})$ where $n_{t,Cj}$ is the number of jobs created in the tth period in BEA sector j, $X_{j(t)}$ is a size measure defined as the average number of jobs within an establishment size category, $(K_{j(t)}/L_{j(t)}) \times log(X_{j(t)})$ is the interaction of the capital-labor ratio in the jth BEA sector at time t and the average number of jobs in an establishment size category in the jth BEA sector at time t, and $\eta_{Cj(t)}$ is a BEA industry-specific residual. Using a seemingly unrelated regression, we jointly estimate a system of 59 BEA sector equations over the period from 1990 through 2005.

Similar to Rossi-Hansberg and Wright (2007a), we focus on the β_{Cj} estimates for the interaction term in equation 11.1 above. The prediction from their structural model is that BEA industries with higher capital-labor ratios will have negative and small coefficient estimates on β_{Cj}'s. Our results for the job creation regressions are reported in table 11.4. As shown, the coefficient estimates on β_{Cj}'s exhibit considerable cross-sectional variability across BEA industry sectors. About 56 percent of the estimated β_{Cj}'s have the anticipated negative sign, but only about 42 percent of those are statistically significantly different from zero at the usual levels. Surprisingly, we also find several sectors that exhibit a positive relationship between size and job creation. The strongest evidence in support of the Rossi-Hansberg and Wright (2007a) prediction—that sectors with factor structures that are characterized by large

TABLE 11.4 Coefficient Estimates from Seemingly Unrelated Regression of the Percentage Change in Job Creation, Between Period $t+1$ and Period t, and the Period t Interaction of the Capital-Labor Ratio and the Natural Log of Average Number of Jobs by Establishment Size, for BEA Industry Classification

BEA label	Average K/L	β_{Cj}	Standard error	BEA label	Average K/L	β_{Cj}	Standard error
Accommodation	4.00	0.091***	0.026	Funds, trusts, other	9.77	-0.001	0.006
Administration, support services	0.41	0.125***	0.031	Furniture, related products	0.68	0.000	0.047
Air transport	5.14	-0.013	0.013	Hospitals, nursing care	2.15	-0.145***	0.049
Ambulatory health care services, health care services	0.98	0.081**	0.035	Information processing	0.59	0.055	0.045
Amusements, gambling	2.80	-0.02	0.014	Insurance carriers, related	1.19	-0.006	0.025
Apparel, leather	0.91	0.011	0.011	Legal services	0.24	0.041	0.341
Broadcasting, telecommunications	7.31	-0.030***	0.007	Machinery	1.71	-0.003	0.008
Chemical products	2.98	0.034	0.019	Management of companies	2.11	-0.039	0.06
Computer systems design	0.49	-0.153***	0.030	Mining (not oil, gas)	6.89	-0.017	0.018
Computers, electronics	1.65	-0.026***	0.008	Mining support	5.07	0.001	0.008
Construction	0.55	0.022	0.063	Miscellaneous manufacturing	1.31	-0.041	0.029
Educational services	2.97	-0.035	0.028	Motor vehicles	1.22	-0.085**	0.036
Electrical equipment, appliances	1.63	-0.140***	0.048	Movies, recording	1.72	0.066	0.038
Fabricated metal	1.54	-0.065**	0.023	Nonmetallic mineral	2.38	0.029	0.027
Federal Reserve, financial intermediation	3.24	0.013	0.011	Oil, gas extraction	31.00	-0.001	0.001
Food services, drinking	1.43	0.071	0.06	Other services	2.14	0.042	0.037
Food, beverage, tobacco	2.69	0.021	0.016	Other transport	2.84	-0.011***	0.004
				Other transport equipment	1.46	-0.026	0.034
				Paper products	3.29	0.027	0.019
				Performing arts, sports	1.84	0.009	0.018

(continued)

TABLE 11.4 (continued)

BEA label	Average K/L	β_{Cj}	Standard error	BEA label	Average K/L	β_{Cj}	Standard error
Petroleum, coal	8.95	−0.018	0.012	Services, miscellaneous	0.48	0.014	0.018
Pipeline transport	16.58	0.001	0.002	Social assistance	0.60	−0.073	0.058
Plastics, rubber	1.71	−0.156**	0.053	Textiles	2.30	0.021	0.024
Primary metals	4.06	0.018	0.018	Transit	3.39	−0.020	0.040
Printing, related	1.22	−0.046	0.035	Truck transport	1.13	−0.018	0.031
Publishing, software	0.77	−0.01	0.041	Utilities	22.24	−0.002	0.004
Railroad transport	15.74	−0.031*	0.018	Warehousing	1.28	−0.130***	0.045
Real estate leasing, sales	8.29	0.000	0.002	Waste management	5.30	−0.002	0.006
Real estate	214.36	−0.001***	0.000	Water transport	11.57	−0.013	0.028
Retail trade	1.68	−0.131***	0.034	Wholesale trade	1.06	−0.163***	0.042
Securities, investments	0.76	0.035	0.031	Wood products	1.56	0.007	0.026

NOTES: The table presents the results of a jointly estimated seemingly unrelated regression for 59 BEA industry categories over 16 years, between 1990 and 2005. The system of equations estimated is the $t + 1^{th}$ and t^{th} period annual percentage change in job growth by establishment size category regressed on an intercept, the tth period value of the natural log of the average number of jobs within each size category in the BEA sector, the tth period lagged interaction of the capital-labor ratio for the BEA sector, and the tth period natural log of the average number of jobs with each size category. We report only the coefficient estimate on the interaction term. In columns two and six of the table, we report the 16-year average capital-labor ratio (K/L) for the BEA sector. BEA = Bureau of Economic Analysis. * = statistically significant at the .10 level; ** = statistically significant at the .05 level; *** = statistically significant at the .01 level.

physical capital shares should exhibit negative scale dependence in job creations—is found for the real estate sector and for other capital-intensive manufacturing sectors such as telecommunications, transportation, and automotive manufacturing. Some BEA sectors generate either ambiguous results, which are due to lack of statistical significance, or in the case of labor-intensive areas sectors, such as Administration and Support Services, there is a reversal of the Rossi-Hansberg and Wright (2007a) prediction and the coefficient estimate on β_{Cj} is found to be statistically significant and positive.

We also test for evidence of size dependence in the job destruction rates within BEA sectors, again following the Rossi-Hansberg and Wright (2007a) specification,

$$
\begin{aligned}
\log(Y_{D_{j(t)}}) = {} & \alpha_{D_j} + \gamma_{D_j} \log(X_{j(t)}) \\
& + \beta_{D_j}(K_{j(t)}/L_{j(t)}) \times \log(X_{j(t)}) + \eta_{D_{j(t)}},
\end{aligned}
\tag{11.2}
$$

where $log(Y_{D_{j(t)}})$ is the log of the job destruction rate for establishment size categories within an industry-specific BEA sector, $Y_{D_{j(t)}}$ is defined as $n_{t+1,Dj}/n_{t,Dj}$ where $n_{t,Dj}$ is the number of jobs destroyed by establishment size in period t in BEA sector j, and $\eta_{D_{j(t)}}$ is a BEA category specific residual. The Rossi-Hansberg and Wright (2007a) long-run structural model emphasizes that the combined effect of mean reversion in stocks of specific factors, such as capital, and a unitary elasticity of substitution leads to a null hypothesis that net exit rates, or rates of job destruction, should decline with establishment size. Similarly, Orr (1974) and MacDonald (1986) find that firms' exit rates are negatively associated with measures of physical capital intensity by industry, although they do not control for the sizes of the firms. This again suggests that the coefficient estimates on the β_{D_j}'s should be negative and smaller for more capital-intensive BEA sectors because larger establishments exhibit lower job destruction rates that are due either to exit or job reductions.

The results from the seemingly unrelated regression of the system of 59 BEA industry sectors from 1990 through 2005 are reported in table 11.5. As shown in the table, we find that, similar to the job creation regression results, about 58 percent of the coefficient estimates are negative, and of those, 47 percent are statistically significant at standard levels. Again, there is considerable heterogeneity across BEA sectors; however, the BEA sectors with the highest physical capital-labor ratios—such as real estate, heavy manufacturing, and broadcasting and telecommunications—exhibit the smallest negative coefficients in keeping with a mean reverting growth dynamic for those

TABLE 11.5 Coefficient Estimates from Seemingly Unrelated Regression of the Percentage Change in Job Destruction, Between Period $t+1$ and Period t, and the Period t Interaction of the Capital-Labor Ratio and the Natural Log of Average Number of Jobs by Establishment Size, for BEA Industry Classification

BEA label	Average K/L	β_{Dj}	Standard error	BEA label	Average K/L	β_{Dj}	Standard error
Accommodation	4.00	−0.047**	0.018	Federal Reserve, financial intermediation	3.24	0.031***	0.011
Administration, support services	0.41	0.022	0.031	Food services, drinking	1.43	−0.147***	0.039
Air transportation	5.14	0.009	0.011	Food, beverage, tobacco	2.69	−0.005	0.013
Ambulatory health care services, health care services	0.98	−0.057*	0.033	Funds, trusts, other	9.77	0.012**	0.006
				Furniture, related products	0.68	0.024	0.046
Amusements, gambling	2.8	0.006	0.012	Hospitals, nursing care	2.15	−0.005	0.039
Apparel, leather	0.91	−0.01	0.008	Information processing	0.59	−0.099**	0.04
Broadcasting, telecommunications	7.31	−0.014**	0.007	Insurance carriers, related	1.19	0.113***	0.025
Chemical products	2.98	−0.014	0.018	Legal services	0.24	−1.290***	0.37
Computer systems design	0.49	−0.114***	0.031	Machinery	1.71	0.002	0.008
Computer, electronics	1.65	0.008	0.006	Management of companies	2.11	−0.209**	0.095
Construction	0.55	0.170**	0.071	Mining (not oil, gas)	6.89	−0.009	0.011
Educational services	2.97	0.026	0.032	Mining support	5.07	−0.004	0.007
Electrical equipment, appliances	1.63	−0.109**	0.05	Miscellaneous manufacturing	1.31	−0.024	0.027
Fabricated metal	1.54	0.019	0.022	Motor vehicles	1.22	−0.105***	0.036
				Movies, recording	1.72	0.011	0.027

Nonmetallic mineral	2.38	−0.003	0.022	Real estate	214.36	−0.0006**	0.000
Oil, gas extraction	31.00	0.001	0.001	Retail trade	1.68	−0.016	0.026
Other services	2.14	−0.419***	0.044	Securities, investments	0.76	−0.150***	0.035
Other transport	2.84	−0.004	0.005	Services, miscellaneous	0.48	0.039**	0.019
Other transport equipment	1.46	0.022	0.031	Social assistance	0.60	−0.045	0.067
Paper products	3.29	−0.024	0.017	Textiles	2.30	0.034*	0.019
Performing arts, sports	1.84	0.005	0.021	Transit	3.39	−0.063**	0.031
Petroleum, coal	8.95	0.01	0.011	Truck transport	1.13	−0.108***	0.034
Pipeline transport	16.58	−0.001	0.002	Utilities	22.24	−0.007	0.004
Plastics, rubber	1.74	0.039	0.046	Warehousing	1.28	−0.061	0.042
Primary metals	4.06	0.011	0.016	Waste management	5.30	0.017**	0.006
Printing, related	1.22	0.044	0.029	Water transport	11.57	0.01	0.033
Publishing, software	0.77	−0.036	0.034	Wholesale trade	1.06	−0.001	0.032
Railroad transport	15.74	−0.014	0.020	Wood products	1.56	0.038	0.030
Real estate leasing, sales	8.29	0.000	0.001				

NOTES: The table presents the results of a jointly estimated seemingly unrelated regression for 59 BEA industry sectors over 16 years, between 1990 and 2005. The system of equations estimated is the $t + 1^{th}$ and t^{th} period annual percentage change in job growth by establishment size category regressed on an intercept, the tth period value of the natural log of the average number of jobs within each size category, the tth period lagged interaction of the capital-labor ratio for the BEA sectors, and the tth period natural log of the average number of jobs with each size category. We report only the coefficient estimate on the interaction term. In columns two and six of the table, we report the 16-year average capital-labor ratio (K/L) for the BEA sector. BEA = Bureau of Economic Analysis.

BEA sectors. Here again, the real estate sector has a relatively small negative coefficient and the coefficients on other capital-intensive manufacturing sectors are also significantly small and negative, a result consistent with the Rossi-Hansberg and Wright (2007a) predictions.

Although many of the BEA sectors appear to follow the Rossi-Hansberg and Wright (2007a) predictions for the relationship between size dynamics and factor input structure, a number of anomalous industries remain, in which the capital-labor ratios do not appear to induce mean reversion in growth rates by establishment sizes. In the next section, we will implement a more flexible random-coefficients model that allows us to exploit the cross-sectional panel nature of our data and to determine the relative effects of the capital-labor ratios and financial capital constraints on the size dynamics of industry job creation and destruction in the United States.

Joint Tests for Physical Capital and Financing Effects

Following the theoretical literature, the key characteristics that distinguish the rate of mean reversion in the growth rates of BEA industrial sectors include the relative intensity of the physical capital (see Rossi-Hansberg and Wright, 2007a) and financial capital market constraints (see Cabral and Mata, 2005; Cooley and Quadrini, 2001). The null hypothesis that we test in this section is that there is no long-run size dependence in job creations or destruction rates for establishments conditioned on survival within each BEA sector. We jointly test whether the intercept, α_{Cj}, and slope coefficients, β_{Cj}, in the job creation regressions are functionally related to the financial flow variables or for the capital-labor ratio within BEA industry sectors. Dropping the time subscripts for notational convenience, we define the intercept, α_{Cj}, in the job creation regression as

$$\hat{\alpha}_{Cj} = \delta_{01} + \delta_{01K}(K/L) + \delta_{01V}V + \delta_{01B}B \tag{11.3}$$

and, similarly, the slope coefficient, β_{Cj}, is defined as

$$\hat{\beta}_{Cj} = \delta_{11} + \delta_{11K}(K/L) + \delta_{11V}V + \delta_{11B}B, \tag{11.4}$$

where K/L is the capital-labor ratio, V is the log of the dollar amount of venture capital investment, and B is the log of the dollar amount of small-business lending.

We also jointly test whether the intercept, α_{Dj}, and the slope coefficient, β_{Dj}, for job destruction rates are functionally related to the financial flow variables and the capital factor intensity of BEA industry-specific sectors. The intercept, α_{Dj}, for the job destruction regression is defined as

$$\hat{\alpha}_{Dj} = \delta_{02} + \delta_{02K}(K/L) + \delta_{02V}V + \delta_{02B}B \tag{11.5}$$

and the slope coefficient, β_{Dj}, for the job destruction regression is defined as

$$\hat{\beta}_{Dj} = \delta_{12} + \delta_{12K}(K/L) + \delta_{12V}V + \delta_{12B}B, \tag{11.6}$$

where, again, K/L is the capital-labor ratio, V is the log of the dollar amount of venture capital investment, and B is the log of the dollar amount of small-business lending.

To estimate the job creation (job destruction) model, we implement a full-information maximum-likelihood version of our estimator using a multi-level random-parameters model and an Expectation-Maximization (EM) algorithm to consistently jointly estimate the full system of parameters for the job creations (job destruction) relationships. We assume that for the jth BEA sector, the job creation (job destruction) regression can be written as (again suppressing the time subscripts for notational convenience)

$$y_j = X_j\gamma_j + \varepsilon_j, \tag{11.7}$$

where

$$\varepsilon_j \sim N(\vec{0}, \sigma_j^2 I_{nj}),$$

and n_j is equal to 21 as we consider 21 average establishment size categories for each of the 59 BEA sectors per year (the panel comprises 11 years of data for 1990 through 2005), σ_j^2 is the error variance associated with the $n_j \times 1$ vector ε_j, γ_j is a 2×2 matrix of coefficients hypothesized to vary randomly across the 59 BEA sectors over each of the 11 years, and X_j is the $n_j \times 2$ matrix of observations consisting of a vector of ones to allow a random-parameter intercept, α_{Cj} and α_{Dj}, for the job creation and job destruction specifications, respectively, and a vector of dimension $n_j \times 1$ of the average of establishment sizes for the jth BEA sector in a given year. The y_j is the $n_j \times 1$ vector of observations on the log rank ordering of establishments of a given size for the jth BEA sector in a given year, and I_{nj} is an $n_j \times n_j$ identity matrix. We are assuming here that the γ_j's for job creation regression are drawn from population distributions with constant means and variances and that the γ_j's for the job destruction regression are also drawn from the populations distributions with constant means and variances.

From the prior discussion of the theoretical literature, the coefficients on establishment size within a BEA sector, γ_j's, should themselves be functions of the financial flow variables for small business and venture capital and for the factor intensity ratio between capital and labor within BEA industry-specific sectors. Let $Z_{j,t-1}$ be a $2 \times L$ block diagonal matrix of these potential constraints on establishment growth rates,

$$
Z_j = \begin{pmatrix} \bar{z}_{j1} & \vec{0} & \vec{0} \\ \vec{0} & \ldots & \vec{0} \\ \vec{0} & \vec{0} & \bar{z}_{jk} \end{pmatrix},
$$

where $\bar{z}_{jk}$ is an ℓ_k-element vector of variables defined as the capital-labor ratio K/L, the level of venture capital V, and the level of small-business lending B. Then the following set of equations determines the random coefficients γ_j:

$$
\gamma_j = Z_j \delta + \omega_j, \tag{11.8}
$$

and

$$
\omega_j \sim N(\vec{0}, \Omega)
$$

for firms $j = 1, \ldots, J$ independently. Where δ is a fixed $L \times 1$ vector of constraints on growth at the establishment level and Ω is a fixed 2×2 disturbance covariance matrix for these effects.[15]

If equation 11.8 is valid, then the firm-level γ_j's are random coefficients drawn from a normal distribution of population parameters centered at $Z_{j,t-1}\delta$. Ordinary least squares (OLS) estimation does not account for the variance component structure, $Var(y_j)$, which is a function of both ε_j and ω_j. Thus, OLS is an inefficient estimator and the standard errors of the estimates would be biased upward (see Hsiao, 1986; Laird and Ware, 1982). In addition, Stein-like estimators have been shown to be a superior method for incorporating prior structural information, again as in equation 11.8 (see Dempster, Rubin, and Tsutakawa, 1981).

Because we're interested in (1) obtaining unbiased and efficient estimates for the γ_j and δ parameters; and (2) drawing population inferences, equation 11.7 is more correctly viewed as a random-coefficients model in which the

---

15. In what follows, we assume that the ε_j and ω_j are uncorrelated. This does not seem unreasonable, given their different origins: the ω_j represent ex ante shocks in aggregate external capital and factor input markets external to the establishments, and the ε_j are ex post shocks to the establishment-level growth decisions.

regression coefficients are assumed to be the dependent variables of another regression such as equation 11.8. Combining these two equations yields a random-coefficients model (general hierarchical model) for each BEA industrial sector, j, as

$$y_j = X_j Z_j \delta + (\varepsilon_j + X_j \omega_j). \tag{11.9}$$

Equation 11.9 is the hierarchical representation of the job creation (job destruction) regression defined by equation 11.1 for job creations and by equation 11.2 for job destructions. The relationship between the constraints and the coefficients on establishment size in the job creation (job destruction) regression can be tested using the estimates of δ. The model also provides estimates of the distribution of the slope coefficient, or the coefficient on the average establishment size, for the job creation (job destruction) regression over the BEA sectors by year, the γ_j's, and their standard errors. Hence, it allows for direct tests of constraints on the growth and exit rates by BEA sectors.

As previously noted, equation 11.9 cannot be estimated by OLS (equivalently, unrestricted maximum likelihood) because the combined error term $(\varepsilon_j + X_j \omega_j)$ is correlated with the independent variables, unless $E\{X_j \omega_j\} = \vec{0}$. The consequence of this correlation is to bias downward the estimates of the variance-covariance matrix of ε_j and ω_j obtained from (unrestricted) maximum-likelihood estimation. We can avoid this bias by using a restricted maximum likelihood (REML) estimator that accounts for the loss in degrees of freedom from estimating δ.

The results for our REML estimates for equation 11.9 for job creation dynamics are reported in the upper panel of table 11.6. The estimated interaction terms for the random intercept, equation 11.3, is reported in the first tier of the table's upper panel. As shown, the overall rate of job creations is negatively related to the capital-labor intensity of BEA sectors, so rates of job creations appear to be more attenuated for more capital-intensive production technologies. Overall, the financial flow variables do not have statistically significant effects on the average job creation rates. We report the results for the random slope coefficient, equation 11.4, in the second tier of table 11.6's upper panel. As shown, larger average-size establishments with higher-capital intensity exhibit lower rates of job creation over the period. This finding suggests that the intensity of the physical factor structure affects growth dynamics within industry sectors, and the effect is in the direction postulated by Rossi-Hansberg and Wright (2007a). This result suggests that we would reject the null hypothesis of the overall scale independence of growth dynamics for capital-intensive production technologies such as those identified in table 11.4.

TABLE 11.6 REML Estimates of the Determinants of the Random-Parameter Estimates for the Intercept and Slope for the Job Creation and Destruction Regressions on Capital-Labor Ratios and the Supply of Capital, 1995–2005

		Job creation estimates	
	Equation (3) coefficients	Coefficient estimates	Standard error
Intercept	δ_{01}	−5.572***	(1.139)
Capital-labor ratio	δ_{01K}	−0.005**	(0.002)
Log of small-business lending	δ_{01B}	−0.066	(0.126)
Log of venture capital flows	δ_{01V}	−0.019	(0.079)
	Equation (4) coefficients	Coefficient estimates	Standard error
Intercept	δ_{11}	0.374	(0.219)
Capital-labor ratio	δ_{11K}	−0.002***	(0.000)
Log of small-business lending	δ_{11B}	−0.023	(0.020)
Log of venture capital flow	δ_{11V}	0.025**	(0.012)
		Job destruction estimates	
	Equation (5) coefficients	Coefficient estimates	Standard error
Intercept	δ_{02}	−8.657***	(1.143)
Capital-labor ratio	δ_{02K}	−0.005***	(0.001)
Log of small-business lending	δ_{02B}	0.139	(0.127)
Log of venture capital flow	δ_{02V}	−0.155**	(0.071)
	Equation (6) coefficients	Coefficient estimates	Standard error
Intercept	δ_{12}	0.417	(0.247)
Capital-labor ratio	δ_{12K}	−0.001***	(0.000)
Log of small-business lending	δ_{12B}	0.015	(0.025)
Log of venture capital flow	δ_{12V}	−0.029	(0.021)

NOTES: The table presents the results for the REML estimates of the random parameters for the job creation and destruction regressions for a panel of 11 years for 59 BEA industries. The job creation regressions include an 11-year panel over 59 BEA industries (the natural log of job growth by establishment size category regressed on the natural log of the average number of jobs within each size sectors), and the job destruction regressions include an 11-year panel over 59 BEA industries (the natural log of the job destruction by establishment size category regressed on the average number of jobs within each size category). The estimated coefficients, by year, for the 59 BEA industries are regressed on the average capital-labor ratio within the BEA industry, a weighted average of the total BEA and state-specific venture capital investments (weights are the proportion of jobs by the BEA industry within a state), and a weighted average of the total dollar value of loans of less than $1 million made by commercial banks within each state (weights are again the proportion of BEA jobs of a given industry within the state). ** = statistically significant at the .05 level; *** = statistically significant at the .01 level.

The log flow of venture capital positively affects the slope coefficient on the average size of establishments and the availability of small bank loans does not have a statistically significant effect. This finding suggests that job creation rates become more sensitive to firm size with access to venture funding. However, our finding that capital intensity and the flow of venture funds differentially affect growth rates over the size distribution of establishments appears to identify a possible causal channel for the mean reversion in growth rates across industry sectors.

The REML estimates for equation 11.9 for job destruction dynamics are reported in the lower panel of table 11.6. In the upper tier of the lower panel, we report the estimated interaction terms for the random intercept, or average job destruction rate (equation 11.5). As shown, the average rate of job destruction is negatively affected by the capital-labor intensity of the BEA sectors, so overall growth is slower in these BEA sectors over the period. In contrast to the job creation results reported in the upper panel of table 11.6, we find that the flow of small-business lending is negatively associated with average job destruction rates over all BEA sectors. The venture capital constraints do not have a statistically significant effect on the rates of job destruction.

We report the estimated slope coefficients for the effect of average establishment size on job destruction rates in the lower tier of the second panel of table 11.6. Again, similar to the results for the job creation regressions, the capital-labor ratio intensity exhibits a strongly negative and statistically significant effect on the estimated coefficient (equation 11.6) on the average size of establishments. As shown, larger average-size establishments with higher capital intensity exhibit lower rates of job destruction over the period. This finding suggests that the intensity of the physical factor structure affects growth dynamics within industry sectors, again in the direction postulated by Rossi-Hansberg and Wright (2007a). This result indicates that we would reject the null hypothesis of the overall scale independence of growth dynamics. The capital flow variables do not have a statistically significant effect on the average size of establishments and job destruction rates. Thus, only the capital factor intensity differentially affects growth rates over the size distribution of establishments.

For each BEA sector for each year (a total of 649 coefficient estimates), we compute the value of the random coefficient for the intercepts and slopes, given the annual levels of the capital-labor ratio for the sector and the annual level of financial flows. We report the summary statistics for these computed random coefficient estimates for the intercept and the slope for the job creation regression in the upper panel of table 11.7. In the upper left quadrant of table 11.7, we report the descriptive statistics for the distribution of the estimated intercept coefficient, $\hat{\alpha}_{Ci}$. As shown, we find that the average rate of

TABLE 11.7   Summary Statistics for the REML Estimates for the Intercept and Slope-Estimated Coefficients for the Job Creation and Destruction Regressions

	Job creation random coefficients estimates	
	Intercept ($\hat{\alpha}_{Cj}$) $\hat{\alpha}_{Cj} = \delta_{01} + \delta_{01K}(K/L) + \delta_{01V}V + \delta_{01B}B$	Slope ($\hat{\beta}_{Cj}$) $\hat{\beta}_{Cj} = \delta_{11} + \delta_{11K}(K/L) + \delta_{11V}V + \delta_{11B}B$
Mean	−6.366	0.151
Standard deviation	1.279	0.258
Kurtosis	−0.549	−0.115
Skewness	0.256	−0.454
Minimum	−9.324	−0.747
Maximum	−2.830	0.721

	Job destruction random coefficients estimates	
	Intercept ($\hat{\alpha}_{Dj}$) $\hat{\alpha}_{Dj} = \delta_{02} + \delta_{02K}(K/L) + \delta_{02V}V + \delta_{02B}B$	Slope ($\hat{\beta}_{Dj}$) $\hat{\beta}_{Dj} = \delta_{12} + \delta_{12K}(K/L) + \delta_{12V}V + \delta_{12B}B$
Mean	−6.519	0.173
Standard deviation	1.284	0.280
Kurtosis	−0.140	−0.118
Skewness	0.103	−0.380
Minimum	−10.471	−0.731
Maximum	−2.386	0.783

NOTE: The table presents the summary statistics for the random coefficient estimates of the intercept and slope for the job creation and destruction regressions for a panel of 11 years for 59 BEA industries. The job creation regression is the natural log of job growth by establishment size category regressed on the natural log of the average number of jobs within each size category. The job destruction regressions, by year, for 59 BEA industries is the natural log of the job destruction by establishment size category regressed on the average number of jobs within each size category.

job creations is negative, as expected given the several episodes of significant decreases in job creation rates that were reported in figure 11.1. The estimated distribution has slight right skewness; however, all the average estimates are negative, as shown in their minimum and maximum values.

In the upper right quadrant of table 11.7, we report the descriptive statistics for the distribution of the slope coefficient, $\hat{\beta}_{Cj}$, on average establishment size. The estimated mean of this distribution is positive. Thus, unconditionally, increases in average establishment sizes are associated with an average 15 percent positive change in job creation rates—a result that would not, on average, be associated with unconditional mean reverting growth rates. Conditional on the capital-labor ratio in a BEA sector, however, the results suggest that larger average establishment sizes in more capital-intensive BEA industries have lower rates of job creations, because the coefficient on establishment size dynamics for these industries would be found in the lower tail of the coefficient distribution. Again, given the results in table 11.6, BEA sectors with lower capital intensity are found in the positive tail of the distribution of the size dynamic coefficients. Again, this result is consistent with the Rossi-Hansberg and Wright (2007a) structural model.

In the lower left quadrant of table 11.7, we report the descriptive statistics for the distribution of the estimated intercept coefficient, $\hat{\alpha}_{Dj}$. Despite the upward trend in job destruction rates that are shown in figure 11.1 over the initial years of the sample, the last four years of the sample period indicate rather sharp decreases in job destruction rates. It is these later trends that appear to drive the negative mean of the intercept distribution. Again, the estimated distribution has very slight right skewness; however, all the average estimates are negative, as shown in their minimum and maximum values.

In the lower right quadrant of table 11.7, we report the descriptive statistics for the distribution of the slope coefficient, $\hat{\beta}_{Dj}$, on average establishment size. The estimated mean of this distribution is positive. Again, this result means that unconditional increases in average establishment sizes are associated with an average 17 percent positive change in job destruction rates—a result that would not, on average, be associated with unconditional mean reverting growth rates. Conditional on the capital-labor ratio in a BEA sector, however, the results suggest that larger average establishment sizes in more capital-intensive BEA industries have lower rates of job destructions, as the coefficient on establishment size dynamics for these industries would be found in the negative tail of the coefficient distribution. Again, given the results in table 11.6, BEA sectors with lower capital intensity are found in the upper tail of the distribution of the size dynamic coefficient for job destruction rates. Again, this result is consistent with the Rossi-Hansberg and Wright (2007a) structural model.

Overall, we interpret the results of the random coefficient estimates to imply that the financial capital flows only modestly influence the relationship between job creation and destruction rates and establishment size dynamics. The availability of bank lending appears to have no statistically significant effect on establishment size and job creations and destructions. Venture capital market flows do have a statistically significant effect on the relationship between establishment size and job creations. The positive sign found for this coefficient suggests that venture capital availability intensifies the advantages of larger establishments.

As discussed above, the intensity of the capital-labor factor structure of BEA industries does appear to have a statistically and economically important effect on the size distribution of job creation and destruction dynamics. Furthermore, the relative stability of the time series of the physical capital factor intensity levels within BEA sectors suggests that factor structure is a fundamental determinant of growth dynamics. Overall, the results suggest important violations of the proportionate growth assumption over the size distribution of establishments for capital-intensive industries, although overall we would accept the null hypothesis that unconditional growth rates appear to be proportional. The physical capital factor intensity of a BEA sector appears to be an important mechanism leading to violations of proportionate job creation and destruction rates by average establishment size. Constraints associated with the availability of capital over the size distribution do not appear to be associated with differential job creation and destruction dynamics. Thus, although both channels appear to have a role, the results on the capital-labor prediction of the Rossi-Hansberg and Wright (2007a) model appear to be supported, whereas the direction of the financial-constraints variable is not consistent with models, such as that of Cooley and Quadrini (2001), that have proposed this mechanism.

SCALE AND THE SIZE DISTRIBUTION OF ESTABLISHMENTS

As already discussed in the section on growth and exit dynamics, recent theoretical work focusing on financial mechanisms—by Albuquerque and Hopenhayn (2004), Cabral and Mata (2005), Clementi and Hopenhayn (2005), Cooley and Quadrini (2001), and the recent paper by Rossi-Hansberg and Wright (2007a), which focuses on the factor scale mechanism—predicts significant cross-sectional differences in the size distribution of establishments across BEA industry sectors. In this section, we test the null hypothesis that the size distribution of total jobs within each BEA sector is Pareto.

Our specification for the Pareto regressions follows the development in Gabaix (1999) and Gabaix et al.(2003). For each BEA industry sector, j, under the null hypothesis that the observed natural log of the total jobs distribution is approximated using a distribution with tails exhibiting the power law decline,

$$P(X_j > s_j) \sim C_j s_j^{-s_j}, C_j, s_j > 0, \tag{11.10}$$

with a tail index $\zeta_j > 0$ where C_j is an absolute constant (see Gabaix, 1999; Gabaix and Ibragimov, 2007); and Gabaix et al., 2003). Assuming a rank ordering over the size of establishments $X_j(1) \geq \ldots \geq X_j(n)$ under the null hypothesis that the distribution satisfies the power law in equation 11.1, we estimate the Pareto exponent ζ_j by running an OLS log-log rank-size regression with $\gamma_j = 0$,

$$\log(t_j - \gamma_j) = \alpha_j - \beta_j \log(X_{j(t)}) + s_j, \tag{11.11}$$

where log is the natural log, t_j is the rank of an establishment greater than a given size in BEA category j, and $X_{j(t)}$ is the establishment's size.[16] Thus, the test for the null that the size distribution of establishments within a BEA sector distributed Pareto is a test that each β_j is one.

The results from estimating the β_j coefficients, the "Pareto exponents," for BEA industry-specific sectors by year are reported in table 11.8. As shown, there is considerable variability in the average values of these coefficients over BEA sector and years. An observed distribution of establishment sizes would be Pareto, if the estimated coefficient, β_j, is found to be equal to one. This finding, of course, implies that growth rates are scale independent. If growth rates depend negatively on size, then the tails of the empirical distribution are thinner than the tails of the Pareto distribution, with coefficient equal to one, and the relationship is concave. Although the related test statistics are not shown, we reject the null hypothesis of $\beta_j = -1$ for all but the BEA sectors for furniture and nonmetallic metals. We thus conclude that, overall, the BEA sectors exhibit a size dependence in the rank ordering of establishments, suggesting that there exists an important channel for mean reversion in growth dynamics.

Joint Tests for Capital Intensity and Financing Effects

We again apply the random-parameters specification developed in the subsection "Joint Tests for Physical Capital and Financing Effects." Our random-parameters specification is again motivated by the Pareto regressions reported in Rossi-Hansberg and Wright (2007a). We define the intercept, α_j, for the random-parameters version of the Pareto regression as

$$\hat{\alpha}_j = \delta_{03} + \delta_{03K}(K/L) + \delta_{03V}V + \delta_{03B}B \tag{11.12}$$

and the slope coefficient, β_j, on the average size of establishments as

---

16. Gabaix and Ibragimov (2007) show that the common assumption that $\gamma_j = 0$ is motivated by the approximate linear relationship $\log(1/N_j) \approx \log(C_j) - \zeta_j \log(X_{j(t)}, t_j = 1, \ldots, n_j$ implied by equation 11.1.

TABLE 11.8 Coefficient Estimates for the Pareto Regressions by BEA Industry Classification by Year, 1990–2005

BEA label	Average K/L	β_i	Standard error	BEA label	Average K/L	β_i	Standard error
Accommodation	4.00	−1.079	0.005	Fabricated metal	1.54	−1.133	0.007
Administration, support services	0.41	−1.432	0.011	Federal Reserve, financial intermediation	3.24	−1.258	0.009
Air transportation	5.14	−0.754	0.003	Food services, drinking	1.43	−1.707	0.017
Ambulatory health care services, health-care services	0.98	−1.893	0.021	Food, beverage, tobacco	2.69	−0.828	0.005
Amusements, gambling	2.80	−1.302	0.008	Funds, trusts, other	9.77	−0.943	0.005
Apparel, leather	0.91	−0.939	0.009	Furniture, related	0.68	−1.005	0.004
Broadcasting, telecommunications	7.31	−0.894	0.007	Hospitals, nursing care	2.15	−0.477	0.004
Chemical products	2.98	−0.686	0.004	Information processing	0.59	−1.132	0.008
Computer systems design	0.49	−1.210	0.013	Insurance carriers, related	1.19	−1.220	0.006
Computers, electronics	1.65	−0.689	0.004	Legal services	0.24	−1.673	0.012
Construction	0.55	−2.423	0.017	Machinery	1.71	−0.886	0.005
Educational services	2.97	−0.774	0.008	Management of comp.	2.11	−0.775	0.010
Electrical equipment, appliances	1.63	−0.669	0.004	Mining (not oil, gas)	6.89	−0.883	0.006
				Mining support	5.07	−1.198	0.006
				Miscellaneous manufacturers	1.31	−1.143	0.006

Industry					Industry			
Motor vehicles	1.22	−0.536	0.003		Real estate leasing, sales	8.29	−1.595	0.008
Movies, recording	1.72	−1.423	0.008		Real estate	214.36	−2.048	0.013
Nonmetallic mineral	2.38	−0.994	0.007		Retail trade	1.68	−1.969	0.018
Oil, gas extraction	31.00	−1.119	0.006		Securities, investments	0.76	−1.090	0.008
Other services	2.14	−2.148	0.018		Services, miscellaneous	0.48	−1.757	0.011
Other transport	2.84	−1.122	0.006		Social assistance	0.60	−1.590	0.012
Other transport equipment	1.46	−0.621	0.003		Textiles	2.30	−0.812	0.006
Paper products	3.29	−0.630	0.005		Transit	3.39	−1.104	0.006
Performing arts, sports	1.84	−1.381	0.009		Truck transport	1.13	−1.526	0.007
Petroleum, coal	8.95	−0.646	0.004		Utilities	22.24	−0.797	0.006
Pipeline transport	16.58	−0.863	0.006		Warehousing	1.28	−1.000	0.005
Plastics, rubber	1.74	−0.796	0.007		Waste management	5.30	−1.357	0.007
Primary metals	4.06	−0.627	0.005		Water transport	11.57	−0.813	0.006
Printing, related	1.22	−1.401	0.007		Wholesale trade	1.06	−1.796	0.010
Publishing, software	0.77	−1.032	0.005		Wood products	1.56	−1.024	0.006
Railroad transport	15.74	−0.631	0.006					

NOTES: The table presents the joint estimates for the Pareto regressions of the size distribution of BEA industry sectors using seemingly unrelated regressions from 1990 through 2005. The dependent variable is the natural log of the probability that an establishment is larger than a given employment size, and the independent variable is the natural log of the average number of jobs in establishments within each size class. K/L = capital-labor ratio.

$$\hat{\beta}_j = \delta_{13} + \delta_{13K}(K/L) + \delta_{13V}V + \delta_{13B}B, \tag{11.13}$$

where K/L is the capital-labor ratio, V is the log of the dollar amount of venture capital investment, and B is the log of the dollar amount of lending to small businesses.

The REML estimates for equation 11.9 for the Pareto regression are shown in table 11.9. In the upper panel of table 11.9, we report the estimated interaction terms for the random intercept (equation 11.12). As shown, neither the capital-to-labor factor intensity nor the financial flow variables is statistically associated with this coefficient. In the lower panel of table 11.9, we report the estimated slope coefficients for the effect of average establishment size category on the rank ordering of establishments. The capital-labor ratio is shown to negatively affect the slope parameter as a function of the average size of establishment size category. This result suggests that BEA industrial sectors with more physical capital intensity do

TABLE 11.9 REML Estimates of the Determinants of the Random-Parameter Estimates for the Intercept and Slope from the Pareto Regressions on Capital-Labor Ratios and the Supply of Capital, 1995–2005

	Equation 11.12 coefficients	Coefficient estimates	Standard error
Intercept	δ_{03}	13.434***	(2.914)
Capital-labor ratio	δ_{03K}	−0.888	(0.101)
Log of small-business lending	δ_{03B}	0.172	(−0.322)
Log of venture capital flows	δ_{03V}	0.01	(0.180)
	Equation 11.13 coefficients	**Coefficient estimates**	**Standard error**
Intercept	δ_{13}	−1.371***	(0.397)
Capital labor ratio	δ_{13K}	−0.079***	(0.014)
Log of small-business lending	δ_{13B}	−0.019	(0.04)
Log of venture capital flows	δ_{13V}	−0.001	(0.024)

NOTES: The table presents the results for the REML estimates of the random parameters for the Pareto regressions for a panel of 11 years for 59 BEA industries. The Pareto regression is the natural log of the probability that an establishment is larger than a given employment size regressed on the natural log of the average number of jobs in establishments within each size class. The estimated coefficients, by year, for the 59 BEA industries are regressed on the average capital-labor ratio within the BEA industry, a weighted average of the total BEA and state-specific venture capital investments (weights are the proportion of jobs by the BEA industry within a state), and a weighted average of the total dollar value of loans of less than $1 million made by commercial banks within each state (weights are again the proportion of BEA jobs of a given industry within the state). *** = statistically significant at the .01 level.

TABLE 11.10 Summary Statistics for the REML Estimates for the Intercept and Slope Coefficients for the Pareto Regressions

	Intercept ($\hat{\alpha}_j$) $\hat{\alpha}_j = \delta_{03} + \delta_{03K} (K\!/\!L) + \delta_{03v} V$ $+ \delta_{03B} B$	Slope ($\hat{\beta}_j$) $\hat{\beta}_j = \delta_{13} + \delta_{13K} (K\!/\!L) + \delta_{13V} V$ $+ \delta_{13B} B$
Mean	14.118	−1.464
Standard deviation	3.338	0.443
Kurtosis	0.331	−0.012
Skewness	0.841	−0.796
Minimum	8.492	−2.797
Maximum	23.787	−0.753

NOTE: The table presents the summary statistics for the random coefficient estimates of the intercept and slope for the Pareto regressions for a panel of 11 years for 59 BEA industries. The Pareto regression, by year, for the 59 BEA industries is the natural log of the probability that an establishment is larger than a given employment size regressed on the natural log of the average number of jobs in establishments within each size class.

not have the unitary slope that would be expected if the size distribution was Pareto. This result suggests that more capital-intensive BEA sectors would be more likely to exhibit mean reverting, rather than proportionate growth rates.

In table 11.10, we report the estimated distributions for the slope coefficient for the Pareto regression from the random coefficient specification. We find the mean slope coefficient of the Pareto regression to be −1.46 with a standard deviation of 0.443. We would accept the null hypothesis of a parameter value of −1.00 for only about 4 percent of the BEA industry sectors. As shown, the distribution of the Pareto slope parameter is quite negatively skewed, and the extreme violations of the Pareto distribution arise in BEA sectors that exhibit higher capital-labor ratios. The slope coefficient is not affected by the financial flows, and this result is, again, more consistent with the Rossi-Hansberg and Wright (2007a) structural model than alternative explanations.

As discussed, the intensity of the capital-labor factor structure of BEA sectors does appear to have a statistically and economically important effect on the size distribution of establishments. Furthermore, the relative stability of the time series of the physical capital factor intensity levels within BEA sectors suggest that factor structure is a fundamental determinant of growth dynamics. Overall, the results suggest important violations of the proportionate growth assumption over the size distribution of establishments.

A REMAINING PUZZLE: THE SCALE INDEPENDENCE OF GEOGRAPHIC AGGREGATES OF BEA SECTORS

Our finding—that the microstructure dynamics of job creation and destruction at the establishment level are characterized by important violations of proportionate growth rates by establishment sizes—appears to be somewhat at odds with the common finding that the growth rates of city populations do not depend on the size of the city. Because our establishment-level data include very detailed geographic indicators, we undertake preliminary tests for scale independence of BEA sector aggregates into their respective geographic location, defined by their urban area or city. The city aggregates are comprised of weighted averages of the factor intensities of the BEA sector and our geographically defined capital flows. Of course, this aggregate exercise may be importantly obscured by potentially confounding effects of agglomeration.[17] Our first measure of cities is the commonly used MSA designation (see Eeckhout, 2004; Gabaix, 1999; Ioannides and Overman, 2003; Krugman, 1996; and Soo, 2005, among others). We have 331 of these centers, and they are defined over large geographic areas that may include a number of distinct city jurisdictions. We also aggregate our establishments into smaller urban jurisdictions using five-digit FIPS codes for counties and cities. We have 3,215 of these FIPS-city/ county units defined as "cities," and they tend to represent a single city or single county.

In table 11.11, we provide a breakdown of the differences between the MSA and FIPS city/county designations. As shown, the San Francisco Bay Area MSA comprises 3,777,498 jobs; however, this "city" includes 10 distinct FIPS urban city/county units. Using the five-digit FIPS designations, we identify 3,215 cities in the NETS Database. The largest FIPS designations in the San Francisco Bay Area is San Mateo County, with 959,464 jobs; the smallest FIPS designation is Napa County, with 64,540 jobs.

We first follow the large existing literature, testing for Zipf's law for cities and whether the geographic aggregates of jobs within cities fit a power law, with an exponent approximately equal to one. As previously discussed, this regularity has been found to be robust over a number of definitions for cities.

---

17. In a preliminary analysis of the possible importance of these effects, we computed the Ellison and Glaser (1997) concentration index at the three-digit SIC level for all establishments in the United States over our sample period. We then computed weighted averages of these agglomeration measures for our 59 BEA sectors. A Pearson's correlation for the average Ellison and Glaser concentration index and the capital-labor ratio for each BEA sector for each year was a very low −.042. Although the two measures do not appear to be highly correlated, we leave an in-depth analysis of the effects of agglomeration on our results to be completed in future work.

TABLE 11.11   MSA and FIPS Geographic Identifiers for San Francisco–Oakland–San Jose

MSA	County/city	City name
7362		San Francisco–Oakland–San Jose, CA
7362		Oakland, CA PMSA
7362	6001	Alameda County
7362	6013	Contra Costa County
7362		San Francisco, CA PMSA
7362	6041	Marin County
7362	6075	San Francisco County
7362	6081	San Mateo County
7362		San Jose, CA PMSA
7362	6085	Santa Clara County
7362		Santa Cruz–Watsonville, CA PMSA
7362	6087	Santa Cruz County
7362		Santa Rosa, CA PMSA
7362	6097	Sonoma County
7362		Vallejo-Fairfield-Napa, CA PMSA
7362	6055	Napa County
7362	6095	Solano County

NOTES: This table reports the Federal Information Processing Standards (FIPS) Codes for Metropolitan Statistical Areas (MSA), state/county codes, and city and county names for the San Francisco–Oakland–San Jose MSA. PMSA = Primary Metropolitan Statistical Area.

Zipf's law is typically verified, following equation 11.9, by regressing the natural log of a city's rank, $log(r)$, on the natural log of city size. Because the city's rank in the empirically observed distribution is given by

$$r = \overline{N} \times \left(\frac{\overline{S}}{S} \right)^{a}, \tag{11.14}$$

where $\overline{N}$ is the number of cities above the truncation point, $\overline{S}$ is the truncation city size, and we set $a = 1$ to satisfy the Pareto distribution. Taking the natural log of equation 11.14 gives us

$$\log (r) = K - a \log (S), \tag{11.15}$$

where $K = \log(\overline{N}) + a \log(\overline{S})$ is the intercept in the regression. The estimated value of the parameter a in equation 11.15 has been shown to be extremely sensitive to the city size that is chosen as the truncation point (see Eeckhout, 2004; Gabaix, 1999; and Gabaix and Ioannides, 2004). Eeckhout (2004) proves that if the true underlying distribution is lognormal, then the estimated parameter, $\hat{a}$, of the Pareto distribution is increasing in the truncated city size, $(d\hat{a}/d\hat{S}) > 0$, and decreasing in the truncated sample population, $d\hat{a}/d\overline{N} < 0$. We report tests for this theoretical prediction in table 11.12, using our two definitions of cities. In the upper panel of the table, we use our MSA definition of establishment aggregates and test whether the size distribution of BEA sector jobs in cities is inversely related to the rank of cities by numbers of jobs. We find that the estimates for $\hat{a}$ systematically deviate from one as we truncate the sample at smaller and smaller MSAs. We find exactly the same results with even more important reductions in the estimated value of $\hat{a}$ when we use the larger sample of FIPS-city/county designations.

Overall, the results reported in table 11.12 are consistent with the proposition of Eeckhout (2004) that the job size distribution of cities is consistent with a lognormal distribution. These results also suggest that the evolution of the size distribution of jobs within cities is likely to satisfy Gibrat's proposition concerning proportionate growth of jobs over the size distribution of cities. Thus, the aggregate effect of mean reversion dynamics leads to a steady-state long-run-growth urban dynamic that is proportionate.

To further consider the validity of this finding, we test whether the constraints identified in the micro-dynamics of establishment job creation and destruction also affect city-level size dynamics. As we can only measure factor intensity and capital market constraints at the MSA level, we carry out our tests using the MSA-defined cities. We estimate a version of equation 11.15 in which we pool the data by time and include time series dummies for each year. The $\hat{a}$ estimates for the four pooled regressions by the four $\overline{S}$ cutoffs match the estimates in table 11.11 to within the third decimal place. We then collect the residuals from these regressions and run them on the constraints identified in the BEA analyses using establishment-level data.

The findings reported in table 11.13, again show that there is structure to the Pareto regression residuals. The statistically significant coefficients for the factor intensity measure indicate that higher capital-labor ratios are associated with larger errors from the Pareto distribution for all but the lowest truncation cutoff. In contrast, we find only modest evidence that the deviations from the Pareto linear regressions are economically and statistically associated with the financial capital constraints. As reported in the bottom panel of table 11.13, we find that at the smallest truncation cutoff for the distribution of cities, there is evidence that the deviations from the Pareto linear regression are associated with venture capital flows and that higher capital flows are associated with larger residuals. Overall, these results suggest that the long-run physical capital intensities of industries induce nonproportionate job growth in larger cities in the United States, whereas growth appears to be proportionate for the full

TABLE 11.12 Pareto Coefficient Regressions for the Size Distribution of Cities

$\overline{N}$	$\overline{S}$	City/county	Year	K (Standard error)	$\hat{a}$ (Standard error) (GI S.E.)	R-squared value
MSA						
135	190,000	Huntsville, AL	1990	18.035 (0.232)	1.07 (0.018)(0.130)	.966
			2005	17.95 (0.235)	1.062 (0.019)(0.129)	.966
182	127,368	Dutchess County, NY	1990	17.037 (0.170)	1.002 (0.014)(0.106)	.967
			2005	17.184 (0.183)	1.006 (0.015)(0.087)	.966
235	83,815	La Crosse, WI	1990	16.293 (0.142)	0.942 (0.011)(0.087)	.967
			2005	16.419 (0.145)	0.949 (0.011)(0.088)	.967
335	27,299	Enid, OH	1990	14.807 (0.117)	0.832 (0.0097)(0.064)	.956
			2005	15.073 (0.118)	0.846 (0.0096)(0.065)	.956
FIPS city/county						
500	47,918	Fayette City, PA	1990	17.751 (0.131)	1.067 (0.011)(0.067)	.918
			2005	18.304 (0.150)	1.104 (0.113)(0.070)	.950
1,000	17,869	Tioga City, NY	1990	16.088 (0.064)	0.931 (0.005)(0.0411)	.959
			2005	16.375 (0.069)	0.946 (0.006)(0.042)	.959
2,000	5,342	Currituck City, NC	1990	14.667 (0.034)	.807 (0.003)(0.026)	.965
			2005	14.795 (0.037)	.809 (0.003)(0.026)	.962
3,215	90	North Providence, RI	1990	12.180 (0.036)	0.564 (0.003)(0.014)	.866
			2005	12.235 (0.032)	0.563 (0.037)(0.014)	.866

NOTES: The table presents the slope and intercept coefficient estimates for the Pareto regressions of the rank-size rule, using various truncation points for the sample of cities. GI S.E. = the Gabaix and Ioannides (2004) Standard Error, $\hat{a}(2/N)^{.5}$; MSA = metropolitan statistical area; FIPS = Federal Information Processing Standards.

TABLE 11.13 Residual Diagnostics on the Pareto Regressions for the Size Distribution of Cities

Variable	Parameter estimate	Standard error	R-squared value
Truncation cutoff = 182			
Intercept	−0.248***	(0.141)	0.004
Log of capital-labor ratio	0.106***	(0.034)	
Log of small-business lending	0.009	(0.013)	
Log of venture capital flow	−0.001	(0.004)	
Truncation cutoff = 182			
Intercept	−3.02***	(0.115)	0.004
Log of capital-labor ratio	0.081***	(0.027)	
Log of small-business lending	0.017	(0.011)	
Log of venture capital flow	0.002	(0.003)	
Truncation cutoff = 235			
Intercept	−0.229**	(0.099)	0.002
Log of capital-labor ratio	0.052**	(0.023)	
Log of small-business lending	0.011	(0.009)	
Log of venture capital flow	0.004	(0.003)	
Truncation cutoff = 334			
Intercept	−0.184	(0.097)	0.002
Log of capital labor ratio	0.03	(0.022)	
Log of small-business lending	0.006	(0.009)	
Log of venture capital flow	0.007**	(0.003)	

NOTES: The table presents regressions of the residual from the Pareto regressions report in table 11.11 on the natural log of the capital-labor ratio, the natural log of small-business lending, and venture capital flows at the city level. ** = statistically significant at the .05 level; *** = statistically significant at the .01 level.

distribution of cities. This result may reflect the unconditional positive coefficients of the average establishment size effects on job creations and destructions that were found in the random-parameters results reported in the section "Scale and the Size Distribution of Establishments." Unconditionally, these results also suggest proportionate growth dynamics that are potentially consistent with the aggregate results. Nevertheless, a clear explanation for aggregate proportionate growth finding remains an outstanding puzzle for future work.

CONCLUSIONS

This chapter has reexamined the dynamics of job creation and destruction in relation to the size of establishments and provided tests for whether establishment size is related to growth rates. The chapter extends prior work by empirically testing for the characteristics of employment growth at the establishment or micro level, and then aggregating the establishment-level employment data into the urban locations of these establishments. Our aggregation strategy allows for tests of the aggregate city-level distributions of employment and job growth dynamics that are consistent with the establishment-level analyses. At both the micro and city level, we jointly test for two potentially related mechanisms that could, on their own, introduce mean reversion in growth and size relationships in the aggregate economy. We implement our tests using a consistent multilevel random effects empirical specification that allows us to fully exploit both the time series and cross-sectional richness of our unique data set. Our results suggest that the industry-specific capital-labor ratios, a proxy for diminishing returns, lead to statistically significant levels of mean reversion in growth rates by establishment sizes at the microestablishment level and at least potentially for city aggregates of BEA sectors. Given our measures of financial capital market flows, we find that financial capital market constraints have a modest effect on size dynamics at the micro level and are statistically unimportant at the aggregate level in other than the smallest cities.

APPENDIX

TABLE 11A.1   BEA Industry Sectors

BEA sector	NAICS	BEA sector	NAICS
Accommodation	721	Fabricated metal manufacturing	332
Administration, support services	5412–5415	Federal Reserve banks, credit	
Air transportation	481	intermediation	521, 522
Ambulatory health care services	621	Food services, drinking	
Amusements, gambling, and		establishments	722
recreation	713	Food, beverage, tobacco	311, 312
Apparel and leather manufacturing	315, 316	Funds, trusts, and other financial	525
Broadcasting and tele-		Furniture and related products	
communications	513	manufacturing	337
Chemical products manufacturing	325	Hospitals, nursing and residential	
Computer systems design	5415	care	622, 623
Computer, electronics		Information and data processing	514
manufacturing	334	Insurance carriers and related	
Construction	23	activities	524
Educational services	61	Legal services	5411
Electrical equipment, appliances		Machinery manufacturing	333
manufacturing	335	Management of companies	55

(continued)

TABLE 11A.1 *(continued)*

BEA sector	NAICS	BEA sector	NAICS
Mining except oil and gas	212	Railroad transportation	482
Mining support	213	Real estate	531, 532
Miscellaneous manufacturing	339	Rental and leasing services	533
Motor vehicles, bodies, trailers	3361–3363	Retail trade	44, 45
Movies and recording	512	Securities, commodities, and	
Nonmetallic mineral	327	investments	523
Oil and gas extraction	211	Services, miscellaneous	5416–5419
Other services	487, 488, 492	Social assistance	624
Other transport	3369	Textiles	313, 314
Other transportation equipment	3364–3366	Transit and ground passenger	485
Paper products	322	Truck transportation	484
Performing arts and sports	711–712	Utilities	22
Petroleum and coal	324	Warehousing and storage	493
Pipeline transportation	486	Waste management and	
Plastics and rubber	326	remediation	561, 562
Primary metals manufacturing	331	Water transportation	483
Printing and related	323	Wholesale trade	42
Publishing and software	511	Wood products manufacturing	321

NOTES: The table presents the 59 BEA industry sectors that are used in all the regressions and the corresponding NAICS classification for each BEA sector. BEA = Bureau of Economic Analysis; NAICS = North American Industry Classification System.

SOURCE: National Income and Product Accounts, Bureau of Economic Analysis.

REFERENCES

Albuquerque, Rui, and Hugo A. Hopenhayn. 2004. "Optimal Lending Contracts and Firm Dynamics." *The Review of Economic Studies* 71: 285–315.

Brakman, Steven, Harry Garretsen, Charles V. Marrewijk, and Marianne V. Berg. 1999. "The Return of Zipf: Towards a Further Understanding of the Rank-Size Distribution." *Journal of Regional Science* 39: 183–213.

Cabral, Luís M. B., and José Mata. 2005. "On the Evolution of the Firm Size Distribution: Facts and Theory." *American Economic Review* 93: 1075–1090.

Clementi, Gian Luca, and Hugo A. Hopenhayn. 2005. "A Theory of Financing Constraints and Firm Dynamics." *The Quarterly Journal of Economics* 121: 229–265.

Cooley, Thomas F., and Vincenzo Quadrini. 2001. "Financial Markets and Firm Dynamics." *American Economic Review* 91: 1286–1310.

Dempster, Arthur P., Donald B. Rubin, and Robert K. Tsutakawa. 1981. "Estimation in Covariance Components Models." *Journal of the American Statistical Association* 76: 341–353.

Dobkins, Linda H., and Yannis M. Ioannides. 2000. "Dynamic Evolution of the U.S. City Size Distribution." In Jean-Marie Huriot and Jacques-François Thisse, eds., *The Economics of Cities*, 417–427. Cambridge: Cambridge University Press.

Dumais, Guy, Glen Ellison, and Edward L. Glaeser. 2002. "Geographic Concentration as a Dynamic Process." *The Review of Economics and Statistics* 84: 193–204.

Dunne, Timothy, Mark J. Roberts, and Larry Samuelson. 1989. "The Growth and Failures of U.S. Manufacturing Plants." *The Quarterly Journal of Economics* 104: 671–698.

Eaton, Jonathan, and Zvi Eckstein. 1997. "Cities and Growth: Theory and Evidence from France and Japan." *Regional Science and Urban Economics* 27: 443–474.

Eeckhout, Jan. 2004. "Gibrat's Law for (All) Cities." *The American Economic Review* 94: 1429–1451.

Ellison, Glen, and Edward L. Glaeser. 1997. "Geographic Concentration in U.S. Manufacturing Industries: A Dartboard Approach." *Journal of Political Economy* 105: 311–316.

Evans, David S. 1987. "Tests of Alternative Theories of Firm Growth." *The Journal of Political Economy* 95: 657–674.

Gabaix, Xavier. 1999. "Zipf's Law for Cities: An Explanation." *The Quarterly Journal of Economics* 114: 739–767.

Gabaix, Xavier, Parameswaran Gopikrishnan, Vasiliki Plerou, and H. Eugene Stanley. 2003. "A Theory of Power-Law Distributions in Financial Markets." *Nature* 423: 267–270.

Gabaix, Xavier, and Rustam Ibragimov. 2007. "Rank-1/2: A Simple Way to Improve the OLS Estimation of Tail Exponents." Working Paper, Department of Economics, Harvard University.

Gabaix, Xavier, and Yannis M. Ioannides. 2004. "The Evolution of City Size Distributions." In V. Henderson and J. Thisse, eds., *Handbook of Regional and Urban Economics*, vol. 4, 2341–2378. Amsterdam: North-Holland.

Garicano, Luis, and Esteban Rossi-Hansberg. 2004. "Inequality and the Organization of Knowledge." *American Economic Review* 94: 1974–2002.

Gibrat, Robert. 1931. *Les inégalités économiques: Applications: Aux inégalités des richesses, à la concentration des entreprises, aux populations des villes, aux statistiques des familles, etc., d'une loi nouvelle, la loi de l'effet proportionnel.* Paris: Librairie du Recueil Sirey.

Glaeser, Edward L., Hedi D. Kallal, Jose A. Scheinkman, and Andrei Shleifer. 1992. "Growth in Cities." *Journal of Political Economy* 100: 1126–1152.

Glaeser, Edward L., Jose A. Scheinkman, and Andrei Shleifer. 1995. "Economic Growth in a Cross-Section of Cities." *Journal of Monetary Economics* 36: 117–143.

Hall, Bronwyn. 1987. "The Relationship Between Firm Size and Firm Growth in the U.S. Manufacturing Sector." *Journal of Industrial Economics* 35: 583–606.

Henderson, Boyan. 1982. "Selection and Evolution of Industry." *Econometrica* 50: 649–670.

Henderson, J. Vernon, A. Kuncoro, and M. Turner. 1995. "Industrial Development of Cities." *Journal of Political Economy* 103: 1067–1090.

Hsiao, Cheng. 1986. *Analysis of Panel Data*. Cambridge: Cambridge University Press.

Ioannides, Yannis M., and Henry G. Overman. 2003. "Zipf's Law for Cities." *Regional Science and Urban Economics* 33: 127–137.

Kalecki, Michael. 1945. "On the Gibrat Distribution." *Econometrica* 13: 161–170.

Kapteyn, Jacobus. 1903. "Skew Frequency Curves in Biology and Statistics." Astronomical Laboratory technical report. Groningen: Noordhoff.

Krugman, Paul. 1996. "Confronting the Mystery of Urban Hierarchy." *Journal of the Japanese and International Economies* 10: 399–418.

Laird, Nan M., and John H. Ware. 1982. "Random Effects Models for Longitudinal Data." *Biometrics* 38: 963–974.

Lucas, Robert E. 1967. "Adjustment Costs and the Theory of Supply." *Journal of Political Economy* 75: 321–334.

———. 1978. "On the Size Distribution of Business Firms." *Bell Journal of Economics* 9: 508–523.

MacDonald, James M. 1986. "Entry and Exit on the Competitive Fringe." *Southern Economic Journal* 52: 640–652.

Orr, Dale 1974. "The Determinants of Entry: A Study of the Canadian Manufacturing Industries." *Review of Economics and Statistics* 56: 58–66.

Overman, Henry G., and Yannis M. Ioannides. 2001. "Cross-Sectional Evolution of the U.S. City Size Distribution." *Journal of Urban Economics* 33: 543–566.

Reed, William J. 2001. "The Pareto, Zipf and Other Power Laws." *Economics Letters* 74: 15–19.

Rosen, Kenneth, and M. Resnick. 1980. "The Size Distribution of Cities: An Examination of the Pareto Law and Primacy." *Journal of Urban Economics* 8: 165–186.

Rossi-Hansberg, Esteban, and Mark L. J. Wright. 2007a. "Establishment Size Dynamics in the Aggregate Economy." *American Economic Review* 97: 1639–1666.

———. 2007b. "Urban Structure and Growth." *Review of Economic Studies* 74: 597–624.

Soo, Kwok Tong. 2005. "Zipf's Law for Cities: A Cross Country Investigation." *Regional Science and Urban Economics* 35: 239–263.

Sutton, John. 1997. "Gibrat's Legacy." *Journal of Economic Literature* 35: 40–59.

Zipf, George K. 1949. *Human Behavior and the Principle of Least Effort*. Cambridge, MA: Addison-Wesley.

Postscript: What's Better than Beating the Yankees?

David Warsh

The inspiring teacher is a well-recognized figure in education, celebrated in fiction from *Goodbye Mr. Chips* to the recently released film *The Great Debaters*, in which a professor motivates students at all-black Wiley College to form a debate team that eventually goes all the way from east Texas to challenge Harvard for the national championship in 1935.

Yet, specialization is relentless, even in education. Especially in research universities, the razor-like maxim often holds: Those who can, do; those who can't, teach.

In recent years, however, the value of stellar educators has become so obvious that, even in big research universities, departments of chemistry, physics, biology, and economics have begun offering tenure to the occasional gifted PhD holder who, over the course of a long career, is expected to concentrate mainly on teaching undergraduates— no commitment to produce cutting-edge research required.

That most certainly was not the situation in the fall of 1971 when Karl "Chip" Case turned up at Harvard. That he turned up at all owed mainly to Harry Landreth, his professor at Miami University in Ohio, for whom Case had taught classes as a senior. Landreth, himself a Harvard PhD, complained to his friend Henry Rosovsky that Case's application had been rejected. Rosovsky, the incoming chairman, arranged a second letter.

Certainly, Case was not a typical graduate student in that year of winding down the war in Viet Nam. He was married, for one thing. He was a passionate outdoorsman. He was not particularly mathematical. And he was just back from a year as an Army lieutenant in Quang Tri, with a colorful vocabulary to show for it.

Yet he was in love with economics; ready to take the math-for-dummies course necessary to form at least a speaking acquaintance with linear algebra and transcendental logarithmic production functions; able to form strong bonds with key older members of the faculty, Richard Musgrave and John Kain in particular; and willing to serve as a source of levity and relief to his fellow students in a department preoccupied with turning itself around.

Case served as head teaching fellow from 1972 until 1976, taught dozens of bright undergraduates (one section demanded that he attend their class's twenty-fifth reunion), then took a job teaching at Wellesley College—a first-rate college 10 miles from two great universities. He would be a ranking, but still-not-quite-first-class, citizen in the capital city of the Republic of Economics.

Before long, it was obvious that he was a master teacher. Wellesley students who were headed for business school thronged to his class. More than a few changed their minds about business school and went to economics departments instead. No fewer than 80 Wellesley women have obtained PhDs in economics in the 30 years since Case began teaching there. Virtually all credit him with having played some part in the process.

Still, he managed to keep a hand in research. As a graduate student, he did fieldwork on the landmark 1975 study *Housing Markets and Racial Discrimination,* by Kain and John Quigley, now of the University of California at Berkeley. This crystallized his lifelong interest in residential real estate markets. Once established at Wellesley, Case signed on as a researcher in regional economics at the Federal Reserve Bank of Boston.

Then, in the 1980s, with Ray Fair of Yale University, he coauthored an introductory economics textbook, *Principles of Economics,* that not only succeeded commercially, but also produced some key changes in the way economics today is taught to college students—microeconomics first, instead of business cycles. (About to appear in its ninth edition, with Sharon Oster as coauthor, *Principles of Economics* is the sixth or seventh most frequently adopted today among all principles texts.)

But it was at the Federal Reserve Bank of Boston that Case struck it rich, first intellectually, then financially. Quigley had remarked to him, probably during a session one evening in the inflationary 1970s, that "the only thing stupider than not owning a house is not owning two houses" (whereupon Case and his wife bought a house in Wellesley). Not until 1986 was the depth of that wisdom borne in on him—when the value of their house went up 40 percent in a single year.

Case checked real estate prices in a dozen cities around the country, looking for similar appreciation in other markets. He found none. He wrote up his findings in an article for the Boston Fed's *New England Economic Review.* Faced with no satisfactory explanation of why prices should be going up so rapidly in Boston but not elsewhere, he ventured that perhaps Boston was caught in the midst of that will-'o-the-wisp, a speculative bubble.

Case did not have much solid evidence to go on; he had even less theory. He asked his macro coauthor, Fair, to recommend an expert on bubbles: look no further than Robert Shiller, across the hall at Yale, Fair replied. Case's wife, Susan, a guidance counselor at suburban Stoneham High School, produced a summer research assistant, Maura Doyle.

What was needed, Case and Shiller agreed, was a proper index of home prices: not the usual jumble of transaction prices, of houses with wings added and sills deteriorating, but of well-maintained yet unmodified single-family homes changing hands regularly over long periods. It was a tall order, but not an impossible one. Doyle spent the summer in deeds offices in six cities and towns around the state. When she was done, the professors had something worth having—the clearest picture ever developed of what a theorist would want to know about developments in a single market.

Another summer of collecting similar prices, in other cities around the country, and Case and Shiller published a paper, "The Efficiency of the Market for Single-Family Homes," in the March 1989 issue of *American Economic Review*. Doyle was on her way, first to Mount Holyoke, then to a Massachusetts Institute of Technology PhD (she is now a lecturer at Dartmouth College). Eventually the paper would become famous, at least in certain circles, as evidence that even the housing market was prone to the kinds of mood swings that seemed to routinely afflict the markets for stocks and bonds. The reason that macroeconomists are interested in such matters should be amply clear in the winter of 2007–2008!

But Case and Shiller did not stop there. If indeed one region of the country could swing up while another swung down, then there were risks to home owning that a prudent investor, especially one who thought he or she might someday move, could hope to hedge against—but only if there were an actual market for such risks. The partners now enlisted a Shiller student, Allan Weiss, and formed a company to create the kinds of dependable indices of home prices in cities around the country on which trading of index-based futures and options could be based. Each put up a few thousand dollars at the beginning. A decade later, when the company had become the market leader in residential housing data and valuation, they would sell it for many millions.

Yet all the while, Case was teaching, driving for hours to attend team games and matches, housing a long succession of "host daughters" from countries around the world (and teaching for short stints in as many of those countries as he could), and becoming a full-fledged Wellesley legend. His wife, who had moved to Milton Academy to serve as college counselor, added a new stream of students. Case began filling in teaching introductory economics at Harvard Law School. His businessman father caught the final lecture one year, and, after the standing ovation at the end of the hour, came to terms with his son's choice of a teaching career.

Throughout, Case invested wisely, speculated even more wisely in fancy wine, drank some of it with friends along the way, and went to as many Boston Red Sox games as possible. In the throes of discussing, recently, the fine points of the route to the 2004 World Series, he punched icons on a personal computer in order to blare out *The Impossible Dream*. Once, in the grandstand, with the Sox up 8–3 over the Yankees, he asked his friend and one-time professor, H. James Brown, "What's better than beating the Yankees?" He paused for effect and then answered, "Nothing!"

In 2007, the Lincoln Institute of Land Policy hosted a two-day meeting in Cambridge to produce a conference volume in honor of Case, now 61. Big names presided, among them Quigley of Berkeley and Edward Glaeser and Dale Jorgenson of Harvard. Dozens of friends and former students turned up. Buzz about the subprime crisis filled the breaks.

The final dinner was a particularly warm occasion. Sharon Oster, Ray Fair, and Robert Shiller spoke. Hermann "Dutch" Leonard sang. Edward Lazear, chairman of the Council of Economic Advisers, spoke. Austan Goolsbee recalled Case's practical jokes. At the end of the long evening, Case returned it all in kind. He did not mention the slowly advancing Parkinson's disease that had dogged him for 17 years. "I'm not going anywhere," he told the audience.

For all the pleasure of the evening, the real climax of the conference had come earlier in the day, when Case's friend Jim Brown (who for many years had been the Lincoln Institute's president) brought the final session to its feet when he sought to convey the character of his friend with some lines from Walt Whitman's *Leaves of Grass*:

> I am of old and young, of the foolish as much as the wise;
> Regardless of others, ever regardful of others,
> Maternal as well as paternal, a child as well as a man,
> Stuff'd with the stuff that is coarse,
> and stuff'd with the stuff that is fine,
>
> . . . .
>
> A learner with the simplest, a teacher of the thoughtfullest;
> A novice beginning, yet experient of myriads of seasons;
> Of every hue and caste am I, of every rank and religion,
> A farmer, mechanic, artist, gentleman, sailor, quaker
> A prisoner, fancy-man, rowdy, lawyer, physician, priest.
>
> I resist anything better than my own diversity
> I breathe the air, but leave plenty after me,
> And am not stuck up, and am in my place.

What's better than beating the Yankees? Maybe that.

Publications by Karl E. Case (1976–2000)

Books

Blackburn, Anthony J., and Karl E. Case. 1985. *FairModel Student Manual: An Economic Laboratory in Theory, Policy, and Forecasting*. Englewood Cliffs, NJ: Prentice-Hall.

Case, Karl E. 1978. *Property Taxation: The Need for Reform*. Cambridge, MA: Ballinger Publishing Company.

———. 1986. *Economics and Tax Policy*. Boston: Oelgeschlager, Gunn and Hain Publishers.

Case, Karl E., and Ray C. Fair. 1989. *Principles of Economics*. Englewood Cliffs, NJ: Prentice-Hall.

Marantz, Janet K., Karl E. Case II, and Herman B. Leonard. 1976. *Discrimination in Rural Housing Markets*. Lexington, MA: Lexington Books.

Articles and Book Chapters

Bradbury, Katherine, Karl E. Case, and Christopher Mayer. 1998. "Chasing Good Schools in Massachusetts." *Regional Review* 8(3): 25–26.

———. 1998. "School Quality and Massachusetts Enrollment Shifts in the Context of Tax Limitations." *New England Economic Review* (July/August): 3–20.

———. 2001. "Property Tax Limits, Local Fiscal Behavior, and Property Values: Evidence from Massachusetts Under Proposition 2 1/2." *Journal of Public Economics* 80(2) (May): 287–311.

Bradbury, Katherine L., Karl E. Case, and Constance R. Dunham. 1989. "Geographic Patterns of Mortgage Lending in Boston, 1982–1987." *New England Economic Review* (September/October): 3–30.

Case, Karl E. 1986. "The Market for Single-Family Homes in Boston, 1979–1985." *New England Economic Review* (May/June): 38–48.

———. 1988. "Observations on the Use of Textbooks in the Teaching of Principles of Economics." *Journal of Economic Education* 19(2) (Spring): 165–168.

———. 1989. "Comments on the Asset Approach to Pricing Urban Land: Empirical Evidence." *Journal of the American Real Estate and Urban Economics Association* 17(2) (Summer): 175–176.

———. 1990. "Principles, Politics, and Budgets." *Journal of Student Financial Aid* 20(2) (Spring): 35–36.

———. 1990. "Regional Economic Cycles: The Massachusetts Downturn in Perspective." In *Bank Regulation, Real Estate and the Massachusetts Economy*. Boston: Massachusetts Bankers Association, May.

———. 1991. "Investors, Developers and Supply-Side Subsidies: How Much Is Enough?" *Housing Policy Debate* 2(2) (April): 341–356.

———. 1991. "The Real Estate Cycle and the Regional Economy: The Consequences of the Massachusetts Boom of 1984–1987." *New England Economic Review* (September/October): 37–46. Revised version in *Urban Studies* 29(2) (Spring 1992): 171–183. Second revision published in French in *Financiere et Economie*, 1994.

———. 1992. "How the Commercial Real Estate Boom Undid the Banks." In Lynn E. Brown and Eric S. Rosengren, eds., *Real Estate and the Credit Crunch*, 57–113. Boston: Federal Reserve Bank of Boston, Conference Series #36, September.

———. 1992. "Taxes and Speculative Behavior in Land and Real Estate Markets." *Review of Urban and Regional Development Studies* 4(2): 226–239. Reprinted in *Research in Urban Economics* 9 (1994): 225–239.

———. 1994. "A Decade of Boom and Bust in the Prices of Single-Family Homes: Boston and Los Angeles: 1983–1993." *New England Economic Review* (March/April): 40–52.

———. 1994. "Housing and Land Prices in the United States: 1950–1990." In Yukio Noguchi and James Poterba, eds., *The Economics of Housing in the United States and Japan*. Chicago: University of Chicago Press.

———. 1997. "Volatility, Speculation and the Efficiency of Land Markets." In H. James Brown, ed., *Land Use and Taxation*. Cambridge, MA: Lincoln Institute of Land Policy.

———. 2000. "Real Estate and the Macroeconomy." *Brookings Papers on Economic Activity* 2: 119–162.

———. 2002. "Reconsidering Critical Concepts in Micro Principles." *American Economic Review* 92(2) (May): 454–458.

———. 2007. "The Value of Land in the United States: 1975–2005." In Gregory K. Ingram and Yo-Hung Hong, eds., *Urban Economics and Public Finance*. Cambridge, MA: Lincoln Institute of Land Policy.

Case, Karl E., and Brock Blomberg. 1997. "The Effect of Economic Events on Votes for President: A State by State Analysis." *Advances in International Macroeconomic Theory* 3 (Winter).

Case, Karl E., and Leah Cook. 1989. "The Distributional Effects of Housing Price Booms: Winners and Losers in Boston, 1980–89." *New England Economic Review* (March/April): 3–12.

Case, Karl E., and James Grant. 1991. "Property Tax Incidence in a Multijurisdictional Neoclassical Model." *Public Finance Quarterly* 19(4) (October): 379–392.

Case, Karl E., and Maryna Marynchenko. 2002. "Home Appreciation in Low and Moderate Income Markets." In Nicolas P. Retsinas and Eric S. Belsky, eds., *Low-Income Homeownership: Examining the Unexamined Goal*, 239–256. Washington, DC: Brookings Institution Press.

——. 2002. "Home Price Appreciation in Low and Moderate Income Markets." *Communities and Banking*, Federal Reserve Bank of Boston (Spring): 8–12.

Case, Karl E., and Christopher Mayer. 1995. "The Housing Cycle in the Boston Metropolitan Area: Variations Among Cities and Towns." *New England Economic Review* (March/April): 24–40.

——. 1996. "Housing Price Dynamics Within a Metropolitan Area." *Regional Science and Urban Economics* 26: 387–407.

Case, Karl E., and John M. Quigley. 2008. "How Housing Booms Unwind: Income Effects, Wealth Effects and Feedbacks Through Financial Markets." *European Journal of Housing Policy* 8(2) (June): 161–180.

Case, Karl E., John M. Quigley, and Robert Shiller. 2003. "Home Buyers, Housing and the Macroeconomy." *Asset Prices and Monetary Policy*, Reserve Bank of Australia (November): 149–188.

——. 2005. "Comparing Wealth Effects: The Stock Market Versus the Housing Market." *Advances in Macroeconomics* 5(1) (March).

Case, Karl E., and Robert Shiller. 1987. "Prices of Single Family Homes Since 1970: New Indexes for Four Cities." *New England Economic Review* (September/October): 45–56.

——. 1988. "The Behavior of Home Buyers in Boom and Post-Boom Markets." *New England Economic Review* (November/December): 29–46.

——. 1989. "The Efficiency of the Market for Single-Family Homes." *American Economic Review* 79(1) (March): 125–137.

——. 1990. "Forecasting Prices and Excess Returns in the Housing Market." *Journal of the American Real Estate and Urban Economics Association* 18(4): 253–273.

——. 1996. "Default Risk and Real Estate Prices: The Use of Index-Based Futures and Options in Real Estate." *Journal of Housing Research* 7(2): 243–258.

——. 2003. "Is There a Bubble in the Housing Market?" *Brookings Papers on Economic Activity* 2: 299–362.

Case, Karl E., Robert J. Shiller, and Allan N. Weiss. 1993. "Index-Based Futures and Options Markets in Real Estate." *Journal of Portfolio Management* 19(2) (Winter): 83–92.

Skeath, Susan E., Ann D. Velenchik, Len M. Nichols, and Karl E. Case. 1992. "Consistent Comparisons Between Monopoly and Perfect Competition." *Journal of Economic Education* 23(3) (Summer): 255–261.

Contributors

Editors

Edward L. Glaeser
Fred and Eleanor Glimp Professor
 of Economics
Harvard University
Cambridge, Massachusetts; and
Research Associate
National Bureau of Economic Research
Cambridge, Massachusetts

John M. Quigley
I. Donald Terner Distinguished
 Professor
University of California
Berkeley

Authors

Andrew Caplin
Professor
Department of Economics
New York University
New York

Ingrid Gould Ellen
Associate Professor of Public Policy
 and Urban Planning
Robert F. Wagner Graduate School
 of Public Service
New York University
New York

Stuart A. Gabriel
Arden Realty Chair and Professor
 of Finance and Director, Richard S.
 Ziman Center for Real Estate
Anderson School of Management
University of California
Los Angeles

William Goetzmann
Edwin J. Beinecke Professor of Finance
 and Management Studies and
 Director, International Center
 for Finance
Yale School of Management
Yale University
New Haven, Connecticut

Joseph Gyourko
Martin Bucksbaum Professor of Real
 Estate and Finance, Chairperson,
 Real Estate Department, and
 Director, Samuel Zell and Robert
 Lurie Real Estate Center
University of Pennsylvania
Philadelphia; and
Research Associate
National Bureau of Economic Research
Cambridge, Massachusetts

Eric Hangen
Independent consultant
Neighborhood Reinvestment Corporation
Washington, DC

Robert Kulick
Manager
Empiris LLC
Washington, DC

Chris Mayer
Senior Vice Dean and Paul Milstein
 Professor of Real Estate
Columbia Business School
New York; and
Research Associate
National Bureau of Economic Research
Cambridge, Massachusetts

Barry Nalebuff
Milton Steinbach Professor
   of Management
Yale University School of Management
Yale University
New Haven, Connecticut

Katherine M. O'Regan
Associate Professor of Public Policy
Robert F. Wagner Graduate School of
   Public Service
New York University
New York

Karen Pence
Senior Economist
Board of Governors of the Federal
   Reserve System
Washington, DC

Elisabeth Prentice
Neighborhood Reinvestment
   Corporation
Washington, DC

Steven Raphael
Professor of Public Policy and Associate
   Dean
Goldman School of Public Policy
University of California
Berkeley

John Rodkin
Professor
University of Chicago Law School
Chicago

Larry A. Rosenthal
Adjunct Professor
Goldman School of Public Policy and
   Executive Director, Berkeley Program
   on Housing and Urban Policy
University of California
Berkeley

Stuart S. Rosenthal
Melvin A. Eggers Economics Faculty
   Scholar
Department of Economics
Syracuse University
New York

Ann B. Schnare
Partner
Empiris LLC
Washington, DC

Robert J. Shiller
Arthur M. Okun Professor of
   Economics
Cowles Foundation for Research in
   Economics
International Center for Finance
Yale University
New Haven, Connecticut; and
Chief Economist, MacroMarkets LLC
Madison, New Jersey

Todd Sinai
Associate Professor of Real Estate
The Wharton School
University of Pennsylvania
Philadelphia; and
Research Associate
National Bureau of Economic
   Research
Cambridge, Massachusetts

Tom Skinner
Real Liquidity
Washington, DC

Matthew Spiegel
Professor of Finance
Yale University School of
   Management
Yale University
New Haven, Connecticut

Ioan Voicu
Office of the Comptroller of the
   Currency
Washington, DC

Nancy E. Wallace
Professor of Real Estate and
   Finance
California Chair of Real Estate and
   Urban Economics
Haas School of Business
University of California
Berkeley

Donald W. Walls
President
Walls & Associates
Oakland, California

David Warsh
Proprietor
Economicprincipals.com
Somerville, Massachusetts

Commentators

Richard K. Green
Professor and Director and Chair
   of the Lusk Center for Real
   Estate
School of Policy, Planning, and
   Development
University of Southern California
Los Angeles

Lawrence D. Jones
Professor Emeritus, Strategy and
   Business Economics
Sauder School of Business
University of British Columbia
Vancouver

Stephen Malpezzi
Lorin and Marjorie Tiefenthaler Professor
James A. Graaskamp Center for Real
   Estate
Wisconsin School of Business
University of Wisconsin
Madison

Daniel P. McMillen
Professor
Department of Economics
University of Illinois
Chicago

Timothy J. Riddiough
Professor and E. J. Plesko Chair of
   Real Estate and Urban Land
   Economics
School of Business
University of Wisconsin
Madison

C. F. Sirmans
Professor and Director, Real Estate
   Center Finance Department
School of Business
University of Connecticut
Storrs

Kerry D. Vandell
Director
Center for Real Estate
Paul Merage School of Business
University of California
Irvine

Robert Van Order
Professor
Stephen M. Ross School of Business
University of Michigan
Ann Arbor

Index

About the Lincoln Institute
of Land Policy

The Lincoln Institute of Land Policy is a private operating foundation whose mission is to improve the quality of public debate and decisions in the areas of land policy and land-related taxation in the United States and around the world. The Institute's goals are to integrate theory and practice to better shape land policy and to provide a nonpartisan forum for discussion of the multidisciplinary forces that influence public policy. This focus on land derives from the Institute's founding objective—to address the links between land policy and social and economic progress—that was identified and analyzed by political economist and author Henry George.

The work of the Institute is organized in four departments: Valuation and Taxation, Planning and Urban Form, Economic and Community Development, and International Studies. We seek to inform decision making through education, research, demonstration projects, and the dissemination of information through publications, our Web site, and other media. Our programs bring together scholars, practitioners, public officials, policy advisers, and involved citizens in a collegial learning environment. The Institute does not take a particular point of view, but rather serves as a catalyst to facilitate analysis and discussion of land use and taxation issues—to make a difference today and to help policy makers plan for tomorrow.

The Lincoln Institute of Land Policy is an equal opportunity institution.

L LINCOLN INSTITUTE
OF LAND POLICY

113 Brattle Street
Cambridge, MA 02138-3400 USA

Phone: 1-617-661-3016 x127 or 1-800-LAND-USE (800-526-3873)
Fax: 1-617-661-7235 or 1-800-LAND-944 (800-526-3944)
E-mail: help@lincolninst.edu
Web: www.lincolninst.edu